Win32 Game Developer's Guide

with

DirectX 3

Jason Kolb

WAITE GROUP PRESS™
A Division of
Sams Publishing
Corte Madera, CA

PUBLISHER: Mitchell Waite
ASSOCIATE PUBLISHER: Charles Drucker

ACQUISITIONS MANAGER: Jill Pisoni
ACQUISITIONS EDITOR: Joanne Miller

EDITORIAL DIRECTOR: John Crudo
PROJECT EDITOR: Andrea Rosenberg
DEVELOPMENTAL EDITOR: Harry Henderson
TECHNICAL EDITOR: Jeff Bankston
GAME DEVELOPER: Richard S. Wright Jr.
COPY EDITOR: Michelle Goodman

PRODUCTION DIRECTOR: Julianne Ososke
PRODUCTION MANAGER: Cecile Kaufman
PRODUCTION EDITOR: Kelsey McGee
SENIOR DESIGNER: Sestina Quarequio
DESIGNER: Karen Johnston
PRODUCTION: Jena Brandt, Paula Lowell, Mark Matthews,
            Lisa Pletka, Laura Smith, Andrew Stone
ILLUSTRATIONS: Casey Price, Marvin VanTiem
INDEXER: Robert Long

Printed in the United States of America
98 99 • 10 9 8 7 6 5 4 3
Library of Congress Cataloging-in-Publication Data
Kolb, Jason, 1980-
    Win32 game developer's guide with DirectX 3 / Jason Kolb.
        p.   cm.
    Includes index.
    ISBN 1-57169-030-1
    1. Computer games--Programming. 2. Microsoft Win32. 3. DirectX.
    I. Title.
    QA76.76.C672K65   1997
    794.8'15268--dc21
                                                         96-52462
                                                            CIP

Dedication

I'd like to dedicate this book to my ever-patient parents, Dad and Mom (or Randy and Louise, as they're commonly called).

About the Author

Jason Kolb lives in Plainfield, Illinois. When he's not on the computer or at college he's usually working out, playing guitar, playing sports, or watching TV. This is his first book.

Table of Contents

Contents

Chapter 13: Artificial Intelligence 377

Chapter 14: Distributing Your Game 391

Chapter 15: Putting It All Together 401

Acknowledgments

Boy, I'm kind of apprehensive about writing the Acknowledgments. Hopefully, I won't leave anyone out, but if I do, let me just give one big acknowledgement to everyone in advance right now. Now nobody has a right to get mad at me for not mentioning them.

First of all, I have to thank God for giving me the ability and patience to write this thing. If it weren't for Him, I'd probably be long dead from a combination of exhaustion and monitor radiation by now.

Next, I have to thank my mom and dad. My dad, Randy, introduced me to computers when I was about 10, and I've been hooked ever since (and he's still teaching me stuff about them to this day). He and my mom, Louise, are the two most important people in my life—a big thanks goes out to these guys.

Thanks to the people who helped put this book together: Keith Weiner, who wrote the three sound chapters; Zane Thomas, who wrote the 2D code; Richard Wright, who wrote the 3D examples and the game; André LaMothe, who supplied sound effects; and Andrea Rosenberg, who kept the whole thing going. Also, thanks to all the other people at Waite Group who helped in some way or another to make this book a reality.

Okay, now I have to thank the rest of my family who supported me throughout the book. (Well, maybe not supported, but they at least talked with me about it every once in a while.) First there's my sister Christie and my brother Jeremy. Then there's Aunt Karen, Uncle Bill (the only other true Beatles fanatic I know), Becky (herself an aspiring author—be on the lookout for future books), and Lauren. And I can't forget Annie, Rosie and Linda—love ya!

Okay, now comes the standard list of family members and others so that no one feels left out. Greetings to Grandma, Grandpa, Uncle Brian, Aunt Diane, Brad, Mark, Aunt Val, Uncle Paul, Agnes, Raymond, Aunt Carol, Alex, Mike, Taylor, Uncle Joe, Aunt Sherie, Skyler, Paige, and all the countless relatives and friends who I'm sorry but I can't remember your names.

I think (I sincerely hope) I got everyone in there. Please forgive me if I forgot you.

Introduction

Thanks for buying the *Win32 Game Developer's Guide with DirectX 3*. This book is intended to teach you how to program with all six of the DirectX components: DirectDraw, Direct3D, DirectSound, DirectPlay, DirectInput, and DirectSetup. By the time you finish reading this book you'll have a pretty good understanding of how to program with DirectX—I hope good enough that you're able to write your own game.

DirectX

DirectX (originally called Game SDK, but later renamed to fit in with Microsoft's new strategy of naming all their technologies with an X, as in ActiveX) was introduced by Microsoft in the Fall of 1995. It presented a huge leap forward in computer game technology, one that finally put PCs on a par with dedicated gaming consoles used by gamers around the world.

Several components make up the DirectX API. These components include:

- DirectDraw, which provides ultra-fast access to video hardware. DirectDraw finally lets Windows games compete with the speed of DOS games. It also provides several advanced features which previously had to be written from scratch by the programmer if the game needed them.

- DirectSound, which allows the programmer to easily add sound effects and music to games.

- DirectPlay, which allows for easier implementation of multi-player games over a network or modem, or even the Internet.

- DirectInput, which provides easy use of joysticks or any other available controller device. DirectInput also provides automatic use of future devices, no matter what they might be.

- Direct3D, which provides optimized 3D capabilities to Windows games. Direct3D also allows games to take advantage of 3D accelerated hardware if it is available without any additional coding by the game developer.

- DirectSetup, which automatically installs the DirectX components on the user's system.

Because DirectX games run under Windows, they also gain additional side benefits that include:

- A built-in user interface. Windows 95 provides programs with a stylish user interface that can be used in any number of ways. There are many controls including buttons, scroll bars, edit boxes, and so on that also can be used by programs. All these components can be customized in various ways to give each program a unique look and feel.

- Pre-written graphics routines. Programs running under Windows get automatic access to the GDI, Windows' graphics library. The GDI provides many functions for performing a wide range of operations. It also provides functions for displaying many different graphic primitives including text, polygons, and bitmaps.

- A wide range of fonts for use by applications. Using GDI routines, you can use any TrueType font available on the user's system to display text. It's also possible to create your own fonts to add a custom feel to the text.

- Automatic hardware setup. Under DOS, games had to worry about the type of video, sound, and input hardware the user had installed, but under Windows 95, none of that is handled by the application. Windows 95 takes care of all hardware setup, and Microsoft or the manufacturer takes all the blame for hardware that doesn't work.

- Use of the Windows API. The Windows API is a set of functions that in itself has a wide range of capabilities. Because programmers can use these functions, they don't have to write their own, and thus save lots of time. There are API functions that perform myriad operations, including file I/O, multitasking, printing, and many others.

Who This Book Is For

This book is aimed at developers (hobbyists and professionals) who want to write great games for Windows 95. More specifically, it's aimed at developers who already know how to program in C and/or C++ and use a Windows compiler. But you certainly don't need to be an expert at game programming, or even Windows programming, because everything you need to know is explained at one point or another in the book.

This book is not just meant for professional game developers. I hope this book will be entertaining and informative to people who write games for the love of writing games (or just for some extra money).

What Sets This Book Apart

No, the cover is not the only thing that separates this book from the rest. First of all, it provides you with everything you need to write a top-notch game. With just this book, a computer, Windows 95, a compiler, the accompanying CD-ROM, and a little time and effort, you can be the person to write the next killer game.

The other thing that sets this book apart from the rest is that it covers the Direct3D API, while most other DirectX books do not. Thus, the *Win32 Game Developer's Guide with DirectX 3* is the one and only book that will thoroughly teach you Windows game programming using all of DirectX.

How This Book Is Organized

This book is organized into 15 chapters and an appendix. Each chapter builds on the previous chapters, so it's recommended that you read through the book in order at least once. After that, or if you're already familiar with much of the subject matter, this book will make a great reference.

Below is a brief overview of the chapters:

Chapter 1: The Basics

This chapter explains the basic concepts inherent to game programming, whether in DOS or Windows. It's a good idea to read this chapter if you're new to graphics programming or if you've dabbled before but are a little unclear on a few topics. This chapter also discusses programming with COM, which you should read if you've never worked with COM before.

Chapter 2: DirectDraw

This chapter starts getting into meaty topics such as explaining the basic components of DirectDraw and Windows 95 game programming. It also covers writing the first example program.

Chapter 3: More DirectDraw

This chapter addresses more of the basic DirectDraw concepts not covered in Chapter 2, many of which have to do with writing DirectDraw programs that run in a window.

Chapter 4: Palettes

This chapter explains how to use palettes in DirectDraw. It also discusses using palettes for special effects such as palette animation.

Chapter 5: Bitmaps

This chapter discusses how to use bitmaps in DirectDraw. You'll learn how to load and display them, and how to use them in a game.

Chapter 6: Sprites

This chapter will teach you how to use animated bitmaps (called sprites). We'll develop a full-featured sprite class during the course of this and following chapters that you can use in your own games.

Chapter 7: DirectInput

This chapter discusses how to interact with the user. You'll learn how to read and utilize the joystick and other input devices the user has installed.

Chapter 8: Advanced DirectDraw

In this chapter we'll wrap up our discussion of DirectDraw by discussing a few miscellaneous techniques such as scrolling bitmaps.

Chapter 9: Direct3D Basics

In this chapter you'll learn how to set up and initialize Direct3D. You'll also learn about the different lighting modules and rendering qualities, and how to implement them.

Chapter 10: A Sound Primer

This chapter teaches you the basics of sound programming and gets you ready to start programming with DirectSound.

Chapter 11: DirectSound

In this chapter you'll learn sound programming via DirectSound. You'll also create a sound class that you can use in your own games.

Chapter 12: DirectPlay

This chapter will show you how to write multiplayer games using DirectPlay.

Chapter 13: Artificial Intelligence

In this chapter you'll learn about various artificial intelligence techniques and how you could implement them in your own game.

Chapter 14: Distributing Your Game

This chapter will give you somewhere to start after you've written a game and you want to sell it. It discusses how to put the finishing touches on your game and lists a few different options you have when it comes time to market and sell your game.

Chapter 15: Putting It All Together

This chapter puts DirectDraw, Direct3D, and DirectSound together to write a complete 3D game. This chapter will teach you some of the more advanced Direct3D techniques and will give you a 3D game engine on which to build your own game.

Appendix: Windows 95 Logo Requirements

This chapter tells you what you need to do if you want the Windows 95 logo on your game.

System Requirements

To run a program using DirectX, you're going to need a system that has at least the following:

- A 486/66 MHz or higher CPU
- 8 MB of RAM
- Windows 95 or Windows NT
- DirectX 3 SDK (included on the CD)
- A decent video card

Important:

The video card and driver you use make a HUGE difference in the way DirectX runs. Always make sure you have the latest version of your video driver installed. And please set your color depth to 256 colors, as the Chapter 15 example game will not run otherwise. Still, there is no guarantee that all the examples will work with your video driver, so you may have to get a new video card if yours is too old.

Although it's not required, it's recommended that you have at least a Pentium/60, 16 MB of RAM, and a 3D accelerator card. Without these (or at least the CPU and RAM), writing DirectX programs could be painfully slow as you wait for your programs to compile and run.

The Accompanying CD

The accompanying CD has all the software you need to write DirectX games besides Windows and a 32-bit Windows compiler. It contains the following:

- The DirectX 3.0 SDK
- Paint Shop Pro 32 (an image editor)

- Cool Edit (a sound editor)
- Sound Kit for Windows (an alternative to DirectSound by Keith Weiner, the author of the sound chapters)
- All the source code from the book

This stuff should provide you with everything you need to write a top-notch game.

Installing the Software

The following section tells you how to install and use the software on the CD.

The DirectX 3.0 Software Development Kit

To install the DirectX SDK, simply change to the **DIRECTX3** directory and type **SETUP**. The setup program will take it from there. Be sure to install the entire development kit and not just the files needed to run DirectX.

The Source Code

The source code is located in the **SOURCE** directory. It's organized into chapters (such as CHAPTER1, CHAPTER2, and so on), and the individual examples are numbered by the chapter number and the order in which they appear in the chapter (EX2-1, EX6-5, and so on). The executable for each file is in the same directory as the source code, and you can copy everything right off the CD to your hard drive.

Paint Shop Pro 32

Paint Shop Pro 32 is in the PSP32 directory. Change to that directory and enter **SETUP** to install it.

Cool Edit

Cool Edit is in the **COOL** directory. Change to that directory and type in **C96SETUP** to enter the setup program and install it.

Sound Kit for Windows

To install the Sound Kit for Windows, copy the files from the **SOUNDKIT** directory to your hard drive.

Conclusion

I hope you enjoy *Win32 Game Developer's Guide with DirectX 3* and find it informative. I hope it will give you somewhere to start in your game programming endeavor, at the very least. As we all know, you can never know all there is to know about programming, especially just from reading one book.

Note: Some of the software included on the bundled CD, including PaintShop Pro 32, Cool Edit, and Sound Kit for Windows, are shareware, provided for your evaluation. If you find any of the shareware products useful, you are requested to register it as discussed in its documentation and/or in the About screen of the application. Waite Group Press has not paid the registration fee for this shareware.

1
The Basics

Before we start learning how to program games using DirectX, there are a few things we need to go over. Once we get these miscellaneous topics out of the way, we'll be all set to start writing some real code (and eventually, games).

In this chapter we're going to review the basic principles behind PC graphics and video card operation, survey some recent developments in PC graphics support, look over the COM architecture, and discuss some issues specific to programming with DirectX. Once you finish this chapter, you'll have a solid understanding of what's going on in the basic system architecture and hardware when writing DirectX code, knowledge you'll soon find immensely valuable.

Graphics Basics

First things first. We need to examine a few fundamental concepts that make up the foundation of all graphics programming.

Pixels

Every image you see on your computer monitor is comprised of *pixels*. A pixel represents the smallest area of the screen that can be set to a specific color. If you've never worked with computer graphics before, you may not have noticed pixels. However, as you can see in Figure 1-1, images on the screen are comprised of thousands of dots (pixels) whose colors combine to form an image on the display.

FIGURE 1-1

Pixels

Each pixel is usually stored in the computer as one byte of memory, although in special instances, more or less memory is used. The byte used by each pixel describes its onscreen color. The bytes making up the image on the screen are stored in memory on the video card itself, as we'll see in a moment.

Screen Coordinates

Screen coordinates are a simple but critical concept to grasp. You'll use them all the time to reference the position of a pixel on the screen, so pay close attention.

Screen coordinates are similar to Cartesian coordinates because they are specified using an ordered pair (x, y). The x coordinate specifies the horizontal position of the pixel on the screen, and the y coordinate designates the pixel's vertical position. Both the x and y coordinates equal zero in the upper-left corner of the display, and their values increase as you move to the right and downward. The x coordinate increases as we progress across the screen from left to right, and the y coordinate grows as we move down the screen. Figure 1-2 illustrates this.

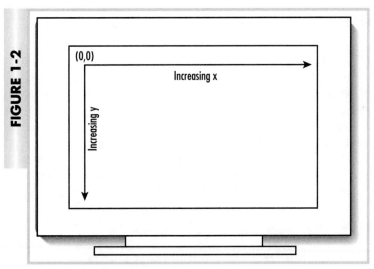

Screen coordinates

The upper-left corner of the screen is located at coordinates (0,0), as mentioned above. The pixel to the right of (0,0) is at (1,0), and the pixel directly below (0,0) is at (0,1). Take a look at Figure 1-3, which shows several pixels from the upper-left corner of the screen.

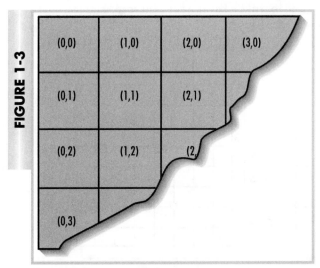

Upper-left corner of the screen

Video Resolution

Resolution is defined as the number of pixels that can be displayed on the screen at once. Resolution is usually expressed as width (x resolution) by height (y resolution), or x by y. More specifically, resolution is expressed as the length in pixels of each dimension. For example, a resolution of 320×200 means that the screen is 320 pixels wide and 200 pixels tall—a total of 64,000 pixels. Figure 1-4 illustrates this concept.

Figure 1-4 above shows two common display resolutions. If you were to count up the pixels in each of these modes (which might take a while), you'd find that the 640×480 resolution contains more than four times as many pixels as the 320×200 mode. This is because the 640×480 mode contains about twice as many pixels in each dimension (x and y) as the 320×200 mode (the y dimension in the 640×480 mode is about 2.4 times larger).

Note

The x resolution will usually be larger than the y resolution. Most monitors are wider than they are tall (the width to height ratio is about 4:3).

There are several resolutions available (you have to pick from a predefined list depending on the individual video card), but you have to be choosy when selecting one for your game. When there are four times as many pixels in a mode (as described above), you have to perform four times as many calculations to display each image. This causes an unpleasant decrease in speed. Ideally, you'd like to have as many pixels onscreen as possible for a crisper image, but in reality you need to strike a balance between speed and resolution so that your game looks nice but isn't too slow.

FIGURE 1-4

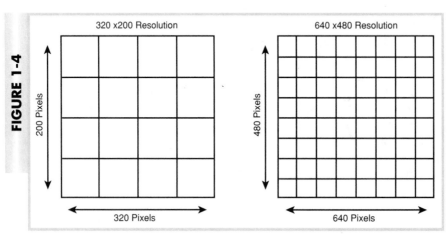

Two common display resolutions

With recent changes in graphics hardware, it *is* possible to have the best of both worlds. Video cards are now being manufactured with up to 4MB of video memory, making resolutions up to, and even greater than, 1024x768 possible without losing too much speed.

Color Depth

Color depth is the number of colors that can be displayed on the screen at one time using pixels. As with display resolution, there is a limited number of color depths from which to choose. The most common color depths are 2 (black & white), 16, 256, and 16 million. Most games use a color depth of 256, meaning that the game can choose from 256 colors when selecting a color for each pixel.

You inform the computer which color depth you want by telling it the number of *bits per pixel* to use. The bits per pixel value tells the computer how many bits to use to describe each pixel. Each bit in the pixel can be set to either one or zero, meaning each bit can represent two different colors. Thus, to calculate the number of colors available for any given bits per pixel value, simply raise two (the number of colors made available by each bit) to the power of the number of bits per pixel being used. For example, in the case of 256 colors, eight bits per pixel are being used ($2^8 = 256$).

The more colors used, the more realistic the image on the screen will appear. This is because the human eye can distinguish literally millions of colors. Again, there is a trade-off between speed and realism because pixels displaying more colors are made up of more bits and take longer to manipulate.

Palettes

Palettes hold the colors used by pixels. Each color in the palette is stored in a *palette entry*, which is the data representation of the color. All the palette entries make up the palette, which is usually represented in code as an array of palette entries. The color contained in each palette entry is then stored as a combination of red, green, and blue values, which blend to form the final color when viewed on the display.

There can only be as many palette entries as there are colors in the current color depth. Any more would be useless, because the video hardware couldn't display them. For example, if the color depth were 8 bits per pixel (256 colors), the maximum number of viewable palette entries would be 256, because only 256 colors can be shown at once.

How do you use palettes? Well, the pixels themselves don't actually hold the color—they're just indexes into the palette's array of entries. Each pixel holds the index of the palette entry storing that pixel's color. Figure 1-5 shows what's going on here, although it's somewhat difficult to portray different colors in black and white.

In this example, the display uses 256 colors. The figure shows the first few bytes of video memory, each of which represents 1 pixel (1 byte = 8 bits = 256 colors). Each pixel contains an integer value that's an index into the array of palette entries. When the screen is updated, the system looks into each pixel, finds the associated palette entry, and displays that color in the pixel's position.

FIGURE 1-5

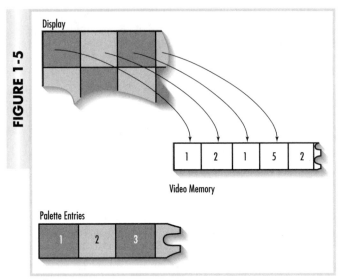

Palette entries

Bits per pixel really come into play when dealing with palettes. When the color depth is 256, each pixel needs 8 bits to hold an index into the palette because 8 bits are needed to hold the integer value 255 (the indexes of the 256 colors range from 0 to 255).

Manipulating palettes is the basis for a number of interesting graphic effects. For example, it's possible to change palette entries on the fly and have each pixel in memory retain its value (an index to a palette entry), even though the color value in the corresponding palette entries change. Many computer games use this attribute of palettes to achieve plasma, fire, and lava lamp effects.

Similarly, it's possible to create more than one palette and switch among them instantaneously, producing the sensation that the pixels on the screen are changing color (because the palette entries' colors are changing). However, the display can only use one palette at a time.

Video Modes

The *video mode* (sometimes called a *display mode*) tells the computer which resolution and color depth to use. The notation for referencing a video mode uses three numbers: the x resolution by the y resolution by the color depth. For example, a common video mode is 320×200×256, meaning that the screen is 320 pixels wide, 200 pixels tall, and 256 colors deep.

Note

The palette is not part of the video mode. The palette is set by functions within the application.

There is a predefined list of video modes supported by the user's video hardware. The list differs from PC to PC, and you always have to make your selection from that list. However, it's not too constraining because there's usually a wide range of video modes from which to choose and many of them are standard. We'll talk more about this subject in the next chapter.

The Video Card

One of the most important things to understand when programming games is how the *video card* works. The video card dictates to the monitor—which is physically connected to the card itself—what should be shown on the screen at any given moment. The application running on the PC tells the video card what to display on the monitor.

When programming computer games, you always deal with the video card, either directly or indirectly. Unlike DOS, the Windows 95 Game SDK lets you work with the video card indirectly by using an API. This lets you bypass mundane tasks such as calling interrupts, which for beginners, can be tedious and extremely confusing.

Video Memory

The video card has its own memory chips, called *video memory*. As you probably know from shopping for a PC, video cards come with different amounts of video memory, usually 1MB or 2MB. One of the advantages of using Windows instead of DOS is that for the most part, Windows takes care of managing this memory. Because of this, you'll rarely have to worry about running out.

I mentioned earlier that the video card tells the monitor what to display. Technically, however, that's not really true because it's actually video memory holding the data that is translated into pictures. Video memory contains the pixels that make up the image on the screen, and the monitor is constantly polling video memory to find out what to display (actually, it has to go through a little hardware first, but that's irrelevant). So, to change the image on the screen, all you need to do is change the contents of video memory! (See Figure 1-6 for an illustration.)

FIGURE 1-6

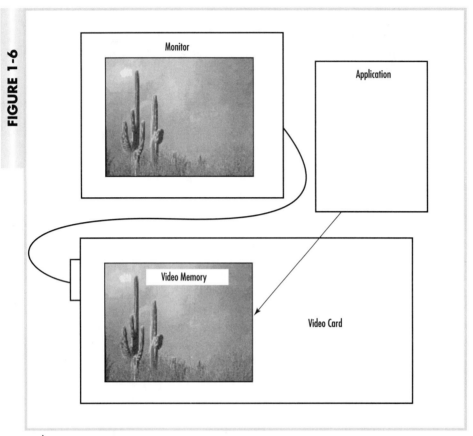

Video memory

Memory Organization

Video memory is organized as a linear array of pixels in memory. Each line of pixels on the screen corresponds to a segment of video memory that's as long as the x resolution of the screen. Once memory reaches the end of one row of pixels, the next line begins, wrapping the video memory around to the following line (see Figure 1-7).

Of course, the x resolution usually isn't set to only 4 pixels wide, but this figure serves as a useful example. The main concept you need to understand is this: Every four pixels, another line on the display begins, but video memory continues in a linear pattern.

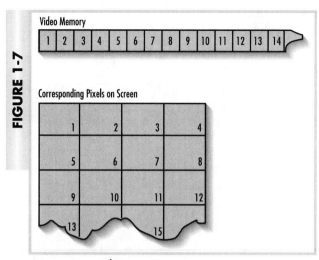

FIGURE 1-7

Wrapping video memory

Pixel Size

Bits per pixel and color depth have a big impact on the data representation of pixels in video memory. When you use a pointer to any type of data (in our case, the pixels in video memory), you need to know how large the data type is. The bits per pixel value tells us how large each pixel is, and therefore, what data type to use for the array.

The most common color depth is 256, meaning each pixel is made up of 8 bits. So what data type should we use to access the array? Well, because a *char* is 8 bits on most systems, we'll just use chars when dealing with pointers to video memory—in 256 colors, of course.

Using Video Memory

Usually we won't deal with video memory itself, but rather some allocated RAM organized in the same way. This type of memory, called a *buffer*, is then copied into video memory, displaying the image on the screen. Buffers are organized in the same wrap-around fashion as video memory, so we'll be able to use the same techniques discussed here to manipulate them.

Ideally, video memory would be arranged so we could access it via a two-dimensional array, but as you saw earlier, that is not the case. We'll need to perform a little math to access memory, and to do that we need to know the x resolution of the screen. We won't go into the actual math involved right now. It's not complex, but it's irrelevant to the topic at hand. To reference a particular pixel in video memory located at (x,y) on the screen, just use the following formula:

```
mem_pointer[y * x_res + x]
```

mem_pointer is the pointer to video memory, which we can use as an array. *y* is obviously the vertical position of the pixel you want to reference, and *x* is the horizontal position. *x_res* is the x-resolution of the screen. Here's another way to access the same pixel:

```
mem_pointer + y * x_res + x
```

All you're really doing is adding a certain number of bytes to the memory address of the first pixel on the screen until reaching the pixel you want. For example, if the screen resolution is 320x200, you could reference the pixel at (24,85) with this bit of code:

```
mem_pointer[85 * 320 + 24];
```

You could also use the following code, which accomplishes the same thing (we'll use this second method in the rest of the book because it's a bit more standard):

```
mem_pointer + 85 * 320 + 24;
```

This code doesn't actually do anything besides reference the pixel at (24,85) in video memory, so if you don't understand it, don't knock yourself out trying to figure it out.

Recall that each pixel contains an index into the palette. Once you obtain the pixel address (using one of the two methods just discussed), you can set the color simply by assigning it an integer value corresponding to one of the palette entries. Let's look at a *very* brief code sample that sets the pixel at (2,2) to the color of the first palette entry (the screen resolution is 320×200):

Listing 1-1 Setting a pixel

```
.
.
.
// Declare a pointer to a char (byte), which will point to the pixel
char* pixel;

// Get a pointer to the pixel at (2,2)
pixel = vid_mem + 2 * 320 + 2;

// Set the pixel value to zero, which is an index to the first palette entry
*pixel = 0;
.
.
.
```

First, a pointer to a char is declared. Then, a pointer to the pixel we want is retrieved using the method described earlier (*vid_mem* is a pointer to the beginning of video memory):

```
pixel = vid_mem + 2 * 320 + 2;
```

Finally, the pixel's value is set to zero, an index into the first palette entry (remember, *pixel* is a *pointer* to the pixel at (2,2)):

```
*pixel = 1;
```

That's all there is to it. Of course, there's a lot more going on here than just the little snippet of code above, but it's all either irrelevant or too complex to explain at this point.

Bitmaps

Bitmaps are an essential part of Windows programming. As far as game programming is concerned, bitmaps are used to hold images of sprites, backgrounds, textures, and any other graphic object.

Bitmaps are arranged in basically the same way as video memory and, therefore, buffers. They are made up of many pixels which are indexes into the palette (actually, they have a palette of their own, but don't worry about that now). Bitmaps also use the same wrap-around memory scheme as video memory. There are some differences among video memory, buffers, and bitmaps, which we'll discuss in a later chapter.

Now, we need to look at some of the underlying architecture behind DirectX, called COM.

COM

DirectX is made up of several components: DirectDraw, Direct3D, DirectSound, DirectPlay, and DirectInput. Each of these components except for DirectInput (for reasons that will become obvious in Chapter 7) is built on the Component Object Model (COM). COM is an object-oriented interface developed by Microsoft for creating objects at the operating system level. Much of Windows 95, including OLE, is based on COM.

One point of confusion has been the relationship between COM and OLE (Object Linking and Embedding). OLE is based on COM, and the two share much of the same technology and interface. But COM is *not* a part of OLE. That said, let's continue.

A *COM object* (sometimes called an *interface*) closely resembles a C++ class and stems from the base class *IUnknown*. In fact, COM objects so closely resemble C++ classes that, when programming in C++, you can access them in exactly the same way as a class. Thus, from a programming standpoint, accessing COM objects is fairly simple. If using C++, you just use the COM object like a class. If you're using C, however, the process is a bit more complex.

Using COM Objects with C

If you decide to use C in your DirectX programs, you'll have a little more work than if you were using C++. You'll have to use an extra parameter for each function call, which is a pointer to the COM object itself, and you must call functions using something called the *vtable*. The vtable is a member (property) of the COM object. It contains pointers to all of the object's functions. To call a function using a vtable, the syntax goes something like this (**pDirectDraw** is the COM object, **lpVtbl** is the vtable, and **Initialize** is the function we're calling):

```
pDirectDraw->lpVtbl->Initialize( pDirectDraw, NULL );
```

This is equivalent to the following C++ code:

```
pDirectDraw->Initialize( NULL );
```

As you can see, when you use C++ you don't have to use the vtable at all or pass the function a pointer to the object. C++ knows that the function requires a pointer to the object and passes it one automatically.

DirectX Macros

Fortunately for you diehard C programmers, Microsoft has kindly included some macros for all the DirectDraw, DirectSound, and DirectPlay functions in their respective header files, which makes life a lot easier. These macros lift a bunch of typing off programmers' shoulders because they automatically call the correct vtable pointer when a function is called. For example, instead of typing the above code, you could instead use (where `Object_Function` is the macro name):

```
Object_Function( pObject, parameter );
```

If you decide to use C in your code, you should look into these macros. They'll save you a ton of time.

Pointer #defines

One more thing about syntax. In its header files, DirectX includes definitions for pointers to DirectX objects. Usually they look something like `LPDIRECTDRAW` or `LPDIRECTSOUND`, with `LP` (long pointer) before the name of the object. For the sake of clarity, we'll always use these definitions in this book.

Releasing COM Objects

After you've finished creating and using COM objects, it's important to release them. To do this, you need to call the *Release* member function, found in all COM objects. A good time to call this function is right after your application's window receives the `WM_DESTROY` message (discussed in the Chapter 2, "DirectDraw"). If you forget to call this function, your user's system resources (memory, GDI handles, and so on) will disappear into the computer twilight zone, and he or she will probably be less than happy with you.

Programming with DirectX

There are a few odds and ends that need clearing up before we can actually program with DirectX. These mostly have to do with the way you use the various DirectX files from within your compiler.

Header Files

DirectX contains several header files that correspond to its various components. Table 1-1 lists each header file and its respective component.

Table 1-1 DirectX header files

Header File	DirectX Component
D3D.H	Direct3D Immediate Mode
D3DRM.H	Direct3D Retained Mode
D3DRMWIN.H	Direct3D Retained Mode with special Windows extensions
DDRAW.H	DirectDraw
DPLAY.H	DirectPlay
DSETUP.H	DirectSetup
DSOUND.H	DirectSound

I recommend that you add the directory containing these files to your compiler's directory path so the sample programs on the CD build without any modifications. You'll find these files in **SDK\INC** off the DirectX SDK root directory.

Library Files

The DirectX SDK contains several library files, which also correspond to specific components. Table 1-2 lists these files and their respective components.

Table 1-2 DirectX library files

Library File	DirectX Component
DDRAW.LIB	DirectDraw
DPLAY.LIB	DirectPlay
DSETUP.LIB	DirectSetup
DSOUND.LIB	DirectSound
D3D.LIB	Direct3D Immediate Mode
D3DRM.LIB	Direct3D Retained Mode

It's a good idea to add the directory that contains these files to your compiler's directory path. This is so the directory can automatically find the files when it tries to compile a project. If you don't, then you'll need to modify the project files on the CD so your compiler knows where to find the library files. Each of the libraries is contained in the **SDK\LIB** directory off the main DirectX directory.

Compilers

In this book we're going to use Microsoft Visual C++, but any compiler will work in its place, provided it's a 32-bit Windows application capable of producing Win32 applications.

However, the project files on the CD are made specifically for Visual C++ and might not work with your compiler. If that is the case, you'll probably have to create new project files to build the sample applications (unless your compiler can import VC++ make files). Below are the steps needed to do this:

1. Create a new project file in your development environment.

2. Add each file in the sample program's directory to that project file.

3. Include the necessary library files in the project file (see Table 1-2).

You'll get a chance to try building a DirectX program in the next chapter.

Summary

Now you know everything needed to begin writing some real code. We've discussed graphics, the video card, COM, and DirectX programming syntax. In the next chapter, we'll begin our in-depth exploration of DirectDraw. You'll learn about some basic DirectDraw objects and use them to write a simple DirectDraw program.

2
DirectDraw

DirectDraw is the heart and soul of DirectX. It is the component that provides graphics applications under Windows 95, with direct access to video memory and video hardware.

Previously, Windows applications had to utilize the Windows GDI (Graphics Device Interface) in order to perform any graphics functions. Direct access to video memory, the standard way of writing games in DOS, was taboo in Windows. Besides being notoriously hard to understand, the GDI was much too slow for any serious game development because it had to go through Windows before accessing the video display. The GDI was not optimized for speed and was shared with other Windows applications, which slowed things down even more. Since games typically need to squeeze as much speed out of the user's computer as possible, things did not bode well for Windows as a gaming platform. As a result, very few commercial game developers released Windows games in the first half of the 1990s.

Then along came the WinG SDK. The WinG SDK was Microsoft's attempt to boost video performance under Windows by using faster bitmap manipulation routines. A few game developers used WinG, but it was rejected by the game programming community at large. Consequently, all the hit games continued to be written for DOS, not Windows. Although a step in the right direction, the WinG SDK was still not as fast as DOS.

But there was hope. Windows 95 was near the release date, and Microsoft was promising that its graphics performance would be leaps and bounds beyond Windows 3.1. Microsoft was developing an API that would enable developers to harness this performance easily: DirectDraw.

DirectDraw Features

DirectDraw provides Windows 95 games with impressive graphics performance and an easy-to-use API. DirectDraw gives programmers many advantages and features, such as:

- Direct access to video memory (see Figure 2-1).
- Use of the new and improved Windows 95 user interface.
- Automatic video hardware configuration.
- Access to a versatile graphics library through the Windows GDI when speed isn't critical. As a bonus, the GDI is faster when used through DirectDraw because it too has direct access to video memory.
- Automatic use of available hardware acceleration without any work at all on the programmer's part.
- Many advanced graphics functions that the programmer can take advantage of without having to reinvent the wheel.

The main advantage of DirectDraw is video memory access. This makes for extremely fast graphics, since working with the bits and bytes of video memory directly is much faster than going through the Windows GDI functions.

Yep, things look pretty bright for Windows 95 as a video game platform. And now you're at the forefront of this new technology, ready to blaze the trail with fast, exciting games.

FIGURE 2-1

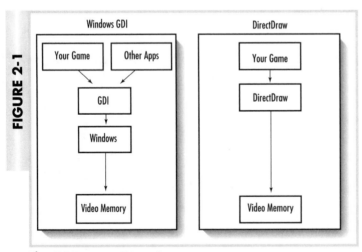

The GDI versus DirectDraw

DirectDraw Architecture

There are several COM objects that make up DirectDraw (see Figure 2-2), all derived from the base class `IUnknown`:

- The `DirectDraw` object itself, COM object type `IDirectDraw`, represents the display device, which is usually a video card. You use a `DirectDraw` object to control some of the fundamental properties of the display device, such as the video mode. DirectDraw object member functions are also used to create the other DirectDraw-related objects listed below.

- `IDirectDrawSurface` objects represent a region of video memory. They are used to store images and display them on the screen, usually by utilizing built-in bitmap functions.

- `IDirectDrawPalette` objects represent palettes. Palette manipulation with them is fairly simple and straightforward. Usually, a `DirectDrawPalette` object is associated with a `DirectDrawSurface` object so the surface knows what colors to use for displaying the image.

- `IDirectDrawClipper` objects prevent applications from drawing outside of a specified area. Clipper objects are usually used when a DirectDraw application is being displayed in a window and therefore should not be allowed to draw outside of the window's client area.

FIGURE 2-2

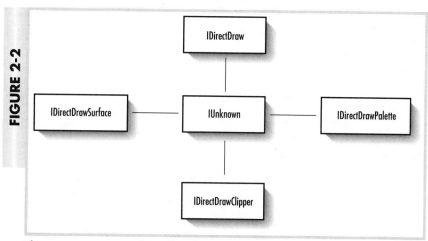

The DirectDraw architecture

DirectDraw HAL

The DirectDraw HAL (Hardware Abstraction Layer) enables DirectDraw to take advantage of any hardware acceleration available on the user's machine. You, the programmer, don't have to deal with the HAL directly unless you are writing device drivers for video hardware. The only scenario in which you might deal with the HAL is if you want to know exactly what capabilities the user's hardware does and does not support. We'll look at how to do this later in the chapter.

DirectDraw Software Emulation

Software emulation, sometimes referred to as HEL (Hardware Emulation Layer), provides capabilities that are not supported by hardware. If a certain function is needed by the application but is not supported by hardware, HEL pieces that functionality together from the capabilities the hardware *does* support. Figure 2-3 gives an illustration of the difference between the execution of functions that the hardware does and does not support.

Note

Since the HEL is piecing together the functionality you want to use from existing hardware functionality, possibly along with a little software code, it's certainly not as fast as functionality directly supported by hardware. You may want to keep this in mind when you decide exactly which hardware capabilities to use in your program (perhaps by detecting the available hardware functionality, as explained in several places throughout this book).

FIGURE 2-3

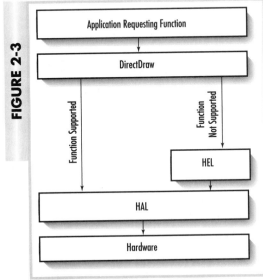

DirectDraw, HAL, and Software Emulation

Using both HAL and software emulation, a DirectDraw application can safely use any function it needs— whether or not the user's hardware supports it. For example, if you need to do some bitmap stretching in your application (we'll actually do this later), you can go ahead and perform the necessary functions without worrying about whether or not your video hardware supports them. This makes for much more fluid and portable programming.

Before we write our first DirectDraw program, we need to review some of the basic concepts inherent to Windows programming.

Example 2-1: Windows Application Essentials

When programming in Windows, you need to keep a few important pieces of information in mind.

First of all, you need to know how to use *instance handles*. Instance handles act sort of like the application's ID, identifying it to Windows. Windows gives each application a unique instance handle for identification (designated at run time when the application first starts up).

Window handles are used the same way as instance handles: They identify each window to the system. Each window that is open in Windows has a unique handle which identifies it to the Windows environment.

We'll keep all the items just mentioned in a neat little package, or more specifically, a neat little structure. This structure is declared in the file **Ex2-1.H** on the CD. Let's take a look the file:

Listing 2-1 **Ex2-1.H**

```
#define WIN32_EXTRA_LEAN
#include <windows.h>
#include <windowsx.h>
#include <mmsystem.h>
#include <ddraw.h>

#include "ddrawex.h"  // Header file for DirectDraw initialization
#include "render.h"  // Header file for actual drawing code
#include "resource.h"  // Header file for resources

typedef struct _GApp
{
 //
 // Global App Data
 //
 HINSTANCE  hinst;
 HWND    hwndApp;
 LPDIRECTDRAW lpdd;
 RECT    wndRect;
 UINT    timerid;
} GApp, * LPGApp;

extern GApp gapp;
```

Several standard header files are also preceded by `#include`:

```
#include <windows.h>
#include <windowsx.h>
#include <mmsystem.h>
#include <ddraw.h>
```

Here's a list explaining what each of the standard headers is for:

- WINDOWS.H is the header file containing the declarations of all the Win32 API functions, structures, and #defines. All Windows programs #include this file at one point or another.

- WINDOWSX.H contains declarations for some low-level functions that can be used by Windows programs. Don't worry though; we'll only be using one of them, one which isn't very complex at all.

- MMSYSTEM.H contains declarations for multimedia components of Windows. For some odd reason, timers are included in this file. We'll be using timers in the future, so we'll need to #include this file.

- DDRAW.H is the header file for DirectDraw. As mentioned in Chapter 1, I recommend you add the directory containing this file to your compiler's path so that the examples on the CD will build without modifications.

After the standard header files come some header files specific to our application:

```
#include "ddrawex.h"
#include "render.h"
#include "resource.h"
```

RESOURCE.H is the header file holding the standard Windows resources, such as menus. We'll be discussing the other two files later in this chapter.

Now comes the actual structure holding information about our application:

```
typedef struct   GApp
{
 //
 // Global App Data
 //
 HINSTANCE  hinst;
 HWND    hwndApp;
 LPDIRECTDRAW  lpdd;
 RECT    wndRect;
 UINT    timerid;
} GApp, * LPGApp;
```

As you can see, the structure has been typedefined as **GApp** and **LPGApp** so that we can declare instances of the structure using cleaner code.

The instance handle of the application is held in the *hinst* member of the structure, and the window handle of the main application window is held in the *hwndApp* member. The next member in line, *lpDD*, is a pointer to the DirectDraw object that we'll use throughout the application. The *wndRect* member holds the location of the window's client area, which is the area inside the borders and menu. The location of a window's client area is often needed in Windows programming. The next member, *timerid*, is the ID of the timer we'll use in future example programs. Timers also have a unique identifier in the Windows environment.

The last little bit of code in the file declares an external instance of the structure we just declared:

```
extern GApp gapp;
```

The actual instance itself is contained in the file **Ex2-1.CPP**. This declaration is present so that the **GApp** object in **Ex2-1.CPP** is visible to the other files in the project.

WinMain

WinMain

```
int WINAPI WinMain( HINSTANCE hInstance, HINSTANCE
hPrevInstance, LPSTR lpCmdLine, int nShowCmd )
```

Every Windows application begins and ends life in the **WinMain** function, similar to **main** in DOS. Windows calls **WinMain** when an application is started, and the application takes over from there.

WinMain gets four parameters passed to it:

1. **hInstance**—The application instance handle.

2. **hPrevInstance**—If another instance of your application is running, its handle is passed in this parameter. However, this parameter is always **NULL** in Win32 because each application runs in its own address space.

3. **lpCmdLine**—The command line that started the application. This parameter is similar to the *argv* parameter to *main* in C.

4. **nShowCmd**—Specifies how the application should be shown when it starts (minimized, maximized, or normal).

WinMain should return **0** if it has to exit prematurely. If the application goes all the way through and does its thing without encountering any problems, it should return another value (which we'll discuss later).

Before you can use **WinMain**, you need to **#include** the header file that declares it: **WINDOWS.H**, the header file for almost the entire Win32 API. In our example program, the file containing **WinMain**, **Ex2-1.CPP**, **#include**s the file **Ex2-1.H**, which **#include**s all of the header files our entire application needs.

Let's take a look at **WinMain** from our example program, and then we'll walk through it. **WinMain** is contained in the file **Ex2-1.CPP** on your CD.

Listing 2-2 `WinMain`

```
int WINAPI WinMain( HINSTANCE hInstance, HINSTANCE hPrevInstance, LPSTR ⇐
lpCmdLine, int nCmdShow)
{
 MSG msg;

 memset((void *)&gapp, 0, sizeof(gapp) );

 if( !WinInit( hInstance, nCmdShow ) )
  return FALSE;
 if( !DrawInit() )
 return FALSE;

 ShowCursor( FALSE );

 while( 1 )
 {
  if( PeekMessage( &msg, NULL, 0, 0, PM_NOREMOVE ) )
  {
   if( !GetMessage( &msg, NULL, 0, 0 ) )
    return msg.wParam;
   TranslateMessage(&msg);
   DispatchMessage(&msg);
  } else {
   WaitMessage();
  }
 }
}
```

First we declare a `MSG` structure, which is used to hold a Windows message:

```
MSG msg;
```

Windows is an event-driven environment, meaning everything that happens is triggered by messages. We'll discuss this later in the chapter.

The next item in the code probably looks a little funny:

```
memset((void *)&gapp, 0, sizeof(gapp) );
```

A `GApp` structure is declared at the top of `Ex2-1.CPP`. Here we're initializing the entire structure to zero so that it doesn't contain any residual garbage values that could potentially mess something up. This is done using `memset`, a standard C library function.

The next bit of code initializes the Windows portion of our application:

```
if( !WinInit( hInstance, nCmdShow ) )
 return FALSE;
```

`WinInit` is a function we'll write that takes care of standard Windows initialization, such as creating a window. It affects the contents of our *gapp* object, declared at the top of `Ex2-1.CPP`. `WinInit` takes the application's instance handle and the state in which the application should be shown as parameters (see the `WinMain` section earlier). `WinInit` returns `TRUE` if successful, `FALSE` if not. When we call `WinInit`, we check to see whether it was successful so we can bail out if it wasn't. We'll be looking at the `WinInit` function in just a little bit.

The same thing is done with DirectDraw initialization:

```
if( !DrawInit() )
  return FALSE;
```

DrawInit initializes the DirectDraw components of our application and returns a Boolean value to inform us whether it was successful. This function initializes the **DirectDraw** object contained in our *gapp* structure, along with a few other things. Again, we'll examine this function shortly.

The line of code that calls **ShowCursor** momentarily hides the cursor. We need to do this here because we won't be redrawing the entire screen, meaning that no matter where the mouse is when we switch to fullscreen, it won't be redrawn (in other words, there will be a cursor-shaped hole in our screen). We'll restore the cursor shortly.

In order to digest the next chunk of code, we'll need to understand the messaging mechanism that Windows uses. Let's pause now for a brief overview. Veteran Windows programmers can skip this next section.

Windows Messaging

Messages are Windows' way of communicating with applications. Windows uses messages to tell applications when to run, when to stop, what the user is doing, and anything else the application should know. Although these are the primary uses, messages are very diverse and can be used for many things (few, if any, apply to game programming, so we won't discuss them).

Windows applications differ from DOS programs because they use messages sent from Windows to determine what the user wants to do, instead of directly accessing hardware. For example, if an application wants to know where the mouse is, it must wait for a message from Windows giving the mouse's position, instead of querying the mouse itself. The same thing happens when the user inputs text with the keyboard. Instead of querying the keyboard itself to retrieve the text, Windows sends a message to the application telling it which keys were hit.

Windows also uses messages to inform applications if they should be performing a certain task. For example, if an application was partly covered by another application's window, it would need to redraw the uncovered portion when the other application's window is closed or moved. In that situation, Windows would send the application that needed to redraw its window a message stating precisely which part needed redrawing. This same principle applies to many other scenarios, several of which we'll deal with in this book.

Messages are stored in *MSG* structures. Along with the message ID, which is an integer value, *MSG* structures hold two values, also called parameters. These parameters hold information pertinent to the message (for example, for a mouse message, the *x* and *y* location of the cursor in the window). These two parameters are called the **WPARAM** and the **LPARAM**, which are held in the *wParam* and *lParam* members of a *MSG* structure.

Note

WinMain always returns the WPARAM of the last message sent to the application.

The Message Loop

Let's go back to **WinMain** in our example. After we hide the cursor, using **ShowCursor**, we enter the main application loop:

```
while( 1 )
{
 if( PeekMessage( &msg, NULL, 0, 0, PM_NOREMOVE ) )
 {
  if( !GetMessage( &msg, NULL, 0, 0 ) )
   return msg.wParam;
  TranslateMessage(&msg);
  DispatchMessage(&msg);
 } else {
  WaitMessage();
 }
}
```

We're going to keep looping until the program terminates in some fashion (thus, the **while(1)** statement). As you'll see later in the code, we'll use a Windows API function to exit the program.

The loop we've created is called a *message loop*. Message loops are used to retrieve messages from Windows and act accordingly.

The first bit of the loop warrants some explanation:

```
if( PeekMessage( &msg, NULL, 0, 0, PM_NOREMOVE ) )
```

PeekMessage is a Windows API function which looks (peeks) into the line of waiting messages, called the *message queue*, to see if there are any messages waiting to be processed. All we're doing in the line above is checking if any are waiting and, if so, proceeding to the *if* statement. For details on **PeekMessage**, consult your Windows API reference. (The Waite Group's *Windows API Bible* is a good book for this purpose.)

If there *are* messages waiting, we move on to this statement:

```
if( !GetMessage( &msg, NULL, 0, 0 ) )
return msg.wParam;
```

What we're actually doing is retrieving the waiting message, using **GetMessage**, a Windows API function, and storing it in our *msg* structure. If, for some reason, **GetMessage** fails, we quit **WinMain** and return the *wParam* member of the *msg* structure.

After we've retrieved the message we need to call **TranslateMessage**, a Windows API function, before proceeding:

```
TranslateMessage(&msg);
```

If the given message is a keyboard message, **TranslateMessage** turns it into a form that is easier to decipher in code—otherwise it leaves the message as is. We'll go into more detail on this subject later.

After calling **TranslateMessage**, we need to call **DispatchMessage**:

```
DispatchMessage(&msg);
```

`DispatchMessage` sends the given message to a special function, called a *callback function,* which actually handles the message. We'll discuss callback functions more a little later when we look at creating windows.

The next chunk of code is contained in the *else* statement:

```
} else {
  WaitMessage();
}
```

Remember that this *else* is only entered if there isn't a message waiting to be processed. The purpose of the call to `WaitMessage`, a Windows API function, is to let other Windows applications have a crack at the CPU when we don't need it. All `WaitMessage` does is pass control to the system until a new message is sent.

Now let's go ahead and take a look at what happens when we call `WinInit` (remember that `WinInit` is called back in `WinMain`, Listing 2-2).

WinInit

`WinInit` is contained in the file **Ex2-1.CPP** on the CD. It's the function in our project that takes care of the Windows portion of initialization. Simply put, this is what it does:

- Registers a window class.

- Creates the main application window using the window class.

A window class simply tells the Windows environment a few basic things about how your window will behave and look. Windows identifies individual window classes by the their names, which are stored as strings. The name of the window class can be any string; there are really no limitations.

Here's the code that comprises `WinInit`:

Listing 2-3 `WinInit`

```
//
// WinInit --- Create window class and create window
//
static BOOL WinInit( HANDLE hInstance, int nCmdShow )
{
  WNDCLASS wc;

  gapp.hinst = hInstance;

  wc.style = CS_DBLCLKS;
  wc.lpfnWndProc = WindowProc;
  wc.cbClsExtra = 0;
  wc.cbWndExtra = 0;
  wc.hInstance = hInstance;
  wc.hIcon = LoadIcon( hInstance, MAKEINTATOM(IDI_GDKAPP));
  wc.hCursor = LoadCursor( NULL, IDC_ARROW );
```

continued on next page

continued from previous page

```
    wc.hbrBackground = GetStockObject(BLACK_BRUSH);
    wc.lpszMenuName =  NULL;
    wc.lpszClassName = "GdkLesson1Class";

      if( !RegisterClass( &wc ) )
          return FALSE;

      gapp.hwndApp =  CreateWindowEx(
    WS_EX_APPWINDOW,
    "GdkLesson1Class",
    "GDK Lesson 1",
    WS_POPUP | WS_VISIBLE,
    0,
    0,
    GetSystemMetrics(SM_CXSCREEN),
    GetSystemMetrics(SM_CYSCREEN),
    NULL,
    NULL,
    hInstance,
    NULL );

  if( gapp.hwndApp == NULL )
     return FALSE;
  else
   return TRUE;
}
```

As you can see, **WinInit** returns a Boolean value. We'll just return **TRUE** if nothing goes wrong, **FALSE** if we hit a snag.

First we need to declare a **WNDCLASS** structure, which we'll call *wc.* **WNDCLASS** structures are used to hold information about window classes.

The next item on the agenda is to store our application instance in the global **GApp** object, *gapp:*

```
gapp.hinst = hInstance;
```

Remember that we grouped all the vital information about the application in the **GApp** structure (defined in **Ex2-1.H**, Listing 2-1).

Now we need to put some information about our window into the *wc* variable:

```
wc.lpfnWndProc = WindowProc;
wc.cbClsExtra = 0;
wc.cbWndExtra = 0;
wc.hInstance = hInstance;
wc.style = CS_DBLCLKS;
wc.hIcon = LoadIcon( hInstance, MAKEINTATOM(IDI_GDKAPP));
wc.hCursor = LoadCursor( NULL, IDC_ARROW );
wc.hbrBackground = GetStockObject(BLACK_BRUSH);
wc.lpszMenuName =  NULL;
wc.lpszClassName = "GdkLesson1Class";
```

We're not going to step through and discuss each member of *wc*, but the **WNDCLASS** structure is fully explained in the Windows API documentation if you want to learn more. The only vitally important members we'll take time to explain are the *lpfnWndProc*, *lpszMenuName*, and *lpszClassName* members.

Callback Functions

The *lpfnWndProc* member of a **WNDCLASS** structure is very important—it's the address of the window class' callback function.

A *callback function* is the function that actually processes messages sent to an application. When we register our window class, we tell Windows that we want all the messages sent by **DispatchMessage** (in **WinMain**) to go to the callback function we specify in *lpfnWndProc*. Figure 2-4 illustrates the path a message takes once it's retrieved by **GetMessage**.

Callback functions must be declared in a specific way or an error will occur when you try to register your window class. We use the conventional names for the function and its parameters. You could use other names, but the syntax must be as follows:

Callback Function Declaration

```
LRESULT CALLBACK WindowProc( HWND hwnd, UINT uMsg,
WPARAM wParam, LPARAM lParam )
```

FIGURE 2-4

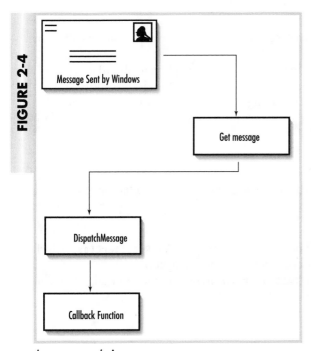

A message's journey

A callback function takes four parameters. These parameters are provided by Windows when `DispatchMessage` is called—you never call a callback function yourself:

1. *hwnd*—the handle of the window to which the message is being sent.

2. *uMsg*—the numerical ID of the message. These IDs are #defined in WINDOWS.H. We'll be using a few of them in just a little bit.

3. *wParam*—the WPARAM of the message. This parameter may or may not be used, depending on the message sent.

4. *lParam*—the LPARAM of the message. This parameter also may or may not be used.

The value returned by callback functions usually varies from message to message.

Menus

The *lpszMenuName* member of a WNDCLASS structure specifies the menu that should be used for windows created from the class (although this can be overridden). The value of the *lpszMenuName* should be the string ID of the menu resource you've created with a resource editor.

The contents of your menu, of course, are up to you, but you'll need to give it a unique string resource ID when you name the menu resource. Our example program will be running in fullscreen mode for now, so we don't need a menu. We'll simply use NULL for *lpszMenuName*.

Class Name

The *lpszClassName* member of the WNDCLASS structure is also very important—it's the name of the window class you're creating.

The name of the class is entirely up to you. For the example, a totally arbitrary value, GdkLesson1Class, is being used. The name of the class helps Windows identify a certain type of window: the window you describe using the rest of the WNDCLASS member variables. When you create the window, you need to supply the name of the window class from which you want the new window created.

Registering the Window Class

Now that we have a window class filled out, we need to register the new class with Windows:

```
if( !RegisterClass( &wc ) )
      return FALSE;
```

To register the window class, we need to use the API function RegisterClass, which simply takes the address of a WNDCLASS structure as the parameter.

If RegisterClass fails, we return FALSE from WinInit to exit the application (remember that WinMain dies if WinInit fails).

Creating a Window

Now that we have a window class registered, we're ready to go ahead and create a window:

```
gapp.hwndApp =  CreateWindowEx(
  WS_EX_APPWINDOW,
  "GdkLesson1Class",
  "GDK Lesson 1",
  WS_POPUP | WS_VISIBLE,
  0,
  0,
  GetSystemMetrics(SM_CXSCREEN),
  GetSystemMetrics(SM_CYSCREEN),
  NULL,
  NULL,
  hInstance,
  NULL );
```

 ## CreateWindowEx

```
HWND CreateWindowEx (DWORD dwExStyle, LPCSTR
lpClassName, LPCSTR lpWindowName, DWORD dwStyle, int
x, int y, int nWidth, int nHeight, HWND hWndParent,
HMENU hMenu, HINSTANCE hInstance, LPVOID lpParam )
```

The Windows API function *CreateWindowEx* is used to create windows. All those parameters look a bit daunting at first, so let's just look at them one at a time:

1. *dwExStyle*—dictates any special behavior the window should have. You don't have to use this parameter at all, but we've used WS_EX_APPWINDOW, which says the window should appear on the taskbar when minimized. The other valid values for this parameter can be found in your Windows API documentation.

2. *lpClassName*—the name of the window class from which the window should be created. We registered the class we're going to use just before calling CreateWindowEx, and we named it GdkLesson1Class.

3. *lpWindowName*—specifies the text that should appear in the title bar of the window and on the task bar when the window is minimized. We'll use GDK Application.

4. *dwStyle*—dictates the basic behavior of the window. There are many possible values for this parameter (all of which can be found in your API documentation); we're using WS_POPUP and WS_VISIBLE. WS_VISIBLE says the window should be visible as soon as the call to CreateWindowEx is complete This avoids having to call another function to make the window visible. WS_POPUP creates a pop-up window, which is essentially a plain window without any of the standard user-interface elements, such as title bars.

5. *x*—specifies the horizontal location of the upper-left corner of the window on the screen. Since we're putting the window at the upper-left corner of the screen, this parameter is zero.

6. *y*—the vertical position of the upper-left corner of the window on the screen. Again, we've used zero.

7. *nWidth*—the width of the window. We're going to use the Windows API function `GetSystemMetrics` to find the width of the entire screen (for more information on `GetSystemMetrics`, consult your API documentation). Thus, the window will take up the entire display.

8. *nHeight*—the height of the window. Again, we've used `GetSystemMetrics` to find the height of the screen so the window will take up the entire display.

9. *hWndParent*—a handle to the parent of this window. Because we're creating a top-level window, this parameter is NULL.

10. *hMenu*—the handle of the menu resource that should be used for the window. If NULL is given for this parameter, the window class' menu is used, which is the one we're going to use.

11. *hInstance*—the handle of the application that will be associated with the window.

12. *lpParam*—specifies any additional information that should be used when creating a window. When a window is created, a message is sent to the callback function saying the window is being created, and this pointer is passed along with it as the LPARAM. Since we don't need to pass any additional information, we'll use NULL.

`CreateWindowEx` returns a handle to the newly created window, which we'll store in our GApp structure:

```
gapp.hwndApp = CreateWindowEx(...
```

If **CreateWindowEx** fails for some reason, it returns **NULL**, so we'll check to make sure that a valid window handle was retrieved and return **FALSE** if it wasn't:

```
if( gapp.hwndApp == NULL )
        return FALSE;
```

If **CreateWindowEx** is successful, we'll return **TRUE** to let **WinMain** know that everything went fine and it's safe to continue:

```
return TRUE;
```

Now that we have a window, we're ready for action, right? Not quite. We still have to take care of some DirectDraw initialization first, and then we have to take a look at our window's callback function. Hold on though; we're getting closer.

DirectDraw Essentials

Now let's cover some of the basic topics concerning DirectDraw. Once we have them out of the way, we'll be able to start writing some code that actually does something!

DrawInit

DrawInit is the function **WinMain** calls to perform DirectDraw initialization. This function will require quite a bit of explanation, so let's take it one bite at a time. Look at the code for **DrawInit** in Listing 2-4:

Listing 2-4 **DrawInit**

```
//
// DrawInit --- Initialize DirectDraw
//
static BOOL DrawInit()
{
 //
 // Create DirectDraw object and initialize helper data
 //
 if( (gapp.lpdd = DDCreate(gapp.hwndApp)) == NULL )
  return FALSE;
 //
 // Fullscreen exclusive mode will be used
 //
 DDSetCooperativeLevel( DDSCL_EXCLUSIVE | DDSCL_FULLSCREEN );
 //
 //  Let 'er rip :-)
 //
 if( DDEnable() == FALSE )
  return FALSE;
 //
 // Initialize rendering code
 //
 if( RenderInit() == FALSE )
  return FALSE;
 return TRUE;
}
```

As you can see, **DrawInit** returns **TRUE** if successful, **FALSE** if not. Now let's look at how the initialization is actually performed.

The DirectDraw Object

The DirectDraw object represents the video display device, typically a video card. All DirectDraw objects are derived from the COM object **IDirectDraw** (similar to the way C++ classes are inherited). The DirectDraw object takes care of a few low-level hardware functions and creates all the other DirectDraw objects in an application. In most applications, you will have only one DirectDraw object, global to the entire application. However, it is possible to have one DirectDraw object for *each* display device on the user's system.

When you declare the DirectDraw object, you usually make your variable of type **LPDIRECTDRAW**. As stated earlier, the DirectDraw header file **DDRAW.H** defines this variable as a pointer to a DirectDraw object. We're going to put our global **LPDIRECTDRAW** variable in a structure, along with a bunch of other objects we need often, as you'll see shortly.

In most cases, you will create and initialize the DirectDraw object near the beginning of your application, after the main application window is created. This is done with a call to the function **DirectDrawCreate**.

 ## DirectDrawCreate

```
HRESULT DirectDrawCreate( GUID FAR* lpGUID,
LPDIRECTDRAW FAR* lplpDD, IUnknown FAR* pUnkOuter )
```

DirectDrawCreate takes three parameters:

1. *lpGUID*—the GUID (Global Unique Identifier) of the display device for which you want to create a DirectDraw object. The identifiers of different devices can be obtained by calling the **DirectDrawEnumerate** function. We'll look at implementing **DirectDrawEnumerate** in the next chapter. If the argument is NULL, **DirectDrawCreate** assumes that you want to create a DirectDraw object for the active display device.

2. *lplpDD*—a pointer to a pointer to a DirectDraw object. No, that isn't a typo. A pointer to a pointer to a DirectDraw object. Remember that the DirectDraw object was declared as type **LPDIRECTDRAW**, which is already a pointer, so we need another pointer to manipulate that pointer. Now all you need to do is pass the address of that pointer to **DirectDrawCreate**, using the & operator. The DirectDraw object to which these pointers point will be initialized with the newly created DirectDraw object.

3. *pUnkOuter*—this parameter shows up in a lot of DirectX function calls. Its purpose is to facilitate future COM features, and it is not presently used. It only appears in current DirectX functions to ensure that future versions are backwards compatible. This argument must be NULL in the current version of DirectX, or the function you're calling will return an error. So until a future release of the Game SDK, just assume that many DirectX function calls end with a NULL argument.

Getting back to **DirectDrawCreate**, take a look at Listing 2-5, which shows an example of it in use:

Listing 2-5 Creating a **DirectDraw** object

```
// Declare a pointer to a DirectDraw object
LPDIRECTDRAW lpDD;
.
.
.
// Declare an HRESULT variable
```

```
HRESULT ret;

// Create a new DirectDraw object
ret = DirectDrawCreate( NULL, &lpDD, NULL );

// Make sure DirectDrawCreate was successful
if( ret != DD_OK )
    return;
```

Let's walk through the code. Just assume that somewhere before the DirectDraw object is declared, a window is created and initialized, and a bunch of other stuff happens.

First, a global pointer to a DirectDraw object named *lpDD* is declared, using the following code:

```
LPDIRECTDRAW lpDD;
```

Somewhere in the program, usually close to the place where the application window is created, `DirectDrawCreate` is called:

```
ret = DirectDrawCreate( NULL, &lpDD, NULL );
```

For the first argument, a **NULL** is passed to indicate the DirectDraw object will be created for the active display device (probably a video card). The second argument is a pointer to our DirectDraw object pointer. This pointer will be initialized with the new DirectDraw object.

After calling `DirectDrawCreate`, its return value (which was stored in the **HRESULT** variable *ret*) is checked to make sure that `DirectDrawCreate` succeeded. If it didn't, we stop.

```
if( ret != DD_OK )
    return;
```

Virtually every DirectX function returns an **HRESULT** value. If the function is successful, the return value will be **DD_OK**. If it is not, the return value will be some other **HRESULT** value, which you can examine if you'd like to have a better idea as to what went wrong.

Creating the DirectDraw Object

When we create the DirectDraw object in our example program, things don't look quite as simple as they did in Listing 2-5. Take a look at the code from **DrawInit** in our example program:

```
if( (gapp.lpdd = DDCreate(gapp.hwndApp)) == NULL )
return FALSE;
```

The reason this call is so brief is that the actual call to `DirectDrawCreate` is contained in a wrapper function, **DDCreate**, making the code more modular. In this book we'll use the same approach with many DirectDraw functions, to make the code easier to read. Before we examine **DDCreate**, we need to look at a few things concerning program organization.

DDRAWEX.H

Let's take a look at the file **DDRAWEX.H**, which defines a structure holding all the vital DirectDraw data for our example program (Listing 2-6):

Listing 2-6 **DDRAWEX.H**

```
//
// DDRAWEX.H
//
typedef struct _DDraw
{
 HWND   hwndApp; // Window to use
 LPDIRECTDRAW  lpdd;   // Pointer to DirectDraw object
 LPDIRECTDRAWSURFACE lpFrontBuffer; // Pointer to front buffer
 BOOL   fEnabled; // DirectDraw enabled
 int    nCooperation; // CooperationLevel
 int    cx;   // Width of window
 int    cy;   // Height of window
 int    bbp;   // Bits per plane
} DDraw, *LPDDraw;

LPDIRECTDRAW  DDCreate(HWND hwndApp);
void    DDDestroy();
BOOL    DDEnable();
void    DDDisable();
LPDIRECTDRAWSURFACE DDGetFrontBuffer();
DWORD   DDColorMatch(LPDIRECTDRAWSURFACE pdds, COLORREF rgb);
int    DDGetWidth();
int    DDGetHeight();
BOOL    DDSetCooperativeLevel(int level);
int    DDGetCooperativeLevel();
```

We haven't covered many of the concepts behind the code in this file, but we need to look at the first several lines, the ones containing the **_DDraw** structure:

```
typedef struct _DDraw
{
 HWND   hwndApp;   // Window to use
 LPDIRECTDRAW  lpdd;    // Pointer to DirectDraw object
 LPDIRECTDRAWSURFACE lpFrontBuffer; // Pointer to front buffer
 BOOL   fEnabled;  // DirectDraw enabled
 int    nCooperation; // CooperationLevel
 int    cx;   // Width of window
 int    cy;   // Height of window
 int    bbp;   // Bits per plane
} DDraw, *LPDDraw;
```

This structure holds virtually all the data we'll need to use DirectDraw. We'll fill it in while initializing the DirectDraw portion of our application (within **DrawInit**). For the moment, don't concern yourself with any of the members of this structure besides *lpdd*, which is a pointer to the main DirectDraw object for our program.

The _DDraw structure is typedefined as both **DDraw** (an instance of the structure) and **LPDDraw** (a pointer to an instance of the structure). We're going to use **LPDDraw** in our code, since it'll be more convenient. The instance of this structure that we'll use in our example is declared in the file **DDRAWEX.CPP** on the CD.

The rest of the file simply declares several functions that we're going to use at one point or another:

```
LPDIRECTDRAW  DDCreate(HWND hwndApp);
void    DDDestroy();
BOOL   DDEnable();
void   DDDisable();
LPDIRECTDRAWSURFACE DDGetFrontBuffer();
DWORD    DDColorMatch(LPDIRECTDRAWSURFACE pdds, COLORREF rgb);
int    DDGetWidth();
int    DDGetHeight();
BOOL    DDSetCooperativeLevel(int level);
int    DDGetCooperativeLevel();
```

We'll use these functions in place of DirectDraw API functions with almost the same name. We're just encapsulating the DirectDraw functions themselves within these wrapper functions to keep the code nice and clean. We're also going to do a few things in several places in the program, so using these wrapper functions lessens our typing load. All these functions are contained in **DDRAWEX.CPP**.

The **DDCreate** Function

Back in our example, we were attempting to create a DirectDraw object:

```
if( (gapp.lpdd = DDCreate(gapp.hwndApp)) == NULL )
return FALSE;
```

Let's take a look at the **DDCreate** function used for just that purpose (Listing 2-7):

Listing 2-7 **DDCreate**

```
LPDIRECTDRAW DDCreate(HWND hwndApp)
{
 HRESULT hr;

 //
 // Destroy existing DDraw object if this is a restart
 //
 if( lpdraw != NULL )
  DDDestroy();
  //
 // Allocate and initialize DDraw object memory
 //
 if( (lpdraw = (LPDDraw)malloc(sizeof(DDraw))) == NULL )
  return NULL;
 memset(lpdraw,0,sizeof(DDraw));
```

continued on next page

continued from previous page

```
//
// Create DirectDraw object
//
    hr = DirectDrawCreate( NULL, &lpdraw->lpdd, NULL );
if( hr == DD_OK )
{
 lpdraw->hwndApp = hwndApp;
 //
 // Initialize defaults
 //
 lpdraw->cx = 640;
 lpdraw->cy = 480;
 lpdraw->bbp = 16;
 } else {
 free(lpdraw);
 lpdraw = NULL;
 return NULL;
 }
 return lpdraw->lpdd;
}
```

If all goes well, **DDCreate** returns a pointer to the newly created DirectDraw object; otherwise it returns **NULL**. Its lone parameter, *hWndApp*, is the window that will display the DirectDraw output.

Up at the top of **DDRAWEX.CPP** is the statement:

```
LPDDraw lpdraw = NULL;
```

This statement creates the single, global DirectDraw structure that we'll use throughout the program. Incidentally, we'll also set *lpdraw* to **NULL** at the same time we declare it, so we know it hasn't been created or initialized yet. In general, we'll use the **NULL** value for any pointers we haven't created or initialized, so that all these objects are easier to keep track of.

The next few lines of code in **DDCreate** ensure the DirectDraw object hasn't already been created. We have to do this so that we can recall **DDCreate** without bringing the system to its knees.

If *lpdraw* has already been created, we destroy it with a call to **DDDestroy**, another function we'll get to soon that frees up the resources associated with the DirectDraw object.

The next several lines allocate and initialize the memory containing the DirectDraw object itself:

```
if( (lpdraw = (LPDDraw)malloc(sizeof(DDraw))) == NULL )
 return NULL;
memset(lpdraw,0,sizeof(DDraw));
```

The first two lines allocate the necessary memory and return **NULL** if **malloc** meets with failure for some reason (presumably, it ran out of memory). **memset** initializes the entire chunk of memory to zero to avoid any nasty surprises that might be hidden. By the way, **MALLOC.H**, which declares the function **malloc**, and **MEMORY.H**, which declares **memset**, are both #included at the top of **DDRAWEX.CPP**.

The next line calls `DirectDrawCreate`:

```
hr = DirectDrawCreate( NULL, &lpdraw->lpdd, NULL );
```

The return value of **DirectDrawCreate** is stored in the **HRESULT** variable *hr.* If we want to, we can then look at *hr* to see if anything went wrong.

The second parameter in the call to **DirectDrawCreate**, *&lpdraw->lpdd*, may look a bit strange. What we're doing is getting a pointer to the **LPDIRECTDRAW** member of our **LPDDraw** structure. Refer back to Listing 2-5 if you forgot what the **LPDDraw** structure looks like.

If all went well and the DirectDraw object was created, we continue on to this line of code:

```
lpdraw->hwndApp = hwndApp;
```

All we're doing here is saving the window handle passed to **DDCreate** in our **LPDDraw** structure. The window handle we saved will come in handy, so it's a good idea to keep it where it can easily be retrieved.

The next two lines of code simply set a size for the application when it's running as a window (not taking up the entire screen):

```
lpdraw->cx = 640;
lpdraw->cy = 480;
```

Next we're going to set the color depth by saving a bit per pixel value (refer to Chapter 1 if you've forgotten what that means):

```
lpdraw->bbp = 16;
```

We're going to use true color for the example applications until we learn how to work with palettes. That way everything will look nice, and we won't have to worry about whether the colors we want to use are available. Although our applications won't get quite the same frame rate as with 256 colors, they'll make much better learning tools.

The last line in that *if* statement (*lpdraw->nBuffers = 2*) deals with another topic we haven't discussed yet, so we'll come back to it later in the chapter.

If the attempt to create the DirectDraw object (using **DirectDrawCreate**) failed, then we move on to the *else* statement:

```
} else {
 free(lpdraw);
 lpdraw = NULL;
 return NULL;
}
```

The call to **free** simply frees the memory we allocated to hold the DirectDraw structure. The next line sets *lpdraw* to **NULL** so that the rest of our application knows it can't legally use the DirectDraw object, since it's not there. The final line returns **NULL** to **DrawInit** (remember, that's the function **WinMain** calls to initialize DirectDraw).

The last line of **DDCreate** simply returns the newly created DirectDraw object (in its **LPDDRAW** structure, of course).

Remember that this line of code won't be reached if the DirectDraw object fails to be created, because the *else* statement returns **NULL**.

SetCooperativeLevel

Back in `DrawInit`, we had this line:

```
DDSetCooperativeLevel( DDSCL_EXCLUSIVE | DDSCL_FULLSCREEN );
```

That line calls the function `DDSetCooperativeLevel`, which is a wrapper for the DirectDraw function `SetCooperativeLevel`. We're going to take some time now to discuss `SetCooperativeLevel`. This is a very important topic, so pay close attention.

After creating the DirectDraw object, you need to make a couple of decisions. First of all, you have to choose whether or not to use *exclusive mode*. Exclusive mode is a condition which tells DirectDraw if your application should be allowed to perform certain operations that affect the system as a whole, not just this application. For example, utilizing exclusive mode allows you to modify the palette and change the display mode. If you need any of these capabilities, you should use exclusive mode.

More than one DirectDraw application can be running at a time, one of the advantages Windows provides. But as the name implies, only one application can use exclusive mode at a time. If you don't really need it, you should be nice to other applications and not use exclusive mode. You also have to be sure that another application is not using exclusive mode when *you* try to use it.

If another application is using exclusive mode, you can still use both DirectDraw and the GDI without any problem; however, you're not permitted to modify the palette or change the display mode. If using exclusive mode is critical to your application, then you should send the user a message telling him or her to close down all other running applications (or something to that effect).

Once you've determined whether or not you need exclusive mode, let DirectDraw know by using the `SetCooperativeLevel` function. Besides informing DirectDraw of your choice about exclusive mode, `SetCooperativeLevel` affects a number of important conditions within your application:

- ModeX—ModeX is a special display mode which has become popular with DOS game programmers in recent years. If you want to use it, you have to tell `SetCooperativeLevel`.

- CTRL+ALT+DEL—If you want to let the user use this infamous key combination as normal, you need to specify it here. Not that they ever will, right?

- Fullscreen mode—Most games run in fullscreen mode. You need to tell `SetCooperativeLevel` whether or not your application will.

Note

It is common practice to call `SetCooperativeLevel` more than once in an application. For instance, many of the example programs we create during the course of this book will switch between windowed and fullscreen mode using a menu. Doing so will require the use of `SetCooperativeLevel` numerous times within the application.

The choices you make when calling this function can have a drastic impact on your game. It would be wise to consider them carefully.

IDirectDraw::SetCooperativeLevel

```
HRESULT SetCooperativeLevel( HWND hWnd, DWORD
dwFlags )
```

SetCooperativeLevel is a member of IDirectDraw. If you are requesting exclusive mode, it would probably be a good idea to glance at the return value (an HRESULT, as mentioned earlier) to make sure another application isn't already using it. If the return value is *DDERR_EXCLUSIVEMODEALREADYSET*, another application has beaten you to the punch, so you'll have to either continue on without exclusive mode or terminate your application.

Besides affecting the conditions mentioned, SetCooperativeLevel connects DirectDraw to your application's main window. This means you have to call SetCooperativeLevel in your game, even if you don't want to specify one of the above conditions. All DirectDraw needs is a basic, *WS_OVERLAPPEDWINDOW*-style window. If you use fullscreen mode, the style window won't be visible anyway, so you usually don't have to worry about how it looks. It's a good idea to give your window a nice name and pretty icon though, so the user can distinguish your application from others when switching tasks.

1. *hWnd*—an HWND handle to your application's main window. This is the window to which DirectDraw will attach.

2. *dwFlags*—a DWORD value that describes the capabilities you want your game to have. A list of values is in Table 2-1. Keep in mind that DWORD values can be combined using the bitwise OR operator, /.

Table 2-1 DWORD values for use with SetCooperativeLevel

Name	Meaning
DDSCL_ALLOWMODEX	Allows the application to use the ModeX display mode.
DDSCL_ALLOWREBOOT	Allows CTRL+ALT+DEL to function within the application.
DDSCL_EXCLUSIVE	Gives the application exclusive mode, if possible.
DDSCL_FULLSCREEN	Allows the application to use the entire screen. Maximizes the window.
DDSCL_NORMAL	Allows the application to behave like a normal Windows application rather than using any of the features given above.
DDSCL_NOWINDOWCHANGES	Prevents DirectDraw from resizing the window.

Note

Using DDSCL_FULLSCREEN causes DirectDraw to ignore the GDI. This means that if any other application's window is visible for some reason, it will not be drawn. This could affect, for example, some of the stay-on-top utilities that have become popular.

A call to `SetCooperativeLevel` looks something like Listing 2-8:

Listing 2-8 Calling `SetCooperativeLevel`

```
// Create the DirectDraw object.
DirectDrawCreate( NULL, &lpDD, NULL );

// Call SetCooperativeLevel.
lpDD->SetCooperativeLevel( hWnd, DDSCL_EXCLUSIVE | DDSCL_FULLSCREEN );
```

First, a DirectDraw object is created, as was explained earlier in the chapter. `SetCooperativeLevel` is then called with arguments that make the application fullscreen in exclusive mode. The *hWnd* variable used in the call is just the handle of the application's window, which would have been created earlier in the code.

Way back in `DrawInit`, the function that `WinMain` calls to perform DirectDraw initialization, we have this line of code:

```
DDSetCooperativeLevel( DDSCL_EXCLUSIVE | DDSCL_FULLSCREEN );
```

That line of code calls the wrapper function `DDSetCooperativeLevel`, which embodies the DirectDraw function `SetCooperativeLevel`. Let's take a look at `DDSetCooperativeLevel` (Listing 2-9, from the file `DDRAWEX.CPP` on the CD):

Listing 2-9 `DDSetCooperativeLevel`

```
BOOL DDSetCooperativeLevel(int level)
{
    BOOL fWasEnabled = lpdraw->fEnabled;

    if( fWasEnabled )
        DDDisable();

    lpdraw->nCooperation = level;

    if( fWasEnabled )
        DDEnable();
    return TRUE;
}
```

`DDSetCooperativeLevel` takes one parameter that specifies the way the application should be displayed. This parameter is equal to the *dwFlags* parameter of `SetCooperativeLevel`.

The first line stores the enabled state of the application in the variable *fWasEnabled*. The *enabled* state of the application tells whether or not the application is currently activated and has the input focus. A Boolean member variable of `DDraw` structures, *fEnabled*, holds the value of this state (**TRUE** if the application has focus, **FALSE** if not).

If the application is enabled, we need to disable it by calling *DDDisable*, a function we'll write shortly. This is because calling `SetCooperativeLevel` twice in a row would kill the system, and we obviously want to avoid that.

The DirectDraw object's new cooperation state is then saved in the member variable *nCooperation*, so when we call `SetCooperativeLevel`, we'll know what state we should put the application into.

Again, the *lpdraw* variable is an instance of an **LPDDRAW** structure holding information vital to DirectDraw. The *nCooperation* member simply holds the *dwFlags* parameter (refer to the `SetCooperativeLevel` section earlier) used to call `SetCooperativeLevel`. The reason we're saving this information in the structure is because it enables us to write a simple wrapper for `SetCooperativeLevel`. We'll come back and change the value of *nCooperation* for later examples.

If the application was enabled when we entered `DDSetCooperativeLevel`, we call `DDEnable`. `DDEnable` is a function we'll be writing shortly that does the actual DirectDraw initialization, including calling `SetCooperativeLevel`.

Finally, we return **TRUE** to the calling function.

Surfaces

Surfaces are chunks of memory used for drawing that are derived from the COM object `IDirectDrawSurface`. Surfaces store images in memory, where you can perform operations on them. As an example, a separate surface is used to hold each graphic object (sprite) in an animated scene, which is then drawn onto another surface, composing the final image (this will be discussed in Chapter 5). See Figure 2-5 for an illustration. Of course, surfaces are not limited to being used as sprites and have many other functions.

Creating Surfaces

Creating a surface is a bit tricky. You'll need to fill in a **DDSURFACEDESC** structure with information describing the surface you're building. This step can be a bit confusing at first, so we'll take a little time to walk through it. Look at Table 2-2, which details the **DDSURFACEDESC** structure. Don't worry if some of the terms look foreign; they'll be explained later.

FIGURE 2-5

Surface holding next frame

Other surfaces holding images

Combining multiple surfaces

Table 2-2 The DDSURFACEDESC structure

Type	Name	Meaning
DWORD	dwSize	The size of the structure in bytes. (Use *sizeof*.)
DWORD	dwFlags	Specifies enabled members.
DWORD	dwHeight	Height of surface.
DWORD	dwWidth	Width of surface.
LONG	lPitch	Number of pixels from one horizontal line of memory to the next.
DWORD	dwBackBufferCount	Number of attached back buffers.
DWORD	dwZBufferBitDepth	Depth, in pixels, of the Zbuffer.
DWORD	dwAlphaBitDepth	Depth, in pixels, of the alpha buffer.
LPVOID	lpSurface	Pointer to surface memory.
DDCOLORKEY	ddckCKDestOverlay	Color key for use by destination overlays.
DDCOLORKEY	ddckCKDestBlt	Color key for use by destination blits.
DDCOLORKEY	ddckCKSrcOverlay	Color key for use by source overlays.

Type	Name	Meaning
DDCOLORKEY	ddckCKSrcBlt	Color key for use by source blits.
DDPIXELFORMAT	ddpfPixelFormat	The pixel format of the surface.
DDSCAPS	ddsCaps	Specifies the surface's capabilities.

When you request a new surface, you must first initialize the *dwSize* member. Then, combine DWORD values using the bitwise OR operator (*|*) to compose the *dwFlags* member. The *dwFlags* member tells DirectDraw which members of the DDSURFACEDESC structure contain valid values. There is a unique DWORD value for each member in the DDSURFACEDESC structure (Table 2-3), save for *dwSize* and *dwFlags*. This scheme saves a lot of time because you only need to fill in the members of the structure you're actually using.

Table 2-3 *dwFlags* values and their corresponding DDSURFACEDESC members

DWORD value	Corresponding member
DDSD_DDSCAPS	ddsCaps
DDSD_HEIGHT	dwHeight
DDSD_WIDTH	dwWidth
DDSD_PITCH	lPitch
DDSD_BACKBUFFERCOUNT	dwBackBufferCount
DDSD_ZBUFFERDEPTH	dwZBufferDepth
DDSD_ALPHABITDEPTH	dwAlphaBitDepth
DDSD_LPSURFACE	lpSurface
DDSD_PIXELFORMAT	ddpfPixelFormat
DDSD_CKDESTOVERLAY	ddCKDestOverlay
DDSD_CKDESTBLT	ddCKDestBlt
DDSD_CKSRCOVERLAY	ddCKSrcOverlay
DDSD_CKSRCBLT	ddCKSrcBlt
DDSD_ALL	All members are valid

Usually, when creating a new surface you will fill in only the width, height, *dwCaps*, and *ddsCaps* members. The other members are for creating specialized surfaces, some of which you'll learn about in later chapters.

The *ddsCaps* member is fairly important when dealing with **DDSURFACEDESC**. It tells **CreateSurface** what kind of surface you are creating. *ddsCaps* is another structure itself, a **DDSCAPS** structure. A **DDSCAPS** structure has only one member, a **DWORD** called *dwCaps*. There are several possible values for *dwCaps*, each describing a different type of surface. These values can, and often must, be combined to create a surface with unique characteristics and capabilities. More on *ddsCaps* later in this section.

 ## IDirectDraw::CreateSurface

```
HRESULT CreateSurface(LPDDSURFACEDESC
lpDDSurfaceDesc, LPDIRECTDRAWSURFACE FAR*
lplpDDSurface, IUnknown FAR* pUnkOuter )
```

To create a new surface, you need to use the **CreateSurface** function, a member of **IDirectDraw**. **CreateSurface** takes three parameters:

1. *lpDDSurfaceDes*—a pointer to a **DDSURFACEDESC** structure with information about the surface you are creating.

2. *lplpDDSurface*—a pointer to the **DirectDrawSurface** object that will be initialized with the new surface.

3. *pUnkOuter*—the useless **NULL** value.

You'll usually want to examine the return value to make sure it's **DD_OK**, because there are quite a few errors that can occur when creating surfaces.

 ## Note

DirectDraw will always put the new surface in video memory unless there isn't enough room or you explicitly ask it to store in plain old system RAM.

Listing 2-10 shows an offscreen surface being created. An offscreen surface is just one that's not visible, but don't concern yourself with that right now.

Listing 2-10 Creating a surface

```
// Declare the surface we're going to create
LPDIRECTDRAWSURFACE lpDDSOffscreen;
      .
      .
      .
// Declare a DDSURFACEDESC structure
DDSURFACEDESC ddsd;
```

```
// Initialize the size member
ddsd.dwSize = sizeof( ddsd );

// Set the dwFlags member so DirectDraw knows the ddsCaps, dwWidth, and
// dwHeight members are valid
ddsd.dwFlags = DDSD_DDSCAPS | DDSD_HEIGHT | DDSD_WIDTH;

// Initialize ddsCaps so it describes a plain offscreen surface
ddsd.ddsCaps.dwFlags = DDSCAPS_OFFSCREENPLAIN;

// Fill in the dimensions (25x25)
ddsd.dwHeight = 25;
ddsd.dwWidth = 25;

// Create the surface using our DDSURFACEDESC structure
lpDD->CreateSurface( &ddsd, &lpDDSOffscreen, NULL );
```

After we fill in the ever-present *dwSize* member, we initialize *dwFlags* so DirectDraw knows the *ddsCaps*, *dwHeight*, and *dwWidth* members are valid:

```
ddsd.dwFlags = DDSD_DDSCAPS | DDSD_HEIGHT | DDSD_WIDTH;
```

Next, we describe the type of surface we're creating, a plain offscreen surface:

```
ddsd.ddsCaps.dwFlags = DDSCAPS_OFFSCREENPLAIN;
```

We then have to let DirectDraw know what size the surface should be—keep in mind that the height and width values of 25×25 were selected arbitrarily:

```
ddsd.dwHeight = 25;
ddsd.dwWidth = 25;
```

Finally, we actually create the surface:

```
lpDD->CreateSurface( &ddsd, &lpDDSOffscreen, NULL );
```

`CreateSurface` is passed a pointer to the `DDSURFACEDESC` structure that was initialized, a pointer to the `DirectDrawSurface` pointer, and the ever-present `NULL`.

Once this bit of code runs, you have a fully functional surface. The only problem is you can't do anything with it yet, because you don't know how to get at the screen. Well, let's take care of that right now.

The Primary Surface

The *primary surface* is the chunk of video memory visible on the display, and it's shared with the GDI if you use the GDI in your game. The primary surface is also shared with the GDI if your game is in windowed mode but the window doesn't take up the entire screen, because the GDI will need to draw the windows lower in the Z-order (underneath the window).

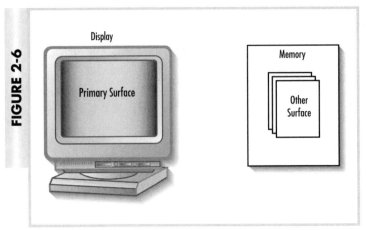

FIGURE 2-6

The primary surface and other surfaces

To create the primary surface, we'll need to fill in a **DDSURFACEDESC** structure (refer to Table 2-4). We'll put the value **DDSCAPS_PRIMARYSURFACE** in the **DDSURFACEDESC**'s *ddsCaps.dwCaps* member. **DDSCAPS_PRIMARYSURFACE** tells `CreateSurface` that a primary surface is being created. There are other values that can be combined with *DDSCAPS_PRIMARYSURFACE*, but we won't discuss them until later.

Note

Do *not* fill in the width and height members of *DDSURFACEDESC* when creating a primary surface. The primary surface is always the size of the display. You change the size of the primary surface by changing the video mode.

Take a look at Listing 2-11, which shows a primary surface being created:

Listing 2-11 Creating a primary surface

```
// Create the DirectDraw object
DirectDrawCreate( NULL, &lpDD, NULL );

// Make the app exclusive in full screen mode
lpDD->SetCooperativeLevel( hWnd, DDSCL_EXCLUSIVE | DDSCL_FULLSCREEN );

// Set the display to 320x200x8 (256 colors)
lpDD->SetDisplayMode( 320, 200, 8 );

// Initialize a DDSURFACEDESC structure with the values for a new primary
// surface
DDSURFACEDESC ddsd;
ddsd.dwSize = sizeof( ddsd );
ddsd.dwFlags = DDSD_DDCAPS; // Only the ddsCaps member is valid
```

```
ddsd.dwCaps.dwCaps = DDSCAPS_PRIMARYSURFACE;

// Create a new primary surface with the DDSURFACEDESC initialized above
lpDD->CreateSurface( &ddsd, &lpDDSPrimary, NULL );
```

First, the DirectDraw object is created, **SetCooperativeLevel** is called, and the display mode is set. A **DDSURFACEDESC** structure, **ddsd**, is then declared, and its **dwSize** member is initialized with its size in bytes. **dwFlags** is set to **DDSD_DDSCAPS** to let DirectDraw know that the **dwCaps** member is valid. After we've done all that, **dwCaps.dwCaps** is set to **DDSCAPS_PRIMARYSURFACE**, which tells DirectDraw a primary surface is being created.

Now that everything is ready to go, we can go ahead and call **CreateSurface**:

```
lpDD->CreateSurface( &ddsd, &lpDDSPrimary, NULL );
```

And that's about it!

DDCreateSurfaces

We're going to write a wrapper function around the DirectDraw API function **CreateSurface**, called **DDCreateSurfaces**, to create all the surfaces we'll be needing at once. It will create a surface using the data in **lpdraw**, and can be called many times to create different types of surfaces. **DDCreateSurfaces** is ultimately called from within **DDEnable** (which, as you'll recall, is called whenever the state of the application is changed or initialization needs to be performed). Let's take a look at **DDCreateSurfaces** (Listing 2-12):

Listing 2-12 **DDCreateSurfaces**

```
static BOOL DDCreateSurfaces()
{
LPDIRECTDRAW    lpdd = lpdraw->lpdd;
DDSURFACEDESC         ddsd;
HRESULT              hr;

memset( (VOID *)&ddsd, 0, sizeof( ddsd ) );

ddsd.dwSize = sizeof( ddsd );
ddsd.dwFlags = DDSD_CAPS;
ddsd.ddsCaps.dwCaps = DDSCAPS_PRIMARYSURFACE;

hr = lpdd->CreateSurface( &ddsd,
    &lpdraw->lpFrontBuffer,
    NULL );

if( hr != DD_OK )
 return FALSE;
else
 return TRUE;
}
```

Like most of our wrapper functions, **DDCreateSurfaces** returns **TRUE** if successful, **FALSE** otherwise.

First, several local variables are declared for use in the function:

```
LPDIRECTDRAW   lpdd = lpdraw->lpdd;
DDSURFACEDESC       ddsd;
HRESULT             hr;
```

lpdd is the pointer to a DirectDraw object that we'll use to access the DirectDraw object stored in our *lpdraw* structure. *Ddsd* is the structure we'll use to describe the surface we want to create to **CreateSurface**. *hr* is a variable we'll use to store the values returned from the DirectDraw functions we will call.

It's always a good idea to clean up the memory we plan to use before doing anything with it, and that's exactly what this line does:

```
memset( (VOID *)&ddsd, 0, sizeof( ddsd ) );
```

Next, we'll need to fill in the *dwSize* member of *ddsd*:

```
ddsd.dwSize = sizeof( ddsd );
```

And for the first example we'll create only a primary surface, so only the *ddsCaps* member of *ddsd* will be valid:

```
ddsd.dwFlags = DDSD_CAPS;
```

And finally, we need to describe the type of surface we're creating:

```
ddsd.ddsCaps.dwCaps = DDSCAPS_PRIMARYSURFACE;
```

For this first example, we'll only use a plain primary surface. Nothing fancy yet; we're just trying to build a bare-bones DirectDraw application.

Now we need to call **CreateSurface**, the DirectDraw API function. We'll call it using *lpdd*, which, as you'll recall, is a pointer to the DirectDraw object held in our **LPDDraw** structure *lpdraw*.

```
hr = lpdd->CreateSurface( &ddsd,
&lpdraw->lpFrontBuffer,
NULL );
```

In an **LPDDraw** structure (Listing 2-5) we called the primary surface *lpFrontBuffer*. We use this name because, as we move through the book, we'll constantly be expanding this sample program. In the next example program, we're going to learn about something called *complex surfaces,* which involve special surfaces called *front buffers.* The primary surface is a kind of front buffer, so that is what it's called in the **LPDDraw** structure.

DDEnable

If you recall from **DDSetCooperativeLevel**, **DDEnable** is the function that does much of the DirectDraw initialization. It's called by this line in **DrawInit** (Listing 2-4):

```
if( DDEnable() == FALSE )
return FALSE;
```

Let's take a look at the code that comprises **DDEnable** (Listing 2-13):

Listing 2-13 `DDEnable`

```
BOOL DDEnable()
{
 HRESULT hr;

 if( lpdraw == NULL )
  return FALSE;

 hr = lpdraw->lpdd->SetCooperativeLevel( lpdraw->hwndApp,
  lpdraw->nCooperation );
 if( hr != DD_OK )
  return FALSE;

 hr = lpdraw->lpdd->SetDisplayMode( lpdraw->cx, lpdraw->cy,
  lpdraw->bbp );
 if( hr != DD_OK )
  return FALSE;

 return DDCreateSurfaces();
}
```

`DDEnable` isn't one of the longest functions we've written, but it's certainly one of the most important.

The first thing `DDEnable` does is check to make sure it has a valid DirectDraw object to work with, and abort if it doesn't (remember that *lpdraw* is our global **LPDDraw** structure).

The next thing you'll notice as you scan the code is that `DDEnable` makes the actual call to `SetCooperativeLevel`:

```
hr = lpdraw->lpdd->SetCooperativeLevel( lpdraw->hwndApp,
lpdraw->nCooperation );
```

Now all those structure and wrapper functions come in handy. All the information we need to call `SetCooperativeLevel` is right here, and the data in the **LPDDraw** structure can be easily changed, should we need to call any of the functions contained in `DDEnable` again.

We need to call `SetCooperativeLevel` using the DirectDraw object pointer stored in our **LPDDraw** structure *lpdraw*, and we'll pass it the window handle stored in the same structure (we saved the window handle back in `DDCreate`). The *nCooperation* member of *lpdraw*, as you'll recall, is the state parameters that should be passed to `SetCooperativeLevel`. Remember that the value of *nCooperation* is set by a call to `DDSetCooperativeLevel`.

After we call `SetCooperativeLevel`, we, as always, make sure it succeeded. The next bit of code sets the display mode:

```
hr = lpdraw->lpdd->SetDisplayMode( lpdraw->cx, lpdraw->cy,
lpdraw->bbp );
```

We'll learn more about setting the display mode in just a moment.

After we've done everything `DDEnable` was supposed to do, we need to call `DDCreateSurfaces` (Listing 2-12) so that the surfaces we're using are up-to-date with the changes we made in `DDEnable`.

Setting the Display Mode

Most Windows users run at high resolution with many colors, which is not suitable for graphics programming. Therefore, most games will need to change the display mode. Remember, you can't change the display mode unless you're using exclusive mode.

There are a number of display modes to choose from. The most common are listed in Table 2-4.

Table 2-4 Common display modes

Resolution	Colors
320×200	256
320×200	16 million
640×400	256
640×400	16 million
640×480	256
640×480	16 million
800×600	256
800×600	16 million
1024×768	256

One thing to remember when choosing a display mode is that not every user's video card supports every display mode. You're probably safe choosing a mode such as 640×480 at 256 colors, but don't go trying to set the display to some obscure mode like 24×740 with 16 million colors.

There is a function, `EnumDisplayModes`, which supplies a list of all the video modes supported by the user's video card. We won't be using this function until the next chapter, where we'll discuss it in detail. For now, we'll just stick with some fairly safe guesses.

 IDirectDraw::SetDisplayMode

```
HRESULT SetDisplayMode( DWORD dwWidth, DWORD dwHeight,
DWORD dwBpp)
```

To set the display mode, use the `SetDisplayMode` function, a member of `IDirectDraw`. It takes three arguments:

1. The width of the screen resolution in pixels. This can be any positive value.

2. The height of the screen resolution in pixels. This also can be any positive value.

3. The bits per pixel (BPP) of the new color depth. Table 2-5 lists common BPP values and their corresponding color depths.

Table 2-5 Bits per pixel

BPP	Colors
1	2 (B&W)
4	16
8	256
16	true color

The most common color depth is 256 colors, since 16 colors looks rather primitive and true color modes tend to be on the slow side.

Let's hop back to our example program for a moment. We were at the function **DDEnable** (Listing 2-13). The line of code that calls **SetDisplayMode** looks like this:

```
hr = lpdraw->lpdd->SetDisplayMode( lpdraw->cx, lpdraw->cy,
lpdraw->bbp );
```

Remember that *lpdraw* is the **LPDDraw** structure holding a bunch of vital DirectDraw information, including the DirectDraw object (the *lpdd* member). This code calls **SetDisplayMode** using the *lpdd* member of the *lpdraw* structure, and uses information from *lpdraw* to set the resolution and color depth. We initialized the *cx*, *cy*, and *bbp* values in **DDCreate** (Listing 2-6).

DDDisable

DDDisable is the function that takes care of DirectDraw cleanup and destruction. We also call it from **DDSetCooperativeLevel** so we don't accidentally create or initialize anything more than once, which would be bad news.

Let's take a look at the **DDDisable** code (Listing 2-14):

Listing 2-14 **DDDisable**

```
void DDDisable()
{
 if( lpdraw == NULL )
  return;

 if( lpdraw->lpFrontBuffer )
 {
  lpdraw->lpFrontBuffer->Release();
  lpdraw->lpFrontBuffer = NULL;
 }

 if( lpdraw->nCooperation & DDSCL_EXCLUSIVE )
  lpdraw->lpdd->RestoreDisplayMode();
}
```

DDDisable doesn't return a value, because if anything goes wrong in this function, you couldn't do anything about it anyway.

The first thing **DDDisable** does is check to make sure it has something to clean up. If *lpdraw* isn't initialized, it has nothing to do, so it just returns.

Next, it checks to make sure the ***lpFrontBuffer*** member of ***lpdraw*** is valid. If it is, **DDDisable** releases the COM object (refer to Chapter 1 for more information) and sets **lpFrontBuffer** to **NULL** so we know it's no longer available.

The last thing we need to do is give up exclusive mode if we were using it. We do this with the **IDirectDraw** member function **RestoreDisplayMode**, which simply restores the display mode that was active before we called **SetDisplayMode**.

The Callback Function

Phew! We're finished with initialization! Now we need to move on to the callback function, which performs most of the user interface work in our applications.

As you may recall, callback functions must be declared in a specific way. You can refer back to the section on **CreateWindowEx** for detailed information. The callback function we'll use in our example program is called **WindowProc**, and is located in the **Ex2-1.CPP** file on the CD. Let's take a look at it in Listing 2-15:

Listing 2-15 **WindowProc**—The callback function

```
//
// WindowProc --- Handles messages for the main application window
//
static long FAR PASCAL WindowProc( HWND hWnd, UINT message, WPARAM wParam, ⇐
LPARAM lParam )
{
 PAINTSTRUCT ps;
 HDC   hdc;
 static BOOL fFirstPaint = TRUE;

 switch( message )
 {
  case WM_SIZE:
  case WM_MOVE:
   GetClientRect(gapp.hwndApp,
    &gapp.wndRect);
   ClientToScreen(gapp.hwndApp,
    (LPPOINT)&gapp.wndRect);
   ClientToScreen(gapp.hwndApp,
    (LPPOINT)&gapp.wndRect+1);
   break;

  case WM_KEYDOWN:
   switch( wParam )
   {
    case VK_ESCAPE:
    case VK_F12:
    PostMessage(hWnd,WM_CLOSE, 0,0);
```

```
       return 0;
     }

   case WM_PAINT:
    hdc = BeginPaint( hWnd, &ps );
    EndPaint( hWnd, &ps );
    Render();
    if( fFirstPaint )
    {
     //
     // This allows the cursor code to retrieve the
     // current background for the cursor instead of
     // using the background which existed before the
     // first paint.
     //
     ShowCursor(TRUE);
     fFirstPaint = FALSE;
    }
    return 1;

   case WM_DESTROY:
    //
    // We're done, clean up and say goodbye
    //
    DDDisable();
    DDDestroy();
    PostQuitMessage( 0 );
    break;
  }
  return DefWindowProc(hWnd, message, wParam, lParam);
}
```

The callback function is probably one of the longest functions we'll run into for a while. Don't let it deter you though; it's really not that complex. We'll just take it a line or two at a time.

The first three lines declare some variables we'll use in different parts of the function. The **PAINTSTRUCT** variable is used for drawing with GDI, as is the **HDC** variable. The **Boolean** variable simply tells us if we're painting the window for the first time, because we'll need to do a little extra work the first time around.

Now we encounter a *switch* statement. For pure C programs, the *switch* statement you see here is the heart and soul of the whole program. This *switch* takes each message received from Windows by the callback function and does whatever it's supposed to do when it receives that type of message. The actual message is passed through the UINT parameter *message* and is the numerical ID of the message.

WM_SIZE and WM_MOVE

Let's take a look at the first two *case* statements within the *switch* statement:

```
case WM_SIZE:
case WM_MOVE:
```

The first two messages we'll handle are the **WM_SIZE** and **WM_MOVE** messages (like all messages, both are actually numerical IDs #defined in WINDOWS.H). We have to handle these, because we need to know the exact position of our window at all times, and the window's position changes whenever the window is sized or moved. We'll just let the same code handle either message:

```
GetClientRect(gapp.hwndApp, &gapp.wndRect);
ClientToScreen(gapp.hwndApp, (LPPOINT)&gapp.wndRect);
ClientToScreen(gapp.hwndApp, (LPPOINT)&gapp.wndRect+1);
break;
```

This code uses a few Windows API functions that we won't discuss, for the sake of brevity. Basically, all it does is fill the window rectangle (in the **gapp** global application structure) with the new position of the window. The calls to **ClientToScreen** simply convert the window's location in window coordinates to the same coordinates on the screen.

WM_KEYDOWN

The next *case* statement handles the **WM_KEYDOWN** message, which is sent whenever the user presses a key:

```
case WM_KEYDOWN:
 switch( wParam )
 {
  case VK_ESCAPE:
  case VK_F12:
   PostMessage(hWnd, WM_CLOSE, 0, 0);
   return 0;
 }
 break;
```

As you can probably guess, we'll use this message a lot in later samples and games. This message replaces DOS **C** functions that check the keyboard buffer, and provides a simple way to interact with the user.

The **WM_KEYDOWN** message makes use of the **WPARAM** message parameter, which we discussed earlier. The **WPARAM** is passed into the callback function through the variable *wParam*, which is actually a type of pointer. We'll use a *switch* statement to handle the various keys the user hits.

Recall that back in WinMain we called **TranslateMessage** before sending the message to the callback function using **DispatchMessage**. What **TranslateMessage** actually does is convert the **WPARAM** of WM_KEYDOWN messages into a more readable form: numerical IDs #defined in WINDOWS.H. The ones we need to handle are named **VK_ESCAPE** (the [ESC] key) and **VK_F12** (the [F12] key). When the user hits either of those keys, we'll quit the application.

The only line of code that does anything substantial in these two *case* statements is

```
PostMessage(hWnd, WM_CLOSE, 0, 0);
```

This code uses the Windows API function **PostMessage** to send another message (**WM_CLOSE**) to the callback function. The **WM_CLOSE** message tells the callback function to close the window. If you'd like more information on **PostMessage**, you can find it in your Windows API documentation.

Finally, we need to return zero to get out of the callback function. When the callback function handles **WM_KEYDOWN** messages, it should always return zero.

WM_PAINT

The **WM_PAINT** message is sent by the Windows environment whenever our window needs to be redrawn. For now we'll draw only with DirectDraw when this message is sent; however, we'll develop some more efficient methods for future programs.

Let's take a look at the *case* statement that handles **WM_PAINT**:

```
case WM_PAINT:
 hdc = BeginPaint( hWnd, &ps );
 EndPaint( hWnd, &ps );
 Render();
 if( fFirstPaint )
 {
  //
  // This allows the cursor code to retrieve the
  // current background for the cursor instead of
  // using the background which existed before the
  // first paint.
  //
  ShowCursor(TRUE);
  fFirstPaint = FALSE;
 }
 return 1;
```

Before we go into the code, we need to sidetrack a bit and learn about the Windows GDI. Sit tight though; we'll be back to coding before you know it.

The Windows GDI

Although the GDI functions aren't very fast, they can do a lot. They have the ability to:

- Draw graphics primitives such as circles, ellipses, rectangles, curves, and any other type of polygon

- Plot individual pixels and lines

- Draw text using TrueType fonts

- Display bitmaps

- Fill areas with patterns and solid colors

- Manage palettes

As you can see, there's a lot of functionality here. The only drawback is the GDI's speed. Although it's faster when running under DirectDraw, it's still not as speedy as we'd like. Obviously, there's going to be a little speed hit when you go through another level of API calls.

We're not going to go into much detail about the Windows GDI; we're just going to learn enough to draw some text. Even though most of the time you won't use the GDI for anything, it does come in handy in a few instances. For example, if you want to put text on your game's screen to display the score or whatever, the GDI is probably the easiest and most flexible way to go.

Device Contexts

Device contexts (DCs) are used to display text and graphics in Windows programs. There are several types of DCs, each serving a unique purpose. The different types of DCs and their functions are listed in Table 2-6:

Table 2-6 Device context types

Device context type	Function
Display	For drawing on the screen.
Printer	For drawing to the printer.
Memory	For drawing to a bitmap in memory.
Information	Retrieves information about a device.

Each type of DC is created in a different way. For our purposes, we only need to learn how to create display DCs. Consult your Windows API manual for more information on the other types of DCs.

DCs are accessed by using handles to device contexts, or HDCs. Display HDCs for drawing on windows are normally obtained by using the `GetDC` function. `GetDC` retrieves an HDC that can be used for drawing to the window, which is passed as an argument.

Retrieving Device Contexts

Usually we'll draw only with device contexts when our callback function receives a `WM_PAINT` message, as it does in our example program. When we receive one of those messages, the first thing we need to do is retrieve a DC that works with our window. We'll do that using the Windows API function `BeginPaint`.

 BeginPaint

```
HDC BeginPaint( HWND hwnd, LPPAINTSTRUCT lppaint );
```

`BeginPaint` simply returns a handle to a valid DC for the given window if successful; otherwise it returns `NULL`. It takes two parameters:

1. The window that will be drawn on using the DC.

2. A PAINTSTRUCT that will be filled with drawing information.

This is the **BeginPaint** code from our sample program:

```
hdc = BeginPaint( hWnd, &ps );
```

As you'll recall, this code is taken from our callback function **WindowProc** from the place that handles the **WM_PAINT** message. *hWnd* is a handle to the window for which the callback function is used (passed in through function parameters), and *ps* is a **PAINTSTRUCT** that we declared at the top of the function. *hdc* is an HDC we also declared at the top of the function.

All we really need to call **BeginPaint** for is retrieving a valid DC handle, and we've done that. But we're still taking up some resources that we allocated using **BeginPaint**, so we'll need to release them. We'll do that by using the Windows API function **EndPaint**, which simply takes the same two parameters as **BeginPaint**:

```
EndPaint( hWnd, &ps );
```

Keep in mind that the HDC we retrieved using **BeginPaint** is still valid, so we're still going to use it to do window painting.

The next line of code in our callback function (in the **WM_PAINT** handler) calls a function we'll be writing named **Render**:

```
Render();
```

Render performs all DirectDraw drawing operations. We'll examine this function shortly.

The next few lines of code in our **WM_PAINT** handler restore the cursor, if this is the first time the **WM_PAINT** message has been received:

```
if( fFirstPaint )
{
//
// This allows the cursor code to retrieve the
// current background for the cursor instead of
// using the background which existed before the
// first paint.
//
ShowCursor(TRUE);
fFirstPaint = FALSE;
}
```

Remember that we had to hide the cursor when we first created the window, to avoid leaving an unsightly black cursor-shaped hole in the middle of the screen (way back in **WinMain**). We now restore the cursor simply using **ShowCursor**. After that, we need to toggle the *fFirstPaint* variable so this bit of code isn't run again.

WM_DESTROY

Windows sends the message **WM_DESTROY** to a window's callback function when the window is being destroyed. Usually, you take care of application cleanup when you receive this message (it's what we'll do here, anyway).

Here's the code from our example that handles **WM_DESTROY**:

```
case WM_DESTROY:
//
// We're done, clean up and say goodbye
//
DDDisable();
DDDestroy();
PostQuitMessage( 0 );
break;
```

The very first thing we do is call **DDDisable** (Listing 2-14), a function we wrote to do some DirectDraw cleanup. The next line of code calls **DDDestroy**, a function we'll examine shortly. **DDDestroy** removes all the various DirectDraw objects from memory, so our application doesn't leave a mess behind when the user quits. The final line calls the Windows API function **PostQuitMessage**, which simply tells Windows that we want to quit and sends the application a **WM_QUIT** message, which should be the last message an application ever receives. By the way, the one parameter that **PostQuitMessage** accepts is the **WPARAM** value that **WinMain** should return to the system.

DDDestroy

We call **DDDestroy** when we're done using DirectDraw and want everything cleaned up. Its code is shown in Listing 2-16:

Listing 2-16 **DDDestroy**

```
void DDDestroy()
{
 if( lpdraw == NULL )
  return;
 if( lpdraw->lpdd != NULL )
  lpdraw->lpdd->Release();
  free(lpdraw);
 lpdraw = NULL;
}
```

The first thing **DDDestroy** does is make sure it has something to clean up, by verifying that *lpdraw* isn't **NULL**.

Next, it calls the DirectDraw object's **Release** function (see Chapter 1 for more information) to remove the DirectDraw object from memory.

Finally, it *frees* the memory we allocated for the DirectDraw object (in **DDCreate**, Listing 2-6) and sets the pointer to **NULL** so we know it isn't there anymore.

DefWindowProc

The very last line of our callback function calls the Windows API function `DefWindowProc` and returns its return value:

```
return DefWindowProc(hWnd, message, wParam, lParam);
```

`DefWindowProc` (Default Window Procedure) is simply a callback function supplied by Windows to handle any message you don't. It performs a default behavior for each message and usually handles messages without any problems. By the way, you can just pass it the same parameters Windows passed to your custom callback function.

Rendering

Okay, we're just about done writing our first DirectDraw application. All we need to do now is write the rendering code, and we'll be ready to compile.

Typically, the rendering code in a game will be *much* more complex than the code we're about to write. But since we're just interested in learning how to get something on the screen right now, our example will suffice. This first program merely places the text "Hello World" in the center of the screen, which admittedly isn't very impressive. When we move on to the next example, later in this chapter, we'll add a little life to our program.

RenderInit

During the course of the book, we'll be using the function `RenderInit` to perform initializations that need to occur before we can draw the window for the first time. `RenderInit` is called from `DrawInit` when the application is first started.

Take a look at the version of `RenderInit` used for this example (Listing 2-17):

Listing 2-17 RenderInit

```
BOOL RenderInit()
{
 LPDIRECTDRAWSURFACE lpFrontBuffer = DDGetFrontBuffer();
 HDC hdc;

 //
 // No sense doing this all the time
 //
 msglen = strlen(msg);

 //
 // GetDC and calculate variables used for centering
 //
 if(lpFrontBuffer->GetDC(&hdc) == DD_OK)
 {
  SIZE size;
  int w = DDGetWidth();
  int h = DDGetHeight();
```

continued on next page

continued from previous page

```
GetTextExtentPoint32(hdc, msg, msglen, &size );

//
// Centered text
//
xmin = (w - size.cx) / 2;
ymin = (h - size.cy) / 2;

lpFrontBuffer->ReleaseDC(hdc);
} else {
return FALSE;
}
return TRUE;
}
```

Basically, this version of **RenderInit** just calculates where to start drawing text (*msg*, which is declared at the top of **RENDER.CPP**) in order for it to be centered.

The first line retrieves a pointer to the primary surface:

```
LPDIRECTDRAWSURFACE lpFrontBuffer = DDGetFrontBuffer();
```

We do this using the function **DDGetFrontBuffer**, which is in the file **DDRAWEX.CPP**. Take a look (Listing 2-18):

Listing 2-18 **DDGetFrontBuffer**

```
LPDIRECTDRAWSURFACE DDGetFrontBuffer()
{
  f( lpdraw == NULL )
  return NULL;
 return lpdraw->lpFrontBuffer;
}
```

DDGetFrontBuffer simply makes sure that the surface pointer contained in our global **LPDDraw** structure *lpdraw* is valid and returns it, if it is.

Now we need to retrieve a device context with which to work. We'll need a device context to measure the text, which we need to do because we're trying to center it on the screen. We'll use a device context specialized for use with the primary surface we created:

```
if(lpFrontBuffer->GetDC(&hdc) == DD_OK)
```

Let's take a short time-out to learn how to retrieve a device context for use with a surface.

Getting Surface DCs

When you need to use the GDI, as we do, you'll need to retrieve a DC used specifically for that purpose. We do this with the DirectDraw API function *GetDC*, an **IDirectDrawSurface** member.

IDirectDrawSurface::GetDC

HRESULT GetDC(HDCFAR* lphDC)

As you can see, **GetDC** takes a pointer to an HDC as its only argument. **GetDC** will return a pointer to an HDC for use on the surface in this parameter.

Once you're done with a DC, you need to release it, to free the resources it is using. This is done using **ReleaseDC**, also a member function of **IDirectDrawSurface**.

IDirectDrawSurface::ReleaseDC

HRESULT ReleaseDC(HDC hDC)

In **RenderInit**, the code for retrieving an HDC looks like this:

```
if(lpFrontBuffer->GetDC(&hdc) == DD_OK)
```

We're simply attempting to retrieve an HDC for use with *lpFrontBuffer* and proceeding into the *if* statement if successful. If we're not successful, the *else* statement returns **FALSE**.

The *if* statement looks like this:

```
SIZE size;
int w = DDGetWidth();
int h = DDGetHeight();

GetTextExtentPoint32(hdc, msg, msglen, &size );

//
// Centered text
//
xmin = (w - size.cx) / 2;
ymin = (h - size.cy) / 2;

lpFrontBuffer->ReleaseDC(hdc);
```

DDGetWidth and **DDGetHeight** get the width and height of the primary surface. We're storing these two values in *w* and *h*, respectively.

The **GetTextExtentPoint32** Window API function finds how many pixels the given text will take up when displayed. It puts the values in the *size* structure, with the *cx* member as the width of the text, and *cy* as the height. For details on **GetTextExtentPoint32**, consult your Windows API reference.

Next, we need to calculate where the text should appear on the screen. When you draw text, you need to specify the upper-left corner of its position. To find the correct upper-left corner position of text on the screen, we simply calculate the length of the screen in each dimension (**x** and **y**) and subtract the length of text divided by 2. The horizontal position where the text should appear is stored in the *xmin* global variable, and the vertical position is stored in *ymin*.

Finally, we need to give the DC we retrieved back to Windows, using `ReleaseDC`.

`RenderInit` is declared in the header file `RENDER.H` and defined in the file `RENDER.CPP`, both off the CD.

Render

As you'll recall, our callback function called the function *Render* whenever the `WM_PAINT` message was received (which means the window needs to be updated). *Render* is in the file `RENDER.CPP`. Let's take a look at `Render` (Listing 2-19):

Listing 2-19 Render

```
void Render()
{
 LPDIRECTDRAWSURFACE lpFrontBuffer = DDGetFrontBuffer();
 HDC hdc;

  //
  // Clear last hello from buffer
  //
 FillBufferRect(lpFrontBuffer, NULL, RGB(0,0,255));

 if(lpFrontBuffer->GetDC(&hdc) == DD_OK)
 {
  //
  // Let GDI put text in the buffer for us
  //
  SetBkColor( hdc, RGB(0,0,255) );
  SetTextColor( hdc, RGB(255,255,255) );
  TextOut(hdc,xmin,ymin,msg, strlen(msg));
  lpFrontBuffer->ReleaseDC(hdc);
 }
}
```

The very first thing *Render* does is retrieve a pointer to our primary surface, using `DDGetFrontBuffer`.

The next thing we need to do is fill the entire surface with a single color (we'll use solid blue). We'll do this using the function `FillBufferRect`, which we'll look at in a moment. We have to pass `FillBufferRect` a `COLORREF` (red, green, and blue) color value, which we'll specify using the macro `RGB`. `RGB` simply takes the red, green, and blue values (0 to 255) as parameters and gives back the equivalent `COLORREF` value.

Filling a Rectangle on a Surface

Let's take a quick look at `FillBufferRect` (Listing 2-20):

Listing 2-20 `FillBufferRect`

```
BOOL FillBufferRect( LPDIRECTDRAWSURFACE lpSurface, LPRECT lprect,
 COLORREF color)
{
DDBLTFX      ddbltfx;
HRESULT      hr;

ddbltfx.dwSize = sizeof( ddbltfx );
ddbltfx.dwFillColor = DDColorMatch(color);

hr = lpSurface->Blt(lprect,
    NULL,
    NULL,
    DDBLT_COLORFILL | DDBLT_WAIT,
    &ddbltfx);

return hr == DD_OK;
}
```

`FillBufferRect` accepts three parameters:

1. *lpSurface*—the surface on which to draw.

2. *lprect*—the rectangle that specifies the area that should be filled.

3. *color*—the color that should fill the given rectangle.

A `DDBLTFX` structure must be used to perform filling operations on surfaces. The two members of our `DDBLTFX` structure *ddbltfx* that we need to fill in are *dwSize* (the size of the structure in bytes) and *dwFillColor* (the color that should be used to draw on the surface). We'll fill them in using this code:

```
ddbltfx.dwSize = sizeof( ddbltfx );
ddbltfx.dwFillColor = DDColorMatch(color);
```

Now, we have a little problem. `Blit` needs a `DWORD` value in *ddbltfx.dwFillColor*, not a `COLORREF` value. The `DWORD` value is the one a pixel of the given `COLORREF` value would have when placed in video memory. So to convert from `COLORREF` to the equivalent `DWORD`, we've written a function called `DDColorMatch`. The workings of `DDColorMatch` are a bit too complex for this stage in the game, so we'll just skim over what it does.

DDColorMatch

Here's the code for **DDColorMatch** (Listing 2-21):

Listing 2-21 **DDColorMatch**

```
DWORD DDColorMatch(LPDIRECTDRAWSURFACE pdds, COLORREF rgb)
{
    COLORREF rgbT;
    HDC hdc;
    DWORD dw = CLR_INVALID;
    DDSURFACEDESC ddsd;
    HRESULT hres;

    //
    //  use GDI SetPixel to color match for us
    //
    if (rgb != CLR_INVALID && pdds->GetDC(&hdc) == DD_OK)
    {
        rgbT = GetPixel(hdc, 0, 0);                  // save current pixel value
        SetPixel(hdc, 0, 0, rgb);                    // set our value
        pdds->ReleaseDC(hdc);
    }

    //
    // now lock the surface so we can read back the converted color
    //
    ddsd.dwSize = sizeof(ddsd);
    while ((hres = pdds->Lock(NULL, &ddsd, 0, NULL)) == DDERR_WASSTILLDRAWING)
        ;

    if (hres == DD_OK)
    {
        dw  = *(DWORD *)ddsd.lpSurface;                      // get DWORD
        dw &= (1 << ddsd.ddpfPixelFormat.dwRGBBitCount)-1;  // mask it to bpp
        pdds->Unlock(NULL);
    }

    //
    //  now put the color that was there back.
    //
    if (rgb != CLR_INVALID && pdds->GetDC(&hdc) == DD_OK)
    {
        SetPixel(hdc, 0, 0, rgbT);
        pdds->ReleaseDC(hdc);
    }

    return dw;
}
```

We haven't covered (and won't, for a while) many of the functions used in **DDColorMatch**. But we'll still quickly skim over what it does, so you have some idea as to what's happening.

First, it puts a pixel in the upper-left corner of the surface, using the Windows GDI. The GDI, unlike us, always knows the correct format to use for putting pixels on a surface (the correct format will differ with color depths). After the pixel is on the surface, we then grab the **DWORD** value of the pixel in the surface's memory (actually, it's being cast to a **DWORD**— it could be an 8-bit byte or a 16-bit **DWORD**, depending on the color depth). Once we have the value (we also need to do some bit-fiddling to make sure it's configured for the right color depth), we put back the pixel that was in the upper-left corner of the surface before **DDColorMatch** was called.

Don't worry about the code involved. We haven't thoroughly discussed some of the topics used in this code yet, but if you want to, you can come back and look at **DDColorMatch** after we do.

Back to **FillBufferRect**. After we get the correct **DWORD** value for the color we want, we need to call the **IDirectDrawSurface** member function **Blt**, which, among many other things, performs filling operations:

```
hr = lpSurface->Blt(lprect,
NULL,
NULL,
DDBLT_COLORFILL | DDBLT_WAIT,
&ddbltfx);
```

IDirectDrawSurface::Blt

HRESULT Blit(LPRECT lpDestRect, LPDIRECTDRAWSURFACE lpDDSurface, LPRECT lpSrcRect, DWORD dwFlags, LPDDBLTFX lpDDBltFx)

Blit takes five parameters:

1. *lpDestRect*—the rectangle to be drawn on.

2. *lpDDSurface*—the source rectangle. If memory is being copied from one surface to another, this is the surface from which it will be copied.

3. *lpSrcRect*—the rectangle from which to be copied on the source surface.

4. *dwFlags*—specifies the operation to be performed.

5. *lpDDBltFx*—specifies how certain operations should be performed.

For the *lpDestRect* parameter, we'll use the rectangle passed to **FillBufferRect** through the *lprect* parameter.

We won't be using the *lpDDSurface* parameter for a while, so we'll just use **NULL**. Same thing for *lpSrcRect*.

dwFlags specifies what operation will be performed and how to do it. We're going to fill a rectangle on the screen with a color, so we'll use the **DDBLT_COLORFILL** option. **DDBLT_WAIT** tells **Blt** that if it can't perform the operation the instant it's called, it should just keep trying until it can.

lpDDBltFx holds operation-specific information—in this case, the color to use when filling the rectangle. **Blit** knows in which member of the **DDBLTFX** structure to look from the *dwFlags* parameter.

FillBufferRect simply returns **TRUE** if **Blit** was successful, **FALSE** if not.

Back to **Render** (Listing 2-19). After filling the surface with a solid color, we need to retrieve a device context specialized for use with our surface.

```
if(lpFrontBuffer->GetDC(&hdc) == DD_OK)
  {
```

We simply retrieve an HDC for the primary surface, which is stored in the *lpFrontBuffer* variable we retrieved, using **GetFrontBuffer**, and proceed into the *if* statement if everything goes smoothly:

```
SetBkColor( hdc, RGB(0,0,255) );
SetTextColor( hdc, RGB(255,255,255) );
TextOut(hdc,xmin,ymin,msg, strlen(msg));
lpFrontBuffer->ReleaseDC(hdc);
```

The **if** statement puts text in the surface, using some GDI functions we haven't discussed yet. The first is the function **SetBkColor**. **SetBkColor** sets the color to be used for the background when drawing with the GDI. We'll work with the same color used for the window background.

SetTextColor sets the color to be used for drawing text. We'll use white in the example, to contrast with our blue background.

TextOut displays text at the given position. It takes five parameters: the HDC with which to draw, the horizontal position at which to draw the text, the vertical position, the text to draw, and the length of the text in bytes. *msg* is declared at the top of **RENDER.CPP** as Hello World! Remember that we calculated the *xmin* and *ymin* variables in **RenderInit** so the text would be centered on the screen.

Now that we've finished drawing into the buffer, we need to call **ReleaseDC** to give the DC we used back to Windows.

All right! We're finally done with a program (Example 2-1), and we're ready to compile. Admittedly, this isn't the simplest Hello World application ever written, but it certainly has the most potential. We'll be using this application as a framework and expanding on it throughout the book and the rest of this chapter.

Compiling Example 2-1

All you really need to do to compile this program is type the code in and save the files or copy them from the CD. Then, simply link **DDRAW.LIB** in with the standard Windows libraries and compile it.

The output of Example 2-1 is shown in Figure 2-7:

If you feel adventurous, you could try playing around with the code a little bit. It might be wise to wait until after the next example, though, when you'll have a little bit more knowledge.

FIGURE 2-7

Hello World!

Example 2-1 output

Example 2-2: Moving On

Let's move on to Example 2-2 by expanding the application we just wrote. When we're finished with this next example, the application will not only look more interesting, it will have much more potential and capability than the one we just wrote.

The only major change we're going to make to our application is its ability to use complex surfaces. Using complex surfaces allows us to add animation to applications, and we'll learn about many other important DirectDraw topics along the way.

Timers

The first thing you'll notice as you look through the code for our second example program is that we're now using timers. For now, we'll use timers as a simple means of knowing when to update the display.

In Windows, timers are usually implemented by employing messages. This means that when the specified interval has elapsed—for example, one-half second—a message (`WM_TIMER`) is sent to the callback function. The callback function can then perform whatever it was supposed to, every time the timer goes off.

In our code, a global timer interval variable has been defined at the top of `Ex2-2.CPP`:

```
static DWORD UpdateDelay = 50;
```

We'll set the timer to go off every 50 milliseconds, which will give our application a pretty fast frame rate. We'll use this value when we set a timer using `SetTimer`, a Windows API function we'll discuss shortly.

Timer intervals are specified in terms of milliseconds. This is usually precise enough for most games, certainly for the example that we're writing now.

Each timer set by an application running under the Windows environment has a unique timer ID. Windows uses this ID to send **WM_TIMER** messages to callback functions when the given interval has elapsed. This ID is an integer value, totally up to you. The ID number doesn't matter at all; it can be totally arbitrary.

Setting a Timer

Setting a timer in Windows is not too complex an operation. It involves the use of the Windows API function `SetTimer`, which is declared in the header file `MMSYSTEM.H`.

SetTimer

```
UINT SetTimer( HWND hWnd, UINT nIDEvent, UINT uElapse,
TIMERPROC lpTimerFunc)
```

`SetTimer` returns the timer ID number you give it as *nIDEvent* and accepts four parameters:

1. *hWnd*—The handle of the window that should be sent timer messages. In the example code, we pass the handle of our main window. Remember that `WinInit` creates the main application window, so *gapp.hwndApp* is a handle to that window.

2. *nIDEvent*—The ID of the timer. This is a non-zero value that you specify (1 in our example). It doesn't really matter what this number is, as long as it's not zero.

3. *uElapse*—The interval during which the time messages are sent—this value is given in milliseconds. In the example, we used *UpdateDelay*, defined at the top of Ex2-1.CPP as 50. This means that every 50 milliseconds a timer message is sent to the main window.

4. *lpTimerFunc*—The address of a function to be called when the specified interval elapses. This can be used instead of sending messages to a window, but we'll use the message method because it's much simpler. A NULL value for this parameter tells `SetTimer` to send messages to the given window.

In our example, the timer is set in `WinMain`. Let's take a look at `WinMain` in Listing 2-22, to see how it's changed since the last example (the new code is in boldface):

Listing 2-22 `WinMain`

```
int PASCAL WinMain( HINSTANCE hInstance, HINSTANCE hPrevInstance, LPSTR⇐
lpCmdLine, int nCmdShow)
{
MSG msg;

memset((void *)&gapp, 0, sizeof(gapp) );

if( !WinInit( hInstance, nCmdShow ) )
 return FALSE;
if( !DrawInit() )
 return FALSE;

gapp.timerid = SetTimer(gapp.hwndApp, 1, UpdateDelay, NULL );

ShowCursor(FALSE);
while( 1 )
{
if( PeekMessage( &msg, NULL, 0, 0, PM_NOREMOVE ) )
        {
   if( !GetMessage( &msg, NULL, 0, 0 ) )
          return msg.wParam;
   TranslateMessage(&msg);
   DispatchMessage(&msg);
        } else {
   WaitMessage();
 }
 }
}
```

The timer is set by this code:

```
gapp.timerid = SetTimer(gapp.hwndApp, 1, UpdateDelay, NULL );
```

As you'll recall, our global **GApp** structure had a member called *timerid*, which we'll use to hold the timer ID number returned by **SetTimer**.

Using Timers

The next major change in our example is in the callback function, `WindowProc` (Listing 2-23):

Listing 2-23 `WindowProc`

```
static long FAR PASCAL WindowProc( HWND hWnd, UINT message, WPARAM wParam,⇐
LPARAM lParam )
{
 PAINTSTRUCT  ps;
 HDC          hdc;
 static BOOL fFirstPaint = TRUE;

 switch( message )
 {
  case WM_TIMER:
   RenderNextFrame();
   DDFlip();
   break;

  case WM_SIZE:
  case WM_MOVE:
   GetClientRect(gapp.hwndApp, &gapp.wndRect);
   ClientToScreen(gapp.hwndApp, (LPPOINT)&gapp.wndRect);
   ClientToScreen(gapp.hwndApp, (LPPOINT)&gapp.wndRect+1);
   break;

  case WM_KEYDOWN:
   switch( wParam )
   {
    case VK_ESCAPE:
    case VK_F12:
     PostMessage(hWnd, WM_CLOSE, 0, 0);
     return 0;
   }
   break;

  case WM_PAINT:
  hdc = BeginPaint( hWnd, &ps );
   EndPaint( hWnd, &ps );
   return 1;

  case WM_DESTROY:
   //
   // We're done, clean up and say goodbye
   //
   DDDisable();
   DDDestroy();
   PostQuitMessage( 0 );
   break;
 }
 return DefWindowProc(hWnd, message, wParam, lParam);
}
```

Since Windows sends a `WM_TIMER` message whenever the specified timer interval has elapsed, we need to implement something to handle it. Therefore, we've added the `WM_TIMER` handler to the *switch* statement:

`RenderNextFrame` and `Flip`, both of which are called from the `WM_TIMER` handler, are two new functions we'll write that update the display. This means whenever we receive a `WM_TIMER` message (every 50 milliseconds), we'll draw a new frame.

That's pretty much all there is to adding timer support to our application. In the future, we'll use different methods for determining when to update the display, but for now we'll just stick with timers.

Complex Surfaces

Now let's move on to what we're going to do when our timer fires. In this new example application we'll still use the primary surface, but we'll use it differently: as a *complex surface*.

In games, drawing is usually not done on the primary surface, but rather on a surface that is not visible. This makes for much smoother animation because all you do to display the image is shuffle around some memory (more on that later), which is much faster than the actual drawing. Using multiple surfaces in this manner usually involves the use of *complex surfaces*.

Complex surfaces consist of buffers, which are simply parts of memory used to store an image, much like a surface. A complex surface is made up of a *front buffer* and one or more *back buffers* (Figure 2-8). The front buffer is the buffer that is active and visible. When performing functions on a complex surface, only the front buffer is affected. However, back buffers can be retrieved so that *they* can be manipulated. They can also be switched with the front buffer so that they are active and visible.

Typically, you use complex surfaces for constructing the next image to display in a back buffer, then make that buffer and its image visible when the image is complete. Once an image is composed in a back buffer, you can switch the front and back buffers, changing the back buffer to the front buffer and vice-versa. Switching the front and back buffers of a complex surface is a time-efficient operation know as *flipping*.

There are ways to retrieve the front and back buffers individually, but from a programming point of view, a complex surface looks like any other. A complex surface is declared as a normal surface, and the same functions are used when manipulating a normal surface. The only obvious difference between complex and normal (or simple) surfaces is how they're created.

Flipping

Flipping is a fairly simple operation. After you have drawn into a back buffer, you call *Flip*, a member function of `DirectDrawSurface` objects. *Flip* switches the back buffer and the front buffer, causing the back buffer to become the front buffer and the front buffer to become the back buffer. When there is more than one back buffer, which is actually pretty common, the complex surface behaves in a sort of circular manner. The front buffer goes to the end of the line, and the next back buffer in line moves up and becomes the new front

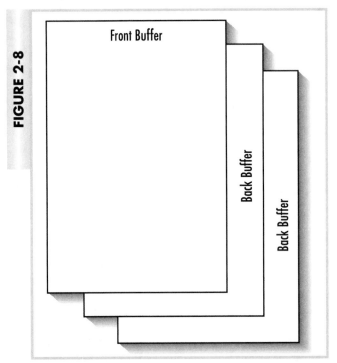

FIGURE 2-8

A complex surface

buffer. Take a look at Figure 2-9 to get a clearer picture. Of course, the number of back buffers isn't limited to two, you can have as many as your heart desires.

Flipping is kind of hard to understand at first, but don't worry, you'll grasp it as time goes on and we start using it.

Creating a Complex Surface

When you create a complex surface, it looks like you're creating only one surface. DirectDraw knows you are building a complex surface and creates the required multiple surfaces. DirectDraw can tell you're creating a complex surface from the values in the *ddsCaps* member in the **DDSURFACEDESC** structure that you pass **CreateSurface**.

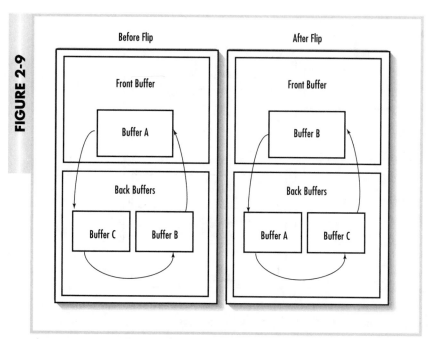

FIGURE 2-9

Flipping a complex surface with two back buffers

Note

One thing to keep in mind when using complex surfaces is that the GDI will continue to use the same surface forever. This means the first primary surface will always appear to be the primary surface to the GDI. Even if the surface is flipped, the GDI will continue to draw into the original primary surface, as shown in Figure 2-10.

We'll deal with the scenario of creating a complex primary surface with one back buffer as an example. This will be fairly simple, as it's basically the same as the code used to create a simple (not complex) primary surface. Listing 2-24 shows the code involved:

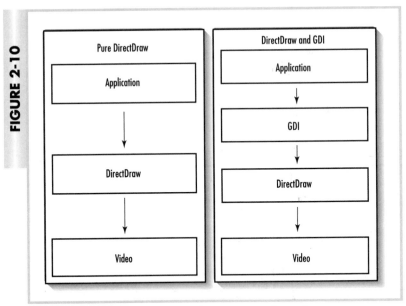

FIGURE 2-10

The GDI will continue to use the same surface forever

Listing 2-24 Creating a complex primary surface

```
// Create the DirectDraw object
DirectDrawCreate( NULL, &lpDD, NULL );

// Make the app exclusive in full screen mode
lpDD->SetCooperativeLevel( hWnd, DDSCL_EXCLUSIVE | DDSCL_FULLSCREEN );

// Set the display to 320x200x8
lpDD->SetDisplayMode( 320, 200, 8 );

// Initialize a DDSURFACEDESC structure with the values for a complex primary
// surface
DDSURFACEDESC ddsd;
ddsd.dwSize = sizeof( ddsd );
ddsd.dwFlags = DDSD_DDSCAPS | DDSD_BACKBUFFERCOUNT;
ddsd.dwCaps.dwCaps = DDSCAPS_PRIMARYSURFACE |
          DDSCAPS_COMPLEX |
          DDSCAPS_FLIP;
ddsd.dwBackBufferCount = 1;

// Create a surface using the DDSURFACEDESC initialized above
lpDD->CreateSurface( &ddsd, &lpDDSPrimary, NULL );
```

The *dwFlags* member has had another value added, *DDSD_BACKBUFFERCOUNT*.

```
ddsd.dwFlags = DDSD_DDSCAPS | DDSD_BACKBUFFERCOUNT;
```

DDSD_BACKBUFFERCOUNT tells DirectDraw that the member specifying the number of back buffers in the complex surface, *dwBackBufferCount*, is valid. You'll always need to use *DDSD_BACKBUFFERCOUNT* and *dwBackBufferCount* when creating with complex surfaces.

dwCaps.dwCaps has also changed:

```
ddsd.dwCaps.dwCaps = DDSCAPS_PRIMARYSURFACE |
        DDSCAPS_COMPLEX |
        DDSCAPS_FLIP;
```

Two new values, *DDSCAPS_COMPLEX* and *DDSCAPS_FLIP*, have been added to the mix. *DDSCAPS_COMPLEX* informs DirectDraw that the surface we're creating is a complex surface, while *DDSCAPS_FLIP* says the surface has flipping capabilities.

Warning

You have to use *DDSCAPS_COMPLEX* whenever you use *DDSCAPS_FLIP*. Also, whenever you use *DDSCAPS_COMPLEX*, the *dwBackBufferCount* member of the DDSURFACEDESC structure must be at least 1.

Let's hop back to our code for a moment to see how to deal with creating complex surfaces.

We'll add a couple members to our global **LPDDraw** structure *lpdraw*, to help us keep track of the complex surface. Take a look at how the **_DDraw** structure looks now (Listing 2-25):

Listing 2-25 **_DDraw**

```
typedef struct _DDraw
{
HWND    hwndApp; // Window to use
LPDIRECTDRAW  lpdd;   // Pointer to DirectDraw object
LPDIRECTDRAWSURFACE lpFrontBuffer; // Pointer to front buffer
LPDIRECTDRAWSURFACE lpBackBuffer; // Pointer to back buffer
BOOL    fEnabled; // DirectDraw enabled
int    nCooperation; // CooperationLevel
int    cx;   // Width of window
int    cy;   // Height of window
int    bbp;   // Bits per plane
int    nBuffers;  // Number of buffers to create
} DDraw, *LPDDraw;
```

We have two new members in this version. First of all, we have *lpBackBuffer*, which we'll use to point to the complex surface's back buffer (we'll learn how to get pointers to back buffers, in a moment). The second is *nBuffers*, which simply keeps a count of all the buffers, including the front one.

We'll add some code to **DDCreate** to initialize the *nBuffers* member. Initializing *lpBackBuffer* will take a little more work and explanation, so we'll put that off until a little later. This is what **DDCreate** looks like now (Listing 2-26):

Listing 2-26 `DDCreate`

```
LPDIRECTDRAW DDCreate(HWND hwndApp)
{
 HRESULT hr;

 if( (lpdraw = (LPDDraw)malloc(sizeof(DDraw))) == NULL )
  return NULL;
 memset(lpdraw,0,sizeof(DDraw));

 //
 // Create DirectDraw object
 //
 hr = DirectDrawCreate( NULL, &lpdraw->lpdd, NULL );

 if( hr == DD_OK )
  {
  lpdraw->hwndApp = hwndApp;
  //
  // Initialize defaults
  //
  lpdraw->cx = 640;
  lpdraw->cy = 480;
  lpdraw->bbp = 8;
  lpdraw->nBuffers = 2;
 } else {
  free(lpdraw);
  lpdraw = NULL;
 }
 return lpdraw->lpdd;
}
```

As you can see, we'll be using one back buffer (one front buffer plus one back buffer equals two buffers). We'll use the value in *nBuffers* when we create the surface using `DDCreateSurfaces`.

Creating the Surfaces

As in the last example, we'll call `DDCreateSurfaces` to create all the surfaces to be used. Let's take a look at how that function has changed (Listing 2-27):

Listing 2-27 `DDCreateSurfaces`

```
static BOOL DDCreateSurfaces()
{
 LPDIRECTDRAW   lpdd = lpdraw->lpdd;
 HRESULT        hr;
 DDSURFACEDESC  ddsd;
 DDSCAPS        ddscaps;

 memset( (VOID *)&ddsd, 0, sizeof( ddsd ) );
```

```
    ddsd.dwSize = sizeof( ddsd );

    ddsd.dwFlags = DDSD_CAPS | DDSD_BACKBUFFERCOUNT;
    ddsd.dwBackBufferCount = lpdraw->nBuffers-1;
    ddsd.ddsCaps.dwCaps = DDSCAPS_PRIMARYSURFACE |
            DDSCAPS_FLIP | DDSCAPS_COMPLEX;

    hr = lpdd->CreateSurface( &ddsd,
        &lpdraw->lpFrontBuffer,
        NULL );

    if( hr != DD_OK )
            return FALSE;

    //
    // get pointer to back buffer
    //
    ddscaps.dwCaps = DDSCAPS_BACKBUFFER;
    hr = lpdraw->lpFrontBuffer->GetAttachedSurface(&ddscaps,
            &lpdraw->lpBackBuffer );

    if( hr != DD_OK )
            return FALSE;
    else
      return TRUE;
}
```

The first thing you'll see has changed is the *dwFlags* member of the **DDSURFACEDESC** structure. We've validated the *dwBackBufferCount* member using the value **DDSD_BACKBUFFERCOUNT**. We need *dwBackBufferCount* to tell **CreateSurface** how many back buffers the complex surface will have.

The second thing we've added is a value to *dwBackBufferCount*:

```
ddsd.dwBackBufferCount = lpdraw->nBuffers-1;
```

Since the *nBuffers* member of *lpdraw* includes the front buffer, we need to subtract 1 from the value to calculate the number of back buffers.

The next item that has changed is the *dwCaps* member of *ddsd.ddsCaps*:

```
ddsd.ddsCaps.dwCaps = DDSCAPS_PRIMARYSURFACE |
        DDSCAPS_FLIP | DDSCAPS_COMPLEX;
```

We've added **DDSCAPS_FLIP** and **DDSCAPS_COMPLEX**, which as you'll recall tell **CreateSurface** to create a flippable complex surface.

After we create the surface, using **CreateSurface**, we need to retrieve a pointer to the single back buffer and store it in the *lpBackBuffer* member of our *lpdraw* structure:

```
ddscaps.dwCaps = DDSCAPS_BACKBUFFER;
hr = lpdraw->lpFrontBuffer->GetAttachedSurface(&ddscaps,
        &lpdraw->lpBackBuffer );
```

Let's take a short time-out and learn how to retrieve pointers to back buffers.

Retrieving Back Buffers

Now that you've created a complex surface, what do you do with it? Well, you need to draw into the back buffers. And to draw into them, you need to access them.

When you access a surface or buffer, you are actually requesting that DirectDraw retrieve it for you. You need to fill out a **DDCAPS** structure, which you can think of as a request form. The structure describes the surface or buffer you are requesting.

DDSCAPS, if you recall, is a member of **DDSURFACEDESC**, which was used when creating surfaces. It's used in much the same way when requesting access to a surface as when creating one. Here, you'll just use its *dwCaps* member to detail the surface you are requesting rather than creating.

Because we're retrieving the back buffer of a complex surface, we're going to fill *dwCaps* with the value *DDSCAPS_BACKBUFFER*, which tells DirectDraw that the surface we're requesting is the next back buffer in the line of buffers. Recall that if there is more than one back buffer in a complex surface, the complex surface behaves as a circular queue.

IDirectDrawSurface:: GetAttachedSurface

```
HRESULT GetAttachedSurface( LPDDSCAPS lpDDSCaps,
LPDIRECTDRAWSURFACE FAR* lplpDDAttachedSurface )
```

To actually access a back buffer, you use the **GetAttachedSurface** function, a member of **IDirectDrawSurface**. It takes two arguments: a pointer to a **DDSCAPS** structure describing the surface, and a pointer to a pointer to a surface. Note the absence of the usual trailing **NULL** in this function.

GetAttachedSurface returns the back buffer in the pointer that you pass into the function as the second argument. You then treat this pointer just as you would any other pointer to a surface.

Listing 2-28 shows a complex surface being created and the back buffer being retrieved. Take a look:

Listing 2-28 Retrieving back buffers

```
// Declare a pointer to the DirectDraw object
LPDIRECTDRAW lpDD;

// Declare a pointer to the primary surface
LPDIRECTDRAWSURFACE lpDDSPrimary;

// Declare a pointer to a surface
LPDIRECTDRAWSURFACE lpDDSBack;
    .
    .
    .

// Initialize a DDSURFACEDESC structure with the values for a complex primary
```

```
// surface
DDSURFACEDESC ddsd;
ddsd.dwSize = sizeof( ddsd );
ddsd.dwFlags = DDSD_DDSCAPS | DDSD_BACKBUFFERCOUNT;
ddsd.dwCaps.dwCaps = DDSCAPS_PRIMARYSURFACE |
            DDSCAPS_COMPLEX |
            DDSCAPS_FLIP;
ddsd.dwBackBufferCount = 1;

// Create a surface using the DDSURFACEDESC initialized above
lpDD->CreateSurface( &ddsd, &lpDDSPrimary, NULL );

// Intialize a DDSCAPS structure with the values for a back buffer
DDSCAPS ddsc;
ddsc.dwCaps = DDSCAPS_BACKBUFFER;

// Get a pointer to a pointer to the back buffer of the complex surface we've
// just created
lpDDSPrimary->GetAttachedSurface( &ddsc, &lpDDSBack );
```

First, as you can see, a global pointer to a **DirectDrawSurface** object is declared in the beginning of the code, along with all the other DirectDraw pointers. Next, a **DDSURFACEDESC** structure is initialized to describe a complex primary surface with one back buffer and flipping capabilities. After the complex surface is created, a **DDSCAPS** structure is initialized to describe a back buffer:

```
DDSCAPS ddsc;
ddsc.dwCaps = DDSCAPS_BACKBUFFER;
```

The **GetAttachedSurface** member of the newly created complex surface is then called to retrieve the back buffer:

```
lpDDSPrimary->GetAttachedSurface( &ddsc, &lpDDSBack );
```

Now we have a pointer to the back buffer in the *lpDDSBack* variable to do with as we wish.

Back in our example, we used this code to retrieve a pointer to the back buffer of our complex surface:

```
ddscaps.dwCaps = DDSCAPS_BACKBUFFER;
hr = lpdraw->lpFrontBuffer->GetAttachedSurface(&ddscaps,
        &lpdraw->lpBackBuffer );
```

Remember that *lpdraw->lpFrontBuffer* is both the primary surface and the front buffer, and *lpdraw->lpBackBuffer* is the pointer in which we want to store the pointer to the back buffer.

Since we now have a pointer to a surface, we'll need to **Release** it once we're done with it. We'll do this in **DDDisable**, where we also **Release** the primary surface.

Rendering

One major difference in this example and the previous one is the rendering code. Using a complex surface when rendering is quite different than using a simple surface.

For this example, we'll add a little bit of movement. (Actually, there's quite a bit of movement—almost enough to make you queasy if you watch long enough.) We'll put Hello World! on the screen, but we'll make it wiggle around in the center.

RenderInit

RenderInit is almost the same as in the last example, but we have to do a little extra math to facilitate the text wiggling. Let's take a look at the new version (Listing 2-29):

Listing 2-29 RenderInit

```
BOOL RenderInit()
{
 LPDIRECTDRAWSURFACE lpFrontBuffer = DDGetFrontBuffer();
 HDC hdc;

 //
 // No sense doing this all the time
 //
 msglen = strlen(msg);

 //
 // GetDC and calculate variables used for wiggling
 //
 if(lpFrontBuffer->GetDC(&hdc) == DD_OK)
 {
  SIZE size;
  int w = DDGetWidth();
  int h = DDGetHeight();

  GetTextExtentPoint32(hdc, msg, msglen, &size );

  //
  // Centered, with wiggle room on all sides
  //
  xmin = ((w - size.cx) / 2) - WiggleRoom;
  xmod = WiggleRoom * 2;
  ymin = ((h - size.cy) / 2) - WiggleRoom;
  ymod = WiggleRoom * 2;

  lpFrontBuffer->ReleaseDC(hdc);
 } else {
  return FALSE;
 }
 return TRUE;
}
```

The four new lines simply calculate the minimum and maximum upper-left corner values for text positions. By the way, *xmod* and *ymod* are two new global integer variables declared at the top of **Ex2-2.CPP**. *WiggleRoom* is #defined as 20.

RenderNextFrame

The **Render** function from the previous example (2-1) has been replaced with **RenderNextFrame**, since now we're working with buffers, or frames. It looks almost the same, except for the fact that it renders into the back buffer and moves the text from frame to frame. Take a look (Listing 2-30):

Listing 2-30 **RenderNextFrame**

```
void RenderNextFrame()
{
LPDIRECTDRAWSURFACE lpBackBuffer = DDGetBackBuffer();
HDC hdc;

//
// Shouldn't be here if no buffers, but avoid GPFs anyway
//
if( lpBackBuffer == NULL )
 return;

//
// Clear last hello from buffer
//
FillBufferRect(lpBackBuffer, NULL, 0x000000FF);

if(lpBackBuffer->GetDC(&hdc) == DD_OK)
{
 int x;
 int y;

 //
 // Get random location for next hello
 //
 x = xmin + rand() % xmod;
 y = ymin + rand() % ymod;

 //
 // Let GDI put text in the buffer for us
 //
   SetBkColor( hdc, RGB(0,0,255) );
 SetTextColor( hdc, RGB(255,255,255) );
 TextOut(hdc,x,y,msg, strlen(msg));
        pBackBuffer->ReleaseDC(hdc);
 }
}
```

The main change since *Render* is the name of the surface pointer used throughout the function.

The one line that has changed significantly is the first:

```
LPDIRECTDRAWSURFACE lpBackBuffer = DDGetBackBuffer();
```

Instead of getting a pointer to the *lpFrontBuffer* member of our *lpdraw* structure, using `DDGetFrontBuffer`, we're now getting a pointer to the back buffer, using the new function `DDGetBackBuffer`. `DDGetBackBuffer` is a fairly simple function and looks almost like a mirror image of `DDGetFrontBuffer`—all it does is return the pointer *lpdraw->lpBackBuffer*.

Other than that, the only thing that has really changed is the code which calculates where the text should appear on the screen:

```
x = xmin + rand() % xmod;
y = ymin + rand() % ymod;
```

We're now using the variables *x* and *y* to put the text on the screen, and we're using the C library function **rand** for a random number generator. We're just getting a value between the maximum and minimum **x** and **y** values for the upper-left corner of the text.

`FillBufferRect`, which is used to fill the back buffer with a solid color, hasn't changed, so there's no need to look at that code.

Flipping the Complex Surface

Take another look at the code from our callback function that handled the **WM_TIMER** message:

```
case WM_TIMER:
 RenderNextFrame();
 DDFlip();
 break;
```

After calling `RenderNextFrame`, it calls `DDFlip`, which flips the complex surface we're using. Let's learn how to flip complex surfaces, then we can examine `DDFlip`.

Using the Flip Interface of `IDirectDrawSurface`

To flip a complex surface, we need to call `Flip`, an interface of `IDirectDrawSurface`.

IDirectDrawSurface::Flip

```
HRESULT Flip( LPDIRECTDRAWSURFACE
lpDDSurfaceOverride, DWORD dwFlags )
```

Flip is a pretty simple function. It takes only two arguments:

1. A pointer to a surface. This argument is an override, and is only used if you wish to flip to a surface other than the next back buffer in line. Ninety-nine percent of the time you won't have any use for this argument, so simply use NULL in its place.

2. A DWORD value. The only value this argument can be set to is *DDFLIP_WAIT*, otherwise it has to be NULL. *DDFLIP_WAIT* tells DirectDraw that if it can't perform the flipping operation when you call Flip, to keep trying until it can. Usually you will use *DDFLIP_WAIT* when calling *Flip*.

Note

You must call Flip as a member of the complex surface (the front buffer). You can't call it as a member of a back buffer you've retrieved, or DirectDraw won't know what you're talking about.

Listing 2-31 shows the code that would call Flip in an application (not from *our* application mind you, this is just a generic piece of code). Keep in mind that Flip is not usually called right after the surface is created, but rather in the body of your program, after you've composed an image in the back buffer and want to display it.

Listing 2-31 Flipping a complex surface

```
// Call Flip. Tell DirectDraw to wait if it can't flip immediately for some
// reason.
lpDDSPrimary->Flip( NULL, DDFLIP_WAIT );
```

Is that simple or what? This code would cause *lpDDSPrimary* to flip the next—and only, in this case—back buffer, *lpDDSBack*.

DDFlip

In our example, the function DDFlip takes care of flipping the surface (in DDRAWEX.CPP). Let's take a look (Listing 2-32):

Listing 2-32 DDFlip

```
BOOL DDFlip()
{
 HRESULT hr;

 hr = lpdraw->lpFrontBuffer->Flip(NULL,DDFLIP_WAIT);

 return hr == DD_OK;
}
```

DDFlip simply calls Flip from the front buffer, returning TRUE if successful.

So basically all we do when the callback function receives a **WM_TIMER** message is draw the next frame into the back buffer using **RenderNextFrame**, and then make the frame visible by calling **DDFlip**. It's as simple as that.

Compiling Example 2-2

Well, you're already finished with your second DirectDraw program. This program, although it doesn't look very snazzy, has a lot more capabilities than the first one did. After a couple more simple programs, you'll know enough to get into some more visually exciting examples, which will be fun, considering the ones we just wrote.

That's it for Chapter 2. Besides learning how to write a skeleton Windows-based program, we pretty much covered all the basics of DirectDraw. You learned how to set up and initialize DirectDraw, use **SetCooperativeLevel**, create and use surfaces, and a whole bunch of other miscellaneous tasks you need to know for programming with DirectDraw. Now that you know the basics, let's move on to some more advanced material. In the next chapter, we'll learn how to further utilize the Windows environment to our application's advantage, and we'll cover some more advanced video mode topics.

3

More DirectDraw

In the last chapter, you learned about the fundamental concepts behind DirectDraw. In this chapter, we'll build on that knowledge and dig into some more complex topics. Some of the topics we'll cover include:

- Writing a windowed DirectDraw application
- Using clippers
- Selecting and enumerating display modes
- Using callback functions for enumeration
- ModeX

After this chapter, you'll understand most of the basics of DirectDraw and be ready to delve into some more complex stuff.

Example 3-1: Adding Windowed Mode

One of the advantages of developing your application in Windows is its user interface. Windows provides you with a simple way to implement menus. Plus, it lets the user easily switch between processes. In Example 3-1, we'll build a simple menu containing an **Exit** option. It doesn't really do that much, but it offers a framework we can build on in this (and other) chapters.

Adding windowed mode support is the next evolutionary step our sample program will take. It'll require quite a bit of work to implement, and we'll spend a good part of this chapter concentrating on it.

One thing that *doesn't* require much work is creating a menu resource. We'll use a menu when working in windowed mode, so you'll have to create a menu resource for the window. In our example, the menu is named **GDKAPPMENU**. It is the resource we used in the **window** class, so it's automatically drawn when we're in windowed mode.

For now, we'll toggle between windowed and fullscreen mode when the user presses [ALT]+[ENTER], the standard Windows key combination for that function.

Note

You cannot flip the primary surface when in windowed mode because no other applications will know the surface has been flipped. (If you need to, refer back to Chapter 2, "DirectDraw," for an explanation of flipping.) We won't need any code changes for fullscreen mode, but we will need to code a work-around for this problem when in windowed mode.

To facilitate using windowed mode, we had to change the **_DDraw** structure a bit from Example 2-2. Take a look at Listing 3-1:

Listing 3-1 **_DDraw** changes

```
typedef struct _DDraw
{
        HWND                    hwndApp;        // Window to use
        LPDIRECTDRAW            lpdd;           // Pointer to DirectDraw object
        LPDIRECTDRAWSURFACE     lpFrontBuffer;  // Pointer to front buffer
        LPDIRECTDRAWSURFACE     lpBackBuffer;   // Pointer to back buffer
        LPDIRECTDRAWCLIPPER     lpClipper;      // Pointer to clipper
        BOOL                    fEnabled;       // DirectDraw enabled
        BOOL                    fFullScreen;    // True when running in
                                                // fullscreen modes
        int                     nCooperation;   //  CooperationLevel
        int                     cx;             // Width of window
        int                     cy;             // Height of window
        int                     bbp;            // Bits per plane
        int                     nBuffers;       // Number of buffers to create
} DDraw, *LPDDraw;
```

Two new members have been added: *lpClipper* and *fFullScreen*. *lpClipper* is a DirectDrawClipper object we'll use in this example (more on this later). *fFullScreen* is a Boolean value that is **TRUE** when our application is running fullscreen, **FALSE** when it's running in windowed mode.

Our **_GApp** application structure has also been modified (Listing 3-2):

Listing 3-2 **_GApp** changes

```
typedef struct _GApp
{
        //
        // Global App Data
        //
        HINSTANCE           hinst;
        HWND                hwndApp;
        LPDIRECTDRAW        lpdd;
        RECT                wndRect;
        UINT                timerid;
        BOOL                fFlippingPaused;
} GApp, * LPGApp;
```

Actually, only one member has been added: *fFlippingPaused*. When our application is in windowed mode, the user can use the menu. If we flip the primary surface when the menu is in use, the screen will get messed up and the user won't know what's going on. Thus, we need to stop flipping until the menu is closed up and no longer in use. *fFlippingPaused* will be **TRUE** when the menu is in use and **FALSE** when its not. We simply won't do any flipping when *fFlippingPaused* is **TRUE**.

The Callback Function

Our callback function has undergone a lot of changes since the last example. Take a look at Listing 3-3, which shows **WindowProc** as it looks now:

Listing 3-3 **WindowProc**

```
static long FAR PASCAL WindowProc( HWND hWnd, UINT message, WPARAM wParam,⇐
LPARAM lParam )
{
    PAINTSTRUCT ps;
    HDC         hdc;

    switch( message )
    {
            case WM_TIMER:
                    if( gapp.fFlippingPaused == FALSE )
                    {
                            RenderNextFrame();
                            DDFlip();
                    }
                    break;

            case WM_SIZE:
            case WM_MOVE:
                    GetClientRect(gapp.hwndApp, &gapp.wndRect);
                    ClientToScreen(gapp.hwndApp, (LPPOINT)&gapp.wndRect);
                    ClientToScreen(gapp.hwndApp, (LPPOINT)&gapp.wndRect+1);
                    break;
```

continued on next page

continued from previous page

```
        case WM_ENTERMENULOOP:
            //
            // Suspend page flipping
            //
            gapp.fFlippingPaused = TRUE;
            //
            // Get GDI's surface back where it's expected!
            //
            gapp.lpdd->FlipToGDISurface();
            //
            // Draw menu
            //
            DrawMenuBar(gapp.hwndApp);
            RedrawWindow(gapp.hwndApp, NULL, NULL, RDW_FRAME);
            break;

        case WM_EXITMENULOOP:
            gapp.fFlippingPaused = FALSE;
            break;

        case WM_COMMAND:
            switch(LOWORD(wParam))
            {
                //
                // File Exit
                //
                case IDM_FILEEXIT:
                    PostMessage(hWnd, WM_CLOSE, 0, 0L);
                    break;
            }
            break;

        case WM_KEYDOWN:
            switch( wParam )
            {
                case VK_ESCAPE:
                case VK_F12:
                    PostMessage(hWnd, WM_CLOSE, 0, 0);
                    return 0;
            }
            break;

        case WM_SYSKEYUP:
            switch( wParam )
            {
                case VK_RETURN:
                {
                    //
                    // ALT+ENTER ... switch between fullscreen
                    // and windowed modes
                    //
                    int nCooperation = DDGetCooperativeLevel();
```

```
                        DDDisable();
                        if( nCooperation & DDSCL_FULLSCREEN )
                                DDSetCooperativeLevel( DDSCL_NORMAL );
                        else
                                DDSetCooperativeLevel( DDSCL_EXCLUSIVE
                                        | DDSCL_FULLSCREEN );
                        DDEnable();
                        RenderInit();
                        break;
                }
        }
        break;

    case WM_PAINT:
            hdc = BeginPaint( hWnd, &ps );
            EndPaint( hWnd, &ps );
            return 1;

    case WM_DESTROY:
            //
            // We're done, clean up and say goodbye
            //
            if( gapp.timerid != 0 )
                    KillTimer(gapp.hwndApp, gapp.timerid);
            DDDisable();
            DDDestroy();
            PostQuitMessage( 0 );
            break;
    }
    return DefWindowProc(hWnd, message, wParam, lParam);
}
```

Let's discuss each of the handlers that have either changed or are altogether new.

WM_TIMER

The first bit of code that has changed is in the **WM_TIMER** handler:

```
case WM_TIMER:
        if( gapp.fFlippingPaused == FALSE )
        {
                RenderNextFrame();
                DDFlip();
        }
        break;
```

Remember that when *gapp.fFlippingPaused* is TRUE, the menu is in use. Each time we receive a timer message we should first check to see whether *fFlippingPaused* is TRUE before rendering the next frame and flipping the surface, which is what we're doing here. This keeps us from rendering anything we're not supposed to.

WM_ENTERMESSAGELOOP

When the user clicks on our window's menu, the Windows environment sends our callback function a **WM_ENTERMENULOOP** message. We need to do a few things when we receive that message:

```
case WM_ENTERMENULOOP:

    //
    // Suspend page flipping
    //
    gapp.fFlippingPaused = TRUE;
    //
    // Get GDI's surface back where it's expected!
    //
    gapp.lpdd->FlipToGDISurface();
    //
    // Draw menu
    //
    DrawMenuBar(gapp.hwndApp);
    RedrawWindow(gapp.hwndApp, NULL, NULL, RDW_FRAME);
    break;
```

The first thing we do is toggle the *gapp.fFlippingPaused* variable so we know not to flip when we receive a timer message.

When you retrieve a DC for a specific surface, it will work with that surface. But the regular Windows GDI that takes care of drawing menus and windows only works with the initial primary surface, that is, the surface visible when the application began. Thus, we need a way to flip back to the initial primary surface before the GDI draws the menu. The DirectDraw API function **FlipToGDISurface** does precisely that, so we need to call it:

```
gapp.lpdd->FlipToGDISurface();
```

Once we flip the complex surface again (probably when we render another frame into a back buffer), the GDI surface won't be visible. So we'll need to call **FlipToGDISurface** every time we get the **WM_ENTERMENULOOP** message.

The next few lines draw the window's menu using a few Windows API functions:
```
DrawMenuBar(gapp.hwndApp);
RedrawWindow(gapp.hwndApp, NULL, NULL, RDW_FRAME);
```

DrawMenuBar simply draws the menu in the window. Then **RedrawWindow** tells the GDI to repaint the entire window.

Although this is a lot of work to get a menu running, the menu will behave exactly as a normal Windows menu should, which is important to users.

WM_EXITMENULOOP

When the user is finished with the menu, Windows sends our callback function the **WM_EXITMENULOOP** message. This is the handler code:

```
case WM_EXITMENULOOP:
    gapp.fFlippingPaused = FALSE;
    break;
```

As you can see, the only thing we need to do is toggle the *fFlippingPaused* variable. If we don't, our rendering code will never update the screen because it will still think the menu is in use.

WM_COMMAND

WM_COMMAND is the message Windows sends when some user interface element—such as a button or menu—is in use. In this case, we check to see whether the user has clicked on our one menu choice, Exit:

```
case WM_COMMAND:
      switch(LOWORD(wParam))
      {
            //
            // File Exit
            //
            case IDM_FILEEXIT:
                  PostMessage(hWnd, WM_CLOSE, 0, 0L);
                  break;
      }
      break;
```

Every menu choice sends a unique WM_COMMAND message when selected (you specify this value when creating the menu using a resource editor). The Exit choice sends the IDM_FILEEXIT value, contained in the low word of *wParam*. We'll use a switch statement to distinguish the different menu commands.

When we receive the IDM_FILEEXIT message, we'll send our callback function a WM_CLOSE message. This will quit our application by closing the window.

WM_SYSKEYUP

Since we need to toggle between windowed and fullscreen mode when the user presses [ALT]+[ENTER], we have to know when that key combination has been pressed. Since [ALT] is a Windows system key—meaning it activates menus—we cannot use the WM_KEYDOWN message to handle it. Whenever the [ALT] key is pressed, Windows sends the WM_SYSKEYDOWN message. When the [ALT] key is released Windows sends the WM_SYSKEYUP message, with any additional pressed keys stored in the WPARAM.

Let's take a look at the handler code for WM_SYSKEYUP:

```
case WM_SYSKEYUP:
      switch( wParam )
      {
            case VK_RETURN:
            {
                  //
                  // ALT+ENTER ... switch between fullscreen
                  // and windowed modes
                  //
                  int nCooperation = DDGetCooperativeLevel();
```

continued on next page

continued from previous page

```
                        DDDisable();
                        if( nCooperation & DDSCL_FULLSCREEN )
                                DDSetCooperativeLevel( DDSCL_NORMAL );
                        else
                                DDSetCooperativeLevel( DDSCL_EXCLUSIVE
                                        DDSCL_FULLSCREEN );
                        DDEnable();
                        RenderInit();
                        break;
                }
        }
        break;
```

The **WPARAM** stores the same type of value sent when the **WM_KEYDOWN** message is sent. Thus, we only need to look for the **VK_RETURN** value in *wParam*. This way, we'll know the user has hit both the [ENTER] and [ALT] keys, our cue to switch display states.

If the user hits [ALT]+[ENTER], we need to toggle display states. First, we need to retrieve the mode that was active at the time of the keypress:

```
int nCooperation = DDGetCooperativeLevel();
```

DDSetCooperativeLevel is simply a function in our example returning the value in the *lpdraw->nCooperation* variable.

Next, we need to disable everything because we have to create it all over again and need a clean slate to work with. To do this, we simply call **DDDisable**.

Finally, we toggle the state of the application between fullscreen and windowed modes:

```
if( nCooperation & DDSCL_FULLSCREEN )
        DDSetCooperativeLevel( DDSCL_NORMAL );
else
        DDSetCooperativeLevel( DDSCL_EXCLUSIVE
                | DDSCL_FULLSCREEN );
```

Here we checking to see if the current mode includes **DDSCL_FULLSCREEN** (fullscreen mode). If it does, we switch the display state to windowed mode, using **DDSCL_NORMAL**. If we're not already in fullscreen mode, we switch to fullscreen exclusive mode using **DDSCL_FULLSCREEN** and **DDSCL_EXCLUSIVE**.

After we've toggled the state of the application, we need to create and initialize everything all over again:

```
DDEnable();
RenderInit();
break;
```

By the time all these functions are called, our application will have toggled its display state and will be ready to render another frame.

DDEnable

DDEnable is the function from the last example that initializes and re-initializes our application. Its called when the application begins, and whenever DDSetCooperativeLevel is called. It has undergone a *lot* of changes since the last example. Let's take a look at Listing 3-4, which shows DDEnable as it looks now:

Listing 3-4 DDEnable

```
BOOL DDEnable()
{
        HRESULT hr;

        if( lpdraw == NULL )
                return FALSE;

        hr = lpdraw->lpdd->SetCooperativeLevel( lpdraw->hwndApp,
                lpdraw->nCooperation );
        if( hr != DD_OK )
                return FALSE;

        if( lpdraw->nCooperation & DDSCL_EXCLUSIVE )
        {
                //
                // Mode changes allowed when DDSCL_EXCLUSIVE is set
                //
                hr = lpdraw->lpdd->SetDisplayMode( lpdraw->cx, lpdraw->cy,
                        lpdraw->bbp );

                if( hr != DD_OK )
                        return FALSE;
        } else {
                //
                // Not exclusive, use the window as is
                //
                RECT rcWork;
                RECT rc;
                HDC hdc;

                hdc = GetDC(NULL);
                lpdraw->bbp = GetDeviceCaps(hdc, PLANES) * GetDeviceCaps(hdc,
                        BITSPIXEL);
                ReleaseDC(NULL, hdc);

                SetRect(&rc, 0, 0, lpdraw->cx, lpdraw->cy);

                AdjustWindowRectEx(&rc, GetWindowStyle(lpdraw->hwndApp),
                        GetMenu(lpdraw->hwndApp) != NULL,
                        GetWindowExStyle(lpdraw->hwndApp));
```

continued on next page

continued from previous page

```
            SetWindowPos(lpdraw->hwndApp, NULL, 0, 0, rc.right-rc.left,
                rc.bottom-rc.top, SWP_NOMOVE | SWP_NOZORDER |
                SWP_NOACTIVATE);

            SetWindowPos(lpdraw->hwndApp, HWND_NOTOPMOST, 0, 0, 0, 0,
                SWP_NOSIZE | SWP_NOMOVE | SWP_NOACTIVATE);

            //
            // make sure our window does not hang outside of the work area
            // this will make people who have the tray on the top or left
            // happy.
            //
            SystemParametersInfo(SPI_GETWORKAREA, 0, &rcWork, 0);
            GetWindowRect(lpdraw->hwndApp, &rc);

            if (rc.left < rcWork.left) rc.left = rcWork.left;
            if (rc.top  < rcWork.top)  rc.top  = rcWork.top;

            SetWindowPos(lpdraw->hwndApp, NULL, rc.left, rc.top,
                0, 0, SWP_NOSIZE | SWP_NOZORDER | SWP_NOACTIVATE);
        }

        return DDCreateSurfaces();
}
```

The first change you'll notice is that we now do two completely different things for windowed and fullscreen mode.

To figure out which mode we're running in, we simply see whether *DDSCL_EXCLUSIVE* is in *lpdraw->nCooperation*. Since we cannot be in exclusive and windowed modes at the same time, we're obviously in fullscreen mode if *DDSCL_EXCLUSIVE* is in there.

The only thing we need to do when we're in fullscreen mode is set the display resolution. The call to `SetDisplayMode` is essentially unchanged since the last example.

When we're in windowed mode, though, things don't look quite so simple. But basically, that big chunk of code does nothing more than position the window on the screen so it's not obstructed and its client area is the right size.

The first three relevant statements find the color depth of the display:

```
hdc = GetDC(NULL);
lpdraw->bbp = GetDeviceCaps(hdc, PLANES) * GetDeviceCaps(hdc,
        BITSPIXEL);
ReleaseDC(NULL, hdc);
```

We need to do this because if we don't explicitly set the display mode when we switch to windowed mode, the display mode will be whatever the user set as the Windows desktop display mode.

To retrieve the color depth, we use the Windows API function `GetDeviceCaps`, which returns the value of the specified system element. For more information on this function, consult your Windows API reference.

The values we stored in the *cx* and *cy* members of our global **GApp** structure are the width and height of the window's *client* area, meaning the portion of the window inside the borders and menu. We need to figure how tall and wide the entire window should be, which is what these two statements do:

```
SetRect(&rc, 0, 0, lpdraw->cx, lpdraw->cy);

AdjustWindowRectEx(&rc, GetWindowStyle(lpdraw->hwndApp),
     GetMenu(lpdraw->hwndApp) != NULL, GetWindowExStyle(lpdraw->hwndApp));
```

The first statement sets the rectangle *rc* to the width and height that the window's client area should be, using the Windows API function **SetRect**. The next statement uses the Windows API function **AdjustWindowRectEx** to find the total—including menus, icons, buttons, and so on—width and height of a window with a client area the size of the rectangle *rc*. For more information on both these functions, consult your Windows API reference.

For your information, rectangles holding the position of a window on the screen are given as follows:

- The upper-left corner of the rectangle (*left*) is the horizontal location of any pixel on the window nearest to the left of the screen.

- The top of the rectangle (*top*) is the vertical location of any pixel on the window nearest to the top of the screen.

- The other two coordinates are the width (*width*) and height (*height*) of the rectangle, not the lower-right corner.

- The coordinates begin with (0,0) at the upper-left corner of the display.

Next we'll position the window in the upper-left corner of the display, using the Windows API function **SetWindowPos**.

```
SetWindowPos(lpdraw->hwndApp, NULL, 0, 0, rc.right-rc.left,
     rc.bottom-rc.top, SWP_NOMOVE | SWP_NOZORDER |
     SWP_NOACTIVATE);

SetWindowPos(lpdraw->hwndApp, HWND_NOTOPMOST, 0, 0, 0, 0,
     SWP_NOSIZE | SWP_NOMOVE | SWP_NOACTIVATE);
```

The first call to **SetWindowPos** puts the window in the upper-left corner of the screen. The second call puts the window at the bottom of the Z-order. We need to put the window below all the others so it becomes invisible for a moment. We'll move the window around a bit, and the user will probably become frustrated trying to use the window while it moves around the screen.

If the user doesn't have the system taskbar configured so it's hidden when not in use, it will occupy some screen real estate. Therefore, we need to check that our window won't be obscured by the taskbar, no matter which of the four sides of the screen it's docked on. To do this, we need to find the portion of the screen the taskbar isn't using, which we'll do with the Windows API function, **SystemParametersInfo**.

```
SystemParametersInfo(SPI_GETWORKAREA, 0, &rcWork, 0);
```

SystemParametersInfo is a function that retrieves miscellaneous information about how the user has set up the system. We'll use it to find the portion of the desktop available for use by our window (the work area).

Next, we'll find the onscreen rectangle our window occupies by using the Windows API function, `GetWindowRect`.

```
GetWindowRect(lpdraw->hwndApp, &rc);
```

Now that we have all the necessary information, we make sure the window isn't obstructed by the taskbar. If it is, we'll move it.

```
if (rc.left < rcWork.left) rc.left = rcWork.left;
if (rc.top  < rcWork.top)  rc.top  = rcWork.top;
```

Finally, we'll put the window into its new position on the screen, although it's only a new position if the window was being obstructed by the taskbar.

```
SetWindowPos(lpdraw->hwndApp, NULL, rc.left, rc.top,
        0, 0, SWP_NOSIZE | SWP_NOZORDER |
        SWP_NOACTIVATE);
```

After most of *DDEnable* has run its course, *DDEnable* returns the return value of *DDCreateSurfaces*.

Now that we've taken care of our window management needs, there are some considerations we must address to make sure drawing only occurs in the proper location—inside the window we just set up.

Clippers

Clipper objects are used, usually in windowed mode, to prevent DirectDraw from drawing on a screen area that shouldn't be drawn on. They are most useful when dealing with windows since windows often overlap. Without clippers, DirectDraw applications that are overlapped by other windows still draw on top of the overlapping windows with no regard for the Z-order. Figure 3-1 shows the consequences of not using clippers and illustrates how DirectDraw applications behave with clippers.

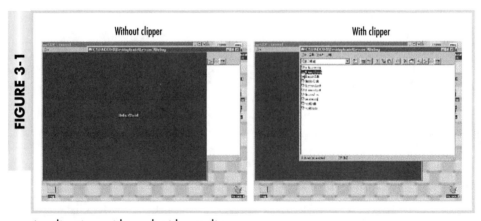

FIGURE 3-1

Application with and without clippers

Clippers are created by building a *clip list*. A clip list is a list of rectangles defining the area on which DirectDraw can draw. A clip list is built either by associating it with a surface or a window (actually, a window handle). When a clipper is associated with a surface, you need to explicitly state which parts (regions) of the surface are visible and available for drawing. When the clipper is associated with a window handle, it automatically keeps track of the visible region by using the window's client area as the only rectangle in the clip list.

Once the clip list is built, you must attach it to the surface to be clipped. Once the clipper—and therefore, the clip list—is attached to the surface, DirectDraw can only draw inside the region the clip list specifies.

Before we go on, here's a brief note on how DirectDraw draws using clippers. Drawing with clippers is not as efficient as drawing without them because DirectDraw must perform more operations for the same amount of work. Take, for example, a situation in which a DirectDraw application's window is being overlapped in the upper-right hand corner by another window (see Figure 3-2).

Usually when a window is being filled, DirectDraw only has to draw one solid rectangle to cover the entire window. However, when a window is being overlapped and a clipper is used, DirectDraw has to draw *two* rectangles to fill the window. This is because DirectDraw cannot draw in the portion being covered (the upper-right corner in our example). Figure 3-3 demonstrates this.

As you can see, it is not economical for time-intensive applications such as 3D games to use clippers. However, there are ways to keep your window on top of all the others. This provides a plausible alternative to using clippers since you no longer need to worry about whether part of your window has been overlapped. Consult your API reference for more information.

In this book, we'll use clippers when in windowed mode since that's the only way our applications will act as expected—aside from keeping the window on top at all times.

Creating the Surfaces

The process of creating the surfaces when in fullscreen mode hasn't changed at all since the last example. When we're in windowed mode, however, it's a different story. Let's take a look at **DDCreateSurfaces** in Listing 3-5 to see the differences.

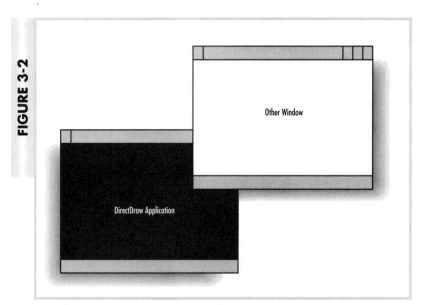

FIGURE 3-2

Overlapping a DirectDraw application's window

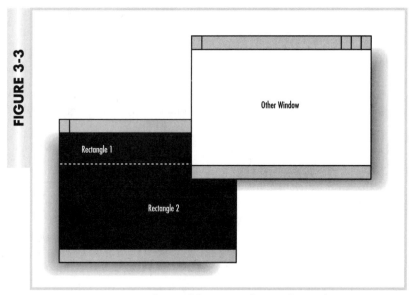

FIGURE 3-3

Drawing two rectangles to fill an overlapped window

Listing 3-5 `DDCreateSurfaces`

```
static BOOL DDCreateSurfaces()
{
        LPDIRECTDRAW    lpdd = lpdraw->lpdd;
        DDSURFACEDESC   ddsd;
        HRESULT         hr;
        DDSCAPS         ddscaps;


        memset( (VOID *)&ddsd, 0, sizeof( ddsd ) );
        ddsd.dwSize = sizeof( ddsd );

    if ( lpdraw->nCooperation & DDSCL_FULLSCREEN )
    {
        //
        // fullscreen case, create a primary (ie front) and
        //      either 1  or 2 back buffers
        //
          ddsd.dwFlags = DDSD_CAPS | DDSD_BACKBUFFERCOUNT;
          ddsd.dwBackBufferCount = lpdraw->nBuffers-1;
          ddsd.ddsCaps.dwCaps = DDSCAPS_PRIMARYSURFACE |
                    DDSCAPS_FLIP | DDSCAPS_COMPLEX;

          hr = lpdd->CreateSurface(&ddsd,
                            &lpdraw->lpFrontBuffer,
                            NULL );

          if( hr != DD_OK )
                return FALSE;

          //
          // get pointer to back buffer
          //
          ddscaps.dwCaps = DDSCAPS_BACKBUFFER;
          hr = lpdraw->lpFrontBuffer->GetAttachedSurface(&ddscaps,
                &lpdraw->lpBackBuffer );

          if( hr != DD_OK )
                return FALSE;
        } else {
            //
              //  window case, create the primary surface
            //  and create a backbuffer in offscreen memory.
            //
            ddsd.dwFlags = DDSD_CAPS;
            ddsd.ddsCaps.dwCaps = DDSCAPS_PRIMARYSURFACE;

              hr = lpdd->CreateSurface( &ddsd, &lpdraw->lpFrontBuffer,
                NULL );

            if( hr != DD_OK )
                return FALSE;
```

continued on next page

continued from previous page

```
                        lpdraw->lpBackBuffer = DDCreateSurface( lpdraw->cx,
                            lpdraw->cy, FALSE );

                        if( lpdraw->lpBackBuffer == NULL )
                            return FALSE;
                //
                // now create a DirectDrawClipper object.
                //
                        hr = lpdd->CreateClipper(0, &lpdraw->lpClipper, NULL);

                        if( hr != DD_OK )
                            return FALSE;

                        hr = lpdraw->lpClipper->SetHWnd(0, lpdraw->hwndApp);

                        if( hr != DD_OK )
                            return FALSE;

                        hr = lpdraw->lpFrontBuffer->SetClipper(lpdraw->lpClipper);

                        if( hr != DD_OK )
                            return FALSE;
                }

            return TRUE;
    }
```

The first thing we do is to check whether we're in fullscreen mode or not. If we are in fullscreen mode, we don't need to do anything different from the last example. If we're in windowed mode, however, that makes quite a difference.

If we're in windowed mode, we won't be able to flip the primary surface (see the section on flipping for an explanation of why). Therefore, we cannot make the primary surface complex. It will just be a plain, simple primary surface.

We'll still render into the former back buffer (*lpdraw->lpBackBuffer*) even though we're not using the complex surface. Once we render into *lpdraw->lpBackBuffer*, we'll just copy (blit) its contents onto the primary surface—an operation almost as fast as flipping.

To create the back buffer, we'll write another little function, **DDCreateSurface**, which simply creates the given surface as a plain vanilla offscreen surface. *Offscreen surfaces* aren't part of the primary surface, and they can have any width and height you wish. Although they *can* be complex, we'll just create the back buffer as a single surface.

Let's take a quick peek at **DDCreateSurface** to see what it looks like (Listing 3-6):

Listing 3-6 **DDCreateSurface**

```
LPDIRECTDRAWSURFACE DDCreateSurface(DWORD width, DWORD height, BOOL sysmem )
{
        DDSURFACEDESC       ddsd;
        HRESULT             hr;
        LPDIRECTDRAWSURFACE lpSurface;
```

```
//
// fill in surface desc
//
memset( &ddsd, 0, sizeof( ddsd ) );
ddsd.dwSize = sizeof( ddsd );
ddsd.dwFlags = DDSD_CAPS | DDSD_HEIGHT |DDSD_WIDTH;

ddsd.ddsCaps.dwCaps = DDSCAPS_OFFSCREENPLAIN;
if( sysmem )
        ddsd.ddsCaps.dwCaps |= DDSCAPS_SYSTEMMEMORY;

ddsd.dwHeight = height;
ddsd.dwWidth = width;

hr = lpdraw->lpdd->CreateSurface( &ddsd, &lpSurface, NULL );

if( hr != DD_OK )
        lpSurface = NULL;
return lpSurface;
}
```

DDCreateSurface accepts three parameters: the width of the surface, the height of the surface, and a Boolean value specifying if the surface should be created in system memory (RAM). **DDCreateSurface** returns the newly created surface.

DDCreateSurface is a fairly simple function. It enables the *ddsCaps*, *ddsHeight*, and *ddsWidth* members of the **DDSURFACEDESC** structure, and fills them in according to the given parameters.

Back to **DDCreateSurfaces** (not **DDCreateSurface**, don't confuse the two). We've just created the (former) back buffer. Now we'll create a clipper, which we'll associate with the application window and attach to the primary surface.

Creating a `DirectDrawClipper` Object

To create a clipper (an `IDirectDrawClipper` object), we'll use the `CreateClipper` function, a member of `IDirectDraw`.

`IDirectDraw::CreateClipper`

```
HRESULT CreateClipper( DWORD dwFlags,  ⇐
LPDIRECTDRAWCLIPPER FAR* lplpDDClipper,  ⇐
IUnknown FAR* pUnkOuter )
```

`CreateClipper` accepts three parameters:

1. *dwFlags*—this parameter is not currently used. It must be zero.

2. *lplpDDClipper*—pointer to a pointer that will be filled in with the address of the newly created `DirectDrawClipper` object.

3. *pUnkOuter*—the NULL value that is in a lot of DirectX calls. Remember, it has to be NULL.

In our example, we have a pointer to a `DirectDrawClipper` object (an `LPDIRECTDRAWCLIPPER`) declared in the *lpClipper* member of our global `LPDDraw` structure, *lpdraw*. We'll initialize that pointer with the `DirectDrawClipper` object. Here's the code that does the job (from `DDCreateSurfaces`):

```
hr = lpdd->CreateClipper(0, &lpdraw->lpClipper, NULL);
```

After we create the `DirectDrawClipper` object, we'll associate it with our application window.

Associating a `DirectDrawClipper` Object

We'll associate the `DirectDrawClipper` object just created with the main application window, created way back in `WinInit`. To associate a `DirectDrawClipper` object with a window we use the function `SetHWnd`, which is a member of `IDirectDrawClipper`.

IDirectDrawClipper::SetHWnd

```
HRESULT SetHWnd( DWORD dwFlags, HWND hWnd )
```

The *dwFlags* parameter is not used and should be zero. The *hWnd* parameter should be a handle to the window to be associated with the `DirectDrawClipper` object.

As you'll recall, a handle to the window is stored in the *lpdraw->hwndApp* member variable. We'll use it when we call `SetHWnd` in `DDCreateSurfaces`.

```
hr = lpdraw->lpClipper->SetHWnd(0, lpdraw->hwndApp);
```

Now that the clipper is created and associated with a window, all that's left to do is attach it to the surface to be clipped. To attach a `DirectDrawClipper` object to a surface, we use the `SetClipper` function, which is a member of `IDirectDrawSurface`.

IDirectDrawSurface::SetClipper

```
HRESULT SetClipper( LPDIRECTDRAWCLIPPER ⇐
lpDDClipper )
```

As you can see, `SetClipper` requires only one parameter, a pointer to the clipper to be attached to the surface. We'll supply `SetClipper` with the pointer to our `DirectDrawClipper` object stored in *lpdraw->lpClipper*.

Now that we're ready to call `SetClipper`, we just need to decide which surface to clip. We'll clip the only visible surface in our application, *lpdraw->lpFrontBuffer*.

```
hr = lpdraw->lpFrontBuffer->SetClipper(lpdraw->lpClipper);
```

And we're ready to roll! *lpdraw->lpFrontBuffer* will now be clipped until `SetClipper` is called using `NULL` as the only parameter, or until either the surface or the clipper are destroyed.

Rendering

Obviously, since our surface structure has changed, our rendering procedure also must change. Most notably, we need to copy the back buffer to the front buffer, instead of flipping it when we run in windowed mode.

Neither `RenderInit` nor `RenderNextFrame` has changed since the last example. `RenderInit` still calculates the wiggle room for the text. `RenderNextFrame` fills the back buffer with a shade of blue and draws the text Hello World! into it.

DDFlip

The function that *has* changed is `DDFlip`. Before all it did was flip *lpdraw->lpFrontBuffer*. But now it has two distinct scenarios to deal with. In the first, our application is in fullscreen mode, flipping is permitted, and the same code from the previous example can be used. In the second, we're in windowed mode, and we need to write a whole new chunk of code.

Let's take a look at the modified `DDFlip` (Listing 3-7):

Listing 3-7 `DDFlip`

```
BOOL DDFlip()
{
        HRESULT hr;

        if( lpdraw->nCooperation & DDSCL_FULLSCREEN )
        {
                hr = lpdraw->lpFrontBuffer->Flip(NULL,DDFLIP_WAIT);
        } else {
                hr = lpdraw->lpFrontBuffer->Blt(&gapp.wndRect, // dest rect
                        lpdraw->lpBackBuffer,            // src surface
                        NULL,                      // src rect (all of it)
                        DDBLT_WAIT,                      // wait if can't blt now
                        NULL);
        }

        return hr == DD_OK;
}
```

As you can see, we still just flip *lpdraw->lpFrontBuffer* if we're running in fullscreen mode. If we're not in fullscreen mode, however, we need to copy the contents of *lpdraw->lpBackBuffer* into *lpdraw->lpFrontBuffer*, because we created them as two separate surfaces rather than one complex surface.

To copy surfaces, we'll use the function `Blt`, a member of `IDirectDrawSurface`. `Blt` is called as a member of the surface being copied to.

IDirectDrawSurface::Blt

```
HRESULT Blt( LPRECT lpDestRect, ⇐
LPDIRECTDRAWSURFACE lpDDSrcSurface, LPRECT⇐
lpSrcRect, DWORD dwFlags, LPDDBLTFX lpDDBltFx )
```

Blit accepts five parameters:

1. *lpDestRect*—the rectangle on the destination surface to be copied to.

2. lpDDSrcSurface—the surface to be copied from.

3. lpSrcRect—the rectangle to be copied from on the source surface. NULL indicates the entire surface.

4. dwFlags—specifies what kind of copy operation is performed, as well as any extra options.

5. *lpDDBltFx*—pointer to a DDBLTFX structure specifying any special effects to be used. NULL if it's not being used.

Keep in mind that if the destination and source rectangle sizes are not the same, Blit will stretch (or shrink) the image from the source surface to make it fit into the destination rectangle. If possible, try to make sure these rectangles are the same size because stretching is a CPU-intensive operation.

Take a look at how we call Blit in our example program:

```
hr = lpdraw->lpFrontBuffer->Blt(&gapp.wndRect, // dest rect
        lpdraw->lpBackBuffer,           // src surface
        NULL,                           // src rect (all of it)
        DDBLT_WAIT,                     // wait if can't blt now
        NULL);
```

We use the window rectangle stored in the **GApp** structure for the destination rectangle and **NULL** for the source rectangle. We copy from the back buffer (*lpdraw->lpBackBuffer*), which is used as the *lpDDSrcSurface* parameter.

For the *dwFlags* parameter, we use **DDBLT_WAIT**. There's a whole slew of possible values for *dwFlags*, each one dictating a specific behavior for Blit. We're not going to cover each, but if you'd like more information on them you can find it in the DirectDraw help file. The value we're using, **DDBLT_WAIT**, tells DirectDraw to wait for an opportune time if it cannot perform the blit the instant Blt is called.

Compiling Example 3-1

We're finished with this example. We've taken quite a step forward from the previous examples, in which the only thing we could do with our application was watch it. Now we can contain it in a fully functional window and switch between windowed and fullscreen mode by pressing ALT+ENTER. Figure 3-4 shows the running application.

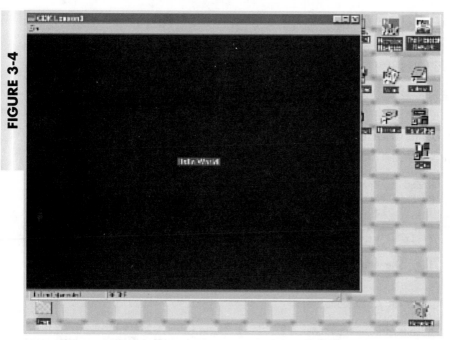

FIGURE 3-4

Example 3-1 in action

We're rapidly moving towards completing our basic coverage of DirectDraw. Next we'll add menu control for the display format, and in the next chapter we'll learn how to code animation (sprites). Pretty soon, you'll know just about all there is to know about DirectDraw!

Excercise 3-2: Display Modes

For our next trick we'll add a menu so the user can choose a display mode simply by clicking on it. Although we'll write a lot of code, we won't actually cover that much new material because a lot of it is just menu code.

WinMain

`WinMain` hasn't changed a whole lot—and probably won't for the rest of the book. Only one line has been added to it, which calls the function `BuildModesMenu`. `BuildModesMenu` is a function we'll write that builds a menu to tack on the one in our main application window.

BuildModesMenu

BuildModesMenu will build a menu containing all the display modes available on the user's system. In order to do this, we need to retrieve information about each mode one at a time and tack a new choice on the end of the menu for each.

Here's the code that makes up BuildModesMenu (Listing 3-8):

Listing 3-8 BuildModesMenu

```
static void BuildModesMenu()
{
        HMENU   hMenu = GetMenu(gapp.hwndApp);
        HMENU   hMenuModes;
        int     nMode;
        //
        // If we've previously build a mode menu toss it
        //
        if( (hMenuModes = GetSubMenu(hMenu, 1)) != NULL )
                DeleteMenu(hMenu, 1, MF_BYPOSITION);
        //
        // Create new mode menu
        //
        hMenuModes = CreateMenu();
        AppendMenu(hMenu,MF_POPUP | MF_ENABLED, (UINT)hMenuModes, "&Modes");
        //
        // Add existing modes to the new menu
        //
        for( nMode = 0; nMode < DDGetDisplayModesCount(); nMode++ )
        {
                DisplayMode dmode;
                char    strbuf[80];

                if( DDGetDisplayMode(nMode, &dmode) == FALSE )
                        break;
                wsprintf(strbuf, "%dx%dx%d", dmode.width, dmode.height,
                        dmode.bpp);
                AppendMenu(hMenuModes, MF_ENABLED, IDM_MODE + nMode, strbuf);
        }
        DrawMenuBar(gapp.hwndApp);
}
```

A lot of Windows API calls modify the menu in this function. We won't go into the specifics of each because this isn't a basic Windows programming book. If you need more information on a certain function, refer to your Windows API documentation or your online SDK help.

Menus are identified by their handles (HMENU variables), much in the same way as windows are. The first thing we do is retrieve a handle to our main application window's menu:

```
HMENU  hMenu = GetMenu(gapp.hwndApp);
```

We simply use the GetMenu API function, which takes the handle of the window the menu is attached to as the single parameter.

Each submenu (each option on the menu bar itself) is also identified with a menu handle. We'll retrieve the handle of the second submenu in our window's menu using the `GetSubMenu` function (remember, the index starts with zero):

```
if( (hMenuModes = GetSubMenu(hMenu, 1)) != NULL )
    DeleteMenu(hMenu, 1, MF_BYPOSITION);
```

All we're doing is deleting the menu if it's already there so that when we add menu choices for each available display mode, we don't fill the menu with a bunch of duplicate choices.

Then, we create a new submenu to stick onto the end of our window's menu:

```
hMenuModes = CreateMenu();
```

`CreateMenu` is an API function that creates a generic menu resource and returns a handle to it.

Next, we'll tack the menu just created, *hMenuModes*, onto the end of the existing window menu (*hMenu*) using the Windows API function `AppendMenu`:

```
AppendMenu(hMenu,MF_POPUP | MF_ENABLED, (UINT)hMenuModes, "&Modes");
```

We'll name the menu `Modes`, with the M underlined (ALT+M then becomes the hotkey to activate the menu).

We then enter a *for* loop that actually sticks menu choices onto the menu. This loop contains a large percentage of the new code in the example (although some of the code is contained in other functions we'll write), so we'll take our time covering it.

```
for( nMode = 0; nMode < DDGetDisplayModesCount(); nMode++ )
{
    DisplayMode dmode;
    char     strbuf[80];

    if( DDGetDisplayMode(nMode, &dmode) == FALSE )
            break;
    wsprintf(strbuf, "%dx%dx%d", dmode.width, dmode.height,
            dmode.bpp);
    AppendMenu(hMenuModes, MF_ENABLED, IDM_MODE + nMode, strbuf);
}
```

The first thing we do is configure the *for* loop so it runs as many times as there are available display modes. We get the number of available display modes using the function `DDGetDisplayModeCount`, which we'll examine momentarily.

Next we declare a variable of type `DisplayMode`, *dmode*. `DisplayMode` is a specific type of structure we've written (in `DDRAWEX.H`) that holds information about a display mode. Here's the definition of `DisplayMode`:

```
typedef struct tagDisplayMode
{
    int          width;
    int          height;
    int          bpp;
} DisplayMode, FAR * LPDisplayMode;
```

As you can see, it holds information about the x resolution, y resolution, and color depth (bpp, or bits per pixel) of a given display mode. We'll use one of these structures whenever we want to hold information about a certain display mode.

The other variable we'll use in the loop is a string called *strbuf*, which holds the actual text appearing on the menu for each choice.

Next, we call the function `DDGetDisplayMode`, which we'll write in a minute or two:

```
if( DDGetDisplayMode(nMode, &dmode) == FALSE )
        break;
```

`DDGetDisplayMode` retrieves information about the display modes available on the user's system and fills a `DisplayMode` structure with information about one of them. In this case, it's filling the `DisplayMode` structure *dmode* with information about a display mode.

After *dmode* is filled with information about an available display mode, we'll put a string in *strbuf* telling the user about the display mode (width * height * color depth):

```
wsprintf(strbuf, "%dx%dx%d", dmode.width, dmode.height, dmode.bpp);
```

The information about the display mode stored in *dmode* is written into the string using the standard C library function `wsprintf`.

Now that we have the text to put on the menu, let's add a new menu choice to our submenu (*hMenuModes*):

```
AppendMenu(hMenuModes, MF_ENABLED, IDM_MODE + nMode, strbuf);
```

`AppendMenu` is a Windows API function that tacks a menu choice onto the given menu. In this case, we're adding a menu choice with the text in *strbuf* to the submenu *hMenuModes*. One important item to notice is the part reading `IDM_MODE + nMode`. When a menu choice is clicked, a `WM_COMMAND` message is sent to the callback function. The value in the third parameter of the call to `AppendMenu` is the value of the low word of the `LPARAM` (a numeric value). We use the low word of the `LPARAM` to distinguish which menu choice was selected when a `WM_COMMAND` message is sent.

After we get out of the loop, we should redraw the menu before leaving, so it'll reflect the changes:

```
DrawMenuBar(gapp.hwndApp);
```

And we're done. We need to go back and look at the two functions used, `DDGetDisplayModesCount` and `DDGetDisplayMode`, which both play an important role in building our menu. But before we do that, we need to cover `EnumDisplayModes`, a DirectDraw API function that retrieves information about the available display modes.

EnumDisplayModes

`EnumDisplayModes`, a member of `IDirectDraw`, provides you with a description of each mode compatible with the user's hardware (or, if you prefer, a list of modes compatible with a specific surface).

IDirectDraw::EnumDisplayModes

```
HRESULT EnumDisplayModes( DWORD dwFlags, ⇐
LPDDSURFACEDESC lpDDSurfaceDesc, LPVOID ⇐
lpContext, LPDDENUMMODESCALLBACK lpEnumCallback )
```

EnumDisplayModes accepts four parameters:

1. *dwFlags*—doesn't do anything in this version of DirectDraw. Must be zero.

2. *lpDDSurfaceDesc*—points to a DDSURFACEDESC structure describing the surface to be checked for compatibility with available modes. If you want to check for all the display modes available on the system, this parameter should be NULL.

3. *lpContext*—points to a piece of data that will be passed to the callback function along with information about the display mode (see *lpEnumCallback*, below).

4. *lpEnumCallback*—points to the callback function that will be called when an available mode is found.

Yep, using EnumDisplayModes requires you use a callback function. Remember that a callback function is a function called every time an event happens. We used one earlier for the window callback function, WindowProc, and we'll write another one that will be called every time a new mode is found on user's system. The callback function that EnumDisplayModes uses must be declared like this:

DDEnumDisplayModes Callback Function

```
HRESULT CALLBACK EnumDisplayModesCallback( ⇐
LPDDSURFACEDESC lp, LPVOID lpContext )
```

The first parameter DirectDraw passes to the callback function is a pointer to a DDSURFACEDESC structure describing the display mode. We'll look further into this shortly.

The second parameter is the same pointer passed to EnumDisplayModes in its third parameter. We aren't going to use it, so it will always be NULL.

DDGetDisplayModesCount

Now we need to backtrack and look at the function BuildModesMenu, which is used to see how many display modes are available on the system. Here it is (Listing 3-9):

Listing 3-9 `BuildModesMenu`

```
int  DDGetDisplayModesCount()
{
        if( nDisplayModes == 0 )
        {
                HRESULT hr = lpdraw->lpdd->EnumDisplayModes(0, NULL, NULL,
                        EnumDisplayModesCallback);

                if( hr != DD_OK )
                        return -1;
        }
        return nDisplayModes;
}
```

Here's our callback function, `EnumDisplayModesCallback` (Listing 3-10):

Listing 3-10 `EnumDisplayModesCallback`

```
static HRESULT CALLBACK EnumDisplayModesCallback(LPDDSURFACEDESC pddsd,
        LPVOID Context)
{
        if( nDisplayModes == MAX_DISPLAYMODES - 1 )
                return DDENUMRET_CANCEL;

        DisplayModes[nDisplayModes].width = pddsd->dwWidth;
        DisplayModes[nDisplayModes].height = pddsd->dwHeight;
        DisplayModes[nDisplayModes].bpp = pddsd->ddpfPixelFormat.dwRGBBitCount;

        nDisplayModes++;

        return DDENUMRET_OK;
}
```

When this function is called (by DirectDraw after we call `EnumDisplayModes`), we'll store information about the display mode described in *pddsd*. To store information about each of these display modes, we declare an array of `DisplayMode` structures at the top of `DDRAWEX.CPP`:

```
static DisplayMode DisplayModes[MAX_DISPLAYMODES];
```

Incidentally, `MAX_DISPLAYMODES` is #defined as 20 in `DDRAWEX.H`.

We've also added a counter to keep track of how many display modes are available, an integer variable called *nDisplayModes*, initialized to zero.

When the callback function is called, we first check that we haven't reached the maximum number of display modes and cancel the display mode enumeration process if we have:

```
if( nDisplayModes == MAX_DISPLAYMODES - 1 )
        return DDENUMRET_CANCEL;
```

DDENUMRET_CANCEL is the value to be returned from the callback function if the enumeration process is canceled. Otherwise, **DDENUMRET_OK** is returned.

Next, we store the information about the display mode in the *DisplayModes* array:

```
DisplayModes[nDisplayModes].width = pddsd->dwWidth;
DisplayModes[nDisplayModes].height = pddsd->dwHeight;
DisplayModes[nDisplayModes].bpp = pddsd->ddpfPixelFormat.dwRGBBitCount;
```

The **DDSURFACEDESC** structure passed to the callback function describes the display mode found. If you need refreshing on the member variables in a **DDSURFACEDESC** structure, refer to Table 2-4 in Chapter 2 or the DirectDraw help file.

Finally, we need to increment the display mode counter and return **DDENUMRET_OK** to DirectDraw.

After DirectDraw calls this callback function as many times as there are available display modes (or 20 times, maximum), we'll have the array of **DisplayMode** structures (*DisplayModes*) filled with information about each mode. Also, *nDisplayModes* will contain the number of available display modes. To ensure that we will look for available display modes whenever the display mode is changed or **DDSetCooperativeLevel** is called, *nDisplayModes* is set to zero in *DDDisable*, which is called whenever one of these operations takes place.

Let's take a quick look back at the loop in **BuildModesMenu**:

```
for( nMode = 0; nMode < DDGetDisplayModesCount(); nMode++ )
{
        DisplayMode dmode;
        char    strbuf[80];

        if( DDGetDisplayMode(nMode, &dmode) == FALSE )
                break;
        wsprintf(strbuf, "%dx%dx%d", dmode.width, dmode.height,
                dmode.bpp);
        AppendMenu(hMenuModes, MF_ENABLED, IDM_MODE + nMode, strbuf);
}
```

As you now see, the *for* statement loops as many times as there are available display modes. Also, the loop index (*nMode*) is used as an index into the *DisplayModes* structure holding information about each available display mode.

DDGetDisplayMode

DDGetDisplayMode is called to retrieve information about a specified display mode. Here's what it looks like (Listing 3-11):

Listing 3-11 `DDGetDisplayMode`

```
BOOL DDGetDisplayMode(int index, LPDisplayMode lpMode )
{
        if( lpdraw == NULL ||
                index >= MAX_DISPLAYMODES ||
                lpdraw->fEnabled == FALSE )
                return FALSE;

        if( nDisplayModes == 0 )
        {
                HRESULT hr = lpdraw->lpdd->EnumDisplayModes(0, NULL, NULL,
                        EnumDisplayModesCallback);

                if( hr != DD_OK )
                        return FALSE;
        }

        if( index < 0 || index > nDisplayModes - 1 )
                return FALSE;
        memcpy( lpMode, &DisplayModes[index], sizeof(DisplayMode) );

        return TRUE;
}
```

The first parameter is an index to the display mode to be retrieved (an index into the *DisplayModes* array). The second is a pointer to the `DisplayMode` structure to be filled with information about the display mode.

The first thing `DDGetDisplayMode` does is check that all the components it needs are in place, have legal values, and are initialized:

```
if( lpdraw == NULL ||
        index >= MAX_DISPLAYMODES ||
        lpdraw->fEnabled == FALSE )
        return FALSE;
```

The *lpdraw* DirectDraw structure cannot be `NULL`, the display mode index cannot be greater than the upper limit of the *DisplayModes* array, and DirectDraw must be enabled (meaning `DDEnable` must have been called).

After that, it checks to make sure *nDisplayModes* isn't zero. If it is, `EnumDisplayModes` hasn't been called yet and must be called using essentially the same code used `DDGetDisplayModesCount`:

```
if( nDisplayModes == 0 )
{
        HRESULT hr = lpdraw->lpdd->EnumDisplayModes(0, NULL, NULL,
                EnumDisplayModesCallback);

        if( hr != DD_OK )
                return FALSE;
}
```

And before we can copy the desired `DisplayMode` structure into the pointer, we need to perform a range check to make sure the index variable won't go outside the array:

```
if( index < 0 || index > nDisplayModes - 1 )
        return FALSE;
```

Finally, we copy the specified `DisplayMode` structure into the *lpMode* `DisplayMode` pointer passed into `DDGetDisplayMode` (using `memcpy`).

```
memcpy( lpMode, &DisplayModes[index], sizeof(DisplayMode) );
```

Now that we've accomplished everything we intended, we just return `TRUE` to the calling function.

The Callback Function

Since we have to deal with the menu built in `BuildModesMenu`, we'll have to handle its messages in the callback function, `WindowProc`. Take a look (Listing 3-12):

Listing 3-12 `WindowProc`

```
static long FAR PASCAL WindowProc( HWND hWnd, UINT message, WPARAM wParam, LPARAM ⇐
lParam )
{
    PAINTSTRUCT ps;
    HDC         hdc;

    switch( message )
    {
            case WM_TIMER:
                if( gapp.fFlippingPaused == FALSE )
                {
                        RenderNextFrame();
                        DDFlip();
                }
                break;
        case WM_SIZE:
        case WM_MOVE:
                GetClientRect(gapp.hwndApp, &gapp.wndRect);
                ClientToScreen(gapp.hwndApp, (LPPOINT)&gapp.wndRect);
                ClientToScreen(gapp.hwndApp, (LPPOINT)&gapp.wndRect+1);
                break;
        case WM_ENTERMENULOOP:
                //
                // Suspend page flipping
                //
                gapp.fFlippingPaused = TRUE;
                //
                // Get GDI's surface back where it's expected!
                //
                gapp.lpdd->FlipToGDISurface();
                //
```

continued on next page

continued from previous page

```
                        // Draw menu
                        //
                DrawMenuBar(gapp.hwndApp);
                    RedrawWindow(gapp.hwndApp, NULL, NULL, RDW_FRAME);
                    break;
            case WM_EXITMENULOOP:
                    gapp.fFlippingPaused = FALSE;
                    break;
            case WM_COMMAND:
                    switch(LOWORD(wParam))
                    {
                            //
                            // File Exit
                            //
                            case IDM_FILEEXIT:
                                    PostMessage(hWnd, WM_CLOSE, 0, 0L);
                                    break;
                        default:
                            //
                            // Check to see if this is a mode menu
                            // command
                            //
                            if(LOWORD(wParam) >= IDM_MODE &&
                                    LOWORD(wParam) < IDM_MODE +
                                    DDGetDisplayModesCount())
                            {
                                    DisplayMode dmode;

                                    if( DDGetDisplayMode(LOWORD(wParam) -
                                            IDM_MODE, &dmode) == TRUE )
                                    {
                                        //
                                        // Valid display mode ---
                                        // disable ddraw and switch mode
                                        //
                                        DDDisable();
                                        DDSetWidth(dmode.width);
                                        DDSetHeight(dmode.height);
                                        DDSetBpp(dmode.bpp);
                                        DDEnable();
                                        RenderInit();
                                    }
                            }
                    }
                    break;
            case WM_KEYDOWN:
                    switch( wParam )
                    {
                            case VK_ESCAPE:
                            case VK_F12:
                                    PostMessage(hWnd, WM_CLOSE, 0, 0);
                                    return 0;
                    }
```

```
                            break;
                case WM_SYSKEYUP:
                        switch( wParam )
                        {
                                case VK_RETURN:
                                {
                                        //
                                        // ALT+ENTER ... switch between fullscreen
                        // and windowed modes
                                        //
                                        int nCooperation = DDGetCooperativeLevel();

                                        DDDisable();
                                        if( nCooperation & DDSCL_FULLSCREEN )
                                                DDSetCooperativeLevel( ⇐
DDSCL_NORMAL );

                                        else
                                                DDSetCooperativeLevel( ⇐
DDSCL_EXCLUSIVE

                                                        | DDSCL_FULLSCREEN
                                                | DDSCL_ALLOWMODEX);
                                        DDEnable();
                                        BuildModesMenu();
                                        RenderInit();
                                        break;
                                }
                        }
                        break;
                case WM_PAINT:
                        hdc = BeginPaint( hWnd, &ps );
                        EndPaint( hWnd, &ps );
                        return 1;
                case WM_DESTROY:
                        //
                        // We're done, clean up and say goodbye
                        //
                        if( gapp.timerid != 0 )
                                KillTimer(gapp.hwndApp, gapp.timerid);
                        DDDisable();
                        DDDestroy();
                        PostQuitMessage( 0 );
                        break;
        }
        return DefWindowProc(hWnd, message, wParam, lParam);
}
```

WM_COMMAND

The major change in this function is the addition of a *default* statement to the
WM_COMMAND message switch. This is hit if the user picks a menu choice (therefore sending a **WM_COMMAND** message with the numeric menu choice ID in the low word of the **WPARAM**)
and the menu ID isn't **IDM_FILEEXIT**, which a *case* statement handles.

First, the *default* statement checks whether the low word of the **WPARAM** is one of the menu command IDs of the mode choices:

```
if(LOWORD(wParam) >= IDM_MODE &&
      LOWORD(wParam) < IDM_MODE +
      DDGetDisplayModesCount())
```

Back when we built the menu, we gave each display mode's menu choice an ID equal to **IDM_MODE** plus that mode's index in the *DisplayModes* array. In the above *if* statement, we make sure the low word of the **WPARAM** is greater than **IDM_MODE** and less than **IDM_MODE** plus the number of available display modes. If it doesn't meet this criteria, the menu choice clicked is not one of the display mode choices.

If a display mode menu choice was clicked, we must retrieve the matching **DisplayMode** structure from the *DisplayModes* array:

```
DisplayMode dmode;
if( DDGetDisplayMode(LOWORD(wParam) -
      IDM_MODE, &dmode) == TRUE )
```

We're simply using the **DDGetDisplayMode** function we wrote to retrieve the display mode corresponding to the menu choice the user clicked. We get the correct array index by subtracting **IDM_MODE** from the value of the low word of the **LPARAM**.

After we get the right display mode, we need to disable DirectDraw so we can set the display mode:

```
DDDisable();
```

The we set the width and height of the primary surface to the screen resolution of the chosen mode using the **DDSetWidth** and **DDSetHeight** functions:

```
DDSetWidth(dmode.width);
DDSetHeight(dmode.height);
```

DDSetWidth and **DDSetHeight** are in **DDRAWEX.CPP**, but we won't discuss them since they're very simple functions—all they do is set the value of *lpdraw->cx* and *lpdraw->cy*.

We need to set the color depth to the right value, using the function **DDSetBpp**, which simply sets *lpdraw->bpp* to the given value:

```
DDSetBpp(dmode.bpp);
```

Now that all the pieces are in place, we'll set the display mode again using **DDEnable**:

```
DDEnable();
```

Remember that **DDEnable** will call **BuildModesMenu** again, so whenever the display mode changes, the menu is rebuilt. We need to do this because certain display modes are not available in windowed mode and, therefore, shouldn't show up on the menu (more on this shortly).

Finally, we call **RenderInit** again to ensure that everything is properly set up to handle the new display mode:

```
RenderInit();
```

WM_SYSKEYUP

Another change has been made to the callback function in the handler of the **WM_SYSKEYUP** message. We only handled **WM_SYSKEYUP** when the **WPARAM** was **VK_RETURN**, meaning ALT+ENTER had been pressed and we were supposed to toggle between fullscreen and windowed mode.

We still do the same thing, but we need to add a few lines. Take a look:

```
case WM_SYSKEYUP:
    switch( wParam )
    {
        case VK_RETURN:
        {
            //
            // ALT+ENTER ... switch between fullscreen
// and windowed modes
            //
            int nCooperation = DDGetCooperativeLevel();

            DDDisable();
            if( nCooperation & DDSCL_FULLSCREEN )
                    DDSetCooperativeLevel( ⇐
DDSCL_NORMAL );
            else
                    DDSetCooperativeLevel( ⇐

DDSCL_EXCLUSIVE
                            | DDSCL_FULLSCREEN
                    | DDSCL_ALLOWMODEX);
            DDEnable();
            BuildModesMenu();
            RenderInit();
            break;
        }
    }
    break;
```

The first thing you'll notice added is the **DDSCL_ALLOWMODEX** flag to the **DDSetCooperativeLevel** call when in fullscreen mode. This allows **ModeX** display modes to be used. They'll also show up on the display modes menu. More on this momentarily.

The second thing added is a call to **BuildModesMenu**. Since the display mode has probably changed and some modes may not be available any more, we need to rebuild the display modes menu.

ModeX

There are usually two available ModeX display modes in DirectDraw: 320×200×8 and 320×240×8. These two modes are exclusively ModeX, so **DDSCL_ALLOWMODEX** must be used in the call to *SetCooperativeLevel* if you plan to use them.

As mentioned earlier, higher resolution display modes take longer to render another frame than lower resolutions, especially when dealing with 3D graphics. When you need lower resolution display modes, you'll probably have to use the ModeX modes (since basically ModeX modes are the available low-resolution modes).

There's a catch to using ModeX, however. The Windows environment doesn't know how to draw on ModeX surfaces, so you can't use ModeX in windowed mode. Because of this, you also have to use exclusive (and fullscreen) mode whenever you use ModeX. The general rule of thumb is this: **DDSCL_ALLOWMODEX** can only be used when both **DDSCL_FULLSCREEN** and **DDSCL_EXCLUSIVE** are also used.

Also, **EnumerateDisplayModes** only enumerates ModeX modes when **DDSCL_ALLOWMODEX** is present in the call to **SetCooperativeLevel**, so we won't have to worry about listing ModeX modes in the menu when they cannot be used.

Another catch is that using ModeX prevents you from doing lots of stuff with the primary surface. You cannot do any of the following when using ModeX:

- Lock the primary surface

- Blit to the primary surface

- Use **GetDC** on the primary surface

Because we used **GetDC** on the primary surface (*lpdraw->lpFrontBuffer*) in a few places throughout the rendering functions, we'll have to go back and change them. Let's do that right now.

Rendering

Render hasn't changed since the last example, so we only have to look at **RenderInit**. Basically, the only difference is that before we retrieved a DC from the front buffer using GetDC, and now we retrieve it from the back buffer. We do this because ModeX modes might be used and, as mentioned above, we cannot get DCs from a ModeX surface.

RenderInit

The only change is that the call to **DDGetFrontBuffer** (which retrieves a pointer to the front buffer) has been replaced with a call to **DDGetBackBuffer** (which retrieves a pointer to the back). Take a look (Listing 3-13):

Listing 3-13 **RenderInit**

```
BOOL RenderInit()
{
        LPDIRECTDRAWSURFACE lpBackBuffer = DDGetBackBuffer();
        HDC hdc;
```

```
//
// Initialize random number generator for wiggling the text around
//
srand( (unsigned)time( NULL ) );

//
// No sense doing this all the time
//
msglen = strlen(msg);

//
// GetDC and calculate variables used for wiggling
//
if(lpBackBuffer->GetDC(&hdc) == DD_OK)
{
        SIZE size;
        int w = DDGetWidth();
        int h = DDGetHeight();

        GetTextExtentPoint32(hdc, msg, msglen, &size );

        //
        // Centered, with wiggle room on all sides
        //
        xmin = ((w - size.cx) / 2) - WiggleRoom;
        xmod = WiggleRoom * 2;
        ymin = ((h - size.cy) / 2) - WiggleRoom;
        ymod = WiggleRoom * 2;

lpBackBuffer->ReleaseDC(hdc);
} else {
        return FALSE;
}
return TRUE;
}
```

The variable *lpFrontBuffer* is renamed *lpBackBuffer* and initialized with a call to **DDGetBackBuffer**. Since we're not using the DC to draw on the surface, it really doesn't matter from which surface **GetDC** is called (unless, of course, its a ModeX surface, which would have bad repercussions).

DDFlip

A quick note about **DDFlip**. When we're in windowed mode, we cannot flip the screen so we just blit the back buffer to the front buffer. ModeX isn't compatible with windowed mode or **Blit**, so this arrangement works out fine. If, however, the entire application were configured to blit the back buffer to the front buffer, even if we were in fullscreen mode, we couldn't use ModeX display modes because ModeX surfaces cannot be blitted to.

Compiling Example 3-2

That's the last example for this chapter. Go ahead and compile it, see what it looks like, and play with it a little. You can switch between video modes by using the menu, and you can toggle between windowed and fullscreen modes using ALT+ENTER. When your in fullscreen mode (except for ModeX modes), you can bring up the menu by pressing ALT. When your in one of the ModeX modes, you can still activate the menu by pressing ALT, but you won't be able to see it.

Summary

Now that you know all about what goes into setting up the environment for DirectDraw, we can dive into some meatier topics. We'll start learning how to put interesting stuff on the screen, instead of just setting up the screen so we can put stuff on it. In the next chapter we'll examine palettes, which are pretty much the foundation for all graphics programming. We'll even get to write some pretty cool examples!

4
Palettes

In this chapter, we'll discuss palettes. We'll learn how to use them and how to perform some of the tricks of the trade. We haven't talked about palettes since Chapter 1, "The Basics," so if you need a refresher on the basics, refer back to that chapter.

In order to keep the first example simple and avoid some of the complications that arise when simultaneously dealing with changing display modes and palettes, we've axed the code that built the display modes menu. This, of course, does not mean we won't encounter any of those complications—we're simply trying to minimize them. ALT + ENTER still works though, at least most of the time (you'll see what that means as we dig into the code).

Example 4-1: Our First Palette Example

The first application we'll build, Example 4-1, begins in either fullscreen or windowed mode. It builds a palette and fills the screen (or client area, as the case may be) with one color at a time from the palette by cycling through its entries. The index of the palette entry is also displayed in the center of the screen. Take a look at Figure 4-1 to get an idea of how the finished product looks.

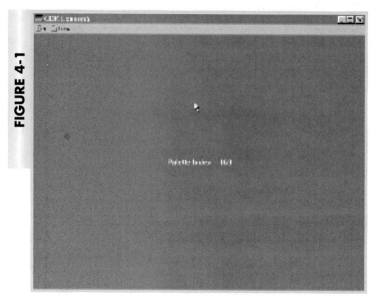

FIGURE 4-1

Example 4-1 in action

Working Around 16 Million Colors

As Chapter 1 mentioned, a display mode using 16 million colors does *not* use a palette. Instead of containing an index to a palette entry, each pixel actually specifies the exact color it should appear as, eliminating the need for a palette. This means that palettes can only be used when running in 256-color or 16-color (not 16 *million* color) mode. Of the 256-color or 16-color modes, only the former is common.

We can't tell from the outset whether or not the user will run Windows 95 in a 256-color mode or a 16-million-color mode. If he or she *is* running in 256 colors, we can run through the rest of the program without any changes. But if 16 million colors are in use, we have to run exclusively in fullscreen mode so we can change to a palletized display mode (one using either 16 or 256 colors).

In order to work around this little problem, a static Boolean variable, named *fCanRunWindowed,* has been added to **DDRAWEX.CPP**. We're going to set *fCanRunWindowed* to **TRUE** if Windows is running in a 256-color mode and we can use windowed mode, or **FALSE** if it's running in 16 million colors. *fCanRunWindowed* is defined as **TRUE** when it's declared, but that may change later in the code.

DrawInit

We've put the code that checks for a palletized display in **DrawInit**. Let's take a look at it (Listing 4-1):

Listing 4-1 `DrawInit`

```
static BOOL DrawInit()
{
 DDSURFACEDESC dddesc;

 //
 // Create DirectDraw object and initialize helper data
 //
 if( (gapp.lpdd = DDCreate(gapp.hwndApp)) == NULL )
  return FALSE;
 //
 // A palette is required, so see if we can run windowed or not //

 memset(&dddesc, 0, sizeof(dddesc));
 dddesc.dwSize = sizeof(dddesc);
 dddesc.dwFlags = DDSD_PIXELFORMAT;
 gapp.lpdd->GetDisplayMode( &dddesc );

 //
 // Assume we can run windowed
 //
 fCanRunWindowed = TRUE;
 if( (dddesc.ddpfPixelFormat.dwFlags & DDPF_PALETTEINDEXED8) == 0 )
 {
  //
  // Can't run windowed since this is not a palettized mode, find
  // another mode
  //
  DisplayMode dmode;
  int mode;
  //
  // Fix previous bad assumption
  fCanRunWindowed = FALSE;
   //
  // Go through the available modes looking for one we can use
  //
  for( mode = 0; mode < DDGetDisplayModesCount(); mode++ )
  {
   if( DDGetDisplayMode(mode, &dmode) == TRUE )
   {
    if( dmode.bpp == 8 )
    {
     //
     // found an eight bit mode, setup and switch
     // to fullscreen
     //
     DDSetWidth(dmode.width);
     DDSetHeight(dmode.height);
     DDSetBpp(dmode.bpp);
     DDSetCooperativeLevel( DDSCL_EXCLUSIVE
      | DDSCL_FULLSCREEN );
     //
```

continued on next page

continued from previous page

```
            // DDEnable (below) will fail if ShowWindow
            // is not called here to effect
           // the switch to full screen mode.  Inside
           // DDEnable the call to
           // DDCreateSurfaces with its call to
           // CreateSurface is the source of
           // the error.  This is a workaround.
           //
           ShowWindow(gapp.hwndApp, SW_SHOW);
           break;
        }
     }
   }
   //
   // Bail if no suitable mode found
   //
    if( mode == DDGetDisplayModesCount() )
    return FALSE;
  } else {
   //
   // Display is palettized, start out windowed
   //
   DDSetCooperativeLevel( DDSCL_NORMAL );
  }

  //
  //  Let 'er rip :-)
  // if( DDEnable() == FALSE )
   return FALSE;
  //
  // Initialize rendering code
  // if( RenderInit() == FALSE )
   return FALSE;
  return TRUE;
}
```

As you can see, there have been quite a few changes in **DrawInit** since the last example. All these changes really only accomplish one goal: making sure our application runs in a 256-color display mode so the palette works correctly.

The first thing we must do is find the color depth of the current display mode. We do this with a call to the DirectDraw API function **GetDisplayMode**, an interface of **IDirectDraw**.

First, we need to fill out a **DDSURFACEDESC** structure telling DirectDraw what to look for when **GetDisplayMode** is called:

```
memset(&dddesc, 0, sizeof(dddesc));
dddesc.dwSize = sizeof(dddesc);
dddesc.dwFlags = DDSD_PIXELFORMAT;
```

We want to know the color depth so we'll set *dwFlags* to **DDSD_PIXELFORMAT**, which, as you'll see shortly, gives us information about the color depth.

Next, we'll call GetDisplayMode, which takes a pointer to a DDSURFACEDESC structure as a parameter. The DDSURFACEDESC parameter should provide the information we're looking for in its *dwFlags* member.

We put DDSD_PIXELFORMAT in *dwFlags*, which makes the DDSURFACEDESC's *ddpfPixelFormat* member valid (a DDPIXELFORMAT structure). After we call GetDisplayMode, the DDPIXELFORMAT's *dwFlags* member indicates the color depth using several different flags. The flag we'd like here is DDPF_PALETTEINDEX8, indicating that there are 8 bits per pixel, or 256 colors.

Even though we don't know what the current color mode is, we'll set *fCanRunWindowed* to TRUE at the outset and change it if we find that the user is running Windows in a different display mode.

Next, we're going to see if the DDSURFACEDESC structure filled in by GetDisplayMode indicates that the user is running in 256 colors, and proceed into the *if* statement if not.

If Windows is *not* running in a 256-color display mode, we move into the *if* statement. We'll have to find a suitable display mode in which to run. To do this, we'll write a loop similar to the one in the BuildModesMenu function of the last example.

Once we're into the *if* statement, we can set *fCanRunWindowed* to FALSE because we now know Windows is running in 16-million-color mode, meaning we can't run windowed.

Next, we create a loop to find a suitable display mode for the palette stuff we want to perform. All we're doing is looping until we either reach the maximum number of display modes without finding one that's decent, or we find one and *break* from the loop.

Once we get a display mode to look at (using DDGetDisplayMode from the last example), we need to see if it's in 256-color mode. If it is, we'll go ahead and use it. We do this by setting the resolution and color depth to the values from the display mode we just found.

Since we just changed the display mode, we can't forget to call DDSetCooperativeLevel. Otherwise, we would just waste a whole bunch of time.

One of the complications (or bugs) that arises when using DirectDraw is that the main application window must be shown at least once before we can successfully switch to fullscreen mode. Therefore, we need to call ShowWindow to show our window before calling DDEnable, which changes the display mode.

Since we identified and set the display mode we want to use we can quit looping, which we do by calling *break*.

If we run all the way through our loop and don't find a suitable display mode, we need to return FALSE to let WinMain know it must abort the program. Since our program only does palette manipulation, there's obviously no point continuing if we can't use palettes.

By the way, if the user is running in a 256-color mode when we enter the function, we can just proceed as in all the previous examples because no new code is used.

Disabling Windowed Mode

If the user is running Windows in 16 million colors and we start running in fullscreen to work around it, we obviously can't just let him or her switch back to windowed mode using [ALT] + [ENTER]. In order disable this, we change the handler code for [ALT] + [ENTER] to look like this (Listing 4-2):

Listing 4-2 The ALT + ENTER handler in **WindowProc**

```
case VK_RETURN:
{
 //
 // ALT+ENTER ... switch between fullscreen
 // and windowed modes
 //
 int nCooperation = DDGetCooperativeLevel();

 //
 // Skip this if we can't run windowed
 //
 if( fCanRunWindowed == FALSE )
 break;
 DDDisable();
 if( nCooperation & DDSCL_FULLSCREEN )
 DDSetCooperativeLevel( DDSCL_NORMAL );
 else
 DDSetCooperativeLevel( DDSCL_EXCLUSIVE
   | DDSCL_FULLSCREEN
   | DDSCL_ALLOWMODEX );
 DDEnable();
 RenderInit();
 break;
}
```

Now that we've disabled that potential hang-up, we're clear of the 16 million color problem and can move on to other things.

The Palette Class

Because there are so many palette operations that you must perform over and over, palettes are well-suited for a C++ class. We'll write a palette class that handles all the routine initialization in the constructor and automatically cleans itself up in the destructor. This class will also have several useful utility functions for such things as filling the palette with a wash of colors, and so on. All apologies to the C purists out there, but palettes really are better suited for C++ classes. Besides, converting the classes to C structures would not require that much work—consider it a challenge.

We'll call the palette class **CDDPalette**, and store it in the files **CDDPAL.H** and **CDDPAL.CPP** on the CD. Now let's get acquainted with the class's declaration, which is basically all of **CDDPAL.H** (see Listing 4-3):

Listing 4-3 `CDDPAL.H`

```
//
// CDDPal.h
//
class CDDPalette
{
protected:
 int    m_nNumColors;
 LPDIRECTDRAWPALETTE m_pDDPalette;
public:
 CDDPalette();
 LPDIRECTDRAWPALETTE CreatePalette(LPDIRECTDRAW lpdd, DWORD dwFlags, ⇐
   LPPALETTEENTRY lpColorTable, int nColors );
 LPDIRECTDRAWPALETTE CreatePalette(LPDIRECTDRAW lpdd, DWORD dwFlags );
 LPDIRECTDRAWPALETTE GetDDPalette();
 BOOL   FadeEntries(COLORREF clrStart, COLORREF clrStop,
    int iFirstEntry, int nEntries, BYTE peFlags);
};
```

The *m_nNumColors* member variable represents the number of colors in the palette, and *m_pDDPalette* holds a pointer to an `IDirectDrawPalette` object—the DirectDraw COM object representing a palette.

Before we get into using these member functions in the code, let's familiarize ourselves with them.

C D D P a l e t t e : : C D D P a l e t t e

The constructor does two simple jobs: It sets the number of colors to zero and initializes the `LPDIRECTDRAWPALETTE` pointer to `NULL`. Nothing too complex, but here they are anyway (Listing 4-4):

Listing 4-4 `CDDPalette::CDDPalette`

```
CDDPalette::CDDPalette()
{
 //
 // Initialize members
 //
 m_nNumColors = 0;
 m_pDDPalette = NULL;
}
```

Now that's out of the way, let's quickly cover the destructor, ~`CDDPalette`.

C D D P a l e t t e : : ~ C D D P a l e t t e

The destructor is even simpler than the constructor. It has one single task: Remove the palette pointer from memory if it's not `NULL`. It does this by calling the universal DirectX function `Release`, the equivalent of the C++ *delete* operator.

Here's the code (Listing 4-5):

Listing 4-5 `CDDPalette::~CDDPalette`

```
CDDPalette::~CDDPalette()
{
 //
 // If a DDraw palette has been created release it
 //
 if( m_pDDPalette != NULL )
  m_pDDPalette->Release();
}
```

Let's move on to the function that takes care of creation and initialization, `CreatePalette`.

CDDPalette::CreatePalette

`CreatePalette` is a member function of our palette class used to build an `IDirectDrawPalette` object. There are two versions of the function: one that builds a palette from an array of predefined colors and one that creates an empty palette. We'll use the latter for now.

Here's the code for `CreatePalette` (Listing 4-6):

Listing 4-6 `CDDPalette::CreatePalette`

```
LPDIRECTDRAWPALETTE CDDPalette::CreatePalette(LPDIRECTDRAW lpdd,
 DWORD dwFlags )
{
 LPDIRECTDRAWPALETTE lpddpal = NULL;
 LPPALETTEENTRY lpEntries;

 if( dwFlags & DDPCAPS_8BIT )
 {
  //
  // Allocate color table and set it to zero
  //
  lpEntries = (LPPALETTEENTRY)malloc(256 * sizeof(PALETTEENTRY));
  memset(lpEntries, 0, 256 * sizeof(PALETTEENTRY));

  //
  // Create the Direct Draw palette
  //
  lpddpal = CreatePalette(lpdd, dwFlags, lpEntries, 256);

  //
  // Release buffer
  //
  free(lpEntries);
 }
 return lpddpal;
}
```

`CreatePalette` takes two parameters: a pointer to the DirectDraw object that will create the palette, and a `DWORD` that holds flags specifying how the palette will behave. It returns a pointer to the newly created palette.

One structure we'll use a lot as we work with palettes is the `PALETTEENTRY` structure, or `LPPALETTEENTRY`, a pointer to the same. A `PALETTEENTRY` structure holds information about a single palette entry in the form of variables that contain the red, green, and blue components of the color and a flag variable. Its declaration is in `WINDOWS.H`, but you can take a look at it right here:

```
typedef struct tagPALETTEENTRY {
 BYTE peRed;
 BYTE peBlue;
 BYTE peGreen;
 BYTE peFlags;
} PALETTEENTRY;
```

As you can probably guess, *peRed*, *peBlue*, and *peGreen* specify the intensity values of the respective colors that make up the final color.

The *peFlags* member specifies how the palette entry should be treated. The only value we're interested in right now is `PC_NOCOLLAPSE`. If you don't put `PC_NOCOLLAPSE` in *peFlags* when specifying a color and another palette entry has the same color value, Windows will simply match any pixels using the duplicate color to the existing color, instead of creating a new palette entry for the duplicate color. This could severely mess up palette animation and other operations, so we'll use `PC_NOCOLLAPSE` as needed.

Back to `CreatePalette`. The first thing we need to do is check that the palette being created contains 256 colors. If it doesn't, we're probably running in 16-million-color mode and there's no use in even creating a palette. If it does, we enter the *if* statement.

The first thing we do inside the *if* statement is allocate space for 256 `PALETTEENTRY` structures to hold the colors in the palette:

```
lpEntries = (LPPALETTEENTRY)malloc(256 * sizeof(PALETTEENTRY));
```

lpEntries is an `LPPALETTEENTRY` variable declared in the beginning of *CreatePalette*.

Since we weren't provided any colors to put in the palette, we're going to set the entire array of palette entries to zero, which is the equivalent of setting them all to black:

```
memset(lpEntries, 0, 256 * sizeof(PALETTEENTRY));
```

Next we'll call `CreatePalette`:

```
lpddpal = CreatePalette(lpdd, dwFlags, lpEntries, 256);
```

What? That's right, we're calling the overloaded version of `CreatePalette` that accepts an array of palette entries and fills them with colors. We'll discuss that one momentarily, after we finish up with this version. (For you C++ newbies, overloaded functions are simply functions that have the same name but accept different parameters or return a different value; C++ determines on the fly which function should be called.)

The other `CreatePalette` will initialize everything we haven't taken care of already, so our job here is done. Now we'll clean up by releasing the memory we've allocated. The other overloaded `CreatePalette` built the `LPDIRECTDRAWPALETTE` object in the `CDDPalette` member variable *lpddpal*, so all we need to do is return it to the calling function.

Now we just need to examine the other `CreatePalette`. This is a bit involved, so we'll take it one step at a time.

The Overloaded CDDPalette::CreatePalette

Here's the code for the other overloaded `CreatePalette` (Listing 4-7):

Listing 4-7 The other CDDPalette::CreatePalette

```
LPDIRECTDRAWPALETTE CDDPalette::CreatePalette(LPDIRECTDRAW lpdd, DWORD dwFlags,⇐
LPPALETTEENTRY lpColorTable, int nColors )
{
LPLOGPALETTE pPal;
HDC     hdc;
HRESULT   hr;

//
// Only 256 entry palettes for now
//
if( nColors != 256 )
 return NULL;
//
// Allocate header and room for palette entries
//
pPal = (LOGPALETTE*)malloc(sizeof(LOGPALETTE) + nColors
  * sizeof(PALETTEENTRY));
//
// Initialize header
//
pPal->palVersion = 0x300;
pPal->palNumEntries = nColors;
//
// Use screen DC to get current palette
//
hdc = GetDC(0);
//
// If the system has no static palette colors just copy everything
//
if( GetSystemPaletteUse(hdc) == SYSPAL_NOSTATIC )
{
 memcpy( pPal->palPalEntry, lpColorTable, nColors
  * sizeof(PALETTEENTRY) );
 for( int i = nColors; i < 256; i++ )
  pPal->palPalEntry[i].peFlags = PC_NOCOLLAPSE;
} else {
//
// Copy callers color table but preserve static system colors
//
```

```
    int nStatic;
    int nUsable;
    int i;
    //
    // Get number of static colors and read entire system palette
    //
    nStatic = GetDeviceCaps(hdc, NUMCOLORS);
    GetSystemPaletteEntries(hdc, 0, 256, pPal->palPalEntry);
    //
    // Set low part of static entry palette flags to zero
    //
    for(i = 0; i < nStatic / 2; i++)
     pPal->palPalEntry[i].peFlags = 0;
    //
    // Now copy over the available part of the system palette
    //
    nUsable = nColors - nStatic;

    memcpy( &pPal->palPalEntry[i], &lpColorTable[i],
     nUsable * sizeof(PALETTEENTRY) );
    //
    // Finish by setting botton part of static entry's palette flags
    //
    for(i += nUsable; i < 256; i++ )
     pPal->palPalEntry[i].peFlags = 0;
  }
  ReleaseDC(0, hdc);
  //
  // Create the Direct Draw palette
  //
  hr = lpdd->CreatePalette(dwFlags, pPal->palPalEntry, &m_pDDPalette,
   NULL);
  //
  // Release temporary memory
  //
  free(pPal);
  if( hr != DD_OK )
   return m_pDDPalette = NULL;
  else
   return m_pDDPalette;
}
```

Let's take a look at the parameters for this function:

1. *lpdd*—a pointer to the DirectDraw object we'll use to create the palette.

2. *dwFlags*—specifies how the palette will behave.

3. *lpColorTable*—an array of palette entries containing the colors in the new palette.

4. *nColors*—the number of colors in the palette.

`CreatePalette` returns a pointer to the newly created palette object.

In a nutshell, this function finds out if it can use all the colors in the palette, copies the colors from the palette entries into the palette, then creates the palette.

The first thing we do is make sure we're dealing with a 256-color palette:

```
if( nColors != 256 )
 return NULL;
```

This function only works with 256 colors, so there's no use continuing if the number of colors is anything else.

Now we need to create a palette. In Windows programming, palettes are usually represented by a **LOGPALETTE** structure. **LOGPALETTE**s have members containing information about the operating system the palette is for, the number of palette entries, and the palette entries themselves. Here's how the structure is declared in **WINDOWS.H**:

```
typedef struct tagLOGPALETTE {
 WORD   palVersion;
 WORD   palNumEntries;
 PALETTEENTRY palPalEntry[1];
} LOGPALETTE;
```

palVersion is the version number of the palette (the *version number* tells which operating system the palette was built for), *palNumEntries* is the number of palette entries, and *palPalEntry* is the array of entries making up the palette.

Anyway, back to the code. We need to build a **LOGPALETTE** structure to represent the palette. We declared a pointer to one in the beginning of *CreatePalette* as *pPal*, which is what we'll use. Before we do, though, we need to allocate space for it:

```
pPal = (LOGPALETTE*)malloc(sizeof(LOGPALETTE) + nColors*sizeof(PALETTEENTRY));
```

The size of the structure equals the size of a **LOGPALETTE** structure plus the number of colors multiplied by the size of a **PALETTEENTRY** structure, because the number of colors equals the number of palette entries needed.

Now we'll initialize *pPal*'s two members which aren't palette entries (the palette version and number of palette entries):

```
pPal->palVersion = 0x300;
pPal->palNumEntries = nColors;
```

The current version number of all Windows palettes is 0x300, because palettes haven't changed since version 3.0 of Windows. Obviously, because we made it this far, the number of colors in the palette will be 256, but we'll use *nColors* to initialize *palNumEntries* anyway. The function tends to be more extensible that way.

There's one problem we have to deal with when creating a palette. Sometimes Windows has some palette entries that need to stay the same in order to draw the user interface with the correct colors. If we changed the colors Windows uses for this, the title bars, menus, and other objects would look a little funny.

To find out if we can change all the palette entries, we need to use some GDI functions that require a legitimate DC. To get the DC, we'll use the Windows API function **GetDC** with zero as the single parameter. Normally **GetDC** takes a window handler as the parameter, but because we don't really want to draw anything with it we can use zero instead.

Now we need to find out whether we can change all the palette entries. To do this, we'll use the Windows API function `GetSystemPaletteUse`:

```
if( GetSystemPaletteUse(hdc) == SYSPAL_NOSTATIC )
```

`GetSystemPaletteUse` returns `SYSPAL_NOSTATIC` if all the palette entries can be changed, `SYSPAL_STATIC` if they can't. We'll deal with the case of `SYSPAL_NOSTATIC` first.

If we *can* change all the palette entries, we proceed into the *if* statement. The first thing we do there is copy the array of palette entries passed into `CreatePalette` to the array of palette entries in the `LOGPALETTE` structure *pPal*:

```
memcpy( pPal->palPalEntry, lpColorTable, nColors * sizeof(PALETTEENTRY) );
```

Remember that the size of the array of palette entries is the size of a `PALETTEENTRY` structure multiplied by the number of colors.

Now we just need to set the flags for the palette entries to `PC_NOCOLLAPSE` so all the palette entries remain as is and Windows doesn't decide to match them to existing colors:

```
for( int i = nColors; i < 256; i++ )
 pPal->palPalEntry[i].peFlags = PC_NOCOLLAPSE;
```

If we *can't* use all the palette entries, we need to keep the ones Windows is using in place and fill the other ones with the colors we need. First, we must find the number of palette entries Windows itself is using, meaning the number of entries that can't be changed:

```
nStatic = GetDeviceCaps(hdc, NUMCOLORS);
```

The Windows API function `GetDeviceCaps` returns a number of different values depending on the parameters. Check your API reference for more information.

Now we'll copy the palette entries Windows is using to the array of palette entries in the `LOGPALETTE` structure, using the Windows API function `GetSystemPalette`:

```
GetSystemPaletteEntries(hdc, 0, 256, pPal->palPalEntry);
```

`GetSystemPalette` copies the palette entries Windows is using into exactly the same position in the array as in the palette initially used by Windows. This is because Windows keeps half the colors it uses in the front of the array of palette entries, and the other half at the end (it's kind of a pain, but we have to live with it).

Now, we'll set the flags for the system colors (the colors that Windows is using) to zero, because `GetSystemPalette` doesn't copy the flags for the palette entries and we don't want residual garbage in there:

```
for(i = 0; i < nStatic / 2; i++)
 pPal->palPalEntry[i].peFlags = 0;
```

Here we just work with the first half of the system colors, because we only loop to half of them. Remember that *nStatic* was the number of system colors as returned by `GetDeviceCaps`.

Now we'll find the number of changeable palette entries by subtracting the number of system colors from the number of total colors (which is, as always, 256). After we find that out, we'll copy as many colors as we can from the array of palette entries passed into `CreatePalette` into the changeable part of the palette we're building:

```
memcpy( &pPal->palPalEntry[i], &lpColorTable[i],nUsable*sizeof(PALETTEENTRY));
```

Remember that *i* is still set to the index of the palette entry after the last system color in the first half of the palette. We're just copying as many palette entries as we can, which is *nUsable* number of palette entries.

We also need to set the flags for the last half of the system colors palette entries to zero. After that we no longer need the DC retrieved earlier, so we release it.

And finally, we create the palette using the DirectDraw object passed into `CreatePalette`:

```
hr = lpdd->CreatePalette(dwFlags, pPal->palPalEntry, &m_pDDPalette, NULL);
```

 IDirectDraw::CreatePalette

```
HRESULT CreatePalette( DWORD dwFlags,
LPPALETTEENTRY lpColorTable,
LPDIRECTDRAWPALETTE* lplpDDPalette, IUnknown*
pUnkOuter )
```

The `CreatePalette` function we call here is a member function of `IDirectDraw`, and it takes four parameters:

1. *dwFlags*—specifies how the palette will behave.

2. *lpColorTable*—an array of `PALETTEENTRY` structures holding the colors to be in the newly created palette.

3. *lplpDDPalette*—a pointer to a pointer to an `IDirectDrawPalette` to be initialized with the palette.

4. *pUnkOuter*—not currently supported, must be `NULL`.

For the parameters, we pass in the *dwFlags* parameter passed into our version of *CreatePalette*, the array of palette entries in our `LOGPALETTE` structure, a pointer to our `LPDIRECTDRAWPALETTE` member *m_pDDPalette*, and `NULL`, respectively.

Before we return from `CreatePalette`, we need to free the `LOGPALETTE` structure for which we allocated memory because it's no longer needed. We'll also return a pointer to the `LPDIRECTDRAW` palette return by `CreatePalette`—provided that, of course, `CreatePalette` was successful.

CDDPalette::GetDDPalette

`GetDDPalette` is one of those standard C++ member functions that returns a pointer to a member protected variable. In this case, we return the member variable that's a pointer to the `IDirectDrawPalette` object. We don't even need to list the code; all it does is return *m_pDDPalette*.

CDDPalette::FadeEntries

FadeEntries is a particularly useful member function. It creates a wash from one color to another at the specified location in the palette, using a given number of colors. (A *wash* is just a bunch of colors that gradually fade from one specific color to another over a given number of palette entries.) We'll use this function a lot when we get into palette animation.

Here's the code for FadeEntries (Listing 4-8):

Listing 4-8 CDDPalette::FadeEntries

```
BOOL CDDPalette::FadeEntries(COLORREF clrStart, COLORREF clrStop,
 int iFirstEntry, int nEntries, BYTE peFlags )
{
LPPALETTEENTRY  lpEntries;
int    i;
float   rStep;
float   gStep;
float   bStep;
float   r;
float   g;
float   b;

//
// Get start red, green, and blue colors
//
r = (float)(clrStart & 0xff);
g = (float)((clrStart >> 8) & 0xff);
b = (float)((clrStart >> 16) & 0xff);
//
// Calculate step for each component
//
rStep = ((float)(clrStop & 0xff) - r) / (float)nEntries;
gStep = ((float)((clrStop >> 8) & 0xff) - g) / (float)nEntries;
bStep = ((float)((clrStop >> 16) & 0xff) - b) / (float)nEntries;
//
// Allocate temporary buffer
//
lpEntries = (LPPALETTEENTRY)malloc(nEntries * sizeof(PALETTEENTRY));
//
// Fill in the entries
//
for( i = 0; i < nEntries; i++ )
{
 lpEntries[i].peRed = (BYTE)r;
 lpEntries[i].peBlue = (BYTE)b;
 lpEntries[i].peGreen = (BYTE)g;
 lpEntries[i].peFlags = peFlags;
```

continued on next page

continued from previous page

```
    r += rStep;
    g += gStep;
    b += bStep;
}
//
// Update Direct Draw palette with color table entries
//
BOOL fResult = m_pDDPalette->SetEntries(0, iFirstEntry, nEntries,⇐
    lpEntries) == DD_OK;

free(lpEntries);

return fResult;
}
```

FadeEntries accepts five parameters:

1. *clrStart*—the color starting the wash, given as a COLORREF value that can be specified with the RGB macro.

2. *clrStop*—the color the wash ends with, also a COLORREF value.

3. *iFirstEntry*—the index of the palette entry the wash starts with.

4. *nEntries*—the number of palette entries to fill with the wash.

5. *peFlags*—the flags to be put in the *peFlags* member of the PALETTEENTRY structures for each palette entry.

One thing you must remember when using this function is that it doesn't check for stupid palette entry indexes. For example, if you told it to start at palette index 250 and continue the wash for 100 palette entries, you'd obviously go outside the 256 range of colors. Since this function doesn't know any better and would do it anyway, you have to watch your step.

In a nutshell, here's how **FadeEntries** works. First, it finds out how much it needs to step for the red, green, and blue values of every palette entry to reach the end value in *nEntries* number of palette entries. Second, it creates the wash in a temporary palette. Last, it updates the real palette with the new values.

One thing to note: When we calculate the colors to be placed in the palette, we can't use a COLORREF value to specify the color. We need to use the same format as when a pixel is placed on a surface, that is, the format in which the red, green, and blue components of the color are specified by individual bits in the byte in the surface.

The format used within surface memory—at least in 256-color modes, it's different with other color depths—looks like Figure 4-2.

As you can see from the figure, there are two bits to designate every red, green, and blue component of the color. The values for each of these bits are given in hexadecimal notation.

The first two bits, the useless ones, always have to be FF. The remaining six bits must range from 00 to FF to dictate the given color. For example, because pure red is the RGB value 0,0,255, the value of the pixel on a surface is 0xFF0000FF.

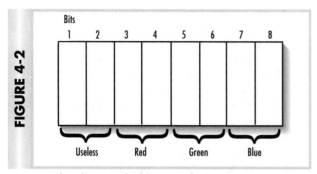

FIGURE 4-2

Pixel values as held in surface memory

DDColorMatch from previous examples was essentially figuring out what we just learned here: It was trying to get the equivalent byte value for the given RGB value. It was simply sticking the color on a surface in the form of a pixel, then reading the byte and returning it as a DWORD. We no longer have to use DDColorMatch, however, because we now know how to do it ourselves.

Anyway, back to the code. We need to get a byte value for the starting color. To do this, we need to extract the red, green, and blue values from the starting color. There's a really simple way to do this: We merely shift the RGB value the correct number of bits and mask the resulting value by 0xFF to fill in the useless bits:

```
r = (float)(clrStart & 0xff);
g = (float)((clrStart >> 8) & 0xff);
b = (float)((clrStart >> 16) & 0xff);
```

In effect, we've made the red, green, and blue values (*r, g,* and *b*) *floats,* so they each contain 16 bits. This means we have to shift twice as many bits as if using plain bytes.

Now that we have the individual byte values, we need to figure out how much to add to each red, green, and blue component of the color to reach the stop color in the given number of palette entries. We'll put the result in the *rStep, bStep,* and *gStep* float variables:

```
rStep = ((float)(clrStop & 0xff) - r) / (float)nEntries;
gStep = ((float)((clrStop >> 8) & 0xff) - g) / (float)nEntries;
bStep = ((float)((clrStop >> 16) & 0xff) - b) / (float)nEntries;
```

We'll do the same thing we did before to extract the individual color values (except we're extracting them from the stop color), then subtracting the start value from each component and dividing by the number of palette entries with which we will create the wash. This will give us color values in *rStep, gStep,* and *bStep* that we can use to add to the start color, so we can come up with a smooth wash to the end color.

Now we allocate an array of *nEntries* palette entries to hold the wash in a temporary palette:

```
lpEntries = (LPPALETTEENTRY)malloc(nEntries * sizeof(PALETTEENTRY));
```

Then we'll fill in the entries with the wash using a *for* loop. The first thing we do in the loop is put the red, green, and blue values into their respective members and stick the flag parameter passed to `FadeEntries` into *peFlags*.

Initially *r, g,* and *b* will be the same red, green, and blue values passed into the function as the start color, but only until we add the step colors to them. Then they'll be one step closer to the end color and one step farther from the start color.

After adding the step values to the previous colors, the loop is finished. If all goes well, the loop will continue on and fill *nEntries* palette entries with colors fading smoothly from the start color to the stop color.

Now that we have the wash in a temporary palette, we just need to update the palette. We do this using the `IDirectDrawPalette` member function `SetEntries`.

 ## IDirectDrawPalette::SetEntries

```
HRESULT SetEntries( DWORD dwFlags, DWORD
dwStartingEntry, DWORD dwCount, LPPALETTEENTRY
lpEntries)
```

`SetEntries` accepts four parameters:

1. *dwFlags*—not used, must be zero.

2. *dwStartingEntry*—the index of the first palette entry to change.

3. *dwCount*—the number of palette entries to set.

4. *lpEntries*—pointer to the array of palette entries from which to take the replacement colors.

We're using many of the same parameters passed to `FadeEntries` in our call to `SetEntries`, because they're declared in pretty much the same way.

All right, now that we're finished, all we have to do is clean up. We just have to free the array of palette entries, *lpEntries,* then return either `TRUE` or `FALSE`, depending on whether or not `SetEntries` succeeded.

Rendering

The rendering process has changed quite a bit, because we can now employ palettes and are rendering a completely different picture on the screen. Now we'll cycle through the palette entries and display them on the screen, along with the index of the current palette entry as a string of text.

First we need to put a global pointer to a `CDDPalette` class at the top of `RENDER.CPP`, called *ddPal*, and initialize it to `NULL`, so we actually have a palette to use. Now that that's out of the way, let's get to the code.

RenderInit

RenderInit has changed quite a bit since the last example, which was in Chapter 3, "More DirectDraw." Now we're creating a wash of colors in the palette, via **FadeEntries**, and setting up the string of text in the center of the screen so we can tell which palette entry is filling it. Take a look at Listing 4-9, which shows the new version of **RenderInit**:

Listing 4-9 **RenderInit**

```
BOOL RenderInit()
{
LPDIRECTDRAWSURFACE lpBackBuffer = DDGetBackBuffer();
HDC hdc;
//
// If we've been here before and allocated a palette toss it
//
if( ddPal != NULL )
 delete ddPal;
//
// Create new palette
//
ddPal = new CDDPalette;
ddPal->CreatePalette(DDGetLPDirectDraw(),
 DDPCAPS_8BIT | DDPCAPS_INITIALIZE);
//
// Associate palette with front buffer
//
DDGetFrontBuffer()->SetPalette(ddPal->GetDDPalette());
//
// Create a wash in the current palette
//
ddPal->FadeEntries(RGB(255,0,0), RGB(255,255,0), 10, 32,
 PC_NOCOLLAPSE);
ddPal->FadeEntries(RGB(255,255,0), RGB(0,255,0), 42, 32,
 PC_NOCOLLAPSE);
ddPal->FadeEntries(RGB(0,255,0), RGB(0,255,255), 74, 32,
 PC_NOCOLLAPSE);
ddPal->FadeEntries(RGB(0,255,255), RGB(0,0,255), 106, 32,
 PC_NOCOLLAPSE);
ddPal->FadeEntries(RGB(0,0,255), RGB(255,0,255), 138, 32,
 PC_NOCOLLAPSE);
ddPal->FadeEntries(RGB(255,0,255), RGB(255,0,0), 170, 32,
 PC_NOCOLLAPSE);
//
// GetDC and calculate variables used for text positioning
//
    if(lpBackBuffer->GetDC(&hdc) == DD_OK)
    {
 char msg[] = "Palette Index = 00";
 SIZE size;
 int w = DDGetWidth();
 int h = DDGetHeight();
```

continued on next page

continued from previous page

```
    GetTextExtentPoint32(hdc, msg, strlen(msg), &size );

    //
    // Calculate location which will center the text
    //
    xmin = (w - size.cx) / 2;
    ymin = (h - size.cy) / 2;

            lpBackBuffer->ReleaseDC(hdc);
  } else {
   return FALSE;
  }
  //
  // Initialize background color index
  //
  BkColorIndex = 10;
  return TRUE;
}
```

The palette will initially be **NULL** when the example firsts begins, so if it's not **NULL** when we get into **RenderInit**, then this is obviously at least the second time it's been called. If that happens, we must delete the palette object—so we can create it again.

After cleaning up the palette, we create the palette using the C++ *new* operator, and create an empty palette using the version of **CreatePalette** that only accepts two parameters. We call it using the **DDPCAPS_8BIT** flag, which tells **IDirectDraw::CreatePalette** the palette should be 8 bits per pixel in color depth, and therefore 256 colors. The **DDPCAPS_INITIALIZE** flag tells it to use the array of palette indexes being passed to it.

Now we have to tell the front buffer to use the palette just created, which we do using the **IDirectDrawSurface** member **SetPalette**. The call to **SetPalette** tells the surface that from now on, it should use the palette passed to **SetPalette** as its active one.

Now we'll create a wash of colors in the palette, using several calls to **FadeEntries**. Each call to **FadeEntries** creates a fade from the previous stop color to another color, until the last color fades to the original start color. We couldn't do all of the washes in one call to **FadeEntries** though, because we want several distinctly different colors in the palette. For example, you can't have a wash from red to blue and have green in the middle. Calling **FadeEntries** makes a nice fade to several different colors in the palette that looks smooth when cycled through on the screen.

Next we get a DC to use for measuring text from the back buffer (using **IDirectDrawSurface::GetDC**) and proceed into the *if* statement. The only thing that's changed in the *if* statement is the text in the message. For now it's initialized to **Palette Index = 00**, but we'll change the text as we render each frame.

One more thing has changed in **RenderInit**:

```
BkColorIndex = 10;
```

We're keeping track of the palette entry we're on in the variable *BkColorIndex*. We'll use it when we cycle through the entries. It's initially 10 because if we can't change the system colors, they won't look right in the fade. The first and last 10 colors in the palette are used by Windows and don't work in the wash at all.

RenderNextFrame

`RenderNextFrame` fills the back buffer with the cycling palette entry, then writes the index of the palette entry into it via a string of text. It's not overly complicated, but here it is for you to review (Listing 4-10):

Listing 4-10 **RenderNextFrame**

```
void RenderNextFrame()
{
LPDIRECTDRAWSURFACE lpBackBuffer = DDGetBackBuffer();
HDC hdc;

//
// Shouldn't be here if no buffers, but avoid GPFs anyway
//
if( lpBackBuffer == NULL )
 return;

//
// Clear last hello from buffer
//
FillBufferRect(lpBackBuffer, NULL, (COLORREF)BkColorIndex);

if(lpBackBuffer->GetDC(&hdc) == DD_OK)
{
 char msg[40];

 wsprintf(msg, "Palette Index = %02d", BkColorIndex);
 //
 // Let GDI put text in the buffer for us
 //
 SetBkMode( hdc, TRANSPARENT );
 SetTextColor( hdc,RGB( 255, 255, 255) );

 TextOut(hdc,xmin,ymin,msg, strlen(msg));
 lpBackBuffer->ReleaseDC(hdc);
}
if( ++BkColorIndex > 201 )
 BkColorIndex = 10;
}
```

As you can see, we're now passing `FillBufferRect` the index of the palette entry that has the color we want to fill the back buffer with, instead of an explicit `COLORREF` value. When the pixels in the buffer are filled with the index, they're painted as the color of the palette entry to which the index refers. We still have to cast it to a `COLORREF` value though, chiefly because `FillBufferRect` still calls GDI functions that need a `COLORREF` value.

We also create a different message each time `RenderNextFrame` is called, displaying the index of the current palette entry that fills the screen. We do this by printing the number of the palette index into the *msg* string with the **wsprintf** function. We're also setting the background color of the text to transparent by passing **SetBkMode** the value **TRANSPARENT** instead of an explicit color value.

After we get the text set up, we finally increment the value of the palette index by 1, until it reaches 201. We're stopping at 201 because if Windows won't let us change all the palette entries, we'd better not assume we can use the upper portion of the palette either. This is just to be on the safe side.

FillBufferRect

The only difference in `FillBufferRect` is that it doesn't call `DDColorMatch` to convert the color passed into a pixel value—because it's now being passed an index to a palette entry, instead of an `RGB` value. We won't even bother looking at the code because this change is so small.

Before we can go on with the code, we need to discuss something called the *vertical blank*, which has to do with the monitor.

The Vertical Blank

The monitor has a little electron gun that zooms back and forth across the screen, continually updating it to reflect the changes to video memory. Well, almost continually. The electron moves the same way we read a book, from top to bottom, left to right. Once it reaches the lower-right pixel on the screen, it has to move back to the upper-left corner of the display before starting to refresh the monitor again. The time it takes the electron gun to move this distance is called the *vertical blank* (also called the *vertical retrace*).

It's common practice in game programming to wait for the vertical blank to update the screen. Otherwise, there is sometimes a noticeable flicker when you copy a new image to video memory and the electron gun is still in the middle of an update.

 Note

Because it occurs at a constant rate, the vertical blank is sometimes used as a highly accurate timer.

In this example, we'll add a menu option to wait for the vertical blank, just so you can see the difference. In all later programs, the vertical blank wait will be hard-coded in.

WindowProc

We'll add both a menu option with the resource ID `IDM_WAITVBLANK` and a corresponding handler the message will send to Example 4-1. Here's the code (from within the `WM_COMMAND` handler) that handles the new menu option (see Listing 4-11):

Listing 4-11 Menu handler

```
case IDM_WAITVBLANK: gapp.fWaitForVerticalBlank = !gapp.fWaitForVerticalBlank;
CheckMenuItem(GetMenu(hWnd),
  LOWORD(wParam), MF_BYCOMMAND | (gapp.fWaitForVerticalBlank ?⇐
    MF_CHECKED : MF_UNCHECKED ));
  break;
```

A Boolean member variable has been added to our global **GApp** structure, called *fWaitForVerticalBlank.* We'll toggle it when the Vertical Blank menu option is selected.

After making sure *fWaitForVerticalBlank* coincides with the user's choice, we need to toggle the checked state of the menu option to reflect the state of *gapp.fWaitForVerticalBlank.* We do this using the Windows API function **CheckMenuItem**. For more information on this function, consult your Windows API reference.

DDFlip

DDFlip is the function in which we actually take the vertical blank period into consideration. Take a look (Listing 4-12):

Listing 4-12 **DDFlip**

```
BOOL DDFlip()
{
 HRESULT hr;

 if( lpdraw->nCooperation & DDSCL_FULLSCREEN )
 {
  hr = lpdraw->lpFrontBuffer->Flip(NULL,DDFLIP_WAIT);
 } else {
  if( gapp.fWaitForVerticalBlank )
   lpdraw->lpdd->WaitForVerticalBlank(DDWAITVB_BLOCKBEGIN,
    NULL);
  hr = lpdraw->lpFrontBuffer->Blt(&gapp.wndRect, // dest rect
     lpdraw->lpBackBuffer,// src surface
     NULL,  // src rect (all of it)
     DDBLT_WAIT,
     NULL);
 }
    return hr == DD_OK;
}
```

If *gapp.fWaitForVerticalBlank* is **TRUE**, we call the **IDirectDraw** member function **WaitForVerticalBlank**, which obviously waits for the vertical blank period to begin.

 ## IDirectDraw::WaitForVerticalBlank

```
HRESULT WaitForVerticalBlank( DWORD dwFlags, HANDLE hEvent)
```

WaitForVerticalBlank's first parameter, *dwFlags*, specifies how to use the function. Table 4-1 lists its possible values.

Table 4-1 WaitForVerticalBlank *dwFlags* values

Value	Meaning
DDWAITVB_BLOCKBEGIN	Return when the vertical blank begins.
DDWAITVB_BLOCKBEGINEVENT	Trigger an event when the vertical blank begins. Not currently supported.
DDWAITVB_END	Return when the vertical blank ends and the display begins.

We'll be using DDWAITVB_BLOCKBEGIN so WaitForVerticalBlank waits until the vertical blank begins to return. As a side note, I mentioned earlier that sometimes the vertical blank period is used as a highly efficient timer. However, that isn't possible under Windows until WaitForVerticalBlank supports triggering events using the DDWAITVB_BLOCKBEGINEVENT value.

The Callback Function

There's one more detail we have to attend to before compiling Example 4-1. We have to make sure that if the palette we're using changes for some reason, we restore it as soon as possible. The palette usually only changes if the user switches to another application needing colors other than the ones we're using, therefore modifying the palette. If that happens, we must be ready to remedy the situation.

Whenever *any* application changes the palette, Windows sends each one a WM_PALETTECHANGED message. So to keep the palette in order, we'll reset the palette whenever we receive this message. There's another palette-related message we'll have to handle, WM_QUERYNEWPALETTE, which is sent whenever our application is about to receive the input focus. This message gives us a chance to restore the palette we're using.

Since we need to do essentially the same thing for each of these two messages—put the colors we want to use back into the palette, we'll let the handler for WM_PALETTECHANGED fall through to the code for WM_QUERYNEWPALETTE. Here's the code for both the handlers (Listing 4-13):

Listing 4-13 Message handlers

```
case WM_PALETTECHANGED:
 if ((HWND)wParam == hWnd)
  break;
 // fall through to WM_QUERYNEWPALETTE
case WM_QUERYNEWPALETTE:
 if(ddPal && ddPal->GetDDPalette())
 {
  HRESULT hr;
  hr = DDGetFrontBuffer()->SetPalette(ddPal->GetDDPalette());
  if( hr == DDERR_SURFACELOST )
  {
   DDGetFrontBuffer()->Restore();
   DDGetBackBuffer()->Restore();
  }
 }
 break;
```

One thing to note is that we're checking the WPARAM of the WM_PALETTECHANGED message before we fall through to the WM_QUERYNEWPALETTE handler code. The WPARAM holds the window handle of the application that changed the palette, and we obviously don't need to reset the palette if our application was the one that changed it.

The first thing the handler code does is make sure we have a valid palette to restore with by checking the pointers to our palette class and the IDirectDrawPalette object. After that, it just resets the palette by associating it with the front buffer.

Since we probably lost the palette from the user switching between applications, there's always the possibility we lost our surfaces too. If we did lose the surfaces, SetPalette will return DDERR_SURFACELOST instead of DD_OK. So before going any further in the code, we check to make sure SetPalette didn't return DDERR_SURFACELOST. If it did, we'll just call Restore to restore the front and back buffers back to healthy states.

The code we just looked at (to handle the palette-related message) will be in all the DirectDraw applications in the book from this point on, because losing the palette is always a possibility.

Compiling Example 4-1

Another example down, one more to go (in this chapter). Go ahead and try out the menu and play around with the example a little bit. The more you learn about palettes, the better.

Example 4-2: Palette Animation

For our next trick, we'll do some palette animation. *Palette animation* simply means drawing something on the screen and changing the colors of the palette entries the image uses, to create the illusion of movement. In this example, we'll draw some random stars on the screen and make them twinkle. Finally, something that's visually interesting! (Example 4-2 is shown in Figure 4-3.)

This is one of the simplest changes we've made to an example so far in the book. The only real changes are in the rendering functions except for one in the **DDFlip** function, which we'll look at right now.

FIGURE 4-3

Example 4-2 in action

DDFlip

Here's the code for `DDFlip` (Listing 4-14):

Listing 4-14 `DDFlip`

```
BOOL DDFlip()
{
HRESULT hr;

 lpdraw->lpdd->WaitForVerticalBlank(DDWAITVB_BLOCKBEGIN, NULL);

 if( lpdraw->nCooperation & DDSCL_FULLSCREEN )
 {
  hr = lpdraw->lpFrontBuffer->Flip(NULL,DDFLIP_WAIT);
 } else {
  hr = lpdraw->lpFrontBuffer->Blt(&gapp.wndRect,  // dest rect
     lpdraw->lpBackBuffer, // src surface
     NULL, // src rect (all of it)
     DDBLT_WAIT,
     NULL);
 }
    return hr == DD_OK;
}
```

As mentioned earlier in the last example, the examples now automatically wait for the vertical blank before rendering. `WaitForVerticalBlank` is still called right at the beginning of `DDFlip`, before anything else can happen.

Rendering

Before we get to the rendering functions, we need to learn how to access the actual pixels making up the image, which is called *surface memory*. Once we have a pointer to the beginning of surface memory, we can do whatever we want to the image by manipulating the values of the individual pixels.

Accessing Surface Memory

To access surface memory, you have to lock and then unlock a surface. *Locking* is the process of obtaining a pointer to either all or a portion of surface memory. *Unlocking* is the process of notifying DirectDraw you are finished using the surface memory.

Anytime the contents of a surface change, the surface is locked—only sometimes it goes on behind the scenes and you don't see it happening. This holds true for anytime DirectDraw does anything with a surface, such as getting a DC, blitting, and so on.

There's one thing you should remember about locked surfaces. When a surface is locked, you really can't do too much with it until it's unlocked, including blitting to or from it. Also, when a surface is locked, Windows must be temporarily frozen to prevent it from trying to draw to the surface. Therefore, you should try to keep the periods when a surface is locked as short as possible.

RenderInit

The only real changes from Example 4-1 are right here in the rendering functions, with **RenderInit** undergoing the most dramatic revision. Let's take a look at it first (Listing 4-15):

Listing 4-15 RenderInit

```
BOOL RenderInit()
{
 LPDIRECTDRAWSURFACE lpBackBuffer = DDGetBackBuffer();
 LPDIRECTDRAWSURFACE lpFrontBuffer = DDGetFrontBuffer();
 LPDIRECTDRAW lpdd = DDGetLPDirectDraw();
 DDSURFACEDESC dddesc;
 HRESULT hr;

 srand( (unsigned)time( NULL ) );

 //
 // If we've been here before and allocated a palette toss it
 //
 if( ddPal != NULL )
  delete ddPal;
 //
 // Create new palette
 //
 ddPal = new CDDPalette;
 ddPal->CreatePalette(lpdd, DDPCAPS_8BIT | DDPCAPS_INITIALIZE);
 //
 // Associate palette with front buffer
 //
 lpFrontBuffer->SetPalette(ddPal->GetDDPalette());
 //
 // Create color wash
 //
 ddPal->FadeEntries(RGB(128,128,196), RGB(196,196,255), 10, 5,
  PC_NOCOLLAPSE);
 ddPal->FadeEntries(RGB(196,196,255), RGB(128,128,196), 15, 5,
  PC_NOCOLLAPSE);
 //
 // Get palette entries for later use
 //
 ddPal->GetDDPalette()->GetEntries(0, 0, 256, entries);
 //
 // Fill buffer with black
 //
 FillBufferRect(lpBackBuffer, NULL, 0);
 //
```

```
// Lock buffer to get pointer to surface memory and surface description
//
memset(&dddesc,0,sizeof(dddesc));
dddesc.dwSize = sizeof(dddesc);
hr = lpBackBuffer->Lock(NULL, &dddesc,
 DDLOCK_WAIT | DDLOCK_SURFACEMEMORYPTR , NULL );
char *p = (char *)dddesc.lpSurface;
//
// Create some stars in the buffer
//
for(int i = 0; i < 500; i++ )
{
 //
 // Pick size location and initial color at random
 //
 int x = (rand() % (dddesc.dwWidth - 2)) + 2;
 int y = (rand() % (dddesc.dwHeight - 2)) + 2;
 int color = (rand() % 10) + 10;
 int size = rand() % 10;
 //
 // Each star is at least on pixel in size
 //
 p[y * dddesc.lPitch + x] = color;
 //
 // Expand for next largest size
 //
 if( size >= 7 )
 {
  p[(y - 1) * dddesc.lPitch + x] = color;
  p[y * dddesc.lPitch + x - 1] = color;
  p[y * dddesc.lPitch + x + 1] = color;
  p[(y + 1)* dddesc.lPitch + x] = color;
 }
 //
 // And once more for the really large one
 //
 if( size == 9 )
 {
  p[(y - 2) * dddesc.lPitch + x] = color;
  p[(y - 1) * dddesc.lPitch + x - 1] = color;
  p[(y - 1) * dddesc.lPitch + x + 1] = color;
  p[y * dddesc.lPitch + x - 2] = color;
  p[y * dddesc.lPitch + x + 2] = color;
  p[(y + 1) * dddesc.lPitch + x - 1] = color;
  p[(y + 1) * dddesc.lPitch + x + 1] = color;
  p[(y + 2) * dddesc.lPitch + x] = color;
 }

}
//
// Done with the buffer so unlock it, always!
//
lpBackBuffer->Unlock(dddesc.lpSurface);
//
```

continued on next page

continued from previous page

```
// Copy over the foreground buffer
//
hr = lpFrontBuffer->Blt(&gapp.wndRect,
    lpBackBuffer,
    NULL,
    DDBLT_WAIT,
    NULL);

return TRUE;
}
```

After the palette has been created, we'll create a palette fade from the 10th palette entry to the 20th.

The 10th palette entry will be dark blue, and the 20th will be a very *light* blue. We'll cycle the color of each start through these 10 palette entries, which will make the stars appear to twinkle.

Next, we grab the palette using the **IDirectDrawPalette** member **GetEntries**. **GetEntries** is used exactly the same way as **SetEntries**. We'll put the palette entries we retrieve in an array of 256 **PALETTEENTRY** structures called *entries*, which is declared at the top of **RENDER.CPP**.

Because we won't actually be drawing anything on any surfaces when *RenderNextFrame* is called—only changing palette entries—we need to fill the back buffer with a solid color. We'll fill it with black so it'll resemble the night sky. To do this, we fill the entire surface with palette entry number zero, which is black unless we change it.

Locking Buffers

Now, we need to lock the back buffer so we can draw some stars into it. When locking a surface, the surface memory and information about it are returned in a **DDSURFACEDESC** structure. Before we actually lock the surface, we need to initialize a **DDSURFACEDESC** structure so it's ready to use.

After getting a **DDSURFACEDESC** structure ready, we call the DirectDraw function that actually locks surface memory, **Lock**.

 ## IDirectDrawSurface::Lock

```
HRESULT Lock( LPRECT lpDestRect,
LPDDSURFACERECT lpDDSurfaceRect, DWORD dwFlags,
HANDLE hEvent)
```

Lock accepts four parameters:

1. *lpDestRect*—a rectangle identifying the area of the surface to lock. If you want to lock the entire surface, simply use **NULL**.

2. *lpDDSurfaceRect*—points to a **DDSURFACERECT** structure filled with details about the surface.

3. *dwFlags*—specifies how the surface will be locked.

4. *hEvent*—handle of an event to trigger when the surface is ready to be locked. We won't use this parameter in this book, and when it's not in use it should always be NULL.

The *dwFlags* parameter is important. Its possible values are listed in Table 4-2:

Table 4-2 Lock *dwFlags* values

Value	Meaning
DDLOCK_SURFACEMEMORYPTR	Lock should return a pointer to the top of the specified rectangle or the top of the surface if no rectangle was specified. This is the default.
DDLOCK_EVENT	An event handle is being passed to lock through the *hEvent* parameter. Trigger it when the surface is ready to be locked.
DDLOCK_WAIT	Sometimes a surface cannot be locked because it is being blitted to. If this flag is set, Lock will keep trying until the surface can be locked or an error occurs.

The only flag we'll use when we call Lock is DDLOCK_WAIT. You'll usually always use this flag when calling Lock, unless you want to set up an event to wait for an opportunity to lock the surface.

The **DDSURFACEDESC** structure that Lock fills in has two important members we'll look at. The first is *lpSurface*, which is a pointer to the surface memory requested. If you locked a rectangle, *lpSurface* will be a pointer to the upper-left corner of that rectangle in surface memory. If you locked the entire surface, *lpSurface* will be a pointer to the first byte of surface memory.

Surface Pitch

The other member we need to pay attention to is *lPitch*, which tells us how many bytes we need to traverse to reach the start of the next line of surface memory, called the *pitch* of the surface (see Figure 4-4).

So to access a pixel at *x, y* using the members given to us in the **DDSURFACEDESC** structure, we simply use *y*lPitch+x*.

Locking the Back Buffer

Back to our example. We just initialized a **DDSURFACEDESC** structure, *dddesc*, to use it with **Lock**. Here's the call to **Lock**:

```
hr = lpBackBuffer->Lock(NULL, &dddesc, DDLOCK_WAIT | DDLOCK_SURFACEMEMORYPTR,
   NULL );
```

As you can see, we'll use both **DDLOCK_WAIT** and **DDLOCK_SURFACEMEMORYPTR** as *dwFlags*. The only reason we use **DDLOCK_SURFACEMEMORYPTR** is for the sake of clarity—it's really not necessary because it's the default. As you probably noticed, we're using **NULL** as the first parameter, meaning we want a pointer to the entire chunk of surface memory, not just a certain rectangle.

Now that we have the pointer to surface memory in *dddesc*, we'll store the pointer in a separate pointer to a char, *p*. We're using a **char** pointer because characters are single bytes, which work very well for 256-color surfaces because each pixel is one byte in size.

Drawing Stars

Now that we have a pointer to surface memory, we'll draw some stars onto the surface. We'll draw 500 stars of random size, color, and position all over. The first thing we do inside the *for* loop that draws the stars is pick a random *x* and *y* location greater than zero but smaller than the surface boundaries, in other words, a location inside the surface. We simply use the *dwWidth* and *dwHeight* members of the **DDSURFACEDESC** structure returned by **Lock**, which give us the width and height of the chunk of surface memory, respectively.

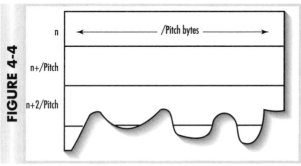

FIGURE 4-4

Surface pitch

After picking a random location for the star, we need to choose a color for it. The color should be somewhere between 10 and 20, because that is where we created a wash in the palette. Anything outside that range would look odd because it would be a completely different color.

Next, we pick a random size for the star. This size isn't the actual size of the star in pixels, but rather a number we'll use to determine how big the star should be when drawn on the screen—kind of like small, medium, and large. The random number will be between 0 and 9, so we'll just use it as an indicator of the star's size.

Since each star will be *at least* 1 pixel in size, we'll plot that first pixel (using the pitch and the *x* and *y* location as shown earlier) right off the bat:

```
p[y * dddesc.lPitch + x] = color;
```

Now, we'll draw some more pixels around the star if the number indicating its size is larger than 7:

```
if( size >= 7 )
{
  p[(y - 1) * dddesc.lPitch + x] = color;
  p[y * dddesc.lPitch + x - 1] = color;
  p[y * dddesc.lPitch + x + 1] = color;
  p[(y + 1)* dddesc.lPitch + x] = color;
}
```

The above code merely draws a pixel above, below, and on either side of the original star pixel. After this is run, the star will end up looking like a small diamond.

If the star's size is 9, the largest possible value, we'll add even more pixels:

```
if( size == 9 )
{
  p[(y - 2) * dddesc.lPitch + x] = color;
  p[(y - 1) * dddesc.lPitch + x - 1] = color;
  p[(y - 1) * dddesc.lPitch + x + 1] = color;
  p[y * dddesc.lPitch + x - 2] = color;
  p[y * dddesc.lPitch + x + 2] = color;
  p[(y + 1) * dddesc.lPitch + x - 1] = color;
  p[(y + 1) * dddesc.lPitch + x + 1] = color;
  p[(y + 2) * dddesc.lPitch + x] = color;
}
```

This code draws more pixels around the entire star, making it look like a slightly bigger diamond.

Unlocking the Buffers

Whenever we lock a surface we need to unlock it. If we don't, it'll wreak havoc with our program because we won't be able to use the surface again.

To unlock a surface, we simply use the `IDirectDrawSurface` member function `Unlock`, `Lock`'s counterpart. `Unlock` takes just one parameter, the pointer to surface memory, which was in the *lpSurface* member of the `DDSURFACEDESC` structure `Lock` filled in.

Unlocking the Back Buffer

This is the code from our example that unlocks the back buffer after we emerge from the star-drawing loop:

```
lpBackBuffer->Unlock(dddesc.lpSurface);
```

Now the surface is back the way it was before we entered `RenderInit`, except that it has a bunch of stars all over it.

Since we'll only change the values in the palette entries to create motion and we won't actually change the contents of any surfaces, we don't need to perform any page flipping or blitting in Example 4-2. Therefore, we need to copy the contents of the back buffer (into which we just drew all the stars) onto the front buffer, so they're visible to the user. We simply blit 'em there using `Blt`.

Now the front buffer is filled with all the stars, which is all we were trying to accomplish in `RenderInit`—besides creating the palette. We didn't draw the stars directly into the front buffer in the first place because if we run in windowed mode, we obviously aren't in exclusive mode and therefore can't lock the primary surface (which is, of course, the front buffer).

This version of `RenderInit` is the most complex new function we've encountered so far, but it also covers the most ground. Learning how to lock, unlock, and draw directly into surfaces are some of the most essential and handy functions you'll learn throughout the course of the DirectDraw chapters in this book.

RenderNextFrame

As we mentioned previously, we won't actually change the contents of any buffers in this version of `RenderNextFrame`—all we'll do is cycle palette entries. This differs from the last example, in which we changed the palette indices of each pixel in the surface.

Here's the code for `RenderNextFrame` (Listing 4-16):

Listing 4-16 RenderNextFrame

```
void RenderNextFrame()
{
 PALETTEENTRY temp = entries[10];
 //
 // Slide all palette entries down one slot, the
 // first one now will later be last.
 //
 for( int color = 10; color < 19; color++ )
  entries[color] = entries[color + 1];
 entries[color] = temp;
 //
 // Update palette with new entry settings
 //
 ddPal->GetDDPalette()->SetEntries(0, 10, 10, &entries[10]);
}
```

First, we store the 10th palette entry so we don't overwrite it when moving all the other palette entries back one position in the array.

After that, we'll slide all the palette entries back one index in the array (keep in mind that the wash only goes from palette entry 10 to palette entry 20). We're simply copying each **PALETTEENTRY** structure from its previous index to its previous index minus 1—essentially just moving the entire wash of colors back in the palette.

After moving all the palette entries back in the *for* loop, we need to copy the palette entry that was previously 10th in the wash to the 20th position. We have to do this to keep the cycle running smoothly, or eventually the entire wash will be replaced by the value of the 20th palette entry.

Finally, we set the 10th through 20th palette entries in the active palette to their new values using the **CDDPalette::SetEntries** function.

PaintFrame

PaintFrame is a new function for this example. Because **RenderNextFrame** doesn't actually paint the screen, the window won't be updated if it ever becomes obscured. Therefore, we need another function to repaint the window whenever it needs to be completely redrawn, so we've written **PaintFrame** (Listing 4-17):

Listing 4-17 **PaintFrame**

```
void PaintFrame()
{
 LPDIRECTDRAWSURFACE lpBackBuffer = DDGetBackBuffer();
 LPDIRECTDRAWSURFACE lpFrontBuffer = DDGetFrontBuffer();

 lpFrontBuffer->Blt(&gapp.wndRect,
      lpBackBuffer,
      NULL,
      DDBLT_WAIT,
      NULL);

}
```

All **PaintFrame** does is grab a pointer to the front and back buffers, then blit the back buffer—which still contains a copy of the starfield—to the front buffer, thus repainting it.

PaintFrame is called when the window callback function receives the **WM_PAINT** message. As you'll recall, Windows sends an application the **WM_PAINT** message when its window needs to be repainted for any reason, so it suits our purpose perfectly.

Compiling Example 4-2

Yep, that's it! Although that was one of the shortest examples so far, we learned more than in any of the previous ones, except maybe the first. We're also getting into some more interesting programs always refreshing after wading through a slew of Hello World programs (although we have one more of those, Example 5-1, which is still much more interesting than any of the previous Hello World programs).

One note about compiling, though. Be sure to add the new source file, `CDDPAL.CPP` to your project. If you don't, the compiler won't know where to find the `CDDPalette` class.

Summary

That's the end of Chapter 4. In this chapter we've learned how to create palettes, use them in a program, and use them safely without bringing the system to a halt. Along the way, we also learned how to write a useful palette class and incorporate some neat tricks, such as palette animation, into it. Now that we've covered palettes, let's move on to Chapter 5, "Bitmaps," which explores bitmaps. Since bitmaps are based on palettes, you already have a pretty good idea of what's going on—so on to Chapter 5!

5
Bitmaps

In the last chapter we learned about palettes. As a continuation of that discussion, this chapter will teach you to load and display bitmaps.

Example 5-1: Bitmaps

We'll create just one more Hello World program. But wait, before you get discouraged, rest assured that it's not another text-wiggler program. This next program puts a ray-traced Hello World on top of our starfield example from Chapter 4, "Palettes," with a little palette animation thrown in to make the stars twinkle. Figure 5-1 shows what the finished product looks like.

The Hello World bitmap is in a file called **HELLO.BMP**. Be sure that after compiling the executable for this example (**Ex51.exe**) it's in the same directory as **HELLO.BMP**. Otherwise, you won't be able to run it since the executable won't find the bitmap.

During the course of writing this example, we'll develop a class for bitmaps, or DIBs (Device Independent Bitmaps) as they're called, that will take care of many of the routine chores usually associated with bitmaps. We'll call this class **CDDDib** and store it in the files **CDDDIB.H** and **CDDDIB.CPP**.

The Bitmap File Format

When saved into files, bitmaps are separated into three main chunks: the file header, the bitmap and color information, and the bitmap data itself. This data is stored as a **BITMAPFILEHEADER** structure, a **BITMAPINFO** structure, and an array of bytes, respectively. All three of these sections are saved in the exact order listed above. Figure 5-2 shows this graphically.

FIGURE 5-1

Example 5-1 in action

FIGURE 5-2

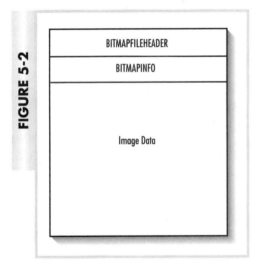

A bitmap file

The **BITMAPFILEHEADER** structure holds general information about the bitmap file itself. This is how a **BITMAPFILEHEADER** structure looks:

```
typedef struct tagBITMAPFILEHEADER {
        WORD    bfType;
        DWORD   bfSize;
        WORD    bfReserved1;
        WORD    bfReserved2;
        DWORD   bfOffBits;
} BITMAPFILEHEADER;
```

The *bfType* member variable specifies the type of the file: It's the first thing read in from the file, and if the *bfType* member isn't **0x4d42**, the file isn't considered a bitmap file. The *bfSize* member gives the size, in bytes, of the entire file. The *bfOffBits* member gives the number of bytes away from the end of the **BITMAPFILEHEADER** structure that the actual bitmap data—the image—begins. This is basically in case you don't want to pay attention to the bitmap information and color data, which would be stupid. The other two member variables, called *bfReserved1* and *bfReserved2*, are useless to us and must always be zero.

After the **BITMAPFILEHEADER** comes a **BITMAPINFO** structure. **BITMAPINFO** structures hold specifics about the bitmap and an array of all the colors used in the bitmap, called the *color table*. **BITMAPINFO** structures are declared like this:

```
typedef struct tagBITMAPINFO {
    BITMAPINFOHEADER bmiHeader;
    RGBQUAD          bmiColors[1];
} BITMAPINFO;
```

The member variable *bmiHeader* contains a lot of specifics about the bitmap, such as its height and width. The other member, the **RGBQUAD** array *bmiColors*, holds the bitmap's color table, one **RGBQUAD** value for each color.

The *bmiHeader* member of the **BITMAPINFO** structure bears more looking into. It's declared as follows:

```
typedef struct tagBITMAPINFOHEADER{
    DWORD   biSize;
    LONG    biWidth;
    LONG    biHeight;
    WORD    biPlanes;
    WORD    biBitCount;
    DWORD   biCompression;
    DWORD   biSizeImage;
    LONG    biXPelsPerMeter;
    LONG    biYPelsPerMeter;
    DWORD   biClrUsed;
    DWORD   biClrImportant;
} BITMAPINFOHEADER;
```

These member variables are very important when using bitmaps. Table 5-1 shows what information each of the members holds.

Table 5-1 BITMAPINFOHEADER structure

Member	Information
biSize	Size of the structure in bytes.
biWidth	The width of the bitmap in pixels.
biHeight	The height of the bitmap in pixels.
biPlanes	Not used, is always zero.
biBitCount	The number of bits per pixel.
biCompression	Specifies what type of compression the bitmap is using—we're only going to accept the value BI_RGB (which means the bitmap is uncompressed) for this member.
biSizeImage	The size of the image data in bytes. Can be zero for BI_RGB compressed bitmaps.
biXPelsPerMeter	Horizontal resolution in pixels per meter.
biYPelsPerMeter	Vertical resolution in pixels per meter.
biClrUsed	The number of colors in the color table actually used by the bitmap.
BiClrImportant	The number of colors in the color table considered important to display the image.

When we read in the bitmap, all this data will be filled in, so we'll have most of the information needed for displaying the bitmap.

The CDDDib Class

The CDDDib class, the class that encapsulates bitmaps, is declared in the header file CDDDIB.H. Let's take a quick glance at it (Listing 5-1):

Listing 5-1 CDDDIB.H

```
//
// CDDDib.h --- Direct Draw CDib class
//
class CDDDib
{
public:
 CDDDib();
```

```
CDDDib( LPCSTR filename );
~CDDDib();
BOOL LoadFile( LPCSTR filename );
DWORD ColorsUsed();
int  Width();
int  Height();
int  RowWidth();
int  Bpp();
void GetPaletteEntries(int first, int count, PALETTEENTRY * entries);
char* m_pBits;
private:
 void  Init();
private:
 BITMAPFILEHEADER m_bmFileHeader;
 LPBITMAPINFO  m_pBmInfo;
};
```

CDDDib has three member variables, two of which are private. The one public member is *m_pBits*, which is a pointer to the bytes making up the image contained in the bitmap, much like *lpSurface* worked with Lock.

The other two member variables are m_bmFileHeader and m_pBmInfo. These are both read in from a bitmap file and used to display the bitmap image.

Let's take a look at the class' constructor.

CDDDib::CDDDib

There are actually two overload constructors for CDDDib. We'll go over the simplest one, the one without any arguments, first. Here's the code for CDDDib::CDDDib (Listing 5-2):

Listing 5-2 CDDDib::CDDDib

```
CDDDib::CDDDib()
{
 Init();
}
```

The only thing this code does is call the member function Init. The code in Init isn't in the constructor because we may need to use it again during the course of the program. Let's take a quick look at Init in Listing 5-3:

Listing 5-3 CDDDib::Init

```
void CDDDib::Init()
{
 memset(&m_bmFileHeader, 0, sizeof(BITMAPFILEHEADER));
 m_pBmInfo = NULL;
 m_pBits = NULL;
}
```

The first thing we do is set the *m_bmFileHeader* structure to zero. This is because we need to identify that the structure isn't initialized, and since it isn't a pointer, we can't set it to **NULL**. Next, we set the other two member variables, which *are* pointers, to **NULL** so we know not to use them.

The Other `CDDDib::CDDDib`

The other constructor, **overloaded**, takes one parameter, the file name of a bitmap. This bitmap will be loaded into the class using another member function called **LoadFile**. Here's the code for the other **CDDDib::CDDDib** (Listing 5-4):

Listing 5-4 The other `CDDDib:CDDDib`

```
CDDDib::CDDDib( LPCSTR filename )
{
 Init();
 LoadFile(filename);
}
```

First Init is called as in the other constructor. Then **LoadFile** is called using the parameter passed into the constructor. **LoadFile** is one of the most interesting new functions around—let's take a look at it.

CDDDib::LoadFile

CDDDib::LoadFile accepts just one parameter, the file name of the bitmap to load, and fully initializes the **CDDDib** class with the bitmap. Let's take a look at the code in Listing 5-5:

Listing 5-5 `CDDDib::LoadFile`

```
BOOL CDDDib::LoadFile( LPCSTR filename )
{
 HFILE hfile = _lopen(filename, OF_READ);
 //
 // bail if fileopen failed
 //
 if( hfile == 0 )
 {
  _close(hfile);
  return FALSE;
 }
 //
 // Read file header
 //
 if( _lread(hfile, &m_bmFileHeader, sizeof(m_bmFileHeader))
  == sizeof(m_bmFileHeader) )
 {
  DWORD colorTableSize;
  //
```

```
// Allocate space for bitmap info, assume 256 entry palette
//
 m_pBmInfo = (LPBITMAPINFO)malloc(sizeof(BITMAPINFO) + 256
 * sizeof(RGBQUAD));
//
// Check magic-cookie and read bitmap info if the cookie's ok
//
if( m_bmFileHeader.bfType != 0x4d42 ||
     lread(hfile, m_pBmInfo, sizeof(BITMAPINFO)-4)
  != sizeof(BITMAPINFO)-4 )
{
 _close(hfile);
 return FALSE;
}
//
// Check the header to see if makes sense as a bitmap
//
BITMAPINFOHEADER *p = &m_pBmInfo->bmiHeader;

if( !((p->biSize == sizeof(BITMAPINFOHEADER)) &&
  (p->biPlanes == 1) &&
    (p->biBitCount == 4) ||
    (p->biBitCount == 8) ||
    (p->biBitCount == 24)
   ) &&
   (p->biCompression == BI_RGB)))
{
   close(hfile);
  return FALSE;
}
//
// Read the color table
//
colorTableSize = ColorsUsed() * sizeof(long);
if( p->biBitCount <= 8 )
{
 if( _lread(hfile, m_pBmInfo->bmiColors, colorTableSize)
!= colorTableSize )
  {
    close(hfile);
    return FALSE;
  }
}
}
   //
 // Looks like we're cooking with gas, read the bitmap bits
 //
 m_pBits = (char *)malloc(m_pBmInfo->bmiHeader.biSizeImage);
 if( m_pBits == NULL )
 {
  _close(hfile);
  return FALSE;
 }
```

continued on next page

continued from previous page

```
BOOL fResult = (_lread(hfile, m_pBits,
 m_pBmInfo->bmiHeader.biSizeImage)
 == m_pBmInfo->bmiHeader.biSizeImage );

_close(hfile);

return fResult;
}
```

We're using the Windows file I/O library functions to read in the bitmap file. We aren't going to discuss the file I/O functions themselves, so if you need more help you should consult your Windows API documentation. Just keep in mind that the read function, **_lread**, returns the number of bytes in which it reads.

The first line of code declares a handle to a file, or an **HFILE**, and opens it in read mode using the given file name and the function **_lopen**. If the file handle returned by **_lopen** is zero, then the file didn't open correctly. In this case, we need to close the file and return.

Next, we need to read in the bitmap file header:

```
if( _lread(hfile, &m_bmFileHeader, sizeof(m_bmFileHeader)) == ⇐
 sizeof(m_bmFileHeader) )
```

We won't use the file header for a little while. First, we need to read in the **BITMAPIN-FO** structure. Before we even do that, though, we need to allocate some memory for the file header since the variable that will hold it, **m_pBmInfo**, is a pointer. Since the color table is included in the **BITMAPINFO** structure, we'll have to allocate memory for that, too. Really, that's the only reason **m_pBmInfo** was made a pointer—so we can allocate enough space for it to hold the color table.

We'll assume the bitmap uses 256 colors. Because the color table is in the form of an **RGBQUAD** array, we'll allocate enough room for 256 **RGBQUADS**, as well as the space needed by the **BITMAPINFO** structure itself:

```
m_pBmInfo = (LPBITMAPINFO)malloc(sizeof(BITMAPINFO) + 256 * sizeof(RGBQUAD));
```

Before we read in the color table, we need to make sure that the bitmap is using the right amount of colors—256 or less. Therefore, we need to read in the **BITMAPINFOHEADER** part of the **BITMAPINFO** structure before reading in the color table. This is because the bitmap's color information is stored in the color table. Therein lies the problem. If you look back at how the **BITMAPINFO** structure is declared, you'll see that it has an array of one **RGBQUAD** structure already in place. That will mess us up if we attempt to read in all 256 colors, because the first one will be missing. In order to solve this problem, we'll have to read in the size of the **BITMAPINFO** structure minus four, which is the size of an **RGBQUAD** structure.

In one fell swoop, we'll read in the **BITMAPINFO** structure and check that the file is a bitmap. Remember that if the *bfType* member of the **BITMAPFILEHEADER** structure isn't **0x4d42**, then the file isn't a bitmap:

```
if( m_bmFileHeader.bfType != 0x4d42 ||
 _lread(hfile, m_pBmInfo, sizeof(BITMAPINFO)-4) !=sizeof(BITMAPINFO)-4 )
 {
 _close(hfile);
 return FALSE;
 }
```

If either of those conditions fails, we close the file and bail.

As mentioned before, we need to check the number of colors used in the bitmap. We'll actually check the bits per pixel value, but it's actually the same thing. First, we need to get a pointer to the **BITMAPINFOHEADER** structure contained in the **BITMAPINFO** structure we just read in:

```
BITMAPINFOHEADER *p = &m_pBmInfo->bmiHeader;
```

Now, we need to check the bits per pixel value of the bitmap. It has to be either 1 (monochrome), 4 (16 colors), 8 (256 colors), or 24 (truecolor). We'll also check that the size of the **BITMAPINFOHEADER** structure is what it should be by checking against its *biSize* member. Plus, we'll make sure it isn't compressed by checking that *biCompression* is BI_RGB. If any of these conditions don't exist, we must exit:

```
if( !((p->biSize == sizeof(BITMAPINFOHEADER)) &&
  (p->biPlanes == 1) &&
  ((p->biBitCount == 1) ||
   (p->biBitCount == 4) ||
   (p->biBitCount == 8) ||
   (p->biBitCount == 24)
  ) &&
  (p->biCompression == BI_RGB)))
{
 _close(hfile);
 return FALSE;
}
```

If we get past that *if* statement, then it looks like everything else will be smooth sailing. Now we'll read in the color table. Before we do that, though, we'll calculate the number of bytes to read in and keep it in a handy place, the temporary variable *colorTableSize*. The size of the color table equals the number of colors multiplied by the size of an **RGBQUAD** structure. To get the number of colors, we've written a function called ColorsUsed that uses a simple switch statement to return the number of colors based on the bits per pixel value. Here's the code that stores the size of the color table:

```
colorTableSize = ColorsUsed() * sizeof(RGBQUAD);
```

If there are more than 256 colors (8 bits per pixel), then there's no need to read in the color table since the bitmap is a truecolor image. We'll check that out before we read in the color table. If we *do* need to read in the color table, we'll simply read it into the *bmiColors* RGBQUAD array in our **BITMAPINFO** structure. We'll read in *colorTableSize* number of bytes and quit if we can't read in that many:

```
if( _lread(hfile, m_pBmInfo->bmiColors, colorTableSize) != colorTableSize )
{
 _close(hfile);
 return FALSE;
}
```

If we successfully read in all the colors, then we're ready to go, except for the fact that we don't have our image data yet. We need to store an array of plain old bytes (`chars`) in our class' member variable *m_pBits*. First, we'll allocate space for it:

```
m_pBits = (char *)malloc(m_pBmInfo->bmiHeader.biSizeImage);
```

Recall that the *biSizeImage* member of the **BITMAPINFOHEADER** structure is the size of just the image data itself, so it serves our purpose well.

Now, all that's left to do is read in the image itself:

```
BOOL fResult = (_lread(hfile, m_pBits, m_pBmInfo->bmiHeader.biSizeImage)
 == m_pBmInfo->bmiHeader.biSizeImage );
```

We're just reading in the same number of bytes that we allocated for the image. If we succeed in reading the image data, then we've successfully loaded the entire bitmap. We just need to close the file and return *fResult* and we're done.

CDDDib::GetPaletteEntries

We need to go over **CDDDib::GetPaletteEntries** because it's fairly important. Here's the code (Listing 5-6):

Listing 5-6 **CDDDib::GetPaletteEntries**

```
void CDDDib::GetPaletteEntries(int first, int count, PALETTEENTRY * entries)
{
 memcpy(entries, &m_pBmInfo->bmiColors[first], count *
  sizeof(PALETTEENTRY) );
}
```

GetPaletteEntries takes three parameters: the index of the first palette entry to copy, how many palette entries to copy, and the pointer to copy the palette entries to. Since **RGBQUAD** and **PALETTEENTRY** structures are structurally identical, the colors will remain intact through the **memcpy**. It's that easy.

CDDDib::GetRowWidth

There's one more member function of **CDDDib** to note. **CDDDib::GetRowWidth** returns the number of bytes in each row of pixels. Because this value varies depending on the bits per pixel value, we need to calculate it differently for each bitmap, which is precisely what this function does.

We won't dig into the code here; we'll just skim over it. Basically, all **GetRowWidth** does is calculate how many bits exist in a row using the bits per pixel value and the number of pixels in a row. **GetRowWidth** then converts that value to bytes with some bit fiddling. Because this value might be a decimal number, it is rounded off to the nearest whole number before being returned.

Rendering

Again, save for the addition of a new class, the rendering code is what has changed the most from the last example in Chapter 4. Most of the code is still here, but now we're slapping a bitmap on top of the stars.

RenderInit

Here's what `RenderInit` looks like now (Listing 5-7):

Listing 5-7 `RenderInit`

```
BOOL RenderInit()
{
 LPDIRECTDRAWSURFACE lpBackBuffer = DDGetBackBuffer();
 LPDIRECTDRAWSURFACE lpFrontBuffer = DDGetFrontBuffer();
 LPDIRECTDRAW lpdd = DDGetLPDirectDraw();
 DDSURFACEDESC dddesc;
 HRESULT hr;
 int i;
 //
 // Load bitmap
 //
 CDDDib* pdib = new CDDDib("hello.bmp");
 //
 // Get the bitmap's palette entries
 //
 pdib->GetPaletteEntries(0, 256, entries);
 //
 // Mark the all as no collapse
 //
 for( i = 10; i < 236; i++ )
  entries[i].peFlags = PC_NOCOLLAPSE;
 //
 // If we've been here before and allocated a palette toss it
 //
 if( ddPal != NULL )
  //
 // Create new palette
 //
 ddPal = new CDDPalette;
 ddPal->CreatePalette(lpdd, DDPCAPS_8BIT | DDPCAPS_INITIALIZE);
 //
 // Associate palette with front buffer
 //
 lpFrontBuffer->SetPalette(ddPal->GetDDPalette());
 //
 // Create color wash
 //
```

continued on next page

continued from previous page

```
ddPal->FadeEntries(RGB(128,128,196), RGB(196,196,255), 100, 5,
 PC_NOCOLLAPSE);
ddPal->FadeEntries(RGB(196,196,255), RGB(128,128,196), 105, 5,
PC_NOCOLLAPSE);
//
// Get palette entries from wash into buffer with bitmap entries
//
ddPal->GetDDPalette()->GetEntries(0, 100, 10, &entries[100]);
//
// Update the palette with all the new entries
//
ddPal->GetDDPalette()->SetEntries(0, 10, 236, &entries[10]);
//
// Fill buffer with black
//
FillBufferRect(lpBackBuffer, NULL, 0);
//
// Lock buffer to get pointer to surface memory and surface description
//
memset(&dddesc,0,sizeof(dddesc));
dddesc.dwSize = sizeof(dddesc);
hr = lpBackBuffer->Lock(NULL, &dddesc,
 DDLOCK_WAIT | DDLOCK_SURFACEMEMORYPTR , NULL );
//
// Copy bitmap to back buffer, center width, 2/5ths of the way down
//
char *p = (char *)dddesc.lpSurface;
int  ydiff = (dddesc.dwHeight - pdib->Height()) * 2 / 5;
int  xdiff = (dddesc.dwWidth - pdib->RowWidth()) / 2;

p += ydiff * dddesc.lPitch + xdiff;

for(int j = 0; j < pdib->Height(); j++ )
 memcpy(&p[j * dddesc.lPitch], &pdib->m_pBits[(pdib->RowWidth())
  * (pdib->Height() - j - 1)], pdib->Width() );
//
// Reset surface pointer
//
p = (char *)dddesc.lpSurface;
//
// Create some stars in the buffer
//
srand( (unsigned)time( NULL ) );
for(i = 0; i < 500; i++ )
{
 //
 // Pick size location and initial color at random
 //
 int    x = (rand() % (dddesc.dwWidth - 2)) + 2;
 int    y = (rand() % (dddesc.dwHeight - 2)) + 2;
 int    color = (rand() % 10) + 100;
 int     size = rand() % 10;
 char * pc = &p[y * dddesc.lPitch + x];
```

```
    //
    // Each star is at least on pixel in size
    //
    SetStarPixel(pc, color);
    //
    // Expand for next largest size
    //
    if( size >= 7 )
    {
      SetStarPixel(pc - dddesc.lPitch, color);
      SetStarPixel(pc - 1, color);
      SetStarPixel(pc + 1, color);
      SetStarPixel(pc + dddesc.lPitch, color);
    }
    //
    // And once more for the really large one
    //
    if( size == 9 )
    {
      SetStarPixel(pc - (2 * dddesc.lPitch), color);
      SetStarPixel(pc - dddesc.lPitch - 1, color);
      SetStarPixel(pc - dddesc.lPitch + 1, color);
      SetStarPixel(pc - 2, color);
      SetStarPixel(pc + 2, color);
      SetStarPixel(pc + dddesc.lPitch - 1, color);
      SetStarPixel(pc + dddesc.lPitch + 1, color);
      SetStarPixel(pc + (2 * dddesc.lPitch), color);
    }

  }
  //
  // Done with the buffer so unlock it, always!
  //
  lpBackBuffer->Unlock(dddesc.lpSurface);
  //
  // Copy over the foreground buffer
  //
  hr = lpFrontBuffer->Blt(&gapp.wndRect,
      lpBackBuffer,
      NULL,
      DDBLT_WAIT,
      NULL);
  delete pdib;
  return TRUE;
}
```

The first thing we do is create a new `CDDDib` object and load the bitmap file `HELLO.BMP` into it using the **overloaded** constructor that takes a parameter:

```
CDDDib* pdib = new CDDDib("hello.bmp");
```

Now, we need to find out which colors the bitmap needs to display properly. We'll store all 256 colors used by the bitmap in the *entries* **PALETTEENTRY** array:

```
pdib->GetPaletteEntries(0, 256, entries);
```

And we'll mark them all **PC_NOCOLLAPSE** so Windows doesn't change them on us (remember, we aren't going to change the first or last 10, because Windows uses them when we're in windowed mode):

```
for( i = 10; i < 236; i++ )
 entries[i].peFlags = PC_NOCOLLAPSE;
```

We'll still have stars, so we still need to create the palette wash. We'll move the wash from palette indexes 10-20 to 100-110, in hopes that the bitmap image will have all its significant colors before palette entry 100:

```
ddPal->FadeEntries(RGB(128,128,196), RGB(196,196,255), 100, 5, PC_NOCOLLAPSE);
ddPal->FadeEntries(RGB(196,196,255), RGB(128,128,196), 105, 5, PC_NOCOLLAPSE);
```

And we need to store the wash in our **PALETTEENTRY** array *entries*, using **CDDPalette::GetEntries.** We'll put palette entries 100-110 into the *entries* array:

```
ddPal->GetDDPalette()->GetEntries(0, 100, 10, &entries[100]);
```

And now, we'll stick our finished set of entries into the palette:

```
ddPal->GetDDPalette()->SetEntries(0, 10, 236, &entries[10]);
```

After that, everything proceeds as before—until we lock the back buffer. Then we need to draw the bitmap into the back buffer. First, we need to get a pointer to the surface memory. Then we need to calculate where the upper-left corner of the bitmap should be when centered on the screen (by the way, **CDDDib::Height** simply returns the height of the palette as it appears in the **BITMAPINFOHEADER** structure):

```
int  ydiff = (dddesc.dwHeight - pdib->Height()) * 2 / 5;
int  xdiff = (dddesc.dwWidth - pdib->RowWidth()) / 2;
```

Now we need to get that pointer to surface memory *p*. We do this in much the same way as we plot a pixel:

```
p += ydiff * dddesc.lPitch + xdiff;
```

Now that the pointer is in position, all we need to do is copy the bitmap:

```
for(int j = 0; j < pdib->Height(); j++ )
 memcpy(&p[j * dddesc.lPitch], &pdib->m_pBits[(pdib->RowWidth())
  * (pdib->Height() - j - 1)], pdib->Width() );
```

What we're doing here is going through each horizontal line of the display (*&p[j * dddesc.lPitch]*) and copying the corresponding line of the bitmap image data (*&pdib->m_pBits[(pdib->RowWidth()) * (pdib->Height - j - 1)]*, which is *pdib->Width()* bytes in length.

Okay, now the bitmap is in the buffer, and we need to draw the stars. We'll just reuse the pointer we drew the bitmap with, so we need to reset it to the beginning of surface memory.

Everything up to the time of actually drawing the stars is pretty much the same, except for the line determining the color of the star:

```
int    color = (rand() % 10) + 100;
```

Before, the color was something between 10 and 20, but now it must fall between 100 and 110 since that's where the stars' palette wash has moved to. So instead of adding 10 to the random number, we add 100.

Also, we're getting a pointer that points straight to the star's location in surface memory:

```
char * pc = &p[y * dddesc.lPitch + x];
```

Doing so makes it easier to use our new macro, **SetStarPixel**. **SetStarPixel** is **#define**d at the top of **RENDER.CPP**. It looks like this:

```
#define SetStarPixel(p,c) if( *(p) == 0 ) *(p) = c
```

SetStarPixel sets the value pointed to by *p* (our pointer to surface memory in this case) to *c*, but only if the value *p* points to is zero. Since zero is conventionally black in a palette, only black pixels will be changed. The background of **HELLO.BMP** is also black. This means we get free transparency, because when we pick a random spot for a star, it doesn't matter if it's on the bitmap or not. If the background is black (has no bitmap), it'll draw a star.

Until the very end of **RenderInit**, the only change is that wherever a pixel should be drawn, **SetStarPixel** is used instead.

At the very end of **RenderInit** we delete the *pdib* pointer. Don't forget to clean up after yourself!

RenderNextFrame

The very last change in this example is in **RenderNextFrame**. The new version is shown in Listing 5-8:

Listing 5-8 **RenderNextFrame**

```
void RenderNextFrame()
{
 PALETTEENTRY temp = entries[100];
 //
 // Slide all palette entries down one slot, the
 // first one now will later be last.
 //
 for( int color = 100; color < 109; color++ )
  entries[color] = entries[color + 1];
 entries[color] = temp;
 //
 // Update palette with new entry settings
 //
 ddPal->GetDDPalette()->SetEntries(0, 100, 10, &entries[100]);
}
```

We had to change this stuff because the palette wash moved to palette entries 100-110. The numbers have changed, but it still does exactly the same thing.

Compiling Example 5-1

This has been another large evolutionary step in your DirectDraw career. Knowing how to load and display bitmaps, especially while managing their palettes, is a very important skill.

We also learned how to cheat our way into getting transparency—by only drawing stars on black pixels—but we'll learn the right way to do it in the next chapter.

Summary

We've covered a lot of ground in this chapter. Learning how to load and display bitmaps isn't easy, but it's essential if you want to do *anything* as far as programming real games goes.

In the next chapter we'll extend our use of bitmaps into sprites and we'll learn quite a bit about different types of surfaces and bitmaps.

6
Sprites

The dictionary defines sprite as *an imaginary being or spirit*. Actually, that definition isn't too far off from its meaning in the world of game programming. *Sprites* are generally thought of as representing characters in a game—the player, an enemy, or any other object that moves.

In programming terms, sprites are just animations that move around. That is, each sprite has several frames (or images) it flips through quickly to create the illusion of movement. The sprite also moves around the screen, which, coupled with the animation, makes it appear to be moving—running, walking, flying, whatever.

Although sprites have taken a back seat to 3D graphics lately, they are still widely used (even in 3D games to a limited extent). Besides, there will always be a market for quality sprite-based games—they possess a distinct look and feel that 3D games just can't duplicate.

The Mechanics

Sprites are animated by storing a sequence of pictures that, when played consecutively and rapidly, depicts them performing some sort of action. There are usually several different animations for each sprite, each portraying a different activity or movement. The animation played is chosen indirectly by the user. More specifically, it is chosen by your code, which the user's input controls.

The sequences of pictures forming the animations are stored in image files, which can be in the format of your choice—bitmap, TARGA, GIF—as long as your program can read images from that type of file. Sometimes all the animations for a sprite are stored in a single image file; sometimes each animation is stored in a separate file. Animations don't even have to be stored in their own files. Each *frame* in an animation can be stored individually. The method you use in your game is really up to you. It's basically just a matter of preference. In this book, we'll store each frame of an animation in its own file for the sake of simplicity. In order to use either of the other methods, there are several extra steps you'd have to take.

Since this next example will be our first dealing with sprites, we want to keep it as simple as possible. With that in mind, the sprite we create will only have one image at first, which means it won't be animated. Don't worry though, we'll add animation in the next example.

Movement

Most sprites, particularly ones representing characters in a game, move. Whether it's up and down, left and right, diagonally, or all of the above, most sprites move in some way.

Although the sprite we'll create in this first example won't move (it will just be static in the center of the screen), we'll give it most of the capabilities needed to move so we can easily add movement later.

Example 6-1: Color Keying

Image files must be saved as rectangles, because there's no way to save them as circles or polygonal shapes; it's just a fact of life. However, most sprites are *not* rectangles. They're usually shaped like humans, mushrooms, toads—anything but rectangles. Because of this, we have to devise a way for the background to show through the holes in sprites. Otherwise, there will be a rectangular block of solid color floating around each sprite as it moves around the screen. Luckily for us, there's a common, easy-to-use solution, called *color keying*.

In color keying, sprites have one color designated as transparent, called the sprite's color key. The color key is usually the color in the very first pixel (the upper-left pixel) of the image file containing the sprite. That color is then used to fill whatever areas on the sprite need to be transparent. When the image (the animation frame) is copied onto the screen—or a surface, as the case may be—the pixels that are the same color as the color key are simply ignored and not copied, as Figure 6-1 shows.

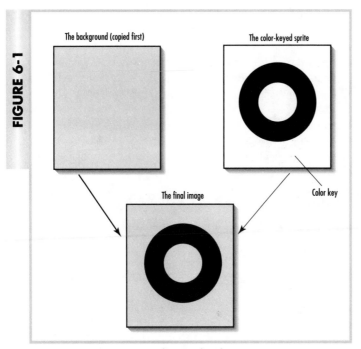

FIGURE 6-1

The background (copied first)   The color-keyed sprite

The final image   Color key

Copying an image with a color key

If the background image of the scene is blitted to the screen first, as in Figure 6-1, it will show through the sprite wherever the color key is on the sprite image.

In DirectDraw, all sprites usually reside in their own individual surface. This means the process of displaying the sprite involves loading an image, copying it into the sprite's surface, blitting the surface to the screen, and loading a new image into the surface whenever the sprite moves (or at a predetermined interval).

When the sprite surface is copied, we need a way to tell DirectDraw which color the color key in the sprite image is. In DirectDraw, it's possible to use a whole range of colors as a color key—that is, use any color in between one color and another. This proves quite handy, for example, when using photographic images, because the background is often not one solid color, but a variation of a color. We'll only use one color for the color key, however, since we know for certain that the bitmap we'll use for the sprite (**HARRIER.BMP** on the CD) has only one color in the background.

In DirectDraw, color keys are represented by *DDCOLORKEY* structures, which are declared as follows:

```
typedef struct _DDCOLORKEY{

DWORD dwColorSpaceLowValue;
DWORD dwColorSpaceHighValue;

} DDCOLORKEY,FAR* LPDDCOLORKEY;
```

The two structure member variables make up the range of colors DirectDraw uses as the color key. The *dwColorSpaceLowValue* member is the low color in the range, and *dwColorSpaceHighValue* is the high color in the range. Any color in between the two is considered part of the color key and therefore, transparent. By the way, don't be afraid to use DWORD interchangeably with COLORREFs (for the two color values). Remember, both have the same number of bits and are configured basically the same way in Windows when used as colors.

After we've filled a DDCOLORKEY structure with the color key information, we need to associate the color key with the surface the sprite image is in. We do this using the IDirectDrawSurface member function SetColorKey.

IDirectDrawSurface::SetColorKey

```
HRESULT SetColorKey( DWORD dwFlags, LPDDCOLORKEY
lpDDColorKey )
```

As you can probably guess, the *lpDDColorKey* parameter is simply a pointer to the DDCOLORKEY structure with the color key information. The other parameter, *dwFlags*, has a lot of bearing on how the color key will work with the surface. Here are its possible values (some of the terms used will be foreign to you, but we'll go over them momentarily):

- DDCKEY_COLORSPACE—specifies that the color key contains a range of colors. Don't use it if only one color is in use.

- DDCKEY_DESTBLT—specifies that the color key will serve as the destination color key for blit operations.

- DDCKEY_DESTOVERLAY—specifies that the color key will serve as the destination color key for overlay operations.

- DDCKEY_SRCBLT—specifies that the color key will serve as the source color key for blit operations.

- DDCKEY_SRCOVERLAY—specifies that the color key will serve as the source color key for overlay operations.

You're probably chockfull of questions by now: What are source and destination color keys, and what's the difference? And what are overlays? In answer to your questions, source and destination color keys are two very different ways of using transparency, and overlays are a special type of transparent surface.

Source color keying is the method of transparency we've been talking about and referring to simply as *transparency*. A surface is created with a color or range of colors that are defined as transparent, that is, not copied when a blit operation is performed. When the color key is blitted onto another surface, any pixels the same color as it aren't copied. As a result, the background shows through the sprite image anywhere that should be transparent.

Destination color keying is something completely different. Destination color keys are used to mark which pixels on a surface can and can't be blitted onto. Only the color (or range of colors) specified in the color key can be changed. This effect is sometimes used to make part of the *background* transparent, useful for window effects in which the sprite walks past a window and is only seen through the glass.

Overlays are surfaces—often used as sprites or backgrounds—which act just like other surfaces, except that they keep track of how they should be drawn in relation to each other. This means they instinctively know which overlay should be drawn above and which below the other one. Each overlay has a Z-order, its depth on the screen in relation to other overlays. Overlays that have a Z-order of zero are the lowest (underneath everything else), and overlays that have the Z-order 4 billion (that means a limit of 4 billion overlays, so don't go crazy with 'em) are the highest. This means an overlay with a Z-order of two would be drawn on top of an overlay with a Z-order of one.

In order to use color keys, or overlays for that matter, you have to call **Blt** using special flags. We'll discuss the relevant ones when we get to that point in our example.

First Cut at the Sprite Class

Sprites have lots of things to do and keep track of, thus they are well-suited to a C++ class. We'll develop a class, called **CDDSprite**, that we'll expand on as we continue our sprite discussion. It would have been nice to inherit this class from the **CDDDib** class created earlier, as sprites and bitmaps have a lot in common, but since we're trying to keep C++ to a minimum, we won't.

The **CDDSprite** class resides in **CDDSPRIT.H** and **CDDSPRIT.CPP**. Here's **CDDSPRIT.H**, which contains the class' declaration:

Listing 6-1 **CDDSPRIT.H**

```
//
// CDDSprit.h
//
class CDDSprite
{
public:
 CDDSprite(LPSTR filename);
 ~CDDSprite();
 void Init();
 void Render(LPDIRECTDRAWSURFACE lpDDSurface, BOOL fTrans);
 void SetX(int newx);
 void SetY(int newy);
 int Width() { return m_w; };
 int Height() { return m_h; };
 void GetPaletteEntries(int first, int count, PALETTEENTRY * entries);

private:
 LPDIRECTDRAWSURFACE m_ddSurface;
```

continued on next page

continued from previous page

```
COLORREF   m_clrTransparent;
PALETTEENTRY  m_aPalEntries[256];
int    m_x;
int    m_y;
int    m_w;
int    m_h;
int    m_nColorsUsed;
};
```

Let's quickly skim over the member variables. *m_ddSurface* is the surface in which the sprite image will reside. We'll blit it to the destination surface to render the sprite, using the member function **Render**.

m_clrTransparent is the color that will act as the sprite's color key. Whenever we need to use a **DDCOLORKEY** structure, for example, when we call **Blt**, we can just fill in using this member.

The *m_aPalEntries* member is an array of palette entries that holds the colors we load from the sprite image file. Again, it would have been nice to have the **CDDDib** class take care of them, but that's not the path we chose, so we need to do it ourselves.

The *m_x* and *m_y* members contain the *x* and *y* location of the sprite on the screen. We'll use these values when we render the sprite and when we add movement in a later example.

The *m_w* and *m_h* members contain the width and height of the sprite image. Knowing the width and height of an image is essential to game programming, and sprites are no exception. We'll use these quite a bit when we load and render the sprite.

The *m_nColorsUsed* member is the number of colors used in the actual image. This value is obtained from the image file.

CDDSprite::CDDSprite

There's only one constructor for our sprite class. It takes the name of the file containing the sprite image as the parameter (this version of the function only accepts DIBs) and proceeds to initialize the sprite using that file. It's shown in Listing 6-2:

Listing 6-2 CDDSprite::CDDSprite

```
CDDSprite::CDDSprite(LPSTR filename)
{
 LPDIRECTDRAW lpdd = DDGetLPDirectDraw();
 DDSURFACEDESC dddesc;
 DDCOLORKEY  ddck;
 //
 // Set defaults
 //
 Init();
 //
 // Load filename as dib
 //
 CDDDib* pdib = new CDDDib(filename);
 //
```

```
// Get colors used
//
m_nColorsUsed = pdib->ColorsUsed();
//
// Get color table, if required
//
if( m_nColorsUsed <= 256 )
 pdib->GetPaletteEntries(0, m_nColorsUsed, m_aPalEntries);
//
// Create a surface for this sprite
//
m_ddSurface = DDCreateSurface(pdib->Width(), pdib->Height(), TRUE);
//
// Lock buffer to get pointer to surface memory and surface description
//
memset(&dddesc,0,sizeof(dddesc));
dddesc.dwSize = sizeof(dddesc);
m_ddSurface->Lock(NULL, &dddesc,
 DDLOCK_WAIT | DDLOCK_SURFACEMEMORYPTR , NULL );
//
// Copy bitmap to surface
//
char *p = (char *)dddesc.lpSurface;

for(int i = 0; i < pdib->Height(); i++ )
 memcpy(&p[i * dddesc.lPitch], &pdib->m_pBits[(pdib->RowWidth())
  * (pdib->Height() - i - 1)], pdib->Width() );
//
// Pick up upper left pixel as default transparent color
//
m_clrTransparent = *(DWORD *)p;
m_clrTransparent &= (1 << pdib->Bpp())-1;
//
// Done with the buffer so unlock it, always!
//
m_ddSurface->Unlock(dddesc.lpSurface);
//
// Get dib width and height
//
m_w = pdib->Width();
m_h = pdib->Height();
//
// We're done with the dib
//
delete pdib;
//
// Set the colorkey
//
ddck.dwColorSpaceLowValue = m_clrTransparent;
ddck.dwColorSpaceHighValue = m_clrTransparent;
m_ddSurface->SetColorKey( DDCKEY_SRCBLT, &ddck );
}
```

Now let's look at the sprite construction process step by step. First we call the member function **Init**, which is similar to the function of the same name in our **CDDDib** class. **Init** simply sets the surface pointer to **NULL** and the sprite's *x* and *y* locations to zero.

Next, we'll create a new **CDDDib** object and load the specified bitmap into it:

```
CDDDib* pdib = new CDDDib(filename);
```

Then we need to create a palette to use. First we'll need to find out how many colors the bitmap actually uses:

```
m_nColorsUsed = pdib->ColorsUsed();
```

If the bitmap doesn't use all 256 colors, we only need to grab the colors it *does* use. We'll assume that the colors it uses are bunched together at the start of the file and start with the first color in the palette:

```
if( m_nColorsUsed <= 256 )
 pdib->GetPaletteEntries(0, m_nColorsUsed, m_aPalEntries);
```

Next, we'll create a surface to hold the sprite using the function **DDCreateSurface**. This function dates back to Example 3-1. As you'll recall, it simply creates a plain offscreen surface using the given dimensions. We'll create an offscreen surface with the dimensions of the bitmap we just loaded and place it in system memory (the surface is created in system memory if the last parameter passed to **DDCreateSurface** is **TRUE**). We'll put the new surface in the member variable *m_ddSurface*:

```
m_ddSurface = DDCreateSurface(pdib->Width(), pdib->Height(), TRUE);
```

Now we need to draw the bitmap into the surface just created. First we **Lock** the surface, then we copy the bitmap image to the surface memory using the same technique in the previous example:

```
char *p = (char *)dddesc.lpSurface;
for(int i = 0; i < pdib->Height(); i++ )
 memcpy(&p[i * dddesc.lPitch], &pdib->m_pBits[(pdib->RowWidth()) *
  (pdib->Height() - i - 1)], pdib->Width() );
```

Now that the bitmap is in the surface, we need to find out what color is in the first pixel of the image so we can use it as the color key. To do this, we'll grab the value of the first pixel and convert it to a **COLORREF** value:

```
m_clrTransparent = *(DWORD *)p;
m_clrTransparent &= (1 << pdib->Bpp())-1;
```

After we've done that, we have to **Unlock** the surface (as always!).

Now we need to store the width and height of the sprite in the *s_h* and *s_w* members. Because our sprite isn't animated yet (the sprite image won't change), it will always have the same dimensions as the loaded bitmap:

```
m_w = pdib->Width();
m_h = pdib->Height();
```

Now that we have the image and dimensions stored away in member variables, we can delete the pointer to the **CDDDib** object we were using:

```
delete pdib;
```

Next we need to set the color key for the surface into which we put the image. There's a **DDCOLORKEY** variable called *ddck* at the top of the constructor we'll use as the color key. We'll only use one color for the color key, so it'll go in both the *dwClrSpaceLowValue* and *dwClrSpaceHighValue:*

```
ddck.dwColorSpaceLowValue = m_clrTransparent;
ddck.dwColorSpaceHighValue = m_clrTransparent;
```

Then we'll set the sprite surface's color key using **SetColorKey**. We'll set it as the source color key for blit operations (destination color keys are only used in rare instances):

```
m_ddSurface->SetColorKey( DDCKEY_SRCBLT, &ddck );
```

Now we have the sprite (almost) all ready to go. We need to go over a couple more member functions, then we'll see how the sprite class is used in the actual program.

CDDSprite::~CDDSprite

The destructor has only one job to do: Release the sprite surface created in the constructor. All it does is make a call to **m_ddSurface->Release()**.

CDDSprite::Render

Render is the function we'll use when we want to draw the sprite onto another surface. It takes two parameters: a pointer to the destination surface and a Boolean value specifying whether or not the sprite should be drawn using transparency. Here's the code (Listing 6-3):

Listing 6-3 **CDDSprite::Render**

```
void CDDSprite::Render(LPDIRECTDRAWSURFACE lpDestSurf, BOOL fTransparent)
{
 RECT destRect = {m_x, m_y, m_x + m_w, m_y + m_h};
 RECT srcRect = {0, 0, m_w, m_h};
 //
 // Copy self to destination surface, transparent if flag set
 //
 lpDestSurf->Blt(&destRect,
   m_ddSurface,
   &srcRect,
   DDBLT_WAIT | (fTransparent ? DDBLT_KEYSRC : 0),
   NULL);
}
```

First of all, we need to calculate the rectangles we'll blit to and from. The destination rectangle is the rectangle on the destination surface to which we'll copy. The upper-left corner of the rectangle is simply the *x* and *y* location of the sprite as stored in *m_x* and *m_y*. The lower-right corner of the rectangle is the *x* and *y* location of the sprite plus the sprite's width and height.

The source rectangle is the rectangle we'll copy from on the sprite surface. Since we want to copy the whole thing, the upper-left corner is **0,0**, and the lower-right corner is the width and height of the sprite (width, height). Figure 6-2 illustrates this:

FIGURE 6-2

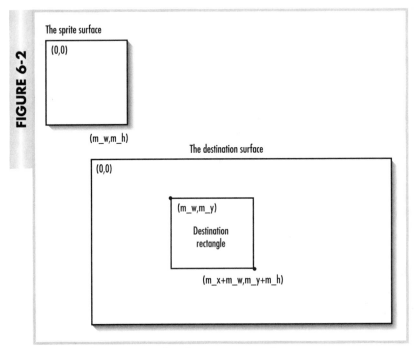

Copying the sprite to the destination surface

Now we'll blit the sprite surface onto the destination surface. If we want to use the source color key, we have to tell **Blt** so by using the flag **DDBLT_KEYSRC**, though it only makes sense to use it if the parameter *fTransparent* (passed in to **Render**) is **TRUE**:

```
lpDestSurf->Blt(&destRect,
  m_ddSurface,
  &srcRect,
  DDBLT_WAIT | (fTransparent ? DDBLT_KEYSRC : 0),
  NULL);
```

That's all there is to it!

Rendering

This time the rendering code won't take nearly as long to go over, because most of it is built right into the sprite class. There are quite a few changes, however, since the graphic output of the program is completely different.

One change that doesn't really involve any specific function is the declaration of a pointer to a **CDDSprite** object at the top of **RENDER.CPP**:

```
CDDSprite *psjet = NULL;
```

As always, it'll be set as **NULL** until created. Initialize this pointer in **RenderInit**, then we'll use it in **RenderNextFrame**.

RenderInit

RenderInit looks drastically different from the **RenderInit** in the last example. This is mostly because we're now initializing a sprite instead of putting a whole bunch of stars in the buffer. Here's the code (Listing 6-4):

Listing 6-4 **RenderInit**

```
BOOL RenderInit()
{
LPDIRECTDRAWSURFACE lpBackBuffer = DDGetBackBuffer();
LPDIRECTDRAWSURFACE lpFrontBuffer = DDGetFrontBuffer();
LPDIRECTDRAW lpdd = DDGetLPDirectDraw();
int i;
//
// Load sprite
//
psjet = new CDDSprite("harrier.bmp");
//
// Place in center of screen
//
psjet->SetX((DDGetWidth() - psjet->Width())/2);
psjet->SetY((DDGetHeight() - psjet->Height())/2);
//
// Get the sprite's palette entries
//
psjet->GetPaletteEntries(0, 256, entries);
//
// Mark all as no collapse
//
for( i = 10; i < 236; i++ )
 entries[i].peFlags = PC_NOCOLLAPSE;
//
// If we've been here before and allocated a palette toss it
//
if( ddPal != NULL )
 delete ddPal;
//
// Create new palette
//
ddPal = new CDDPalette;
ddPal->CreatePalette(lpdd, DDPCAPS_8BIT | DDPCAPS_INITIALIZE, entries,
 256);
//
// Associate palette with front buffer
//
lpFrontBuffer->SetPalette(ddPal->GetDDPalette());
return TRUE;
}
```

A lot of the old is gone, and there's not much new. First, we create the `CDDSprite` object and load the file `HARRIER.BMP` into it:

```
psjet = new CDDSprite("harrier.bmp");
```

Next we calculate the *x* and *y* position of the sprite so it's centered on the screen:

```
psjet->SetX((DDGetWidth() - psjet->Width())/2);
psjet->SetY((DDGetHeight() - psjet->Height())/2);
```

And then we retrieve the sprite's colors and stick them into the palette we're building:

```
psjet->GetPaletteEntries(0, 256, entries);
```

And that's just about it. On to `RenderNextFrame`.

RenderNextFrame

`RenderNextFrame` has been almost completely changed. Take a look at it in Listing 6-5:

Listing 6-5 `RenderNextFrame`

```
void RenderNextFrame()
{
 LPDIRECTDRAWSURFACE lpBackBuffer = DDGetBackBuffer();
 //
 // Clear last image from buffer
 //
 FillBufferRect(lpBackBuffer, NULL, RGB(0,0,255));
 psjet->Render(lpBackBuffer, TRUE);
}
```

All it's doing is getting a pointer to the back buffer, filling the buffer with blue, then rendering the sprite (transparently) into the buffer. Of course, the code is greatly simplified by the fact that the sprite isn't moving, which we'll change as we progress in the chapter.

One thing to take note of here: Since we aren't passing `FillBufferRect` a palette index as the fill color, we need to change `FillBufferRect`, so it once again calls `DDColorMatch` before filling the buffer with the color. If we don't do this, the color `FillBufferRect` fills the buffer with won't be the correct type of value and will probably just turn out black.

Compiling Example 6-1

That's it! Figure 6-3 shows this latest and greatest example in action. Learning how to use color keys is one of the most important things to know when programming with sprites, so this has been a very productive lesson.

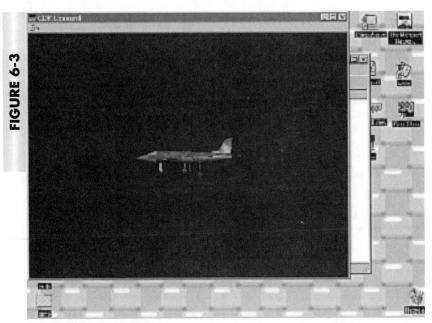

FIGURE 6-3

Example 6-1 in action

When you compile this program, remember to add the file `CDDSPRIT.CPP` to your project, which is the file containing the definitions for most of the `CDDSprite` member functions.

Example 6-2: Adding Animation

Let's expand on our sprite example by adding animation and a little motion to it. We'll add a background for the sprite to move around on. The sprite is now a 3D-rendered helicopter that rotates a little in each frame of animation. We'll also bounce it around the background while it's animating. See Figure 6-4 for a screenshot. It doesn't have a rotor yet, but that's because we'll add it as a separate sprite later. There isn't any interaction with the user yet, but we're still taking a big evolutionary step forward because animation is a significant part of sprite programming.

We'll save each frame in the helicopter animation to a separate bitmap file for the sake of simplicity. Loading in a bunch of frames from a single file is a somewhat complex procedure, and in this example we're simply trying to get an animation to play on the screen.

FIGURE 6-4

Example 6-2 doing its thing

To keep track of the animation, we need to know which frame is being displayed and which comes next. One of the easiest ways to do this is to create a linked list that holds the image for a frame in a node. A *linked list* allows for an unlimited number of frames, and it provides us with an easy way to move from one frame to the next.

In case you aren't familiar with the concept of linked lists, here it is in a nutshell. The basic idea is that a structure is created to store data. Along with the members holding the data, the structure contains a pointer to another structure of the same kind: the next structure in the linked list. Each structure in the list is called a *node*. To create the list you simply declare one instance of the structure, called the *base*. You can then traverse the list using the base, because each node has a pointer to the next one. When you get to the end of the list, the pointer to the next node is **NULL**. That's about all there is to linked lists, although there are books and chapters of books written on the subject. If you're still foggy on the concept, don't worry about it—it'll become clearer as time goes on.

Listing 6-6 shows the code for the animation linked list structure, which we'll name **Frame** (taken from **CDDSPRIT.H** on the CD):

Listing 6-6 The **Frame** structure

```
typedef struct tagFrame
{
 struct tagFrame * next;
 char * pbits;
} Frame;
```

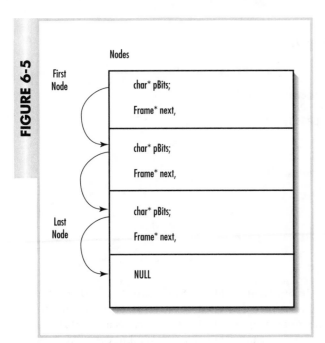

FIGURE 6-5

Nodes

First Node

char* pBits; Frame* next,
char* pBits; Frame* next,
char* pBits; Frame* next,
NULL

Last Node

The `Frame` linked list

Each node contains only two members: a pointer to the next node and a pointer to the image for that frame. Figure 6-5 illustrates how the linked list works.

The Animated Sprite Class

In order to handle animation, we first have to add some more members to our sprite class. Take a look at Listing 6-7, which shows the modified class:

Listing 6-7 `CDDSprite`

```
class CDDSprite
{
public:
 CDDSprite(LPSTR filename);
 ~CDDSprite();
 void  Init();
 void  Render(LPDIRECTDRAWSURFACE lpDDSurface, BOOL fTrans);
 void  SetX(int newx);
 void  SetY(int newy);
 void  SetXScale(float xScale) { m_xScale = xScale; };
 void  SetYScale(float yScale) { m_yScale = yScale; };
 int  Width() { return m_w; };
 int  Height() { return m_h; };
 void  GetPaletteEntries(int first, int count,
```

continued on next page

continued from previous page

```
     PALETTEENTRY * entries);
 BOOL  AddFrame( CDDDib * pdib );
 BOOL  SetFrame(int i);

private:
 LPDIRECTDRAWSURFACE m_ddSurface;
 COLORREF  m_clrTransparent;
 PALETTEENTRY  m_aPalEntries[256];
 int    m_x;
 int    m_y;
 int    m_w;
 int    m_h;
 float   m_xScale;
 float   m_yScale;
 int    m_nColorsUsed;
 Frame*   m_pFrames;
 int    m_rowwidth;
 int    m_iCurFrame;
};
```

The members *m_xScale*, *m_yScale*, SetXScale, and SetYScale have been added so we can stretch the sprite image when it's rendered if needed. These members will be multiplied by the width and height of the sprite image to calculate the scaled rectangle that will be blitted to on the destination surface. We won't use them right now, but we'll add them anyway since they go hand in hand with what we're doing.

The *m_pFrames* Frame structure pointer points to the base of our linked list. To create the base, all we have to do is allocate space for *m_pFrames*.

For simplicity's sake, we won't allow one frame's image to be a different size than that of another. That way, we don't need to complicate the Frame structure with extra members to keep track of the image's size. With this in mind, *m_rowwidth* is the width of every sprite image (in pixels). We don't need to keep track of the sprite image's height, for reasons that will become apparent when we get into the rendering code.

The last new member variable, *m_iCurFrame*, is the index of the frame currently being displayed. We'll use and update it when changing from one frame to the next.

CDDSprite::CDDSprite

The constructor now has a few extra member variables to fill in, so it's a little longer. You can see what's been added in Listing 6-8:

Listing 6-8 CDDSprite::CDDSprite

```
CDDSprite::CDDSprite(LPSTR filename)
{
 LPDIRECTDRAW lpdd = DDGetLPDirectDraw();
 DDSURFACEDESC dddesc;
 DDCOLORKEY  ddck;
 //
 // Set defaults
 //
```

```
Init();
//
// Load filename as dib
//
CDDDib* pdib = new CDDDib(filename);
//
// Get colors used
//
m_nColorsUsed = pdib->ColorsUsed();
//
// Get color table, if required
//
if( m_nColorsUsed <= 256 )
 pdib->GetPaletteEntries(0, m_nColorsUsed, m_aPalEntries);
//
// Create a surface for this sprite
//
m_ddSurface = DDCreateSurface(pdib->Width(), pdib->Height(), TRUE);
//
// Lock buffer to get pointer to surface memory and surface description
//
memset(&dddesc,0,sizeof(dddesc));
dddesc.dwSize = sizeof(dddesc);
m_ddSurface->Lock(NULL, &dddesc,
 DDLOCK_WAIT | DDLOCK_SURFACEMEMORYPTR , NULL );
//
// Copy bitmap to surface
//
char *p = (char *)dddesc.lpSurface;

for(int i = 0; i < pdib->Height(); i++ )
 memcpy(&p[i * dddesc.lPitch], &pdib->m_pBits[(pdib->RowWidth())
  * (pdib->Height() - i - 1)], pdib->Width() );
//
// Pick up upper left pixel as default transparent color
//
m_clrTransparent = *(DWORD *)p;
m_clrTransparent &= (1 << pdib->Bpp())-1;
//
// Done with the buffer so unlock it, always!
//
m_ddSurface->Unlock(dddesc.lpSurface);
//
// Get dib width and height
//
m_rowwidth = pdib->RowWidth();
m_w = pdib->Width();
m_h = pdib->Height();
//
// Set the colorkey
//
ddck.dwColorSpaceLowValue = m_clrTransparent;
ddck.dwColorSpaceHighValue = m_clrTransparent;
```

continued on next page

continued from previous page

```
m_ddSurface->SetColorKey( DDCKEY_SRCBLT, &ddck );
//
// add first frame
//
AddFrame(pdib);
//
// We're done with the dib
//
delete pdib;
}
```

Init also has to do some additional initialization. It now must set the pointer to the base node to **NULL** in order to show that it hasn't been allocated yet. Plus, it must set both scale factors (*x* and *y*) to **1** so that by default, no stretching is done.

The first change in the constructor is this one:

```
m_rowwidth = pdib->RowWidth();
```

As you'll recall, **CDDDib::RowWidth** calculates the width of the image in pixels, which is exactly what we need for the *m_rowwidth* member.

Since we only let each bitmap file contain a single frame, we can just add the bitmap passed to the constructor as a frame. To do this, we use a member function called **AddFrame**, which we'll discuss momentarily. In a nutshell, **AddFrame** takes a pointer to a **CDDDib** class and tacks the image onto the end of the linked list as a new frame of animation.

And the last thing we've changed is the position of the statement:

```
delete pdib;
```

Originally we deleted *pdib* before we set the color key, but since we add it to the linked list *after* we set the color key, we need to keep it around until then.

CDDSprite::Render

Render isn't too different, because all we have to do is add code to calculate the destination rectangle using the scale factors (which will always be **1** for right now, but we want them to be extensible so we'll add the code anyway). Here's what it looks like now (Listing 6-9):

Listing 6-9 CDDSprite::Render

```
void CDDSprite::Render(LPDIRECTDRAWSURFACE lpDestSurf, BOOL fTransparent)
{
 RECT destRect = {m_x,
    m_y,
    m_x + (long)((float)m_w * m_xScale),
    m_y + (long)((float)m_h * m_yScale)};
 RECT srcRect = {0, 0, m_w, m_h};
 //
 // Copy self to destination surface, transparent if flag set
 //
 lpDestSurf->Blt(&destRect,
   m_ddSurface,
```

```
          &srcRect,
          DDBLT_WAIT | (fTransparent ? DDBLT_KEYSRC : 0),
          NULL);
    }
```

As you can see, all we need to do to calculate the new rectangle is multiply the width and height of the sprite image by the scaling factors to find the new width and height.

CDDSprite::AddFrame

As discussed briefly, **AddFrame** adds a new frame to the animation by tacking a new **Frame** structure onto the end of the linked list. Here's the code (Listing 6-10):

Listing 6-10 **CDDSprite::AddFrame**

```
BOOL CDDSprite::AddFrame( CDDDib * pdib )
{
 Frame * cur = m_pFrames;
 Frame * prev = NULL;
 int  i;

 if( m_ddSurface == NULL )
  return NULL;

 while( cur != NULL )
 {
  prev = cur;
  cur = cur->next;
 }
 if( prev == NULL )
  cur = m_pFrames = new Frame;
 else
  cur = prev->next = new Frame;
 cur->next = NULL;

 cur->pbits = new char[m_rowwidth * m_h];

 for(i = 0; i < m_h; i++ )
  memcpy(&cur->pbits[i * m_rowwidth],
   &pdib->m_pBits[m_rowwidth * (m_h - i - 1)], m_w );
 return TRUE;
}
```

AddFrame returns **TRUE** if it succeeds, **FALSE** if it doesn't (about the only reason it wouldn't succeed is if it ran out of memory, which isn't likely under Win32). **AddFrame** takes as its only parameter a pointer to a **CDDDib** structure containing the image for the frame.

To add a new frame we'll need two pointers to a **Frame** structure:

```
Frame* cur = m_pFrames;
Frame* prev = NULL;
```

We'll need to move down the linked list to the last node, so we can stick a new one on the end. As we traverse the list, *cur* will point to the current frame, and ***prev*** will point to the previous one. Since *cur* starts out pointing to the base node, *m_pFrames*, there are no previous nodes, and *prev* is therefore NULL.

The first thing we need to do is make sure the sprite surface is really valid. Things could get nasty if we tried to render a frame of animation and there isn't a surface on which to draw it:

```
if( m_ddSurface == NULL )
 return NULL;
```

Now we need to reach the end of the linked list. All we have to do is keep going until *cur* is equal to NULL, because a NULL pointer to the next node means we've reached the end of the line. As we go through the list, we'll keep ***prev*** pointed at the previous node:

```
while( cur != NULL )
{
 prev = cur;
 cur = cur->next;
}
```

After we get through this list, *cur* will be NULL, and ***prev*** will be pointed at the last real node (or it could still be NULL if the *m_pFrames* pointer is still NULL, because there aren't any nodes in the list yet).

Now we need to allocate memory for the new frame. If *prev* is NULL, there aren't any nodes in the list yet, so we can simply allocate space for *m_pFrames*. If it's not, then *cur* will be pointed at the node after the last (***prev->next***), so we'll allocate space for it. Either way, we'll set *cur* to point at the node we just allocated:

```
if( prev == NULL )
 cur = m_pFrames = new Frame;
else
 cur = prev->next = new Frame;
```

Now we need to set the ***next*** member of the node we just allocated to NULL, so we know where to stop next time:

```
cur->next = NULL;
```

Next we need to allocate space for the new frame's image. The size of the image is the length of each row multiplied by the image's height (we're getting these values from the sprite class' member variables):

```
cur->pbits = new char[m_rowwidth * m_h];
```

Now we'll copy the image from the CDDDib structure:

```
for(i = 0; i < m_h; i++ )
memcpy(&cur->pbits[i * m_rowwidth],
&pdib->m_pBits[m_rowwidth * (m_h - i - 1)], m_w );
```

We now have a new node with the image data in its **pbits** member. In case you were wondering what we do with all this allocated memory after we're done with it, we *delete* it in the destructor.

After we return **TRUE**, we're all done.

CDDSprite::SetFrame

SetFrame is a function that sets the visible frame in the animation to one of the frames in the linked list. Basically, all this entails is copying the image for the specified frame from the **Frame** structure to the sprite surface. Here's the code (Listing 6-11):

Listing 6-11 CDDSprite::SetFrame

```
BOOL CDDSprite::SetFrame(int frame)
{
 LPDIRECTDRAW lpdd = DDGetLPDirectDraw();
 DDSURFACEDESC dddesc;
 Frame * cur = m_pFrames;
 int i = frame;

 if( frame == m_iCurFrame )
  return TRUE;
 while( cur != NULL && frame-- )
  cur = cur->next;
 if( cur == NULL )
  return FALSE;
 m_iCurFrame = i;
 //
 // Lock buffer to get pointer to surface memory and surface description
 //
 memset(&dddesc,0,sizeof(dddesc));
 dddesc.dwSize = sizeof(dddesc);
 m_ddSurface->Lock(NULL, &dddesc,
  DDLOCK_WAIT | DDLOCK_SURFACEMEMORYPTR , NULL );
 //
 // Copy bits to surface
 //
 char *p = (char *)dddesc.lpSurface;

 for(i = 0; i < m_h; i++ )
  memcpy(&p[i * dddesc.lPitch], &cur->pbits[m_rowwidth * i], m_w );
 //
 // Done with the buffer so unlock it, always!
 //
 m_ddSurface->Unlock(dddesc.lpSurface);

 return TRUE;
}
```

SetFrame takes one parameter, the index of the frame, to make it visible. It returns **TRUE** or **FALSE** depending on whether or not it's successful.

First we need to find the `Frame` structure corresponding to the index *frame*, which was passed to `SetFrame`. To do this, we'll need a pointer to the base node of the linked list:

```
Frame * cur = m_pFrames;
```

We'll also need to save the value of the index passed in:

```
int i = frame;
```

m_iCurFrame is an integer member variable holding the index of the current frame of animation and was originally set to zero in `Init`. Before we go traversing through the list, we should check that the index passed to `SetFrame` isn't the same as the current frame. If it is, we don't have to do anything because that frame is already visible.

Now we'll loop until there aren't any more nodes or we've reached the node corresponding with the index *frame:*

```
while( cur != NULL && frame-- )
 cur = cur->next;
```

If *cur* is `NULL` after we emerge from this loop, then we don't have enough nodes to get to the one corresponding to the index and we'll return `FALSE`.

Now we need to update *m_iCurFrame* to match the index of the new current frame:

```
m_iCurFrame = i;
```

Then all we have to do is put the right image into the sprite surface. To do that, we first need to `Lock` the sprite surface's memory. All that's left is to copy the pixel data from the frame's *pbits* member to the sprite surface memory (*dddsc.lpSurface*):

```
char *p = (char *)dddesc.lpSurface;
for(i = 0; i < m_h; i++ )
 memcpy(&p[i * dddesc.lPitch], &cur->pbits[m_rowwidth * i], m_w );
```

With the frame's image in the sprite surface, we can `Unlock` it and return `TRUE` because we're finished:

```
m_ddSurface->Unlock(dddesc.lpSurface);
return TRUE;
```

That's all there is to it. We're pretty much done discussing changes in the sprite class, so let's move on to the rendering code, where the rest of the action is taking place.

Rendering

What we're rendering this time is dramatically different from last time. Instead of a jet sitting on a plain blue surface, we now have a helicopter flying (spinning) over terrain. It's much more interesting, from both visual and programming points of view.

When we initialize the rendering code, we'll have to load the bitmap for the terrain and each frame of the helicopter animation (there are 32 frames in all). Each time we render we'll blit the background bitmap onto the surface, then blit the current frame of the animation on top of it. We'll also move the helicopter each time so it bounces around the screen.

Of course, we'll implement the helicopter as a sprite, but we'll also declare the background image as a sprite. It's not necessary to do it like this, but the sprite class has the image-handling routines built right into it, so it's a little more convenient:

```
CDDSprite *psBackground = NULL;
CDDSprite *psHelicopter;
```

psBackground points to the background, and *psHelicopter* points to the helicopter.

RenderInit

Here's how `RenderInit` looks now (Listing 6-12):

Listing 6-12 **RenderInit**

```
BOOL RenderInit()
{
 LPDIRECTDRAWSURFACE lpBackBuffer = DDGetBackBuffer();
 LPDIRECTDRAWSURFACE lpFrontBuffer = DDGetFrontBuffer();
 LPDIRECTDRAW lpdd = DDGetLPDirectDraw();
 int i;
 //
 // Load sprites
 //
 psBackground = new CDDSprite("backgrnd.dib");
 psHelicopter = new CDDSprite("heli00.dib");
 for( i = 1; i <= 31; i++ )
 {
  char strbuf[20];

  wsprintf(strbuf,"heli%02d.dib",i);
  psHelicopter->AddFrame(new CDDDib(strbuf));
 }
 psHelicopter->SetXScale(1.0f);
 psHelicopter->SetYScale(1.0f);
 psHelicopter->SetX(50);
 psHelicopter->SetY(100);
 //
 // Place in center of screen
 //
 psBackground->SetX((DDGetWidth() - psBackground->Width())/2);
 psBackground->SetY((DDGetHeight() - psBackground->Height())/2);
 //
 // Get the sprite's palette entries
 //
 psBackground->GetPaletteEntries(0, 256, entries);
 //
 // Mark all as no collapse
 //
 for( i = 10; i < 236; i++ )
  entries[i].peFlags = PC_NOCOLLAPSE;
 //
 // If we've been here before and allocated a palette toss it
 //
```

continued on next page

continued from previous page

```
 if( ddPal != NULL )
  delete ddPal;
 //
 // Create new palette
 //
 ddPal = new CDDPalette;
 ddPal->CreatePalette(lpdd, DDPCAPS_8BIT | DDPCAPS_INITIALIZE, entries,
  256);
 //
 // Associate palette with front buffer
 //
 lpFrontBuffer->SetPalette(ddPal->GetDDPalette());
 return TRUE;
}
```

First of all, we need to load the sprites and allocate memory for them. It's easy to do both these things at the same time using the sprite class constructor:

```
psBackground = new CDDSprite("backgrnd.dib");
psHelicopter = new CDDSprite("heli00.dib");
```

Files with **.DIB** extensions are exactly the same as regular bitmap files with the more common **.BMP** extension, so no code changes are needed to read them. The helicopter files go from **HELI00.DIB** to **HELI31.DIB**, so all we're doing here is loading the first frame of the animation at the same time we create the sprite.

Now we need to grab the other 31 frames of helicopter animation. We'll do that by looping 30 times and printing the filename of the 30 files into a temporary string buffer. Once we have the filename in a buffer, we can create a new **CDDDib** object loaded with the bitmap, using the **CDDDib** constructor with the appropriate string. We'll then use **CDDSprite::AddFrame** to add another frame to the frames list:

```
for( i = 1; i <= 31; i++ )
{
 char strbuf[20];

 wsprintf(strbuf,"heli%02d.dib",i);
 psHelicopter->AddFrame(new CDDDib(strbuf));
}
```

Now, just to be safe, we'll set the sprite *x* and *y* scale factors to **1**:

```
psHelicopter->SetXScale(1.0f);
psHelicopter->SetYScale(1.0f);
```

We'll start the helicopter at (**50,100**) on the screen. We do this with the **CDDSprite** member functions **SetX** and **SetY**, which simply change the sprite's *m_x* and *m_y* to the given value:

```
psHelicopter->SetX(50);
psHelicopter->SetY(100);
```

Now we'll place the background sprite in the center of the screen:

```
psBackground->SetX((DDGetWidth() - psBackground->Width())/2);
```

```
psBackground->SetY((DDGetHeight() - psBackground->Height())/2);
```

And we'll grab the background's palette entries to use as the palette:

```
psBackground->GetPaletteEntries(0, 256, entries);
```

The helicopter bitmaps and the background bitmap have been carefully set up to use the same colors. Sometimes this is a great way to do things, but most of the time it doesn't work so well. We'll discuss how to load bitmaps that use different colors later.

RenderNextFrame

Besides displaying the sprites, **RenderNextFrame** now has another task: calculating the position of the bouncing helicopter. To do this it needs some extra variables, which we'll declare globally in the body of **RENDER.CPP**, just above **RenderNextFrame**:

```
static int frame = 0;
static int spindir = 1;
static int x = 50;
static int xinc = 10;
static int y = 100;
static int yinc = 1;
```

frame is the index of the current animation frame. *spindir* will determine in which direction the helicopter spins (by telling us what value to add to the value in *frame*—a value of –1 would make the animation play backward, 1 would make it play forward). *x* and *y* are the location of the helicopter, and *xinc* and *yinc* are the values by which to increment the *x* and *y* location of the sprite each time **RenderNextFrame** is called.

Here's the code for **RenderNextFrame** (Listing 6-13):

Listing 6-13 **RenderNextFrame**

```
void RenderNextFrame()
{
 LPDIRECTDRAWSURFACE lpBackBuffer = DDGetBackBuffer();

 FillBufferRect(lpBackBuffer, NULL, RGB(0,0,255));
 psBackground->Render(lpBackBuffer, FALSE);
 psHelicopter->Render(lpBackBuffer, TRUE);
 psHelicopter->SetFrame((frame += spindir) & 0x1f);

 psHelicopter->SetX(x += xinc);
 if( x >= 300 || x <= 50 )
  xinc = -xinc;
 psHelicopter->SetY(y += yinc);
 if( y >= 200 || y <= 100 )
 {
  yinc = -yinc;
  spindir = -spindir;
 }
}
```

First, the background and the current frame of the helicopter sprite are rendered:

```
psBackground->Render(lpBackBuffer, FALSE);
psHelicopter->Render(lpBackBuffer, TRUE);
```

Next, we set the current frame of the helicopter animation to the current frame plus (or minus, if *spindir* is a negative number) *spindir:*

```
psHelicopter->SetFrame((frame += spindir) & 0x1f);
```

Then we need to set the *x* location of the helicopter to its current location, plus the *xinc* increment value:

```
psHelicopter->SetX(x += xinc);
```

Of course, we need to keep the helicopter on the screen, so we have to keep the location in check. If the *x* location gets to **300** or **50** (just arbitrary values), we'll reverse the helicopter's direction of travel:

```
if( x >= 300 || x <= 50 )
 xinc = -xinc;
```

We also have to do the same thing for the *y* location of the helicopter. If the *y* location goes out of bounds, we'll reverse the direction of the spin (just to make things more interesting).

This isn't the way movement is usually implemented in games, of course. Movement is usually determined either by interaction with the user or by the game's artificial intelligence routines, in the case of nonplayer-controlled objects. Since we haven't covered DirectInput yet, we'll just have to wait until Chapter 7, "DirectInput," to make our animation interactive.

Compiling Example 6-2

We're done with yet another example. We've learned a lot about animation—arguably the most important aspect of sprites—and transparency. We'll learn a lot more about sprites and how to use them in the next several lessons.

Example 6-3: Refining the Sprite Engine

Admittedly, the sprite engine we built in the last example wasn't very sophisticated. We had to manually keep track of which frame we were on and move the sprite ourselves. In this next example, we'll refine the engine by building much of that functionality into the sprite class itself.

Unless your vision is considerably worse than 20/20, you probably noticed our helicopter in the last program didn't have any rotors (how it managed to fly around without them is still a mystery). In this example, we'll add a rotor sprite to the scene, which will spin independently of the helicopter. It will stay positioned on top of the helicopter as they both bounce around the screen, but it will keep track of its own frames and speed of animation. Figure 6-6 shows Example 6-3 in action.

The Self-Tracking Sprite Class

A *lot* has been added to the sprite class since last time. Most of the changes involve keeping track of where the sprite is and where it should move to next. The rest of the changes deal with keeping track of which frame the sprite should display. Here's what CDDSPRIT.H looks like now (Listing 6-14):

Listing 6-14 CDDSPRIT.H

```
//_____
// CDDSprit.h
//
typedef struct tagFrame
{
 struct tagFrame * next;
 char * pbits;
} Frame;

class CDDSprite
```

continued on next page

FIGURE 6-6

Example 6-3 in action

continued from previous page

```
{
public:
 CDDSprite(LPSTR filename);
 ~CDDSprite();
 void  Init();
 void  Render(LPDIRECTDRAWSURFACE lpDDSurface, BOOL fTrans);
 void  SetX(int newx);
 void  SetY(int newy);
 int   GetX() { return m_x; };
 int   GetY() { return m_y; };
 void  SetXScale(float xScale) { m_xScale = xScale; };
 void  SetYScale(float yScale) { m_yScale = yScale; };
 int   Width() { return m_w; };
 int   Height() { return m_h; };
 void  GetPaletteEntries(int first, int count,
    PALETTEENTRY * entries);
 BOOL  AddFrame( CDDDib * pdib );
 BOOL  SetFrame(int i);
 BOOL  SetFrameRange(int first, int last);
 void  AdvanceFrame(int n = 1);
 void  SetDX(int dx) { m_dx = dx; };
 void  SetDY(int dy) { m_dy = dy; };
 int   GetDX() { return m_dx; };
 int   GetDY() { return m_dy; };
 void  Move();

private:
 LPDIRECTDRAWSURFACE m_ddSurface;
 COLORREF  m_clrTransparent;
 PALETTEENTRY  m_aPalEntries[256];
 int     m_x;
 int     m_y;
 int     m_dx;
 int     m_dy;
 int     m_w;
 int     m_h;
 float   m_xScale;
 float   m_yScale;
 int     m_nColorsUsed;
 Frame *  m_pFrames;
 int     m_rowwidth;
 int     m_iTotalFrames;
 int     m_iCurFrame;
 int     m_iFirstFrame;
 int     m_iLastFrame;
};
```

Let's take a look at the member variables—we'll get to the member in a minute. Here's a list of the new ones:

- *m_dx*—This is the distance the sprite moves horizontally every time it's updated.

- *m_dy*—This is the distance the sprite moves vertically each update.

- *m_iTotalFrames*—The total number of frames used by the sprite animation.

🔘 *m_iFirstFrame*—The index of the frame the animation should begin with.

🔘 *m_iLastFrame*—The index of the frame the animation should end with. After this frame, the animation will loop back to the frame *m_iFirstFrame* points to.

To handle all this new information, we have made changes to many functions and added several new ones. Let's go over them now.

CDDSprite::CDDSprite

There's only been one addition since the last version of the constructor, so insignificant we won't even bother to list the code. Right before returning, the *m_iCurFrame* member is set to **0** so that the animation starts on the first frame.

CDDSprite::AddFrame

The only change here is that each time the function is called, the *m_iTotalFrames* member is incremented by **1**. We have to do this to keep track of how many frames are in the animation. Incidentally, *m_iTotalFrames* is now initialized to zero in **CDDSprite::Init**.

CDDSprite::SetFrameRange

SetFrameRange is one of the new member functions. It serves the purpose of setting the first and last frame of the animation. Another function, called **AdvanceFrame**, which we'll examine in the next section, uses the values set in **AdvanceFrame** to loop from the first frame to the last frame, and then back to the first frame (by advancing one frame each time it's called).

SetFrameRange proves a very useful function in the long run. Although we aren't going to use it now, this function lets us store several different animations in a single sprite. All we have to do is pile each animation up, one on top of the other in the linked list, and set the range to correspond to the desired animation. For example, if frames one through five contained an animation of a jet performing a barrel roll, and frames six through eight contained an animation of the jet diving, you could easily switch between the two animations using **SetFrameRange**. You can also play an animation backwards by reversing the first and last frames when you call **SetFrameRange**.

Here's the code for **SetFrameRange** (Listing 6-15):

Listing 6-15 **CDDSprite::SetFrameRange**

```
BOOL CDDSprite::SetFrameRange(int first, int last)
{
 m_iFirstFrame = first;
 m_iLastFrame = last;
 SetFrame(first);

 return TRUE;
}
```

This is a pretty simplistic function. All it does is set the *m_iFirstFrame* and *m_iLastFrame* member variables to the parameters that were passed in (the index of the first and last frame, respectively), and set the current frame to the first frame in the sequence.

CDDSprite::AdvanceFrame

AdvanceFrame is a more complex function than **SetFrameRange**, but not by much. Listing 6-16 shows the code:

Listing 6-16 **CDDSprite::AdvanceFrame**

```
void CDDSprite::AdvanceFrame(int n)
{
 if( n > 0 )
 {
  if( m_iCurFrame == m_iLastFrame )
   SetFrame(m_iFirstFrame);
  else
   SetFrame((m_iCurFrame + n) % m_iTotalFrames);
 } else {
  if( m_iCurFrame == m_iFirstFrame )
   SetFrame(m_iLastFrame);
  else if( m_iCurFrame + n < 0 )
   SetFrame(m_iTotalFrames + m_iCurFrame + n );
  else
   SetFrame(m_iCurFrame + n);
 }
}
```

AdvanceFrame's single parameter is the number of frames to advance the animation by. It can be either a positive or negative number. A positive number will play the animation normally, while a negative number will play it in reverse. The number can also be larger than one, which will advance the animation by more than one frame at a time, making it seem faster.

Let's step through the code. If the number of frames to advance is greater than zero, we'll move forward. The first thing we do then is check whether we're already on the last frame. If we are, we need to move on to the first frame:

```
if( m_iCurFrame == m_iLastFrame )
 SetFrame(m_iFirstFrame);
```

If we aren't already on the last frame, we'll advance *n* number of frames:

```
else
 SetFrame((m_iCurFrame + n) % m_iTotalFrames);
```

The modulus expression **% m_iTotalFrames** simply ensures that we stay in the bounds of the linked list. If you need more information on the modulus operator (%), consult your C or C++ language reference.

If we're being asked to play the animation in reverse (*n* is less than zero), we need to check whether we're already at the first frame and if we are, go to the last frame:

```
if( m_iCurFrame == m_iFirstFrame )
 SetFrame(m_iLastFrame);
```

If we aren't at the first frame, we have to try going back *n* frames in the animation. If going back *n* number of frames puts us out of bounds (at a frame index below zero), however, we need to wrap around to the end of the animation. To calculate the correct index for the new frame, we'll take the total number of frames in the animation (set by SetFrameRange), plus the current frame (which will be smaller than *n*), and add *n* to the total (thus subtracting, since *n* is negative):

```
SetFrame(m_iTotalFrames + m_iCurFrame + n );
```

This leaves us somewhere before the last frame in the animation. We can then continue playing the animation backward if AdvanceFrame is called again using a negative number as *n*.

If the first two *if* statements don't advance the animation, then it's all right to go ahead and advance it normally because advancing *n* frames back still keeps us in bounds:

```
else
 SetFrame(m_iCurFrame + n);
```

That's it. If this function is called consistently over and over (using a timer, most likely), it will animate the sprite either forward or backward with varying speed, depending on how it is called.

One note on AdvanceFrame. Take a close look at the way it's declared:

```
void  AdvanceFrame(int n = 1);
```

Because *n* is defined as 1 in the function declaration, AdvanceFrame can be called without any parameters and will advance just one frame (forward). Just another of the small ways in which C++ proves very useful.

CDDSprite::Move

CDDSprite::Move moves the sprite on its x and y axes according to its *m_dx* and *m_dy* values, respectively. It simply adds each to the sprite's current *x* and *y* position, so they will be drawn in the new position next time they're rendered. It's up to the program to error check so that the sprite doesn't wander off the screen though, so be careful when calling it.

Here's the code for Move (Listing 6-17):

Listing 6-17 CDDSprite::Move

```
void CDDSprite::Move()
{
 m_x += m_dx;
 m_y += m_dy;
}
```

Miscellaneous `CDDSprite` Member Functions

There are a few member functions we won't bother to step through or list because of their triviality. These functions include `SetDX` and `SetDY`, which set the *x* and *y* direction (velocity) of the sprite, respectively. Their counterparts, `GetDX` and `SetDX`, return the *x* and *y* direction of the sprite, respectively. The *x* and *y* values these four functions modify are used by `CDDSprite::Move` to move the sprite.

Rendering

Even though we now have to render the rotor sprite just above the helicopter, the rendering process has actually become *less* complex because of the new member functions we've added to the sprite class. We still have to keep the sprite on the screen, but other than that everything's been pretty much automated.

One thing to note: Because we're using another sprite for the rotor, we have to add another global `CDDSprite` pointer to the top of `RENDER.CPP`.

```
CDDSprite *psRotor;
```

`RenderInit`

`RenderInit` must build the rotor sprite, but that's about the only change. Here's the code (Listing 6-18):

Listing 6-18 `RenderInit`

```
BOOL RenderInit()
{
 LPDIRECTDRAWSURFACE lpBackBuffer = DDGetBackBuffer();
 LPDIRECTDRAWSURFACE lpFrontBuffer = DDGetFrontBuffer();
 LPDIRECTDRAW lpdd = DDGetLPDirectDraw();
 int i;
 //
 // Load sprites
 //
 psBackground = new CDDSprite("backgrnd.dib");
 psHelicopter = new CDDSprite("heli00.dib");
 for( i = 1; i <= 31; i++ )
 {
  char strbuf[20];

  wsprintf(strbuf,"heli%02d.dib",i);
  psHelicopter->AddFrame(new CDDDib(strbuf));
 }
 psHelicopter->SetXScale(1.0f);
 psHelicopter->SetYScale(1.0f);
 psHelicopter->SetX(50);
 psHelicopter->SetY(100);
```

```
psHelicopter->SetFrameRange(0, 31);
psHelicopter->SetDX(10);
psHelicopter->SetDY(1);

psRotor = new CDDSprite("rotor00.dib");
for( i = 1; i <= 14; i++ )
{
 char strbuf[20];

 wsprintf(strbuf,"rotor%02d.dib",i);
 psRotor->AddFrame(new CDDDib(strbuf));
}
psRotor->SetXScale(1.0f);
psRotor->SetYScale(1.0f);
psRotor->SetX(70);
psRotor->SetY(105);
psRotor->SetFrameRange(0, 14);
psRotor->SetDX(10);
psRotor->SetDY(1);

//
// Place in center of screen
//
psBackground->SetX((DDGetWidth() - psBackground->Width())/2);
psBackground->SetY((DDGetHeight() - psBackground->Height())/2);
//
// Get the sprite's palette entries
//
psBackground->GetPaletteEntries(0, 256, entries);
//
// Mark all as no collapse
//
for( i = 10; i < 236; i++ )
 entries[i].peFlags = PC_NOCOLLAPSE;
//
// If we've been here before and allocated a palette toss it
//
if( ddPal != NULL )
 delete ddPal;
//
// Create new palette
//
ddPal = new CDDPalette;
ddPal->CreatePalette(lpdd, DDPCAPS_8BIT | DDPCAPS_INITIALIZE, entries,
 256);
//
// Associate palette with front buffer
//
lpFrontBuffer->SetPalette(ddPal->GetDDPalette());
return TRUE;
}
```

After we've loaded all 31 frames in the helicopter sprite, we must tell it which ones to use by calling `SetFrameRange`. Since all 32 frames (`0, 31`) make up a single animation, we'll tell `SetFrameRange` to use them all:

```
psHelicopter->SetFrameRange(0, 31);
```

We also need to give the helicopter some direction in which to move. We want it to move about ten times as far in the *x* direction as in the *y* direction—so it'll move faster in the *x* direction:

```
psHelicopter->SetDX(10);
psHelicopter->SetDY(1);
```

Now we need to create the rotor bitmap. We'll allocate a new sprite and load the first rotor image into it (`ROTOR00.DIB`):

```
psRotor = new CDDSprite("rotor00.dib");
```

There are 15 rotor images, `ROTOR00.DIB` through `ROTOR14.DIB`. We need to load each of them into the sprite:

```
for( i = 1; i <= 14; i++ )
{
 char strbuf[20];

 wsprintf(strbuf,"rotor%02d.dib",i);
 psRotor->AddFrame(new CDDDib(strbuf));
}
```

We also set the sprite's scale factors to **1** so it doesn't get stretched.

After doing that, we must set the rotor's initial position. We'll place the rotor at the same horizontal position as the helicopter, but we'll put it about 20 pixels higher so it looks like it's resting on top of the helicopter.

Now we'll make all 15 frames we loaded useable by calling `SetFrameRange`:

```
psRotor->SetFrameRange(0, 14);
```

When we set the sprite's *x* and *y* direction, we use the same values as the helicopter sprite because we want them to stick together when we call `Move`.

Everything's ready to go now, so let's move on to `RenderNextFrame`.

RenderNextFrame

Aside from having to keep the helicopter on the screen, `RenderNextFrame`'s job is much easier because of all the new `CDDSprite` member functions we added. Listing 6-19 shows the code.

Listing 6-19 RenderNextFrame

```
void RenderNextFrame()
{
 LPDIRECTDRAWSURFACE lpBackBuffer = DDGetBackBuffer();

 psBackground->Render(lpBackBuffer, FALSE);
```

```
psRotor->Render(lpBackBuffer, TRUE);
psRotor->AdvanceFrame(4);
psRotor->Move();

psHelicopter->Render(lpBackBuffer, TRUE);
psHelicopter->AdvanceFrame(spindir);
psHelicopter->Move();

if( psHelicopter->GetX() >= 300 || psHelicopter->GetX() <= 50 )
{
 psHelicopter->SetDX(-psHelicopter->GetDX());
 psRotor->SetDX(psHelicopter->GetDX());
}
if( psHelicopter->GetY() >= 200 || psHelicopter->GetY() <= 100 )
{
 psHelicopter->SetDY(-psHelicopter->GetDY());
 psRotor->SetDY(psHelicopter->GetDY());
 spindir = -spindir;
}
}
```

The global variable *spindir*, the only remnant from the last example, is still present. It's used to reverse the direction in which the helicopter is spinning, by reversing the order in which the frames are played. Note that the rotor always spins in the same direction, because it isn't affected by *spindir*.

First we render the rotor sprite, using transparency so that the rotor looks like a blur with the background visible through it.

The next line warrants some explanation:

```
psRotor->AdvanceFrame(4);
```

You'd think that we'd call **AdvanceFrame** with a value of **1**—or with nothing at all, which is equivalent to **1**—to advance the animation one frame. That is, in fact, how we call **AdvanceFrame** for the helicopter sprite. It wouldn't make sense for the helicopter to move at the same speed as the rotor, though—it should move a *lot* faster. All we're essentially doing by passing **AdvanceFrame** a value of **4** instead of **1** is making the animation move faster, which makes the whole scene much more realistic.

After we move the rotor (by simply calling **Move**), we render the helicopter, advance its animation, and move it:

```
psHelicopter->Render(lpBackBuffer, TRUE);
psHelicopter->AdvanceFrame(spindir);
psHelicopter->Move();
```

Notice that we call **AdvanceFrame** using *spindir* as the parameter. We do this so *spindir* will still affect the direction in which the helicopter rotates. *spindir* will always be either **1** or **-1**, so the animation will always play at the right speed no matter what direction it moves in.

Now we need to make sure both sprites stay in bound. We'll use basically the same code as before, but we'll update it to include the new member functions:

```
if( psHelicopter->GetX() >= 300 || psHelicopter->GetX() <= 50 )
{
 psHelicopter->SetDX(-psHelicopter->GetDX());
 psRotor->SetDX(psHelicopter->GetDX());
}
if( psHelicopter->GetY() >= 200 || psHelicopter->GetY() <= 100 )
{
 psHelicopter->SetDY(-psHelicopter->GetDY());
 psRotor->SetDY(psHelicopter->GetDY());
 spindir = -spindir;
}
```

Notice that we change the direction of travel for the rotor sprite whenever we change it for the helicopter sprite. This keeps the rotor sprite on top of the helicopter sprite at all times. It would look a little odd if the helicopter blades were spinning around in midair while the helicopter was off doing its own thing somewhere else.

Compiling Example 6-3

We're pretty close to having an industrial strength sprite engine on our hands. Just a little more fine-tuning, and it'll be finished. Aside from optimization, we still need to add projectiles, collision detection, and layered, scrolling backgrounds before we have a complete sprite engine.

Example 6-4: Fine Tuning the Sprite Engine

Our sprite engine works, but not as well as it could. In the next example, we'll learn a few tricks for speeding up our engine (it'll end up being about twice as fast in some cases). We'll implement a more accurate timer and a dirty rectangle scheme, both of which speed up rendering time significantly.

So that we can appreciate how much these new optimizations improve the rendering process, we'll add a menu option to toggle them on and off. We'll also add a counter to the title bar of our application to tell us how long it's taking to render each frame (this is also a very useful thing to know and is often used when testing and debugging games).

High-Resolution Timers

The timers we've used so far (the normal Windows timers) aren't very accurate. Windows itself manages these messages and, in typical Windows fashion, gives other applications time to work even if it interferes with other processes. This often throws off timers, which is not good for applications like games that need to remain consistent as they update the screen. What we need is a timer that is always precise no matter what any other application, or even Windows itself for that matter, does.

Luckily for us, the Windows API includes a multimedia library for handling time-intensive operations, such as animation and sound. The library also includes some high-resolution timer functions that serve our purpose quite nicely. These timer functions are *very* accurate, almost as accurate as we can get without monitoring the system clock itself. (Monitoring the system clock itself can be extremely difficult under Windows, which is why we *aren't* doing it.)

The library file containing these functions is `WINMM.LIB`, which you should add to your project file. The functions are declared in the header file `MMSYSTEM.H`.

The multimedia timer functions don't set a timer like the Windows timer functions do. Windows always has a multimedia timer running, although usually it's not used. The timer functions simply tell it how accurate to be (what its resolution is) and where to send the timer messages (usually to a callback function).

Multimedia timers need a callback function, just like the window callback function or the callback function that finds the available display modes. The only difference is that the timer callback function just receives timer messages.

Determining Timer Resolution

As mentioned earlier, the timer resolution determines how often the timer checks the time. Essentially, it determines the accuracy of the timer. Before we set the timer resolution, we have to find the maximum resolution (smallest amount of time) the timer itself supports. To do this, we need to use the function `timeGetDevCaps`, which is one of the multimedia functions.

timeGetDevCaps

```
MMRESULT timeGetDevCaps( LPTIMECAPS ptc, UINT cbtc )
```

`timeGetDevCaps` takes two parameters: *ptc*, which is a pointer to a `TIMECAPS` structure, and *cbtc*, which is the size of the structure to which *ptc* points. `timeGetDevCaps` will fill the *ptc* with information about the timer device on the system.

The only member of the `TIMECAPS` structure we're interested in is the *wPeriodMin* member, which tells us the minimum interval (and thus the maximum resolution) the timer supports. This value is given in milliseconds, and we'll use it when we set the timer resolution.

Setting the Timer Resolution

Our call to *timeGetDevCaps* found out the maximum *supported* timer resolution, but didn't *set* the timer resolution itself. We now have to tell the timer how often to check the time, which we do using the function `timeBeginPeriod`.

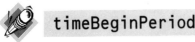

timeBeginPeriod

```
MMRESULT timeBeginPeriod( UINT uPeriod )
```

All we have to do is pass **timeBeginPeriod** the interval the timer should wait before checking the timer. We'll usually use the same value as when we found the maximum timer resolution. You have to be careful not to call **timeBeginPeriod** using a value smaller than the maximum timer resolution, because it'll spit an error back at you.

The Timer Callback Function

After we've told the timer how often to check the time (the maximum timer resolution), we need to tell it how often to send timer messages and where to send them. We do this using the function **timeSetEvent**.

timeSetEvent

```
MMRESULT timeSetEvent( UINT uDelay, UINT
uResolution, LPTIMECALLBACK lpTimeProc, DWORD
dwUser, UINT fuEvent )
```

timeSetEvent accepts five parameters:

1. *uDelay*—the interval between timer messages. Must be greater than or equal to the maximum resolution the timer supports.

2. *uResolution*—the frequency with which the time should be checked, in milliseconds. The lower this value, the higher the timer accuracy. So, 0 means the maximum resolution the timer supports.

3. *lpTimeProc*—a pointer to the callback function to which the timer messages will be sent.

4. *dwUser*—user-specified data that will also be sent to the callback function.

5. *fuEvent*—the event type. There are two values: TIME_ONESHOT, which means the timer message will only be sent once, and TIME_PERIODIC, which means a timer message will be sent every *uDelay* milliseconds. We'll use TIME_PERIODIC.

timeSetEvent returns the ID of the timer event. This ID is used almost the same way as the timer IDs we've used so far (just a way to identify individual timers). In fact, we'll still store it in *gapp.timerid* when we call **timeSetEvent**.

We'll write a function, **StartTimer**, that does all the timer initialization, including setting the timer resolution and the callback function. **StartTimer**'s counterpart **StopTimer** will take care of clean up, which involves killing the callback function.

Adding a High-Resolution Timer

Adding a high-resolution timer to our program will require a lot more code than using the normal Windows timers. Let's look at `StartTimer`, which is called by `WinMain` to set up the high-resolution timer. Here's the code (Listing 6-20):

Listing 6-20 `StartTimer`

```
static void StartTimer()
{
 TIMECAPS caps;

 timeGetDevCaps( &caps, sizeof(caps) );
 timeBeginPeriod( caps.wPeriodMin );

 timeBeginPeriod( caps.wPeriodMin );

 gapp.timerid =
        timeSetEvent( 10 / caps.wPeriodMin,
    caps.wPeriodMin,
    TimerFunc,
    0,
    (UINT)TIME_PERIODIC );
}
```

First we have to determine the maximum resolution supported by the timer, which we do by calling `timeGetDevCaps`:

```
timeGetDevCaps( &caps, sizeof(caps) );
```

The information about the supported resolution is now in the *caps* `TIMECAPS` structure. Now we'll use that information to set the timer's resolution to the maximum possible:

```
timeBeginPeriod( caps.wPeriodMin );
```

Next we need to set the callback function:

```
 gapp.timerid =
 timeSetEvent( 10 / caps.wPeriodMin,
   caps.wPeriodMin,
   TimerFunc,
   0,
   (UINT)TIME_PERIODIC );
```

We'll store the timer event ID in the same place as the timer ID in the previous examples, *gapp.timerid.* Sending messages every 10 milliseconds would put an unnecessary burden on the CPU, so we'll request that messages are sent at an interval somewhat longer than the maximum timer resolution. The callback function is called `TimerFunc`, and we'll examine it in a moment. The `0` means we aren't using any user-defined data. We're using `TIME_PERIODIC` to ensure that timer messages are sent periodically instead of just once.

StopTimer

Sometime before we exit the program we need to tell the timer to stop sending messages to the callback function. We do this using the function `timeKillEvent`.

timeKillEvent

```
MMRESULT timeKillEvent( UINT uTimerID )
```

`timeKillEvent` takes the timer ID returned by the matching call to `timeSetEvent` as its lone parameter.

The function from which we'll call `timeKillEvent` is named `StopTimer`, which we'll call at the end of `WinMain`. Here's the code (Listing 6-21):

Listing 6-21 `StopTimer`

```
static void StopTimer()
{
    if( gapp.timerid != 0 )
    {
        timeKillEvent( gapp.timerid );
        gapp.timerid = 0;
    }
}
```

Before it kills the timer event using `timeKillEvent`, `StopTimer` checks that the ID returned by `timSetEvent` isn't zero. We have to do this because `timeSetEvent` returns 0 upon failure, and calling `timeKillEvent` using a nonexistent ID could be disastrous.

TimerFunc

Timer callback functions are declared as follows:

TimerFunc

```
void CALLBACK TimerProc( UINT nID, UINTuMsg, DWORD
dwUser, DWORD dw1, DWORD dw2)
```

The first parameter is the timer ID returned by `timeSetEvent`. All the others except *dwUser* are reserved; in other words, Windows doesn't want you to do anything with them, and you might get a nasty surprise if you do. *dwUser*, the only parameter you can use, is the value passed to `timeSetEvent` as the user-defined data.

Here's the code for `TimerFunc`, the timer callback function in our example (Listing 6-22):

Listing 6-22 `TimerFunc`

```
static void CALLBACK TimerFunc( UINT wID, UINT wUser, DWORD dwUser, DWORD dw1, ⇐
DWORD dw2 )
{
 if( gapp.fPostPending == FALSE )
 {
  gapp.fPostPending = TRUE;
  ::PostMessage( gapp.hwndApp, WM_USER, 0, (DWORD)0 );
 } else {
  gapp.timerTicksMissed++;
 }
}
```

One of the rules of using these high-resolution timers is that you can't call any Windows functions from within the callbacks, save for a select few. One of the few allowed is **PostMessage**, which we'll use to send a message telling the window callback function that the timer event went off. The window callback then can perform whatever actions are necessary in response. If you try calling other functions directly, you'll leave your program in shambles.

Because we must post a message to the window callback every time we receive a timer message, there may be some backup of pending messages. If we're sending messages too fast for the window callback to handle them, we'll wind up missing some messages, which would be bad.

To get around this sticky problem, two new members have been added to the global **GApp** class: *fPostPending*, a Boolean variable, and *timerTicksMissed*, an integer. We'll set *fPostPending* to **TRUE** right after we post a message, and set it back to **FALSE** once the window callback has received the message. That way we'll know when the window callback is ready for another message (when *fPostPending* is **FALSE**), and when it isn't (when *fPostPending* is **TRUE**). If we get to the timer callback and *fPostPending* is **TRUE**, we'll increment *timerTicksMissed* to keep track of how many timer events the window callback has missed since we last sent it a timer message. When we see that *timerTicksMissed* in the timer callback is greater than zero, we'll render the necessary number of frames to catch up. Then we'll reset *timerTicksMissed* to 0.

Back to the callback function. First, we have to check to see if we can send a message to the window callback:

```
if( gapp.fPostPending == FALSE )
 {
```

If we can, we must set *fPostPending* to **TRUE** to ensure the messages don't start backing up:

```
gapp.fPostPending = TRUE;
```

And finally, we'll post a message to the window callback. We'll post the message **WM_USER**, which is **#defined** in the resource file **LESSON11.RC**:

```
::PostMessage( gapp.hwndApp, WM_USER, 0, (DWORD)0 );
```

If *fPostPending* was FALSE when we entered the timer callback, we can't send a message so we'll just settle for incrementing *gapp.timerTicksMissed*:

```
} else {
  gapp.timerTicksMissed++;
}
```

Let's take a look at what happens in the window callback function when a WM_USER message is received.

The Callback Function

A handler for the message WM_USER has been added to the window callback function. Here's the added code (Listing 6-23):

Listing 6-23 Handler code for WM_USER

```
case WM_USER:
 if( gapp.fFlippingPaused == FALSE )
 {
  UINT tStartRender;
  UINT tEndRender;
  char strbuf[80];

  tStartRender = timeGetTime();
  RenderNextFrame(gapp.timerTicksMissed);
  DDFlip();
  tEndRender = timeGetTime();
  gapp.timerTicksMissed = 0;

  wsprintf(strbuf,"Render time: %4d", tEndRender - tStartRender );
  SendMessage(gapp.hwndApp,WM_SETTEXT, 0, (LPARAM)strbuf);
 }
 gapp.fPostPending = FALSE;
 break;
```

This code takes the place of the code for the normal Windows timer we used previously. That means our job is still to render the scene, but we don't want to render if page flipping is paused (presumably because the user has chosen to disable it, via the menu). If page flipping is paused, none of the rendering code is executed and everything stands still until page flipping resumes.

To put a rendering time counter in the title bar, we must look at the time immediately before and after rendering the scene and measure how much has elapsed. We'll use unsigned integers to store the before and after times:

```
UINT tStartRender;
UINT tEndRender;
```

First we grab the current time using timeGetTime, which returns the amount of time since Windows was started (probably when the user booted up the system), in milliseconds:

```
tStartRender = timeGetTime();
```

Now all we have to do is render the scene. `RenderNextFrame` has been modified to accept one value, the number of timer ticks elapsed since the last time it was called. We won't use this value in `RenderNextFrame` for now, but if you want to render something at a very accurate, constant rate, it'll come in handy. In light of that, we'll simply pass `RenderNextFrame` *gapp.timerTicksMissed*:

```
RenderNextFrame(gapp.timerTicksMissed);
DDFlip();
```

Now that the scene has been rendered, we must look at the time immediately to see how many milliseconds have passed:

```
tEndRender = timeGetTime();
```

tEndRender minus *tStartRender* is now equal to the number of milliseconds taken to render the scene. Since we already used it and it needs to be reset anyway, we'll set *timerTicksMissed* back to zero:

```
gapp.timerTicksMissed = 0;
```

All that's left at this point is putting the number of milliseconds taken to render the scene in the window's title bar. To do this, we need to compose a string buffer containing the text we want to appear in the title bar:

```
wsprintf(strbuf,"Render time: %4d", tEndRender - tStartRender );
```

Now we must send the **WM_SETTEXT** message to the window. A **WM_SETTEXT** message tells a window to change its title bar text to the string in its **LPARAM**:

```
SendMessage(gapp.hwndApp,WM_SETTEXT, 0, (LPARAM)strbuf);
```

The last thing we do in the **WM_USER** handler code is set *gapp.fPostPending* to **FALSE** so the handler can receive more messages. We do this even if page flipping is paused; otherwise we'll never get another message, essentially freezing the game:

```
gapp.fPostPending = FALSE
```

So that's it. This new timer scheme will definitely improve game performance, as well as give us an easy way to monitor the frame rate.

A Dirty Rectangle Painting Scheme

If you've worked with computer animation before, you probably know what a dirty rectangle scheme means. *Dirty rectangle schemes* are popular in computer animation because of the dramatic speed boosts they yield, which also makes them popular with game programmers.

The idea behind a dirty rectangle scheme is that you don't have to redraw what hasn't changed. In sprite-based games, you have a limited number of sprites on the screen at one time. Each time the scene is rendered, they all move (probably). The background, however, does not usually move, and rarely changes. If we redraw the entire background, as we've done so far, then we're needlessly redrawing parts of the screen that haven't changed. A dirty rectangle scheme will eliminate this time-consuming inefficiency.

Dirty rectangle schemes calculate exactly which areas of the screen need redrawing, updating only those regions. Each sprite that moves will have some area around it which needs redrawing. To find out exactly where that area is, we take the rectangle the sprite occupied in the previous frame and combine it with the rectangle the sprite occupies now. Figure 6-7 illustrates this concept. The resulting rectangle, called a *dirty rectangle,* is the only part of the scene that needs redrawing (of course, if other sprites are moving, their dirty rectangles will also need to be redrawn). Only redrawing the dirty rectangles is much more efficient than redrawing the entire screen.

Figure 6-7 illustrates a sprite moving down and to the right—just to the point where it overlaps its previous rectangle. As you can see, there are two little areas that haven't changed but will still be redrawn because they're in the dirty rectangle. Although we can't avoid drawing them, it's a small price to pay for not having to redraw the entire screen.

FIGURE 6-7

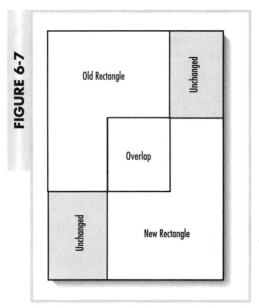

The dirty rectangle being calculated

Implementing Dirty Rectangles

To implement dirty rectangles we'll have to use *clippers*. As you'll recall, clippers prevent DirectDraw from drawing on certain areas of a surface. More accurately, they tell DirectDraw which areas it *can* draw on, using the *cliplist*. The cliplist, as you might remember, is a list of rectangles on a surface that are designated as drawable. We'll use clippers to implement our dirty rectangle scheme by compiling a list of dirty rectangles and sticking them into the cliplist. This will prevent DirectDraw from drawing on any part of the surface that isn't in a dirty rectangle.

We'll use a special data type to provide the clipper with a list of dirty rectangles. This data type is `RGNDATA`, used to designate a series of rectangles called a *region*. It's declared as follows:

```
typedef struct _RGNDATA {
 RGNDATAHEADER rdh;
 char    buffer[1];
} RGNDATA;
```

A `RGNDATA` structure has two members: *rdh*, a `RGNDATAHEADER` structure containing information about the `RGNDATA` structure, and *Buffer*, a pointer to the array of `RECT` structures making up the list. The *rdh* member, as just noted, is a `RGNDATAHEADER` structure declared as follows:

```
typedef struct _RGNDATAHEADER {
 DWORD dwSize;
 DWORD iType;
 DWORD nCount;
 DWORD nRgnSize;
 RECT  rcBound;
} RGNDATAHEADER;
```

The `RGNDATAHEADER` structure is a little more complex than the `RGNDATA` structure. Here's a list of its members:

- *dwSize*—the size, in bytes, of the `RGNDATAHEADER` structure.

- *iType*—the type of the region. This must be `RDH_RECTANGLES`.

- *nCount*—the number of rectangles making up the region.

- *nRgnSize*—the size of the buffer holding the rectangles. You can use zero if you don't know the size (but it's safer to use the size of the buffer).

- *rcBound*—a bounding rectangle for the region, that is, a rectangle enclosing all other rectangles in the region.

We need to initialize a `RGNDATA` structure and its member `RGNDATAHEADER` structure before we can start building a dirty rectangle.

Let's modify **CDDSprite::Move** so it takes a pointer to a **RGNDATA** structure as a parameter. It can then calculate the dirty rectangle formed when the sprite is moved and add it to the **RGNDATA** structure's rectangle list. This way we can move a whole series of sprites and have each add their dirty rectangles to the same list as they move.

CDDSprite::Move

Listing 6-24 shows the new version of **Move**:

Listing 6-24 **CDDSprite::Move**

```
void CDDSprite::Move(LPRGNDATA lpRgnData)
{
 LPRECT lpRect;

 if( lpRgnData != NULL )
 {
  lpRect = &((LPRECT)(lpRgnData->Buffer))[lpRgnData->rdh.nCount];

  lpRgnData->rdh.nCount++;
  lpRgnData->rdh.nRgnSize += sizeof(RECT);
  lpRect->left = m_x;
  lpRect->top = m_y;
 }
 m_x += m_dx;
 m_y += m_dy;
 if( lpRgnData != NULL )
 {
  lpRect->right = m_x + m_w;
  lpRect->bottom = m_y + m_h;
 }
}
```

As just mentioned, **Move** takes a pointer to the list of dirty rectangles in its only parameter. It adds a new one to the list, as long as the pointer is valid.

We need to declare a temporary pointer to a **RECT** structure, called *lpRect*, so we have something in which to build the dirty rectangle. If the pointer passed in isn't **NULL**, we'll set the address of the temporary **RECT** structure to the last dirty rectangle in the list:

```
lpRect = &((LPRECT)(lpRgnData->Buffer))[lpRgnData->rdh.nCount];
```

Remember that *lpRgnData->Buffer* is the address of the list of **RECT** structures making up the region, and *lpRgnData->rdh.nCount* is the **RGNDATAHEADER** member telling us how many dirty rectangles the list contains.

Next we'll increment the dirty rectangle count and move the list pointer to the next **RECT** structure in the list—essentially creating a new dirty rectangle:

```
lpRgnData->rdh.nCount++;
lpRgnData->rdh.nRgnSize += sizeof(RECT);
```

Our *lpRect* pointer points to the dirty rectangle we just created. We'll build our dirty rectangle there.

Okay, now we have everything initialized. All that's left to do (with the dirty rectangle, anyway) is to build the dirty rectangle itself. First, we'll set the upper-left corner of the rectangle to the sprite's old position (remember, the position hasn't been changed yet):

```
lpRect->left = m_x;
lpRect->top = m_y;
```

Now we'll move the sprite:

```
m_x += m_dx;
m_y += m_dy;
```

Then we need to set the bottom-left corner of the rectangle, which will be the sprite's new position plus the width and height of the sprite:

```
lpRect->right = m_x + m_w;
lpRect->bottom = m_y + m_h;
```

That's all we do to the sprite class to implement dirty rectangles. Now we need to move on to the rendering code, where a large majority of the changes have been made.

Rendering

To implement dirty rectangles, we'll need to build another **IDirectDrawClipper** object (besides the one already used to clip the window in windowed mode). In order to set up the new menu option, we'll also add a few global variables to toggle the clipping on and off.

The two toggles are located at the top of **RENDER.CPP**:

```
static fFullFrameUpdate = TRUE;
BOOL fForceFullFrameUpdate = FALSE;
```

fForceFullFrameUpdate is the one toggled by the new menu option. When it's **TRUE**, we'll draw the entire scene *without* using clippers. Occasionally, we'll have to redraw the whole screen, even if clippers are enabled (such as when the window needs repainting). For this purpose we have the variable *fFullFrameUpdate*, which we'll set to **TRUE** when we have to redraw the entire scene. We'll reset it back to **FALSE** once we're done drawing. *fFullFrameUpdate* is initially set to **TRUE** because we need to update the scene at least once when we start up.

We also should briefly look at the **IDirectDrawClipper** object that we'll use as the list of dirty rectangles. It's declared at the top of **RENDER.CPP**:

```
LPDIRECTDRAWCLIPPER lpDDClipper = NULL;
```

We'll initialize it in **RenderInit**, but for right now it's set to **NULL** so we know we can't use it yet.

RenderInit

RenderInit is usually the function that undergoes the most change as we implement new features in our examples. However, that's not the case this time. All we have to do now is create the clipper we'll use for our dirty rectangle work. Here's the code (Listing 6-25):

Listing 6-25 RenderInit

```
BOOL RenderInit()
{
 LPDIRECTDRAWSURFACE lpBackBuffer = DDGetBackBuffer();
 LPDIRECTDRAWSURFACE lpFrontBuffer = DDGetFrontBuffer();
 LPDIRECTDRAW lpdd = DDGetLPDirectDraw();
 int i;
 //
 // Load sprites
 //
 psBackground = new CDDSprite("backgrnd.dib");
 psHelicopter = new CDDSprite("heli00.dib");
 for( i = 1; i <= 31; i++ )
 {
  char strbuf[20];

  wsprintf(strbuf,"heli%02d.dib",i);
  psHelicopter->AddFrame(new CDDDib(strbuf));
 }
 psHelicopter->SetXScale(.75f);
 psHelicopter->SetYScale(.75f);
 psHelicopter->SetX(50);
 psHelicopter->SetY(100);
 psHelicopter->SetFrameRange(0, 31);
 psHelicopter->SetDX(10);
 psHelicopter->SetDY(1);

 psRotor = new CDDSprite("rotor00.dib");
 for( i = 1; i <= 14; i++ )
 {
  char strbuf[20];

  wsprintf(strbuf,"rotor%02d.dib",i);
  psRotor->AddFrame(new CDDDib(strbuf));
 }
 psRotor->SetXScale(.75f);
 psRotor->SetYScale(.75f);
 psRotor->SetX(70);
 psRotor->SetY(105);
 psRotor->SetFrameRange(0, 14);
 psRotor->SetDX(10);
 psRotor->SetDY(1);

 //
 // Place in center of screen
 //
```

```
psBackground->SetX((DDGetWidth() - psBackground->Width())/2);
psBackground->SetY((DDGetHeight() - psBackground->Height())/2);
//
// Get the sprite's palette entries
//
psBackground->GetPaletteEntries(0, 256, entries);
//
// Mark all as no collapse
//
for( i = 10; i < 236; i++ )
 entries[i].peFlags = PC_NOCOLLAPSE;
//
// If we've been here before and allocated a palette toss it
//
if( ddPal != NULL )
 delete ddPal;
//
// Create new palette
//
ddPal = new CDDPalette;
ddPal->CreatePalette(lpdd, DDPCAPS_8BIT | DDPCAPS_INITIALIZE, entries,
 256);
//
// Associate palette with front buffer
//
lpFrontBuffer->SetPalette(ddPal->GetDDPalette());
//
// Create a clipper
//
lpdd->CreateClipper(0, &lpDDClipper, NULL );
lpBackBuffer->SetClipper(lpDDClipper);

 return TRUE;
}
```

Everything proceeds as before until the very end. There, we first create a new clipper object using `IDirectDraw::CreateClipper` and associate with the back buffer:

```
lpdd->CreateClipper(0, &lpDDClipper, NULL );
lpBackBuffer->SetClipper(lpDDClipper);
```

When we created the first clipper, the one that clips the window, we associated it with the front buffer, because it was the one the back buffer (the one we render to) was being blitted or flipped to. This time, however, we need to clip what's being rendered into the back buffer. So that's the buffer with which we associate the clipper.

RenderNextFrame

Most of the code in `RenderNextFrame` is now spent calculating dirty rectangles. Let's take a look (Listing 6-26):

Listing 6-26 RenderNextFrame

```
void RenderNextFrame(UINT)  // ticks missed isn't used in lesson11
{
 LPDIRECTDRAWSURFACE lpBackBuffer = DDGetBackBuffer();
 LPRGNDATA lpRgnData = (LPRGNDATA) new char[sizeof(RGNDATAHEADER)
  + RGNRECTS * sizeof(RECT)];
 //
 // Init data structure for clipper region
 //
 memset(lpRgnData,0, sizeof(RGNDATAHEADER) + RGNRECTS * sizeof(RECT));
 lpRgnData->rdh.dwSize = sizeof(RGNDATAHEADER);
 lpRgnData->rdh.iType = RDH_RECTANGLES;
 //
 // If fullscreen draw is selected or if it's needed, do it
 //
 if( fForceFullFrameUpdate || fFullFrameUpdate == TRUE )
 {
  LPRECT lpRect = (LPRECT)lpRgnData->Buffer;
  //
  // Only using one rect in fullscreen update case
  //
  lpRgnData->rdh.nCount = 1;
  lpRgnData->rdh.nRgnSize = sizeof(RECT);
  lpRect->top = 0;
  lpRect->left = 0;
  lpRect->bottom = psBackground->Height();
  lpRect->right = psBackground->Width();
  //
  // Give region to clipper
  //
  lpDDClipper->SetClipList(lpRgnData,0);
  delete lpRgnData;
  lpRgnData = NULL;
  fFullFrameUpdate = FALSE;
  //
  // If we're running full screen we need to update
  // the currently flipped out buffer
  //
  if( DDGetCooperativeLevel() & DDSCL_FULLSCREEN )
  {
   psBackground->Render(lpBackBuffer, FALSE);
   DDFlip();
  }

 }
 //
 // Move sprites, let them tell us what regions to update
 //
 psRotor->Move(lpRgnData);
 psHelicopter->Move(lpRgnData);
 //
 // If we're doing a fullscreen update then lpRgnData will now be NULL
 //
```

```
 if( lpRgnData != NULL )
 {
  //
  // Use sprite's calculation of what regions to update
  //
  lpDDClipper->SetClipList(lpRgnData,0);
  delete lpRgnData;
 }
 //
 // Do the rendering
 //
 psBackground->Render(lpBackBuffer, FALSE);
 psRotor->Render(lpBackBuffer, TRUE);
 psHelicopter->Render(lpBackBuffer, TRUE);
 //
 // Advance frames
 //
 psRotor->AdvanceFrame(4);
 psHelicopter->AdvanceFrame(spindir);
 //
 // Change directions as required
 //
 if( psHelicopter->GetX() >= 500 || psHelicopter->GetX() <= -100 )
 {
  psHelicopter->SetDX(-psHelicopter->GetDX());
  psRotor->SetDX(psHelicopter->GetDX());
  spindir = -spindir;
 }
 if( psHelicopter->GetY() >= 200 || psHelicopter->GetY() <= 0 )
 {
  psHelicopter->SetDY(-psHelicopter->GetDY());
  psRotor->SetDY(psHelicopter->GetDY());
  spindir = -spindir;
 }
}
```

We need to allocate a new **RGNDATA** structure to keep a list of the dirty rectangles. There are a couple of steps we need to take in order to do this. First off, we need to know how many rectangles will be in the list. To make life easier, we'll create a **#define**, called **RGNRECTS**, equal to the number of sprites in the scene (which is two). Since there will only be one dirty rectangle per sprite, we can easily use that value to find out how many dirty rectangles exist. Of course, when *you* implement dirty rectangles in your game, you'll probably want the number of dirty rectangles maintained dynamically, because there is seldom a constant number of sprites on the screen.

Anyway, to allocate a new **RGNDATA** structure we'll simply allocate the amount of memory occupied by a **RGNDATAHEADER** structure, plus the size of the **#define RGNRECTS** (two) RECT structures:

```
LPRGNDATA lpRgnData = (LPRGNDATA) new char[sizeof(RGNDATAHEADER) + RGNRECTS
 * sizeof(RECT)];
```

Then we'll zero out all that memory, so we can start with a clean slate:

```
memset(lpRgnData,0, sizeof(RGNDATAHEADER) + RGNRECTS * sizeof(RECT));
```

Before we can use the **RGNDATA** structure, we need to initialize the **RGNDATAHEADER**'s *dwSize* member and set the type of region to **RDH_RECTANGLES**:

```
lpRgnData->rdh.dwSize = sizeof(RGNDATAHEADER);
lpRgnData->rdh.iType = RDH_RECTANGLES;
```

Now we have two distinct scenarios to deal with: Either we redraw the entire scene, or we just render the dirty rectangles. Let's look at each.

Redrawing the Entire Scene

If we need to redraw the entire scene (either because the user has selected the menu option forcing us to do so, or the window needs repainting), we first need to get a pointer to the first rectangle in the region:

```
LPRECT lpRect = (LPRECT)lpRgnData->Buffer;
```

Since we'll be redrawing the entire scene, we'll only have one rectangle in the region (the window):

```
lpRgnData->rdh.nCount = 1;
```

For that same reason, the size of the list of rectangles will equal the size of one **RECT** structure:

```
lpRgnData->rdh.nRgnSize = sizeof(RECT);
```

As mentioned earlier, the dirty rectangle is the size of the surface itself since we're rendering the entire scene. With that in mind, we can just use the members of the background sprite (which is the same size as the application window) to set the size of the dirty rectangle:

```
lpRect->top = 0;
lpRect->left = 0;
lpRect->bottom = psBackground->Height();
lpRect->right = psBackground->Width();
```

Now we'll tell the clipper associated with the back buffer to use the region just initialized as the cliplist. We'll do this using the **IDirectDrawClipper** member function **SetClipList**.

IDirectDrawClipper::SetClipList

```
HRESULT SetClipList( LPRGNDATA lpClipList, DWORD
dwFlags )
```

The *dwFlags* parameter isn't used in this version of DirectDraw and must be **NULL**. The *lpClipList* parameter, however, points to the region making up the cliplist. If *lpClipList* is **NULL**, then **SetClipList** removes the cliplist, if there is one.

We'll call `SetClipList` with the region we initialized in *lpClipList* and zero as *dwFlags*:

```
lpDDClipper->SetClipList(lpRgnData,0);
```

Now that the clipper's set, we have no more use for the region, so we can delete it. We can also set the pointer to **NULL** since we won't use it anymore.

Even though we're rendering the whole scene, the sprites still need to be moved. All we have to do is call `CDDSprite::Move` with *lpRgnData* (which we set to **NULL**), because **Move** is written so it doesn't modify the cliplist if the region pointer passed to it is **NULL**.

If we're redrawing the entire surface because the window is being repainted (*fFullFrameUpdate* is **TRUE**), we need to reset *fFullFrameUpdate* to **FALSE** so we don't continuously render the entire scene.

Finally, we have to redraw the background if running in fullscreen mode. We need to do this because when we use fullscreen mode, we flip the buffers rather than blit to them, so we need to redraw both the front *and* back buffers:

```
if( DDGetCooperativeLevel() & DDSCL_FULLSCREEN )
{
 psBackground->Render(lpBackBuffer, FALSE);
 DDFlip();
}
```

That takes care of the scenario in which we must redraw the entire scene. Now, onto the other half of the *if* statement.

Rendering with Dirty Rectangles

With the cliplist already initialized, all we have to do to compile the dirty rectangle list is pass the region pointer to `CDDSprite::Move` for each of the sprites:

```
psRotor->Move(lpRgnData);
psHelicopter->Move(lpRgnData);
```

Remember, if *lpRgnData* is **NULL** when we call `CDDSprite::Move`, it won't be modified. The only possible reason for setting it to **NULL** is if we're redrawing the entire scene.

If we aren't redrawing the entire scene, then we need to set the cliplist to the region calculated in `CDDSprite::Move` (which ended up in *lpRgnData*). We can also get rid of *lpRgnData* because after we move its data into the cliplist, we're done with it:

```
if( lpRgnData != NULL )
{
 //
 // Use sprite's calculation of what regions to update
 //
 lpDDClipper->SetClipList(lpRgnData,0);
 delete lpRgnData;
}
```

Since the cliplist is initialized and associated with the back buffer, we can go ahead and render all the sprites:

```
psBackground->Render(lpBackBuffer, FALSE);
psRotor->Render(lpBackBuffer, TRUE);
psHelicopter->Render(lpBackBuffer, TRUE);
```

The use of dirty rectangles in the three lines above has an impact on the entire program. Most notable is the line rendering the background sprite, *psBackGround*. Because the other two sprites had dirty rectangles calculated for them, the background sprite is only drawn if included in one of these dirty rectangles. Because of this, not much of the background sprite will be rendered, which saves a lot of time.

Amid all the discussion about dirty rectangles, we can't forget to move the two sprites onto their next frame of animation:

```
psRotor->AdvanceFrame(4);
psHelicopter->AdvanceFrame(spindir);
```

The rest of `RenderNextFrame` proceeds as usual.

PaintFrame

`PaintFrame` makes a reappearance because we must redraw the entire scene if the window receives a `WM_PAINT` message. This time, however, we won't blit the back buffer to the front buffer. Instead, `PaintFrame` simply tells `RenderNextFrame` to redraw the entire scene by setting *fFullFrameUpdate* to `TRUE`. Listing 6-27 shows the code:

Listing 6-27 `PaintFrame`

```
void PaintFrame()
{
 //
 // Take the easy way out, just let the next render take care of
 // updating the entire window
 //
 fFullFrameUpdate = TRUE;
}
```

That's all there is to it.

Adding a Fullscreen Drawing Menu Toggle

We can't forget about the menu option that lets us toggle dirty rectangle usage on and off. Hopefully, it'll help you appreciate the speed increase we get from dirty rectangles.

First of all, you must edit the menu resource in your project to add a new menu option, which we'll call `Fullframe Update`. We'll give it the menu resource ID `IDM_OPTIONSFULLFRAMEUPDATE`, which we'll use to write the message handler code in the callback function.

Speaking of the handler code, let's take a quick look at it in Listing 6-28:

Listing 6-28 Fullframe update menu option handler

```
case IDM_OPTIONSFULLFRAMEUPDATE:
{
 fForceFullFrameUpdate =
  !(GetMenuState(GetMenu(gapp.hwndApp),
     IDM_OPTIONSFULLFRAMEUPDATE,
     MF_BYCOMMAND) & MF_CHECKED);

 CheckMenuItem(GetMenu(gapp.hwndApp),
     IDM_OPTIONSFULLFRAMEUPDATE,
     fForceFullFrameUpdate ? MF_CHECKED : MF_UNCHECKED);
 break;
}
```

The first statement toggles *fForceFullFrameUpdate* depending on whether the menu item is checked. The second statement toggles the checked state of the menu item itself. Consult your Windows API reference for help on any of these functions.

Compiling Example 6-4

That's one more example down. Now we have a fairly efficient sprite engine; although, we'll keep adding to it for the remainder of this chapter. Don't forget to add the library file for the high-resolution timers, **WINMM.LIB**, to your project.

Example 6-5: Adding Missiles

For the next example, we'll give the helicopter the ability to shoot little missiles. To make things easier, we'll hold the helicopter in place, and it won't be animated—though the rotor sprite will still be animated. We'll also build more of the animation code into the sprite class itself. (We won't stop tweaking this sprite engine until the end of the chapter, darn it!)

We keep tweaking the sprite class to make it more self-contained, so main program is much less cluttered. Although it worked just fine in the last example, the code reads much more clearly when the sprite class is completely self-contained.

Figure 6-8 shows this new example program (Example 6-5) in action.

The Self-Animating Sprite Class

As just mentioned, we'll move a lot of the animation code into the sprite class itself. We'll write a new member function, called **Tick**, that moves the sprite and advances the animation each time it's called by some internal member variables. **CDDSprite::Tick** will take the place of **CDDSprite::Move**, which means it'll have to calculate the dirty rectangle as well.

Because the whole class is self-contained now, we'll add a couple of functions to the sprite class specifying how fast the sprite should move and the animation should be played. We'll need this capability if we want some sprites to move and animate faster than others, as we've done with the helicopter and the rotor.

FIGURE 6-8

Example 6-5 in action

Several new member variables were added to **CDDSprite** in order to add the new functions. Listing 6-29 shows the **CDDSprite** class declaration:

Listing 6-29 The **CDDSprite** class

```
class CDDSprite
{
public:
 CDDSprite(LPSTR filename);
 ~CDDSprite();
 void  Init();
 void  Render(LPDIRECTDRAWSURFACE lpDDSurface, BOOL fTrans);
 void  SetX(int newx);
 void  SetY(int newy);
 int  GetX() { return m_x; };
 int  GetY() { return m_y; };
 void  SetXScale(float xScale) { m_xScale = xScale; };
 void  SetYScale(float yScale) { m_yScale = yScale; };
 int  Width() { return m_w; };
 int  Height() { return m_h; };
 void  GetPaletteEntries(int first, int count,
    PALETTEENTRY * entries);
 BOOL  AddFrame( CDDDib * pdib );
 BOOL  SetFrame(int i);
 BOOL  SetFrameRange(int first, int last);
```

```
void   AdvanceFrame(int n = 1);
void   SetDX(int dx) { m_dx = dx; };
void   SetDY(int dy) { m_dy = dy; };
int  GetDX() { return m_dx; };
int  GetDY() { return m_dy; };
void   Move(LPRGNDATA lpRgnData = NULL);
void   SetFrameRate(UINT ticksPerFrame, int framesPerTick = 1);
void   SetSpeed(UINT ticksPerMove);
void   Tick(LPRGNDATA lpRgnData);
private:
LPDIRECTDRAWSURFACE m_ddSurface;
COLORREF   m_clrTransparent;
PALETTEENTRY   m_aPalEntries[256];
int     m_x;
int     m_y;
int     m_dx;
int     m_dy;
int     m_w;
int     m_h;
float     m_xScale;
float     m_yScale;
int     m_nColorsUsed;
Frame *   m_pFrames;
int     m_rowwidth;
int     m_iTotalFrames;
int     m_iCurFrame;
int     m_iFirstFrame;
int     m_iLastFrame;
UINT     m_nTicksPerFrame;
int     m_nFramesPerTick;
UINT     m_nTicksPerMove;
UINT     m_nFrameCounter;
UINT     m_nMoveCounter;
};
```

Here's a list of the new member variables and what they represent:

- *m_nTicksPerFrame*—how many clock ticks (timer events) to wait before changing the animation frame.

- *m_nFramesPerTick*—how many frames to advance each time *m_nTicksPerFrame* clock ticks elapse.

- *m_nTicksPerMove*—how many clock ticks to wait before moving the sprite itself.

- *m_nFrameCounter*—used to count down clock ticks until the animation must be advanced.

- *m_nMoveCounter*—used to count down clock ticks until the sprite must be moved.

Two new member functions, `SetFrameRate` and `SetSpeed`, initialize these five new variables. Let's look at them now.

CDDSprite::SetFrameRate

`SetFrameRate` sets the speed at which the sprite's animation will be played. Listing 6-30 shows the code:

Listing 6-30 `CDDSprite::SetFrameRate`

```
void CDDSprite::SetFrameRate(UINT ticksPerFrame, int framesPerTick)
{
 m_nFrameCounter = m_nTicksPerFrame = ticksPerFrame;
 m_nFramesPerTick = framesPerTick;
}
```

`SetFrameRate` takes two parameters: the number of clock ticks to wait before advancing the animation, and the number of frames to advance once that number has elapsed.

Since *m_nFrameCounter* keeps track of the time until we need to advance the animation, we'll set it to the same value as *m_nTicksPerFrame*. We'll just keep decreasing it each clock tick until it reaches zero, at which time we'll advance the animation. We'll then reset it to *m_nTicksPerFrame* again, and the cycle will repeat itself.

The other two member variable initializations are fairly self-explanatory.

One thing you should note in `SetFrameRate` is its declaration, `void SetFrameRate(UINT ticksPerFrame, int framesPerTick = 1)`.

As you can see, *framesPerTick* is initialized to **1**. This means that `SetFrameRate` can be called using just one parameter, *ticksPerFrame*, and *framesPerTick* will be automatically initialized to **0**.

CDDSprite::SetSpeed

`SetSpeed` is used to control how fast the sprite itself moves. Listing 6-31 lists the code:

Listing 6-31 `CDDSprite::SetSpeed`

```
void CDDSprite::SetSpeed(UINT ticksPerMove)
{
 m_nMoveCounter = m_nTicksPerMove = ticksPerMove;
}
```

`SetSpeed` accepts one parameter, the number of clock ticks to wait before moving the sprite, and both *m_nMoveCounter* and *m_nTicksPerMove* are initialized using this value. *m_nMoveCounter* counts down every clock tick until it reaches zero, at which time we'll move the sprite.

CDDSprite::Tick

As mentioned moments ago, Tick will replace Move. But besides just moving the sprite, Tick also has to advance the animation. Here's the code (Listing 6-32):

Listing 6-32 CDDSprite::Tick

```
void CDDSprite::Tick(LPRGNDATA lpRgnData)
{
 //
 // Check frame counter
 //
 if( m_nTicksPerFrame > 0 && --m_nFrameCounter == 0 )
 {
  //
  // Time for a frame change
  //
  if( m_iFirstFrame <= m_iLastFrame )
   AdvanceFrame(m_nFramesPerTick);
  else
   AdvanceFrame(-m_nFramesPerTick);
  m_nFrameCounter = m_nTicksPerFrame;
  //
  // If this sprite won't be moving this tick then update
  // region here
  //
  if( (lpRgnData != NULL) && (m_nTicksPerMove == 0
   || m_nMoveCounter != 1))
  {
   LPRECT lpRect = &((LPRECT)(lpRgnData->Buffer))
    [lpRgnData->rdh.nCount];

   lpRgnData->rdh.nCount++;
   lpRgnData->rdh.nRgnSize += sizeof(RECT);
   lpRect->left = m_x;
   lpRect->top = m_y;
   lpRect->right = m_x + m_w;
   lpRect->bottom = m_y + m_h;
  }
 }
 //
 // Check movement counter
 //
 if( m_nTicksPerMove > 0 && --m_nMoveCounter == 0 )
 {
  //
  // Time to move, let Move function take care of the update region
  //
  Move(lpRgnData);
  m_nMoveCounter = m_nTicksPerMove;
 }
}
```

As you can see, a lot of the functionality previously implemented in `RenderNextFrame` has been built into `CDDSprite::Tick`. `Tick` pretty much takes the place of `Move` as far as any code outside of the sprite class is concerned. `Tick` even takes the exact parameter as `Move`, a region, and fills it with the exact value, a dirty rectangle.

First we have to see if we should advance the animation:

```
if( m_nTicksPerFrame > 0 && --m_nFrameCounter == 0 )
```

If *m_nTicksPerFrame* was set to 0, then we'll just advance the animation every time `Tick` is called. Otherwise, we'll only advance the animation if *m_nFrameCounter* is down to 0 (notice that we decrease *m_nFrameCounter*'s value while we check whether it's reached 0).

If we have to advance the animation, we'll do it by *m_nFramesPerTick* number of frames:

```
if( m_iFirstFrame <= m_iLastFrame )
 AdvanceFrame(m_nFramesPerTick);
else
 AdvanceFrame(-m_nFramesPerTick);
```

We check whether *m_iFirstFrame* is less than *m_iLastFrame* because we don't want any funny frame orders (for whatever reason we decide to set them) to hang up our program. If the starting frame is less than the ending one, we simply advance *m_nFramesPerTick* number of frames in the opposite direction.

Now we need to reset the frame counter. If we forget, the animation will advance every time `Tick` is called:

```
m_nFrameCounter = m_nTicksPerFrame;
```

If the sprite isn't going to move this time around (*m_nMoveCounter* isn't down to 0 yet, and *m_nTicksPerMove* isn't 0), we'll calculate the dirty rectangle right here. Notice we're still checking that the region pointer isn't `NULL` before modifying it:

```
if( (lpRgnData != NULL) && (m_nTicksPerMove == 0 || m_nMoveCounter != 1))
{
 LPRECT lpRect = &((LPRECT)(lpRgnData->Buffer))[lpRgnData->rdh.nCount];

 lpRgnData->rdh.nCount++;
 lpRgnData->rdh.nRgnSize += sizeof(RECT);
 lpRect->left = m_x;
 lpRect->top = m_y;
 lpRect->right = m_x + m_w;
 lpRect->bottom = m_y + m_h;
}
```

Once we break free of the *if* statement determining whether we must advance the animation, we'll move the sprite if *m_nMoveCounter* is down to 0:

```
if( m_nTicksPerMove > 0 && --m_nMoveCounter == 0 )
{
 //
 // Time to move, let Move function take care of the update region
 //
 Move(lpRgnData);
 m_nMoveCounter = m_nTicksPerMove;
}
```

We'll just let **Move** calculate the dirty rectangle (remember, **Move** isn't *completely* gone, you just don't need to call it from anywhere outside the sprite class). We'll also reset *m_nMoveCounter* to equal *m_nTicksPerMove* (don't forget, it's very important!).

Rendering

This time we won't be animating or moving the body of the helicopter. The rotor will still spin, but it will remain stationary directly above the helicopter. The only sprite that *will* move is the new missile sprite, declared up at the top of **RENDER.CPP**:

```
CDDSprite *psMissle;
```

The code that bounced the helicopter and rotor around the screen is gone, since the helicopter is now stationary. This makes it easier to determine where the missile should be coming from and cuts down the amount of code a bit. (We will move the helicopter and rotor later, though.)

RenderInit

Listing 6-33 shows the code for **RenderInit**:

Listing 6-33 **RenderInit**

```
BOOL RenderInit()
{
  LPDIRECTDRAWSURFACE lpBackBuffer = DDGetBackBuffer();
  LPDIRECTDRAWSURFACE lpFrontBuffer = DDGetFrontBuffer();
  LPDIRECTDRAW lpdd = DDGetLPDirectDraw();
  int i;
  //
  // Load sprites
  //
  psBackground = new CDDSprite("backgrnd.dib");
  psHelicopter = new CDDSprite("heli24.dib");
  psHelicopter->SetXScale(.75f);
  psHelicopter->SetYScale(.75f);
  psHelicopter->SetX(400);
  psHelicopter->SetY(100);
  psHelicopter->SetSpeed(0);
  psHelicopter->SetFrameRate(0);

  psRotor = new CDDSprite("rotor00.dib");
  for( i = 1; i <= 14; i++ )
  {
    char strbuf[20];

    wsprintf(strbuf,"rotor%02d.dib",i);
    psRotor->AddFrame(new CDDDib(strbuf));
  }
```

continued on next page

continued from previous page

```
psRotor->SetXScale(.75f);
psRotor->SetYScale(.75f);
psRotor->SetX(412);
psRotor->SetY(104);
psRotor->SetFrameRange(0, 14);
psRotor->SetDX(0);
psRotor->SetDY(0);
psRotor->SetSpeed(0);
psRotor->SetFrameRate(1, 4);

psMissle = new CDDSprite("missle00.dib");
psMissle->SetX(490);
psMissle->SetY(145);
psMissle->SetDX(-20);
psMissle->SetDY(0);
psMissle->SetSpeed(1);
psMissle->SetFrameRate(0);


//
// Place in center of screen
//
psBackground->SetX((DDGetWidth() - psBackground->Width())/2);
psBackground->SetY((DDGetHeight() - psBackground->Height())/2);
//
// Get the sprite's palette entries
//
psBackground->GetPaletteEntries(0, 256, entries);
//
// Mark all as no collapse
//
for( i = 10; i < 236; i++ )
 entries[i].peFlags = PC_NOCOLLAPSE;
//
// If we've been here before and allocated a palette toss it
//
if( ddPal != NULL )
 delete ddPal;
//
// Create new palette
//
ddPal = new CDDPalette;
ddPal->CreatePalette(lpdd, DDPCAPS_8BIT | DDPCAPS_INITIALIZE, entries,
 256);
//
// Associate palette with front buffer
//
lpFrontBuffer->SetPalette(ddPal->GetDDPalette());
//
// Create a clipper
//
lpdd->CreateClipper(0, &lpDDClipper, NULL );
lpBackBuffer->SetClipper(lpDDClipper);

return TRUE;
}
```

Since the helicopter is motionless now, we only need to load the first frame of animation. We also aren't giving the sprite a frame range, because it only needs to render the first frame. We do, however, set its speed and animation speeds to **0**, just in case we accidentally call **Tick** or **AdvanceFrame**:

```
psHelicopter->SetSpeed(0);
psHelicopter->SetFrameRate(0);
```

The rotor sprite *will* be animated, so we'll call **SetFrameRate** with a value of **1** to indicate it should update the animation every time **Tick** is called. We'll still play the animation at the same speed as before (four frames per clock tick). The rotor sprite won't move either, though, so we'll call **SetSpeed** using **0**:

```
psRotor->SetSpeed(0);
psRotor->SetFrameRate(1, 4);
```

Now we need to create the missile sprite. Because the helicopter is on the right of the screen facing left, the missile should look like it's shooting out the front of the helicopter, moving from left to right until it's completely invisible. We'll then move it back to its original position, where it can start all over again.

The missile sprite only contains one frame, **MISSLE00.DIB**. We can load the image into the sprite when we create it, as we did with the others:

```
psMissle = new CDDSprite("missle00.dib");
```

We'll position the missile right in front of the helicopter sprite and tell it to move 20 pixels to the left each time:

```
psMissle->SetX(490);
psMissle->SetY(145);
psMissle->SetDX(-20);
psMissle->SetDY(0);
```

We'll tell the missile to move every clock tick. We also have to tell it never to advance the animation, since it only has one frame:

```
psMissle->SetSpeed(1);
psMissle->SetFrameRate(0);
```

One last thing about **RenderInit**. The values in the calls to **SetXScale** and **SetYScale** have changed from **1.0** to **0.75**, which has the effect of shrinking the sprites to _ of their original size. This has changed so that the missile must travel farther, making it more visible.

That's everything needed to initialize the scene. Now let's take a look at **RenderNextFrame**, which animates it.

RenderNextFrame

RenderNextFrame has been considerably shortened from last time, mainly because it's been relieved of its sprite-bouncing duties, which took up a lot of code.

Here's **RenderNextFrame** as it looks now (Listing 6-34):

Listing 6-34 **RenderNextFrame**

```
void RenderNextFrame()
{
 LPDIRECTDRAWSURFACE lpBackBuffer = DDGetBackBuffer();
 LPRGNDATA lpRgnData = (LPRGNDATA) new char[sizeof(RGNDATAHEADER)
  + RGNRECTS * sizeof(RECT)];
 //
 // Init data structure for clipper region
 //
 memset(lpRgnData,0, sizeof(RGNDATAHEADER) + RGNRECTS * sizeof(RECT));
 lpRgnData->rdh.dwSize = sizeof(RGNDATAHEADER);
 lpRgnData->rdh.iType = RDH_RECTANGLES;
 //
 // If fullscreen draw is selected or if it's needed, do it
 //
 if( fForceFullFrameUpdate || fFullFrameUpdate == TRUE )
 {
  LPRECT lpRect = (LPRECT)lpRgnData->Buffer;
  //
  // Only using one rect in fullscreen update case
  //
  lpRgnData->rdh.nCount = 1;
  lpRgnData->rdh.nRgnSize = sizeof(RECT);
  lpRect->top = 0;
  lpRect->left = 0;
  lpRect->bottom = psBackground->Height();
  lpRect->right = psBackground->Width();
  //
  // Give region to clipper
  //
  lpDDClipper->SetClipList(lpRgnData,0);
  delete lpRgnData;
  lpRgnData = NULL;
  fFullFrameUpdate = FALSE;
  //
  // If we're running full screen we need to update
  // the currently flipped out buffer
  //
  if( DDGetCooperativeLevel() & DDSCL_FULLSCREEN )
  {
   psBackground->Render(lpBackBuffer, FALSE);
   psHelicopter->Render(lpBackBuffer, TRUE);
   DDFlip();
  }
 }
 //
 // Move sprites, let them tell us what regions to update
 //
 psRotor->Tick(lpRgnData);
 //
 // Check bounds for missle
 //
```

```
if( psMissle->GetX() + psMissle->Width() + abs(psMissle->GetDX()) < 0 )
 psMissle->SetX(490);
psMissle->Tick(lpRgnData);
//
// If we're doing a fullscreen update then lpRgnData will now be NULL
//
if( lpRgnData != NULL )
{
 //
 // Use sprite's calculation of what regions to update
 //
 lpDDClipper->SetClipList(lpRgnData,0);
 delete lpRgnData;
}
//
// Do the rendering
//
psBackground->Render(lpBackBuffer, FALSE);
psRotor->Render(lpBackBuffer, TRUE);
psMissle->Render(lpBackBuffer, TRUE);
psHelicopter->Render(lpBackBuffer, TRUE);
}
```

Because the helicopter sprite stays in the same place now, it won't be included in any dirty rectangles unless a sprite moves over it. If we're running in fullscreen mode at the time **RenderNextFrame** is called, we need to draw it on the flipped-out buffer or it will be invisible whenever it's the primary surface (remember, this is the code that gets executed if we redraw the entire scene):

```
if( DDGetCooperativeLevel() & DDSCL_FULLSCREEN )
{
psBackground->Render(lpBackBuffer, FALSE);
psHelicopter->Render(lpBackBuffer, TRUE);
DDFlip();
}
```

Instead of calling **Move** and **AdvanceFrame**, all we have to do to update the rotor sprite is call **Tick** (we're passing **Tick** the address of the region allocated for the dirty rectangle list):

```
psRotor->Tick(lpRgnData);
```

The only bounds-checking we have to do this time is for the missile. We have to make sure it doesn't go off the left of the screen (its *x* position is less than zero). If it does, we reset its *x* position to the sprite's original *x* position of **490**:

```
if( psMissle->GetX() + psMissle->Width() + abs(psMissle->GetDX()) < 0 )
 psMissle->SetX(490);
```

We also have to update the missile sprite at some time in **RenderNextFrame**, and this is as good a time as any:

```
psMissle->Tick(lpRgnData);
```

The last change is the addition of the code rendering the missile sprite into the back buffer. The area of the buffer to which it gets rendered is already included in the dirty rectangle list, since we just called `Tick`.

The rotor sprite's animation has advanced, and the missile sprite has been updated and rendered. Our job here is done.

Compiling Example 6-5

That's another sprite example out of the way. All we have to do now is add collision detection and some neat explosions, and we'll be all set.

Example 6-6: Collision Detection

Let's expand a little on our last example. We'll add a flying saucer that moves up and down the screen, which will occasionally get hit by the missiles fired from the helicopter. When the saucer gets hit, it'll explode. Figure 6-9 shows Example 6-6 in action.

Collision detection is a method of finding out when two sprites are touching (colliding with) each other. We'll use it to see when the missile sprite and the saucer hit each other, which is the saucer's cue to explode.

For now, we'll implement collision detection by seeing if the rectangles containing the sprites overlap. If they overlap, we'll assume the sprites are colliding (see Figure 6-10).

FIGURE 6-9

Example 6-6 in action

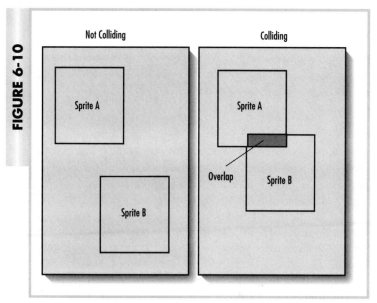

FIGURE 6-10

Rectangle collision detection

To implement collision detection, we'll add a couple of new member functions to the `CDDSprite` class. Let's do that right now.

The Collision-Detecting Sprite Class

We'll add two new member functions to `CDDSprite`.

The first function, `CollisionTest`, performs a test to determine if the sprite is colliding with another one, which is passed in through a parameter. This function does most of the actual collision detection.

The second function, `GetRegion`, calculates the rectangle the sprite occupies and adds it to a region. We need a function that does this because once the missile sprite hits the saucer, we must immediately replace it at the front of the helicopter using `CDDSprite::SetX`. Since we can't use `CDDSprite::Tick` or `CDDSprite::Move` if we move it immediately, we'll have to get the old dirty rectangle somehow, so we'll use `GetRegion`.

CDDSprite::CollisionTest

`CollisionTest` is a pretty simple function. It takes the rectangles of itself and another sprite and compares them to see if they're overlapping any. If they are, then it returns **TRUE** to indicate the sprites have collided. If not, it returns **FALSE**. Listing 6-35 lists the code:

Listing 6-35 `CDDSprite::CollisionTest`

```
BOOL CDDSprite::CollisionTest(CDDSprite *pSprite)
{
 RECT rectMe = { m_x, m_y, m_x + m_w, m_y + m_h };
 RECT rectSprite = { pSprite->m_x, pSprite->m_y, pSprite->m_x +
  pSprite->m_w, pSprite->m_y + pSprite->m_h };
 RECT rectIntersect;

 return IntersectRect(&rectIntersect, &rectMe, &rectSprite);
}
```

`CollisionTest` first calculates its own rectangle in *rectMe*. Then it calculates the rectangle of the other sprite, passed in through *pSprite* in *rectSprite*. It declares one more temporary `RECT` structure we'll use to determine if the other two rectangles are intersecting.

To determine if *rectMe* and *rectSprite* overlap, we can use the Windows API function `IntersectRect`, which takes pointers to the two rectangles to test in the last two parameters. The first parameter will be filled with the overlap rectangle, if there is one. `IntersectRect` returns `TRUE` if the rectangles passed in the last two parameters intersect and `FALSE` if they don't, so we can return `IntersectRect`'s return value from `CollisionTest`.

CDDSprite::GetRegion

`GetRegion` does the same thing as the code in `CDDSprite::Tick` that calculates the sprite's dirty rectangle. In fact, the code is exactly the same. You might even want to write a function that does this and simply call it whenever you need to find the sprite's dirty rectangle. Listing 6-36 shows `GetRegion`'s code:

Listing 6-36 `CDDSprite::GetRegion`

```
void CDDSprite::GetRegion(LPRGNDATA lpRgnData)
{
 LPRECT lpRect;

 if( lpRgnData != NULL )
 {
  lpRect = &((LPRECT)(lpRgnData->Buffer))[lpRgnData->rdh.nCount];

  lpRgnData->rdh.nCount++;
  lpRgnData->rdh.nRgnSize += sizeof(RECT);
  lpRect->left = m_x;
  lpRect->top = m_y;
  lpRect->right = m_x + m_w;
  lpRect->bottom = m_y + m_h;
 }
}
```

`GetRegion` only takes one parameter: the region to which it will add the dirty rectangle.

As mentioned earlier, this code is exactly the same as the code calculating the dirty rectangles in `CDDSprite::Tick`. Since we already went over it, we won't waste time on it again.

Rendering

The rendering functions have a little bit more to do than last time. `RenderInit`, of course, sets up the saucer sprite. `RenderNextFrame` checks if the missile and saucer sprites have collided and changes the saucer sprite's image to an explosion if they have. It also must take care of bouncing the saucer sprite up and down on the screen.

RenderInit

As just noted, `RenderInit` must take care of initializing the flying saucer sprite. Besides that, though, not much is different. Take a look at it in Listing 6-37:

Listing 6-37 `RenderInit`

```
BOOL RenderInit()
{
LPDIRECTDRAWSURFACE lpBackBuffer = DDGetBackBuffer();
LPDIRECTDRAWSURFACE lpFrontBuffer = DDGetFrontBuffer();
LPDIRECTDRAW lpdd = DDGetLPDirectDraw();
int i;
//
// Load sprites
//
psBackground = new CDDSprite("backgrnd.dib");
psHelicopter = new CDDSprite("heli24.dib");
psHelicopter->SetXScale(.30f);
psHelicopter->SetYScale(.30f);
psHelicopter->SetX(400);
psHelicopter->SetY(100);
psHelicopter->SetSpeed(0);
psHelicopter->SetFrameRate(0);

psRotor = new CDDSprite("rotor00.dib");
for( i = 1; i <= 14; i++ )
{
  char strbuf[20];

  wsprintf(strbuf,"rotor%02d.dib",i);
  psRotor->AddFrame(new CDDDib(strbuf));
}
psRotor->SetXScale(.30f);
psRotor->SetYScale(.30f);
psRotor->SetX(412);
psRotor->SetY(104);
psRotor->SetFrameRange(0, 14);
```

continued on next page

continued from previous page

```
psRotor->SetDX(0);
psRotor->SetDY(0);
psRotor->SetSpeed(0);
psRotor->SetFrameRate(1, 4);
//
// Load missle
//
psMissle = new CDDSprite("missle00.dib");
psMissle->SetXScale(.50f);
psMissle->SetYScale(.50f);
psMissle->SetX(450);
psMissle->SetY(115);
psMissle->SetDX(-20);
psMissle->SetDY(0);
psMissle->SetSpeed(1);
psMissle->SetFrameRate(0);
//
// Load saucer
//
psSaucer = new CDDSprite("saucer.dib");
psSaucer->SetX(25);
psSaucer->SetY(350);
psSaucer->SetDX(0);
psSaucer->SetDY(-5);
psSaucer->SetSpeed(1);
psSaucer->SetFrameRate(0);
psSaucer->AddFrame(new CDDDib("boom.dib"));
//
// Place in center of screen
//
psBackground->SetX((DDGetWidth() - psBackground->Width())/2);
psBackground->SetY((DDGetHeight() - psBackground->Height())/2);
//
// Get the sprite's palette entries
//
psBackground->GetPaletteEntries(0, 256, entries);
//
// Mark all as no collapse
//
for( i = 10; i < 236; i++ )
 entries[i].peFlags = PC_NOCOLLAPSE;
//
// If we've been here before and allocated a palette toss it
//
if( ddPal != NULL )
 delete ddPal;
//
// Create new palette
//
ddPal = new CDDPalette;
ddPal->CreatePalette(lpdd, DDPCAPS_8BIT | DDPCAPS_INITIALIZE, entries,
 256);
//
```

```
// Associate palette with front buffer
//
lpFrontBuffer->SetPalette(ddPal->GetDDPalette());
//
// Create a clipper
//
lpdd->CreateClipper(0, &lpDDClipper, NULL );
lpBackBuffer->SetClipper(lpDDClipper);

return TRUE;
}
```

First, notice all the calls to `CDDSprite::SetScale`. We're now scaling down the heli-copter and rotor sprites to about 30 percent of their normal size and the missile sprite to half its normal size. We're doing all this so more images fit on the scene. If we left all the sprites at their original size, we'd run out of screen real estate real fast.

There are two flying saucer animation frames: **SAUCER.DIB**, which is a picture of a fly-ing saucer, and **BOOM.DIB**, which is a picture of the flying saucer exploding. We'll load them both into the sprite, so when the saucer is hit we can just switch the frames. Here's the code that loads the sprite:

```
psSaucer = new CDDSprite("saucer.dib");
psSaucer->SetX(25);
psSaucer->SetY(350);
psSaucer->SetDX(0);
psSaucer->SetDY(-5);
psSaucer->SetSpeed(1);
psSaucer->SetFrameRate(0);
psSaucer->AddFrame(new CDDDib("boom.dib"));
```

We're setting the initial position of the sprite somewhere near the lower-left corner of the scene. Initially it won't move horizontally, and it'll move five pixels a clock tick verti-cally. When the sprite reaches the bottom or top of the screen, we'll simply reverse its direction of travel.

RenderNextFrame

Each time `RenderNextFrame` is called, we must bounce the saucer around and check if the missile and saucer sprites have collided. If the missile and saucer collide, we'll change the saucer sprite's image to an explosion and send the missile sprite back to the helicopter so it can start shooting again.

Take a look at `RenderNextFrame` in Listing 6-38:

Listing 6-38 `RenderNextFrame`

```
void RenderNextFrame()
{
 LPDIRECTDRAWSURFACE lpBackBuffer = DDGetBackBuffer();
 LPRGNDATA lpRgnData = (LPRGNDATA) new char[sizeof(RGNDATAHEADER)
 + RGNRECTS * sizeof(RECT)];
 //
 // Init data structure for clipper region
 //
 memset(lpRgnData,0, sizeof(RGNDATAHEADER) + RGNRECTS * sizeof(RECT));
 lpRgnData->rdh.dwSize = sizeof(RGNDATAHEADER);
 lpRgnData->rdh.iType = RDH_RECTANGLES;
 //
 // If fullscreen draw is selected or if it's needed, do it
 //
 if( fForceFullFrameUpdate || fFullFrameUpdate == TRUE )
 {
  LPRECT lpRect = (LPRECT)lpRgnData->Buffer;
  //
  // Only using one rect in fullscreen update case
  //
  lpRgnData->rdh.nCount = 1;
  lpRgnData->rdh.nRgnSize = sizeof(RECT);
  lpRect->top = 0;
  lpRect->left = 0;
  lpRect->bottom = psBackground->Height();
  lpRect->right = psBackground->Width();
  //
  // Give region to clipper
  //
  lpDDClipper->SetClipList(lpRgnData,0);
  delete lpRgnData;
  lpRgnData = NULL;
  fFullFrameUpdate = FALSE;
  //
  // If we're running full screen we need to update
  // the currently flipped out buffer
  //
  if( DDGetCooperativeLevel() & DDSCL_FULLSCREEN )
  {
   psBackground->Render(lpBackBuffer, FALSE);
   psHelicopter->Render(lpBackBuffer, TRUE);
   DDFlip();
  }
 }
 //
 // Check for collision
 //
 if( psSaucer->CollisionTest(psMissle) )
 {
  //
  // Saucer hit, switch to explosion
```

```
   //
   psSaucer->SetFrame(1);
   //
   // Pick up missle's current region so it will be overwritten
   // with the background
   //
   psMissle->GetRegion(lpRgnData);
   //
   // Move the missle back
   //
   psMissle->SetX(450);
}
//
// Move rotor
//
psRotor->Tick(lpRgnData);
//
// Check saucer bounds, then move it
//
if( psSaucer->GetY() > 350 )
{
 psSaucer->SetDY(-5);
 psSaucer->SetFrame(0);
} else if( psSaucer->GetY() < 20 ) {
 psSaucer->SetDY(5);
 psSaucer->SetFrame(0);
}
psSaucer->Tick(lpRgnData);
//
// Check bounds for missle, then move it
//
if( psMissle->GetX() + psMissle->Width() + abs(psMissle->GetDX()) < 0 )
 psMissle->SetX(450);
psMissle->Tick(lpRgnData);
//
// If we're doing a fullscreen update then lpRgnData will now be NULL
//
if( lpRgnData != NULL )
{
 //
 // Use sprite's calculation of what regions to update
 //
 lpDDClipper->SetClipList(lpRgnData,0);
 delete lpRgnData;
}
//
// Do the rendering
//
psBackground->Render(lpBackBuffer, FALSE);
psRotor->Render(lpBackBuffer, TRUE);
psMissle->Render(lpBackBuffer, TRUE);
psHelicopter->Render(lpBackBuffer, TRUE);
psSaucer->Render(lpBackBuffer, TRUE);
}
```

After we draw the background—if we're being forced to redraw the entire scene—we check for a collision between the missile and saucer sprites using this code:

```
if( psSaucer->CollisionTest(psMissle) )
{
 //
 // Saucer hit, switch to explosion
 //
 psSaucer->SetFrame(1);
 //
 // Pick up missle's current region so it will be overwritten
 // with the background
 //
 psMissle->GetRegion(lpRgnData);
 //
 // Move the missle back
 //
 psMissle->SetX(450);
}
```

First we use **CDDSprite::CollisionTest** to see if there actually *was* a collision. If there was, we change the saucer sprite's image to the second frame, which is the explosion. Since we'll move the missile sprite back to its initial position in front of the helicopter, we add its dirty rectangle to the list using **CDDSprite::GetRegion** so the background gets repainted where the missile hit the saucer. We then replace the missile in front of the helicopter. (One thing to note: The missile's initial **x** position moved from 490 to 450 because the helicopter sprite was scaled down.)

After moving the rotor, we bounce the saucer using this code:

```
if( psSaucer->GetY() > 350 )
{
 psSaucer->SetDY(-5);
 psSaucer->SetFrame(0);
} else if( psSaucer->GetY() < 20 ) {
 psSaucer->SetDY(5);
 psSaucer->SetFrame(0);
}
```

This code reverses the saucer's direction every time it hits the top or bottom of the screen. It also sets the saucer's image to the first frame of the animation (the normal flying saucer image) when it hits the top or bottom of the screen. We have to do this so that when the saucer is hit by the missile and changes to the explosion image, it returns the original saucer image. Otherwise, it would remain an explosion forever.

After we bounce the saucer, we have to call **Tick** so that its dirty rectangle gets added to the list. This brings us to an important point. Back when we allocated the region, *lpRgnData*, we used the **#define RGNRECTS** as the number of dirty rectangles to allocate memory for. We now have two new dirty rectangles to add to the list. The first is the dirty rectangle that gets added to when we manually move the missile sprite (when it hits the saucer). The other is the dirty rectangle the saucer leaves. To allocate enough memory for these new rectangles, **RGNRECTS** has been **#define** as 5 instead of 2.

The last little change in `RenderNextFrame` is at the very end. We must add a call to `Render` for the saucer sprite so it gets drawn. Otherwise, even though the sprite is moving it wouldn't be drawn, so the user would never even know it.

Compiling Example 6-6

That's the last example for Chapter 6. Go ahead and play around with it. Tweak it. The more you mess around with these example programs, the more you'll learn.

We're not quite done refining the sprite engine. In Chapter 8, "Advanced DirectDraw," we'll add scrolling backgrounds and a better collision detection scheme. After that, you'll have a commercial quality sprite engine you can easily use in your own games. Or, at the very least, you'll have a solid understanding of how to build one.

Summary

That just about wraps up Chapter 6. This has been a *very* informative chapter. Even though we really only covered one new feature of DirectDraw (color keying), you learned more about game programming itself than in all the other chapters combined. You learned about animation, dirty rectangles, movement, missiles, and collision detection—all of which are vital to game programming. The next chapter introduces a key element of game design—the player—and discusses how to respond to his or her actions using DirectInput.

7
DirectInput

Now that you've learned how to add elements such as moving animated sprites to programs, something that looks very much like a game is starting to take shape. Before further refining our graphics techniques, let's look at how to actually involve the player in the game. In other words, let's learn how to detect and respond to user actions like moving a mouse or joystick. In order to do this, we'll take a short break from DirectDraw for a while and look at another component of DirectX, DirectInput.

DirectInput lets us take advantage of any input devices available on the user's system. DirectInput is not only a handy API for joystick programming, it provides one *huge* advantage over joystick programming in DOS. Namely, it supports any joystick that could ever be produced—provided that the joystick manufacturer writes a DirectInput driver for the product.

This means if your game has been on shelves for months and a hardware manufacturer suddenly comes out with an amazing new input device—a virtual reality glove, some kind of futuristic steering wheel, whatever—your game can automatically use it without any change in the code whatsoever. This also means you only have to write code to handle input from one type of device and it will work with any other. If you've ever written joystick code in DOS you know what a welcome feature this is, since you probably spent days writing code to handle input from a slew of different joysticks.

This is all assuming, of course, that the manufacturer writes a DirectInput driver for its device. If the manufacturer doesn't, then your users are out of luck since a driver is the only way DirectInput will know how to use the device. As Windows 95 becomes a more common gaming platform, however, it's almost certain any new piece of hardware will come bundled with a DirectInput driver. If it doesn't, the hardware manufacturer will miss out on a huge chunk of the market and probably have its support lines swamped by thousands of irate consumers. Besides, Microsoft writes its own drivers for almost everything, so there's no need to worry.

Since Windows 95 takes care of configuring joysticks, you don't have to worry about calibration either. *Calibrating* is testing how far the joystick moves in each direction so you can correctly read input from it. If you played DOS games at all, you probably remember moving joysticks to the upper-left and lower-right corner every time you wanted to play a new game. Windows 95 handles that now, letting the user calibrate a joystick just once when it's installed. This takes care of calibration for all the Windows 95 games on the system—including yours.

Example 7-1: Joysticks

You probably already know what a joystick is or you wouldn't be a game programmer. However, there are a few joystick terms you'll need to know as we work through DirectInput that aren't part of the common gameplayer's vocabulary. Let's briefly run through them.

There are two types of joysticks: *analog* and *digital*. The difference between the two is in how they detect where the joystick is moving (when the term *moving* is used in relationship to joysticks, it's usually regarding the main directional control). Analog joysticks, the newer of the two, have greater accuracy because they can tell precisely how far in each direction the user is moving the joystick. Digital joysticks, on the other hand, can only detect whether the joystick is moving in a certain direction or not—they can't tell how far. This obviously makes analog joysticks the more desirable of the two because they're more accurate. However, there are strings attached. Analog joysticks take more processing power than digital joysticks because they have to constantly keep track of their position.

DirectInput can handle up to two analog joysticks with four axes, or directions, of movement and four buttons. It can also handle up to four analog joysticks with four buttons as long as the joysticks only move on *two* axes. If the user is using *digital* joysticks, DirectInput can handle up to 16 of them with up to 6 axes and 32 buttons each.

The API

In DirectX 2, the previous version of DirectX, DirectPlay was simply another name for the Win32 joystick API. In DirectX 3, however, DirectInput installs its own replacement device driver, giving it some capabilities above and beyond what the Windows API offers.

 Note

Since DirectInput is just a better joystick device driver, Windows uses it automatically. So there's no need to link another library into your project when you build DirectInput applications.

DirectInput consists of several functions. We'll talk about most of them as we work through Example 7-1. First, though, we need to look at some of the structures used by DirectInput.

The **JOYCAPS** Structure

The **JOYCAPS** structure is used by DirectInput to describe an input device. It has a myriad of members, each describing one aspect of the device such as the number of axes it supports, the number of buttons it has, the device's product name, and so on. We'll only talk about the members we use here.

The **JOYINFOEX** Structure

The **JOYINFOEX** structure contains information about the current state of the joystick. That is, it tells us where the joystick is and which buttons the user is pressing. One of the functions we'll look at shortly fills this structure with information about the state of the joystick, so we can read the values we need from it. Again, there are quite a few members in this structure, so we'll just discuss the ones we use.

Implementing DirectInput

To demonstrate implementing DirectInput, we'll work it into the helicopter example built in the last chapter. We'll let the joystick's directional control move the helicopter and have the helicopter fire a missile when the user presses a joystick button.

JoystickInit

The first thing we must do is write a function to initialize the joystick. We'll call it **JoystickInit** and call it from **WinMain** right after **WinInit**. Listing 7-1 shows the code:

Listing 7-1 **JoystickInit**

```
static BOOL JoystickInit()
{
 JOYINFOEX joyinfo;
 UINT nValid = 0;

 gapp.joystickid = 0;

 if( joyGetNumDevs() == 0 )
  return FALSE;

 memset(&joyinfo,0,sizeof(JOYINFOEX));
 joyinfo.dwSize = sizeof(JOYINFOEX);
 joyinfo.dwFlags = JOY_RETURNBUTTONS | JOY_RETURNX | JOY_RETURNY;

 if( joyGetPosEx(JOYSTICKID1, &joyinfo) != JOYERR_UNPLUGGED )
  gapp.joystickid = JOYSTICKID1;
 else if( joyGetPosEx(JOYSTICKID2, &joyinfo) != JOYERR_UNPLUGGED )
  gapp.joystickid = JOYSTICKID2;
 else
  return FALSE;
```

continued on next page

continued from previous page

```
gapp.fJoyButton1Down = ((joyinfo.dwButtons & 1) != 0);
gapp.fJoyButton2Down = ((joyinfo.dwButtons & 2) != 0);
gapp.wJoyXPos = WORD(joyinfo.dwXpos);
gapp.wJoyYPos = WORD(joyinfo.dwYpos);

joySetThreshold(gapp.joystickid, 100);
joySetCapture(gapp.hwndApp, gapp.joystickid, 100, TRUE);

return TRUE;
}
```

Joysticks are identified by a zero-based index. This means the first joystick attached to the system is number zero, the second joystick is number one, and so on. **MMSYSTEM.H #defines** two joystick identifiers for us, **JOYSTICKID1** and **JOYSTICKID2**, which identify the first and second joystick on the system, respectively.

To keep things simple, we'll only let one joystick move the helicopter around and shoot missiles. We'll keep its ID (or zero-based index) in a new member of our global application structure **GApp** named *joystickid*. If there is only one joystick attached to the system, *joystickid* will contain its identifier. If there are two or more, *joystickid* will contain the first joystick's identifier. However, keep in mind that the index corresponds to the physical connection by which the joysticks are plugged into the system's I/O or game card. If there's a joystick plugged into the second joystick port but not the first, then **JOYSTICKID2** will represent that joystick, and **JOYSTICKID1** simply won't exist.

Anyway, back to the code. To prevent *joystickid* from containing a garbage value, we set it to zero at the outset of **JoystickInit**. We then check whether there are *any* joysticks attached to the system using the function **joyGetNumDevs**. JoyGetNumDevs doesn't accept any parameters and simply returns the number of joysticks available on the system. If the return value is zero, we bail from **JoystickInit** by returning **FALSE**, since there aren't any joysticks to initialize.

Next we need to initialize a **JOYINFOEX** structure. First, we clean out the memory it's using to get rid of any residual garbage. After doing that, we set its *dwSize* member, which plays the same role as the *dwSize* members in any of the other DirectX structures we've worked with, to the size of the entire structure in bytes.

Next, we need to tell the structure which members are valid. This works similarly to how we tell a **DDSURFACEDESC** structure which members are valid, by using a different flag for each valid member and combining the flags in the *dwFlags* member:

```
joyinfo.dwFlags = JOY_RETURNBUTTONS | JOY_RETURNX | JOY_RETURNY;
```

Each of these three flags validates a different structure member variable. We'll discuss the members validated by each in just a moment.

Now we'll use that **JOYINFOEX** structure just initialized to see which joysticks, if any, are attached to the system. We'll only look for the first two joysticks. If they aren't there, we'll assume **joyGetNumDevs** goofed for some reason and return **FALSE**. Of course, the user could have the joysticks plugged into some other port, such as the third or fourth, which would mess up **JoystickInit**. But that's highly unlikely.

To find out whether a joystick is attached to the first or second port, we'll use the function **joyGetPosEx**. Since **joyGetPosEx** fills in a **JOYINFOEX** structure, we'll use it whenever we want information about a joystick, such as its position or whether it even exists. **joyGetPosEx** takes two parameters: the identifier of the joystick to query (its index), and a pointer to a **JOYINFOEX** structure indicating what you're trying to find out about the joystick. Table 7-1 lists the return values of **joyGetPosEx**, each of which is quite important.

Table 7-1 joyGetPosEx return values

Return Value	Meaning
MMSYSERR_NODRIVER	The joystick driver isn't present.
MMSYSERR_INVALPARAM	One of the parameters was invalid.
MMSYSERR_BADDEVICEID	The joystick identifier is invalid.
JOYERR_UNPLUGGED	The specified joystick isn't connected to the system.

To find out which joystick is attached to the system (remember, we'll only use the first one), we'll call **joyGetPosEx** and look for the **JOYERR_UNPLUGGED** return value to come back, meaning a certain joystick is disconnected. Initially, we'll query the first (index zero) joystick, and if it's not attached, we'll query the second (index one). We set *gapp.joystickid* to the identifier of the first valid joystick we find, and return **FALSE** if we don't find one at all.

We have to add a few more members to our **GApp** structure (besides the joystick identifier) so we can actually use the joystick in our example. Here's what the structure declaration looks like now (Listing 7-2):

Listing 7-2 The **GApp** structure

```
typedef struct _GApp
{
 //
 // Global App Data
 //
 HINSTANCE  hinst;
 HWND     hwndApp;
 LPDIRECTDRAW  lpdd;
 RECT     wndRect;
 UINT     timerid;
 BOOL     fFlippingPaused;
 BOOL     fWaitForVerticalBlank;
 BOOL     fPostPending;
 UINT     ticksPerSecond;
 UINT     joystickid;
 WORD     wJoyXPos;
 WORD     wJoyYPos;
 BOOL     fJoyButton1Down;
 BOOL     fJoyButton2Down;
} GApp, * LPGApp;
```

Of course, we've already discussed *joystickid*. The *wJoyXPos* and *wJoyYPos* members hold the *x* and *y* location of the joystick (we'll talk more about this when we get to the rendering code). The *fJoyButton1Down* and *fJoyButton2Down* Booleans are toggled according to whether the first and second joystick buttons are pressed.

We'll use a few members from the **JOYINFOEX** structure to initialize the new members of our **GApp** structure. Remember, this is the structure whose members are validated by flags in its *dwFlags* member, the same way as **DDSURFACEDESC**.

The first **JOYINFOEX** member we need is *dwButtons*, which is validated by the **JOY_RETURNBUTTONS** flag in the *dwFlags* member. After calling **joyGetPosEx**, *dwButtons* will contain flags indicating which buttons are being pressed. The flags making up *dwButtons* are simply the indexes of the buttons pressed. Keep in mind that button indexes are *not* zero-based like joystick indexes. So if the first button is pressed *dwButtons* will contain the value 1, and if the second button is pressed it will contain the value 2, and so on. There are also **#defines** you can use for the first four buttons in **MMSYSTEM.H** in the form **JOY_BUTTON***n*, where *n* is the button's index.

The two other members of **JOYINFOEX** we're concerned with right now are *dwXPos* and *dwYPos*, the *x* and *y* positions of the joystick. We'll use these two members to initialize the *wJoyXPos* and *wJoyYPos* members of our **GApp** structure. Again, there will be more on this when we cover rendering.

Remember we filled in the *dwFlags* member of the **JOYINFOEX** structure (*joyinfo*) before calling **joyGetPosEx** to find out which joystick is attached. This means *joyinfo* will already have all the members we requested filled with information when we get to the next section of code, which transfers the information to our **GApp** members.

It would be nice if we could have some kind of notification mechanism in which DirectInput lets us know when the user presses a button, instead of constantly calling **joyGetPosEx** (which results in a lot of unnecessary function call overhead). Thankfully, DirectInput *does* provide us with such a mechanism. Using DirectInput, we can arrange to send a message to our window's callback function whenever the joystick moves, which is obviously the most efficient way of doing things. To do this though, we must use a few joystick functions that aren't in the DirectX help file, so pay close attention.

First, we need to call **joySetThreshold**, which sets the distance the specified joystick must move before a message is sent:

```
joySetThreshold(gapp.joystickid, 100);
```

joySetThreshold takes the ID of the joystick in the first parameter and the distance it must move before a message is sent. We'll talk more about joystick distances when we get to the rendering code.

Next, we'll use the **joySetCapture** function to set up a message that's sent whenever the joystick moves the distance given to **joySetThreshold**:

```
joySetCapture(gapp.hwndApp, gapp.joystickid, 100, TRUE);
```

joySetCapture takes the handle of the window containing the callback function to which you want to send the messages as the first parameter. The second parameter is the ID of the joystick being monitored. The third is the interval, in milliseconds, that the joystick should be checked for movement. The fourth and final parameter is a Boolean value indicating whether or not joystick messages should only be sent when the joystick has moved the distance specified in the call to `joySetThreshold`. If this value is `FALSE`, messages will be sent periodically even if the joystick hasn't moved. If it's `TRUE`, messages will only be sent when there's some movement. What you give for the fourth parameter will depend on how you write the rest of your joystick code. We've used `TRUE` for reasons that will become apparent when we look at the callback function.

 Note

A message is sent to the callback function any time a button is pressed, even if the joystick hasn't moved.

The Callback Function

Depending on how many joysticks you want to handle, there are quite a few messages you must keep track of. This is because there are at least three messages for each joystick (we'll discuss them in a moment), and that number grows quickly if you let the user have more than one or two joysticks. However, since we'll only use one joystick in our example, it won't be too difficult.

Button Messages

There are two types of button messages that get sent to the callback function: those telling you a button has been pressed and those telling you a button has been released. Button down (pressed) messages take the form `MM_JOY`*n*`BUTTONDOWN`, in which *n* is the (*not* zero-based) index of the joystick sending the message. Button up (released) messages take the form `MM_JOY`*n*`BUTTONUP`, in which *n* is again the index of the joystick sending the message. The index of the button triggering the message is contained in the `LPARAM` of both messages.

Joystick Moved Messages

Joystick moved messages are sent when the joystick's directional control moves the distance specified in the call to `joySetThreshold` (or periodically, depending how you called `joySetCapture`). They take the form `MM_JOY`*n*`MOVE`, in which *n* is the (again, not zero-based) index of the joystick triggering the message. The *x* position of the joystick is contained in the high word of the `LPARAM`, the *y* position in the low word (remember, `LPARAM`s are double words).

The Message Handler

Since we're only using one joystick for our example, we don't need to have a separate handler for each joystick's messages. We can just bunch them all together and use the same handler, as Listing 7-3 shows:

Listing 7-3 The joystick message handler

```
case MM_JOY1BUTTONDOWN:
case MM_JOY2BUTTONDOWN:
case MM_JOY1BUTTONUP:
case MM_JOY2BUTTONUP:
case MM_JOY1MOVE:
 gapp.fJoyButton1Down = ((wParam & JOY_BUTTON1) != 0);
 gapp.fJoyButton2Down = ((wParam & JOY_BUTTON2) != 0);
 gapp.wJoyXPos = LOWORD(lParam);
 gapp.wJoyYPos = HIWORD(lParam);
 return 0;
```

As you can see, all we need to do is extract the information from the **LPARAM** and stick it in the correct **GApp** member. We won't actually use the new information until a little later.

First, in the handler code, we find out which buttons are being pressed by seeing whether either **JOY_BUTTON1** (the first button) or **JOY_BUTTON2** (the second) are in the **WPARAM**. Then we set *gapp.wJoyXPos* (the joystick's *x* position) to the low word of the **LPARAM** and *gapp.wJoyYPos* (the *y* position) to the high word of the **LPARAM**. This will give us all the information needed to react to the user's input.

Rendering

The code that does the rendering is basically the same because we haven't changed anything affecting how the game looks. We must, however, do a few extra things in **RenderInit**. Plus, there's a new function to monitor the joystick and move the sprites, since we now only need to update the sprites when the user moves the joystick.

Movement

As mentioned earlier, analog joysticks more accurately detect the joystick's location than digital ones. When an analog joystick is moved, it can register at any position between the center and the extremities of movement on any given axis (see Figure 7-1). Assuming the

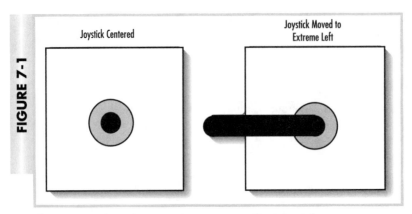

FIGURE 7-1

The centered and extreme positions of a joystick

joystick has four axes, the position of an analog joystick is its *x* and *y* location anywhere between the upper-left and lower-right extremities of movement. But for digital joysticks, the joystick can only be at one of the extremities, or centered—there's no in-between.

All joysticks have a range of movement, from the centered (or neutral) position on each axis to the extremities of each direction. The directional extremities are the farthest the joystick can move on each axis, numbers set by the joystick driver. Again, analog joysticks can assume any value between those two numbers, while digital joysticks can only be centered or located at an extremity.

Joystick Coordinate Systems

With most joysticks, the coordinate system is set up similarly to a screen coordinate system, with zero at the left extremity on the **x** axis and the top extremity on the **y** axis (the most upper-left position to which the joystick can be moved). The centered position is half the joystick's range of movement. Figure 7-2 better illustrates this written description.

Now that you understand joystick coordinate systems a little better, let's move on to `RenderInit`.

RenderInit

The only difference in `RenderInit` from last time is that it must initialize a few more variables. Here's an excerpt showing the new code (Listing 7-4).

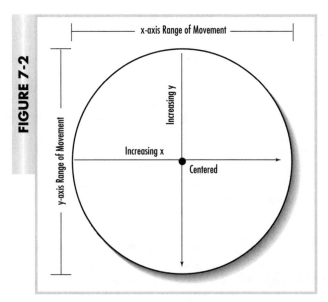

FIGURE 7-2

Joystick coordinates

Listing 7-4 **RenderInit** excerpt

```
JOYCAPS joycaps;

joyGetDevCaps(gapp.joystickid, &joycaps, sizeof(joycaps));

joyXDivisor = (WORD)(joycaps.wXmax - joycaps.wXmin) / 9;
joyYDivisor = (WORD)(joycaps.wYmax - joycaps.wYmin) / 9;
joyLastX = 0;
joyLastY = 0;
```

This code is executed just before **RenderInit** returns **TRUE** to the calling function. Basically, it finds out what one-ninth of the joystick's range of movement is, so we can use that value to move the helicopter sprite at a constant speed when the user moves the joystick.

First have **joyGetDevCaps** fill in a **JOYCAPS** structure with information about the joystick's ID we saved in *gapp.joystickid*. **joyGetDevCaps** takes the joystick ID to query as the first parameter, a pointer to the **JOYCAPS** structure to put the information into as the second, and the size of the **JOYCAPS** structure the second parameter points to as the third.

Once the **JOYCAPS** structure is filled in by **joyGetDevCaps**, we can extract the necessary information by reading its members. Right now we want to know the minimum and maximum x and y locations of the joystick (in other words, its range of movement). That information is contained in the members **wXmax** (the maximum x location), **wXmin** (the minimum x location), **wYmax** (the maximum y location), and **wYmin** (the minimum y location).

We'll set up two variables equal to one-ninth the distance of the joystick's range of movement on each axis:

```
joyXDivisor = (WORD)(joycaps.wXmax - joycaps.wXmin) / 9;
joyYDivisor = (WORD)(joycaps.wYmax - joycaps.wYmin) / 9;
```

We'll use the *joyXDivisor* and *joyYDivisor* variables when we check the joystick to find out how far it moved. Because the joystick's location is given in a unit determined by its manufacturer, we have no idea how large it will be. Sometimes the extremities of the joystick's range of movement get into the hundreds (in coordinate units) for more accuracy. Because we'll move the sprite using the value the joystick driver returns (in those same huge coordinate units), we don't want it quite so large, otherwise the sprite will move unrealistically fast. That's why we divide the range of movement by nine in this bit of code and store it in these variables—we need some more manageable numbers to use for moving the sprites. If you want the sprites to move faster, decrease the number used to divide the range of movement. If you want them slower, increase the number. Of course, if you're dealing with a digital joystick, none of this makes any difference, because there are no positions between the centered and extreme ones.

The other two new variables we're initializing, *joyLastX* and *joyLastY*, represent the joystick's current location. We'll update these variables whenever we get a joystick message and use them to find out whether the joystick has moved since the last message was sent, or whether the message was only sent because a button was pressed. Because this is the first time around, we'll just initialize them to (0,0).

JoyCheck

Instead of putting the code checking the joystick and moving the sprites in `RenderNextFrame`, we lump it all in another function, `JoyCheck`, which we call from `RenderNextFrame`. Listing 7-5 lists `JoyCheck`'s code:

Listing 7-5 **JoyCheck**

```
static void JoyCheck(void)
{
 int x = (gapp.wJoyXPos / joyXDivisor) - 4;
 int y = (gapp.wJoyYPos / joyYDivisor) - 4;
 //
 // Bail if the joystick hasn't moved significantly
 //
 if( x == joyLastX && y == joyLastY )
  return;
 //
 // Otherwise save current position for next try
 //
 joyLastX = x;
 joyLastY = y;
 //
 // Set horizontal speed according to joystick position
 //
 psRotor->SetDX(x);
 psHelicopter->SetDX(x);
 //
 // Set vertical speed according to joystick position
 //
 psRotor->SetDY(y);
 psHelicopter->SetDY(y);
 //
 // Set clock divisor as required
 //
 if( x != 0 || y != 0 )
 {
  psRotor->SetSpeed(1);
  psHelicopter->SetSpeed(1);
 } else {
  psRotor->SetSpeed(0);
  psHelicopter->SetSpeed(0);
 }
}
```

Every time `JoyCheck` is called, we'll see whether the joystick has moved a significant distance since the last time. If it has, we adjust the sprites' directions and speeds. If it hasn't moved significantly, the sprites should be fine using their member functions to move in their previous directions and speeds.

To find out whether the joystick has moved a significant distance since the last time `JoyCheck` was called, we first need to find out where the joystick is at the moment:

```
int x = (gapp.wJoyXPos / joyXDivisor) - 4;
int y = (gapp.wJoyYPos / joyYDivisor) - 4;
```

Instead of using the joystick's location as is, we divide its *x* and *y* position by the *x* and *y* division units, respectively (remember that the division units equal the range of movement divided by nine). This makes the distances smaller so the sprites won't move as fast. Because the joystick coordinates start at zero, the joystick location can't be negative. Because we'll use the joystick location to set the direction of the sprites (as you'll see in a moment), we need to be able to get negative values in order for the sprites to move left or up. For this reason, we subtract 4 from the result of the division (you can use a larger number if you want the sprites to move faster, or a smaller number if you want them slower). For example, if the *x* coordinate of the joystick is 0 (the left extremity) and we subtract 4 from it, the sprites will move left at the rate of 4 pixels per clock tick.

Next we have to see whether the joystick has moved at all since the last time `JoyCheck` was called (remember, *joyLastX* and *joyLastY* hold the *x* and *y* position of the joystick the last time `JoyCheck` was called).

```
if( x == joyLastX && y == joyLastY )
 return;
```

If we get past that statement, it means the joystick has moved a significant distance and we should move the sprites. Before we go on though, we need to save the old *x* and *y* position of the joystick in *joyLastX* and *joyLastY* for the next time `JoyCheck` is called.

After making sure we need to move the sprites, we set the sprites' directions to the *x* and *y* variables we calculated at the outset of `JoyCheck`. Then we take a look at the *x* and *y* position of the joystick. If the *x* and *y* position of the joystick are both zero, the two sprites aren't going anywhere. If they shouldn't move, we set their speeds to zero. Otherwise, we tell them to move every clock tick, using the *x* and *y* movement values we just gave them.

This function might seem a little confusing a first, but just go back and look it over again. Joystick programming is somewhat confusing because the coordinate system isn't organized in the best way. Ideally, (0,0) would be right at the center, so you could use the joystick's position you get from `joyGetPosEx` to set the sprites' directions. However, it's not quite that straightforward, so we must do some awkward stuff to get the sprites moving correctly.

Compiling Example 7-1

Because there's not much to learn about joystick programming, this is the only example program in the chapter. We're finally interactive though!

If you want to, apply the same techniques you just learned to using the mouse. Because using the mouse as an input device is more of a basic Windows programming topic, we won't cover it in this book. But all you'd have to do is handle the mouse messages the same way we did in `JoyCheck`.

Remember, DirectInput isn't a new component—it's just a new device driver. So there's no need to include another library file into your project. Just make sure you `#include` `MMSYSTEM.H` and link in `WINMM.LIB`.

Summary

Truthfully, there isn't much to DirectInput, which is why this chapter was so short. However, it's an important part of game programming, one you'll probably use no matter what type of game you write.

In this chapter you learned to find input devices, initialize them, translate their coordinate systems, and utilize their movement information. In the next chapter we'll wrap up bitmap graphics programming, then move on to 3D graphics (Direct3D).

8

Advanced DirectDraw

In the last chapter we took a brief hiatus from DirectDraw. In this one, we'll wrap up our discussion of DirectDraw and bitmap graphics. Most of this chapter will be spent discussing various ways to improve our bitmaps graphics engine and make it the most versatile engine possible.

Example 8-1: Scrolling

For the first example in this chapter, we'll scroll the background (the mountains) when the user moves the joystick, which makes it look as though the helicopter—not the background—is moving. This is the best way of doings things (in our example, at least) since the helicopter will never reach the edge of the screen and seems to fly on forever. Figure 8-1 shows a screenshot of Example 8-1 in action.

To facilitate the scrolling, the background bitmap is the length of the entire scene. This way, part of the background runs off the edge of the screen whenever the joystick moves (since we'll move the background, not the helicopter). Then, we can just draw (wrap) the part of the background that went off the screen onto the screen's other side. As long as the background bitmap basically looks the same on both sides (there isn't a seam when the two ends sit next to each other), the mountains will look like one continuous bitmap.

FIGURE 8-1

Example 8-1

The Sprite Class Revisited

We'll create the background as an instance of the sprite class we developed in Chapter 6, "Sprites." In order to do the wrapping though, we'll have to add a few things to the sprite class.

First of all, we'll add a Boolean variable, *m_fWrap*, indicating whether the sprite should wrap when it goes off the edge of the screen. If *m_fWrap* is **TRUE**, we'll wrap the sprite when it moves off the screen. Otherwise, we'll just let it disappear, which is called *clipping* the sprite. We'll also add a simple member function, **SetWrap**, that sets *m_fWrap* to **TRUE** or **FALSE**.

There's one other new member function, **CalcRects**, that calculates the rectangles occupied by the sprite when the bitmap appears on both sides of the screen due to wrapping. We'll call **CalcRects** whenever we need to know where to draw the sprite. Let's take a quick look at it now.

CDDSprite::CalcRects

CalcRects calculates the rectangles to which we should blit the sprite on the screen. It calculates the sprite's destination and source rectangles (the rectangles that will be blitted to and from, respectively), taking wrapping into consideration. However, it only allows the sprite to wrap in the **x** coordinate, meaning sprites can only go off the sides of the screen—not the top and bottom. If we wanted to also let `CalcRects` handle sprites wrapping vertically, we'd have to add a few more parameters and a lot more code.

Listing 8-1 shows the code for `CalcRects`:

Listing 8-1 `CalcRects`

```
void CDDSprite::CalcRects(LPRECT dst1, LPRECT src1, LPRECT
dst2, LPRECT src2 )
{
 int  scrWidth = gapp.wndRect.right - gapp.wndRect.left;
 int  clippedWidth = abs(m_x + m_w - scrWidth);

 dst1->left = m_x;
 st1->top = m_y;
 dst1->right = m_x + (long)((float)m_w * m_xScale);
 dst1->bottom = m_y + (long)((float)m_h * m_yScale);
 src1->left = 0;
 src1->top = 0;
 src1->right = m_w;
 src1->bottom = m_h;

 memset(dst2,0,sizeof(RECT));
 memset(src2,0,sizeof(RECT));


 if( clippedWidth != 0 && m_fWrap)
 {
  dst2->top = dst1->top;
  dst2->bottom = dst1->bottom;
  src2->top = src1->top;
  src2->bottom = src1->bottom;

  if( m_x > 0 )
  {
   dst2->left = 0;
   dst2->right = clippedWidth;
   src2->left = m_w - clippedWidth;
   src2->right = m_w;
  } else if( m_x < 0 ) {
   dst2->left = scrWidth - clippedWidth;
   dst2->right = scrWidth;
   src2->left = 0;
   src2->right = clippedWidth;
  }
 }
}
```

`CalcRects` accepts four parameters, although we may not necessarily use them all. Incidentally, all these parameters are filled in by `CalcRects`, so you don't have to supply them. They are

- *dst1*—the destination rectangle (on the surface we want to blit to) for the unwrapped area of the sprite. This is where the first half of the sprite (or the whole thing, if the sprite isn't being wrapped) should be blitted to on the destination surface.

- *src1*—the source rectangle (on the sprite image) for the unwrapped area of the sprite. This is where the first half of the sprite should be *taken* from on the sprite image itself.

- *dst2*—the destination rectangle for the wrapped area of the sprite. This is where the second half of the sprite should be blitted to.

- *src2*—the source rectangle for the wrapped area of the sprite. This is where the second half of the sprite should be taken from (on the sprite bitmap).

Because *dst2* and *scr2* are the rectangles containing the wrapped part of the sprite, they won't be used if the sprite doesn't wrap at all (since *dst1* and *src1* will contain the entire sprite). If this happens, all the members in *dst2* and *src2* are set to zero. *dst1* and *src1* will always be used, so we don't have to worry about them being valid.

We won't spend too much time on `CalcRects`; rather, we'll just quickly step through it.

First of all, we need to find the width of the display and stick it in *scrWidth* (so we know what point on the screen at which to wrap). We also need to find the width of the area of the sprite that's offscreen (and should be wrapped) and put it in *clippedWidth*.

Next, we calculate *dst1*, the sprite's destination rectangle. We're not concerned with wrapping at this point, so we basically use the same routine as before for finding the sprite's destination rectangle.

We then calculate *src1*, the source rectangle for the unwrapped portion of the sprite. This is the entire area of the sprite for now.

There's one thing you should note about the first source and destination rectangles. Since DirectDraw won't draw off the side of the screen, we don't need to modify these two rectangles from the last example. We can simply let them hang off the edge of the screen and we'll be none the worse for wear.

After calculating the first two rectangles, we set *dst2* and *scr2* to zero, just in case the sprite doesn't need any wrapping. We won't change these values unless the sprite *does* need to wrap, so it's important to initialize them to zero before we move into the wrapping code.

If the sprite is supposed to be wrapped when it goes off the screen (if *m_fWrap* is TRUE) and it's indeed partially or wholly off the screen, we move on to the wrapping code itself. Since we're only handling horizontal wrapping, the top and bottom members of the second set of rectangles will always be the same as the first. So, first we copy the *top* and *bottom* members from the first source and destination rectangles to the second set of rectangles.

Next, we calculate the area of the sprite bitmap that moved off the screen and fill in the second set of source and destination rectangles accordingly. As you can see, we must perform different calculations depending on whether the sprite is moving off the left or right of the screen. After these calculations, the second set of rectangles will contain the coordinates of the clipped portion of the sprite image, both on the bitmap and the screen. By blitting both the first and second set of rectangles, we can easily wrap the sprite.

CDDSprite::Render

We have to modify `Render` so it uses the rectangles we get from `CalcRects`. If we forget to do this, the function we just wrote obviously won't help us at all. Listing 8-2 shows the new code for `Render`:

Listing 8-2 `CDDSprite::Render`

```
void CDDSprite::Render(LPDIRECTDRAWSURFACE lpDestSurf, BOOL
fTransparent)
{
 ECT dst1, src1, dst2, src2;

 CalcRects(&dst1,&src1,&dst2,&src2);

 lpDestSurf->Blt(&dst1,
   m_ddSurface,
   &src1,
   DDBLT_WAIT | (fTransparent ? DDBLT_KEYSRC : 0),
   NULL);
 if( dst2.right != 0 && src2.right != 0 )
  lpDestSurf->Blt(&dst2,
    m_ddSurface,
    &src2,
    DDBLT_WAIT | (fTransparent ? DDBLT_KEYSRC : 0),
    NULL);
}
```

First, we get the two rectangles we must blit to, using `CalcRects`. Since the first set of rectangles is always valid, we can go ahead and use them to blit to the destination surface.

Now comes the wrapping part of the code. If the *right* member of the second source and destination surfaces is zero, `CalcRects` is able to fit the entire bitmap into the first set of rectangles and we don't need to worry about blitting with the second set.

If the *right* member of either the second source or destination rectangles is not zero, we can blit from the sprite surface to the destination surface using the second set of rectangles. This will effectively wrap the sprites.

CDDSprite::Move

Wrapping doesn't only take place in the drawing code. When a sprite goes completely off one side of the screen, we need to move it back to the other side. Otherwise, it will keep going off the screen's edge until the user moves it the other way, which will have disastrous effects on our `CalcRects` code. For this reason, we need to modify our `Move` functions. Listing 8-3 shows the new code:

Listing 8-3 `CDDSprite::Move`

```
void CDDSprite::Move(LPRGNDATA lpRgnData)
{
 //
 // Make the move
 //
 m_x += m_dx;
 m_y += m_dy;
 //
 // If this is a wrapping sort of sprite then check for reset of origin
 //
 if( m_fWrap && (m_x + m_w < 0 || m_x > gapp.wndRect.right
  - gapp.wndRect.left ) )
  m_x = 0;
 //
 // Calculate update regions
 //
 if( lpRgnData != NULL )
 {
  RECT dst1, src1, dst2, src2;
  LPRECT lpRect;
  //
  // Get areas which will be blitted to
  //
  CalcRects(&dst1, &src1, &dst2, &src2);
  //
  // Update first region
  //
  lpRect = &((LPRECT)(lpRgnData->Buffer))[lpRgnData->rdh.nCount];

  lpRgnData->rdh.nCount++;
  lpRgnData->rdh.nRgnSize += sizeof(RECT);
  lpRect->left = dst1.left - m_dx;
  lpRect->top = dst1.top - m_dy;
  lpRect->right = dst1.right + m_dx;
```

```
    lpRect->bottom = dst1.bottom + m_h;
    //
    // If there's a second region update it too
    //
    if( m_fWrap && dst2.right != 0 && src2.right != 0 )
    {
     lpRgnData->rdh.nCount++;
     lpRgnData->rdh.nRgnSize += sizeof(RECT);
     lpRect++;
     lpRect->left = dst2.left - m_dx;
     lpRect->top = dst2.top - m_dy;
     lpRect->right = dst2.right + m_dx;
     lpRect->bottom = dst2.bottom + m_h;
    }
  }
 }
```

To handle sprite wrapping, we first check to see whether the sprite has moved completely off the screen. If it has, we move it back to zero, on its **x** coordinate. Of course, this only happens if *m_fWrap* is **TRUE**.

Next, we find out where we should blit to using **CalcRects**. Then, using the first destination rectangle from **CalcRects**, we calculate the dirty rectangle. If the sprite wraps, we have to add another dirty rectangle to cover the part of the sprite being wrapped. To calculate *that* dirty rectangle, we simply use the second destination rectangle.

Rendering

We now have another sprite to deal with: the mountains. As mentioned earlier, the mountains are themselves a sprite, separate from the ground bitmap, which is the background sprite. The mountains are now in a sprite called *psMountains*.

RenderInit

There aren't many changes to **RenderInit**. These lines were added to **RenderInit** to initialize the *psMountains* sprite:

```
psMountains = new CDDSprite("mounts.dib");
psMountains->SetY(192);
psMountains->SetFrameRate(0,0);
psMountains->SetWrap(TRUE);
```

This code, **MOUNTS.DIB**, loads the mountains image, sets its height to 192, and tells itself not to animate. We call **SetWrap** with **TRUE** because this is the sprite for which we wrote all the wrapping code in the first place, so we definitely want it to wrap.

RenderNextFrame

A couple of lines were added to **RenderNextFrame** to handle the new mountain sprite. First of all, we must draw it into the flipped-out buffer if we're doing a full redraw and are in fullscreen mode (otherwise it will disappear when we flip the surface):

```
if( DDGetCooperativeLevel() & DDSCL_FULLSCREEN )
{
 psBackground->Render(lpBackBuffer, FALSE);
 psMountains->Render(lpBackBuffer, TRUE);
 psHelicopter->Render(lpBackBuffer, TRUE);
 DDFlip();
}
```

We also have to call **Tick** so that the mountains move. Although they're not animated, they still need to move in order to scroll. The direction variable is initially set to zero, but we'll give them some momentum when the user moves the joystick (since the direction of scrolling depends on which way the user moves the joystick). Calling **Tick** also adds the mountains to the dirty rectangle list. Most of the time, this adds two rectangles because the mountains will wrap, creating two regions to update.

The last change we must make is adding a call to **Render** at the very end of **RenderNextFrame** so *psMountains* gets drawn:

```
psBackground->Render(lpBackBuffer, FALSE);
psMountains->Render(lpBackBuffer,TRUE);
psRotor->Render(lpBackBuffer, TRUE);
psMissile->Render(lpBackBuffer, TRUE);
psHelicopter->Render(lpBackBuffer, TRUE);
```

We call **Render** with a value of **TRUE** as the second parameter because we want it drawn transparently. Remember, the mountains were removed from the background. So to make the background show through the mountains, we need to draw the mountain sprite transparently.

JoyCheck

Here's where we actually move the background sprite. Instead of moving the helicopter (and the rotor sprite, too, remember) when the user moves the joystick, we scroll the mountain sprite and leave the helicopter in place. Because our **CalcRects** routine doesn't handle vertical scrolling, unfortunately we can only let the user move the mountains horizontally. This means when the joystick is moved up or down, nothing happens.

When the user moves the joystick left or right, we set the mountain sprite in the same direction. We also set the mountain sprite's speed to 1, provided the joystick isn't centered. That's all there is to moving the mountain sprite. Because **Move** takes care of wrapping the sprite's position and **CalcRects** takes care of wrapping its image, we don't have to do anything else in **JoyCheck**.

Compiling Example 8-1

Hopefully, you now have a better understanding of how to wrap bitmaps from one side of the screen to the other. It's an important concept in side-scrolling games in which bitmaps are used for just about everything. Now, let's learn how to use more than one scrolling (and wrapping) bitmap to create a sort of 3D effect in bitmap scenes.

Example 8-2: Adding Multiple Scrolling Layers

We can easily create the illusion of depth by placing more than one scrolling object in a scene's background—or foreground—and making them scroll at different speeds. To demonstrate this, we'll add two tree stumps to the foreground of our helicopter program. These stumps will scroll along with the mountains when the user moves the joystick. Figure 8-2 shows a screenshot of the finished product.

There are a couple of rules we need to observe when deciding where to put the stumps and how fast they should scroll when the user moves the joystick. First of all, objects closer to the viewer should always look larger than objects farther back in the scene

FIGURE 8-2

Example 8-2

(assuming they're supposed to be the same size, of course). Second, objects closer to the viewer always move faster than objects farther back. These rules relate to how objects move in three dimensions and how our eyes perceive them. We'll explore this sort of thing further when get into Direct3D in the next chapter.

To add the two stumps, we'll put two more sprite objects into our rendering code. Since we've loaded and initialized sprites before, we won't bother to even list this code—we'll just skim over the process and note anything of interest.

The sprite appearing closest to the viewer, *psStump1*, will have a *y* value of 400. This puts it not that far above the bottom of the screen—assuming we run in a high-resolution mode like 640×480. The sprite uses **STUMP1.DIB** for its image file.

The sprite that's farther away in the scene, *psStump2*, has a *y* value of 300. This puts it above the first stump, but below the mountains. Its image file, **STUMP2.DIB**, contains a smaller image than **STUMP1.DIB**, thus abiding by the rule that objects in the background should appear smaller than objects in the foreground. Although this method works fine, we could just as well scale the first sprite down to achieve the same effect—try it if you have the time.

Incidentally, both of these sprites have their *m_fWrap* members set to **TRUE**, so they wrap when reaching either side of the screen.

Initializing the Sprites

There really aren't any significant changes in the sprite class, so let's move on and see how to initialize the new sprite.

The sprite initialization, as you'll recall, takes place in **RenderInit**. Here's the only new code:

```
psStump1 = new CDDSprite("stump1.dib");
psStump1->SetY(400);
psStump1->SetFrameRate(0,0);
psStump1->SetWrap(TRUE);
psStump2 = new CDDSprite("stump2.dib");
psStump2->SetY(300);
psStump2->SetFrameRate(0,0);
psStump2->SetWrap(TRUE);
psStump2->SetXScale(.75f);
psStump2->SetYScale(.75f);
```

We do the same thing for both sprites. We basically load in the bitmap, set the sprite's vertical position onscreen, set wrapping to **TRUE**, and scale the sprite if necessary. Since there's no animation, we also set the frame rate to zero.

Rendering

There's nothing too interesting in the rendering department this time. We do the same thing for the stump sprites as we did with the mountain sprite, calling the same functions and using the same values.

JoyCheck

There may not be anything different in `RenderNextFrame`, but there are one or two differences to note in `JoyCheck`.

When the user moves the joystick, we need to call `SetDX` to make the mountains move in the opposite direction. Now we also need to move the stumps in the opposite direction, only at a faster speed since they're closer to us than the mountains:

```
psMountains->SetDX(-x);
psStump1->SetDX(-x * 3);
psStump2->SetDX(-x * 2);
```

psStump1 is the larger, closer stump, so we'll make it move the fastest. To achieve this, we'll move it three times faster than the mountains. *psStump2* is smaller and farther back, so we'll have it move faster than the mountains but slower than the first stump, at twice the mountains' speed.

Compiling Example 8-2

Well, that was sure a quickie! That's okay though, because all we did was use the sprite class from the last example for a few more sprites. Yet the scene looks much better, and if you wanted to, you could write a complete game with this sprite engine.

Summary

Although this chapter was brief, it was quite beneficial. You learned how to use sprites to perform scrolling operations and how to make sprites appear as if they're at varying distances from the viewer. Now that we've finished our sprite class, feel free to tweak it and even write a small game with it. It's incredibly flexible, and you can do so much with it. Plus, it's easily extendible by adding C++ members functions.

That wraps up our discussion of DirectDraw. Now we'll move on to Direct3D, which we'll eventually use to write a complete game.

9

Direct3D Basics

3D—the future of video games. With all the new games boasting cutting-edge 3D graphics, you don't want to be left out. Not to worry, because the Direct3D API not only brings you up to speed with the DOS developers out there, it gives you a big edge.

Direct3D is a library for writing high performance 3D applications for Windows 95 and Windows NT. Right now it's an add-on component (as is the rest of DirectX), but Microsoft has plans to build Direct3D into the next version of Windows (and Windows NT). This will almost certainly make Direct3D an industry standard, so you can rest assured you aren't learning some obscure API that will die out in a few years (a la WinG).

As a DirectX component, Direct3D works perfectly well alongside DirectDraw, DirectSound, DirectPlay, and DirectInput. In fact, it works *very* closely with DirectDraw to get the fastest possible screen updates on the user's system. It does this by rendering to a DirectDraw surface, which you can then use however you want. Besides displaying the surface on the screen, you can also use it as a sprite, the background for a sprite-based game, a texture in another 3D scene, or any other way you dream up. We'll learn how to use Direct3D and DirectDraw together in Chapter 15, "Putting It All Together."

In this chapter, we'll look at the basics of Direct3D and build four example programs that put what we're learning to use. Chapter 15 will expand on what we learn in this chapter and harness our newfound knowledge to build a complete 3D game.

3D Graphics Fundamentals

Any way you slice it, 3D graphics is the single most complex area of computer programming. This is mostly due to the heavy math involved. Don't worry, though; you don't necessarily have to do a whole bunch of math to crank out awesome 3D graphics. If you want it to, Direct3D will shield you from all math so that you can just concentrate on the game aspect.

This section gives you an overview of the fundamentals of 3D graphics. It won't go into any math since, as just mentioned, Direct3D handily provides you with a way around it. There are plenty of good books on the math end of 3D programming, though, so feel free to look it up if you want more control over the rendering process.

3D Coordinate Systems

The first thing you need to understand is the concept of a 3D coordinate system. We've only used a 2D coordinate system until now, so you'll have to get used to using another dimension when you identify a point.

In 3D coordinate systems, usually x is still the horizontal axis and y is still the vertical axis. However, we still need one more axis to describe the other (third) dimension: the axis called z. If you're looking at a piece of paper with the standard Cartesian x and y coordinate system on it, the z axis will point into *or* out of the paper. That's the confusing part—some 3D coordinate systems have the positive z axis pointing *into* the paper, away from the viewer, and some have it pointing *out*, towards the viewer (x and y are sometimes rearranged too, which makes it even more confusing). This doesn't help things much when you're just learning how to program in 3D.

The most common 3D coordinate system is called the left-handed system, in which the positive z axis points into the paper. Direct3D uses this system, as do most 3D graphics libraries. Figure 9-1 illustrates the left-handed system. The other common system is called the right-handed system, in which the positive z axis points out of the paper. The right-handed system isn't used nearly as much as the left-handed system, so don't worry about it.

Keep in mind that all the axes are relative to an origin, which was at the top left of the screen in the 2D coordinate system we used. In 3D systems, remember as you move past the origin on each axis, your location on that axis will change its sign. For example (using the left-handed system, as we always will from now on), if you take a point on the z axis past the origin (thus, on the positive side of the origin) and continue to move it toward you, its z position becomes negative the instant it passes the origin.

Polygons and Objects

3D objects are made up of polygons, which are, in turn, made up of 3D points called vertices (3D points that are part of a polygon). Each of these 3D entities (objects, polygons, and vertices) are represented by a different structure in Direct3D. We'll look at them when we get to the coding part of this chapter.

In 3D programming, everything is made up of vertices. *Vertices* (the plural of vertex) are simply 3D points connecting to form polygons and objects. You'll see vertices used quite a bit in every aspect of 3D programming.

Polygons, as just noted, are made up of connected vertices (Figure 9-2). Polygons can have any number of vertices, as long as they aren't concave (they must be convex, because it's extremely difficult to efficiently render concave polygons). The area between the vertices, called the face of the polygon, can look however you want. What you decide to put on the face of the polygon is called a *material*. Besides having a texture (a bitmap, a solid color, or anything that can be put into a DirectDraw surface), materials also have other properties such as how reflective they are, whether light will shine out of them, and so on.

FIGURE 9-1

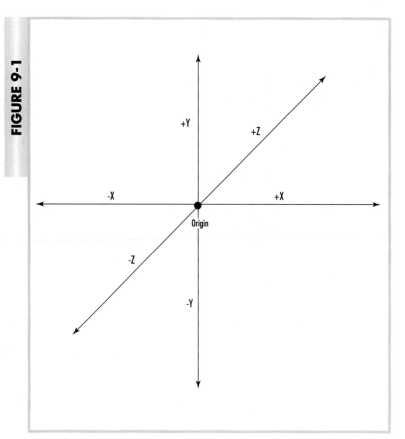

The left-handed 3D coordinate system

FIGURE 9-2

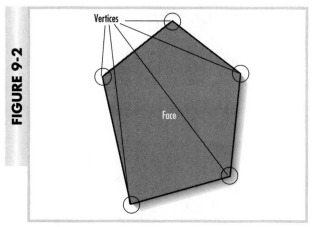

A polygon

Objects, in turn, are made of polygons. Objects are really just a convenient way to think of polygons, because from a programming standpoint, we can't tell if a polygon is in one object or another. As we go through code, you'll see that objects are only formed by polygons which are carefully placed—you don't program with objects, only with polygons and vertices. You could even consider each individual polygon a separate object, perhaps if you were creating an explosion or a similar special effect, where individual polygons move in different directions.

Transformations

There are three types of transformations (movements) that you can perform on polygons: rotation, translation (moving), and scaling (resizing). Transformations aren't strictly limited to polygons, however. There are several other objects you can also use them on, such as the camera (the user's viewpoint—which we'll discuss a little later). Transformations are really our only means of animating a 3D scene, and are therefore, quite important.

Rendering

Polygon rendering is Direct3D Immediate Mode's main job (we'll discuss Direct3D Immediate Mode in a moment). In order to fully understand what we're doing when we start coding, we need to go over a little background about rendering first.

There are usually hundreds, if not thousands, of polygons in a 3D scene (world). Before Direct3D can render them, it has to determine which are visible and what order in which to render them. If it renders polygons that aren't visible, it will waste time uselessly rendering things the user can't see. If it renders them in the wrong order, things will look a little funny because polygons that should be in the back of the scene will be drawn on top of polygons very close to the camera, and vice versa. Either case is bad news.

Determining which polygons are visible (called *clipping*) is a complex task. If you use Immediate Mode, you'll have to do some of it yourself. On the other hand, Retained Mode takes care of it for you (again, we'll discuss both of these at length in just a moment). Direct3D, however, *will* perform one kind of clipping for you for free no matter which mode you use. When you send it a bunch of polygons to render, it makes sure their vertices are visible to the camera. If they aren't, it just disregards them. Though you'll have to do a bit more clipping to get a scene to render correctly, this clipping is incredibly fast, and you can get it automatically.

When Direct3D renders a scene, it has to determine the Z-order of the polygons (the order in which the polygons should be drawn). It uses a Z-buffer for this purpose—in fact, it's the same Z-buffer DirectDraw uses. Basically, this means Direct3D first renders the polygons farthest away, then works its way up. This is an extremely accurate method of rendering and fairly fast. The only drawback is that it tends to slow down pretty fast if the scene contains a lot of polygons; however, it works well for most games. There are several other ways to deal with the Z-order problem, but they're pretty complex, and we won't go into them in this book.

When you tell Direct3D to render a polygon, it must calculate the 2D screen location (x, y) of all its vertices. This is called *projecting coordinates*. Once a polygon has been projected onto the screen, all Direct3D has to do is fill it with something.

The most common thing with which to cover the face of a polygon is a texture (bitmap). Textures look great and can be rendered quickly, especially with the new 3D accelerator boards now on the market. Almost every game you see uses textures to render its polygons. You could also just use a solid color, but that method is (and looks) a bit dated. You'll probably want to use textures in your game unless you're going for some kind of special effect, such as a metallic surface.

Lighting

Lighting is *very* important to the look and feel of your game. However, lighting is also probably the most complex aspect of rendering because of the many different methods.

The most commonly used lighting method right now is *Gouraud*. Gouraud shading calculates the color of each vertex in a polygon by finding out how much light shines on each, then adding that light to the original color (or texture) of that vertex. Gouraud shading produces a nice round look by filling the polygons with a wash of colors between each vertex. For example, if a triangle's top vertex is blue, its lower-left vertex red, and its lower-right vertex white (all from different colored lights shining on the polygon), rendering the polygon would create a wash between blue and red on its left, a wash between blue and white on the right, a wash between red and white on the bottom, and a blend of all three colors in the middle. Gouraud rendering is both fast and attractive, which is why it's now the most common rendering method.

Another rendering method gaining popularity fast is *Phong shading*. Phong shading is the highest quality rendering method because it considers where each light is located and creates a *specular highlight* on the polygon for each. A specular highlight is the shine you see on reflective surfaces when a light is bouncing off them. Adding specular highlights makes a scene look realistic, but it's also pretty slow. You'll probably only want to use this method if the user has a 3D accelerator board installed (one that supports Phong shading).

The oldest method, and probably least commonly used, is *flat shading*. Flat shading simply calculates one color for the entire surface, resulting in a sharp, choppy look. This method was used back when 386's were the dominant PC and is pretty much outdated now. If you have a scene in which you need something rendered as fast as possible, however, this is the best option because it *is* the fastest of the three methods (sometimes it's also used to create a different look for the scene).

Direct3D Hardware Use

3D accelerator cards are becoming increasingly popular and powerful. It would be ugly if one of your users had just bought your game to use with his hot new 3D card, but your game wasn't written to use it. Thankfully that scenario pretty much disappeared with DOS, because if you use Direct3D, you automatically use whatever hardware is available.

I strongly recommend you get a 3D accelerator card for Direct3D programming—not just because it will make your applications look nicer and run better, but because the *Debug* version of Direct3D (the version that gives you detailed error messages) is much slower than the *Retail* version (the one for users). If you decide to go without a 3D board, you'd better have a souped-up monster of a system or a ton of patience to run and debug your game.

If you need a 3D board, try to find one supporting most of Direct3D's features. Several manufacturers make good Direct3D-compatible boards and graphics such as S3, ATI, 3DFx, S-MOS, and many others.

Direct3D HAL and HEL

Since 3D cards (and even most normal video cards by now) have 3D acceleration built into them, it would be nice to take advantage of it instead of doing everything in software. The Direct3D HAL (Hardware Abstraction Layer) does just that, much like the HALs of the other DirectX components. If there is no hardware acceleration, Direct3D has its own software implementation (Hardware Emulation Layer, or HEL), which is also very fast and very optimized. Either way you win because you don't have to write the 3D routines yourself.

All of this is assuming the user has his or her board properly installed and the manufacturer has written a decent driver for it. The former depends entirely on the user—you can't help it if the user can't install his or her board right or didn't install the right driver. The latter depends on the board manufacturer—if your game can't use the board because the driver doesn't work, there's nothing you can do about it. Hopefully, though, everything will work out fine and you'll be able to use the board.

Immediate and Retained Modes

As briefly mentioned earlier, Direct3D can function in either Immediate or Retained Mode (or both, as you'll soon see). Immediate mode is very low level, and you have to do a lot of work yourself when using it. This mode is quite handy if, for instance, you're porting an existing DOS game to Windows 95, or you simply want more control over the rendering process than Retained Mode allows.

The second and more complex mode is Retained Mode. Retained Mode is a full-featured 3D graphics library, making it easier to manage 3D scenes and control the objects in them. Retained mode gives you less control over the whole process, but you don't have to work nearly as much as if you were using Immediate Mode exclusively.

Note

Retained Mode was once a commercial 3D graphics library. It used to be called Reality Lab and was purchased by Microsoft from a company called RenderMorphics. In fact, Microsoft didn't even start to call it Direct3D Retained Mode until well into the DirectX 2 beta program.

Immediate and Retained Modes are closely related and can even be used together. Retained Mode, even though it's a different set of functions, still uses Immediate Mode to perform the rendering. This goes along with the DirectX principle that all components are created equal and can work together.

The fact that you can use Immediate and Retained Modes (and even other DirectX components, such as DirectDraw) together makes for almost endless possibilities. You could use Retained Mode to manage your scene, while using custom rendering processes to make Immediate Mode render it how you want. You could also use Retained Mode for everything except a few items, which Immediate Mode could render directly. You can then use DirectDraw to render text and cartoons on top of the 3D scene. The list goes on and on.

In this book we'll use Retained Mode exclusively, because you must be fairly experienced in 3D graphics development to use Immediate Mode. Everything you learn about Retained Mode can also be applied in almost the same way to Immediate Mode. The only difference is that Immediate Mode doesn't provide all the free features of Retained Mode (although you could write them in yourself if you wanted).

The Rendering Pipeline

Before we continue looking at Retained Mode, you should first understand what's happening under the hood of Immediate Mode. That way it will be simpler to understand Retained Mode concepts. It will also make it easier for you to program using Immediate Mode, should you eventually decide to take that route.

When you want Direct3D Immediate Mode to render a scene, you have to send it an *execute buffer*, which is basically a request to render something. Execute buffers contain two parts: a list of vertices making up all the polygons in a scene, and a series of commands telling Direct3D how to render the polygons.

The part of an execute buffer that tells Direct3D how to render a scene usually also tells Immediate Mode where the camera is, how the view should be set up, and how to move the polygons in the list. You don't *have* to include these things in the execute buffer, but you most often will.

When you send an execute buffer to Immediate Mode telling it to render a scene, it goes through the *rendering pipeline*. The rendering pipeline is made up of three separate parts, or *modules:* the transformation module, the lighting module, and the rendering module. Just so you know, Retained Mode uses the rendering pipeline automatically, meaning you don't even have to mess with it if you decide to skip Immediate Mode.

Each of the modules can be called directly without using the others. This comes in handy if you've written your own specially optimized modules to use in place of one of the standard ones. Most of the time, though, you'll just use the modules Direct3D provides since they work so well.

The Transformation Module

The transformation module, the starting point of the rendering pipeline, transforms the camera and the objects in the polygon list. You can do this yourself if you want. In fact, you probably will if you're porting a DOS application to Windows and don't want to modify the old engine too drastically. However, the Direct3D transformation module is very well optimized, and you probably won't get better performance than it gives.

The transformation module also determines which vertices are in the view (meaning it does the clipping). This is an extremely important job, because it has a huge impact on performance. To perform the clipping, the transformation module finds out which vertices are visible and only gives those to the rendering module.

The Lighting Module

The lighting module keeps track of all the lights in a scene and calculates what color each vertex should be. Although you could write your own lighting module, Direct3D comes with two lighting modules—**Ramp** and **RGB**—that should meet all your needs.

The *RGB module* considers the color of all the lights in a scene when calculating the color of each vertex in a polygon. This produces much more realistic results, but is also considerably slower. This makes the **RGB** color model quite uneconomical in terms of CPU usage, unless it's supported in hardware (which is becoming more and more common).

The second lighting module, *Ramp*, only uses lights colored a shade of gray between white and black. Since it doesn't have to calculate the red, green, and blue components of the light, it's much faster than the **RGB** module, but not quite as realistic. If you're only using white or gray lights it won't matter which module you use, because the output will look the same. But, again, if the user's hardware supports the **RGB** model you'll probably want to use that one, since anything in hardware is probably faster than the software.

The Rendering Module

The rendering module, also called the *rasterization module*, renders the scene with vertex information generated by the transformation module and lit by the lighting module. There are many options you can set for the rendering module to reflect your rendering needs—it's pretty easy to make the output look just the way you want it.

As mentioned before, you won't have to worry about the rendering pipeline if you only use Retained Mode, but it's good to know about it anyway. Let's look at what's involved in getting a Retained Mode scene up and running.

The Building Blocks of a Direct3D World

When you create a 3D world using Direct3D Retained Mode, you have to create and initialize several different Direct3D components. All of these components work together to build, move, and render a scene.

The Direct3D Object

The Direct3D object is *not* the same thing as the DirectDraw object. The DirectDraw object represents the display device, while the *Direct3D* object simply creates other Direct3D objects. You'll always have one of these objects around somewhere, because you need it to create and destroy all the other Direct3D objects you use.

The Direct3D Device

The *Direct3D device* resembles a DirectDraw object more than the Direct3D object does. It represents the rendering destination, or display surface. You also set rendering options, such as rendering quality, using the Direct3D device.

There can be more than one Direct3D device, enabling you to show more than one view of a scene at a time. Several possible uses for more than one device in an application include modeling programs, rearview mirrors, and remote cameras. This will also come in very handy if, for example, virtual reality goggles with one tiny monitor for each eye come into vogue. All you'd need to do to use the goggles is to render the same scene to the two devices as seen from a slightly different position in each eye, creating an illusion of depth.

Frames

A *frame* is basically just something that tells Direct3D how an object should look or act. The name frame is perhaps misleading, because a frame really isn't something you can see or manipulate (in other words, it's not an object). A frame is just a data representation of an object's state.

You can use a frame for one or several objects (and by the way, the word *object* means anything you can manipulate, including lights and cameras). In fact, you can think of frames as a way to group objects behaving in the same way.

To expand on that last idea, frames can also have children and parents. This means if several objects are associated with (contained in) the same frame, each can have its own frames (called *child frames* of the first frame, which is the *parent frame*).

As an example, let's say we're building a model of the sun, the earth, and the moon. Let's first put the sun in a frame, as in Figure 9-3 (remember, a frame really isn't something you can draw, but we have to represent them somehow).

Because the earth is always in the same vicinity as the sun, let's stick it in the same frame (Figure 9-4).

Okay, the earth, of course, should revolve around the sun, so let's put it in a frame revolving around the sun (actually, it will revolve around the point in 3D space that's the center of the sun). The moon revolves around the sun, too, so we can stick it in the same frame (Figure 9-5).

FIGURE 9-3

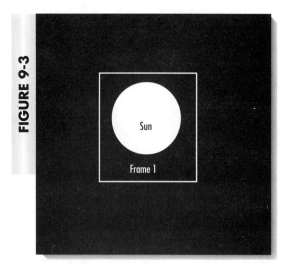

The sun in a frame

FIGURE 9-4

The sun and earth

Now that the frame containing the earth and moon is rotating (or orbiting, if you prefer) around the sun, all that's left is making the moon rotate around the earth. To do this, we simply put the moon in its own frame, which then rotates around the center of the earth (Figure 9-6).

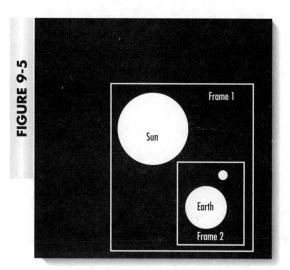

The sun, earth, and moon in their frames

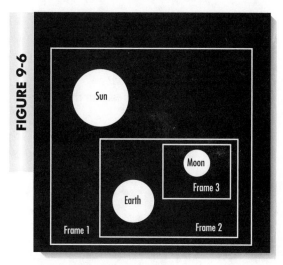

The final scene

When we set the finished scene into action, the sun, earth, and moon will all stay in the same general area since they're contained in the same parent frame (Frame 1 in the illustration). The earth and moon will also rotate around the sun, since they're contained in the same frame (Frame 2), which rotates around the sun. The moon will orbit the earth since it's contained in its own frame rotating around the earth. With frames, everything stays together in a nice neat package. No matter where the sun moves, the earth and moon will orbit around it and each other since we stuck them in frames relative to one another. There's really no way to mess up the scene since we used frames, which is basically the whole point.

If you don't completely understand frames yet, don't worry. They *are* somewhat confusing, but you will understand them more as we work through the examples later.

The Viewport

The *viewport* defines how and where the virtual scene is rendered. The viewport essentially acts as a camera or a window into the 3D world. When you create a viewport, you define where it is located and what it can see. You then attach it to a device, onto which it then renders the scene.

The Examples

The Direct3D examples will look a bit different from any of the previous ones, because Direct3D is vastly different from anything else covered so far. You won't see any of the familiar functions or variables we've been using (with a few exceptions), so don't try to translate what we're writing now back to what we wrote before.

Okay, we covered the basics, so let's get started.

Example 9-1

Example 9-1 is basically a wireframe model in a window the user rotates with the arrow keys. Take a look at Figure 9-7 for a screenshot:

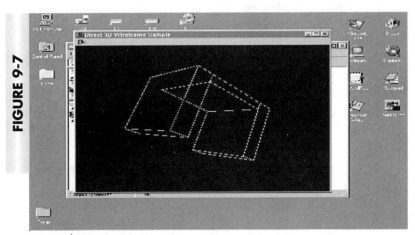

FIGURE 9-7

Example 9-1

This first example may not look very impressive, but it's a foundation we'll use to build the three increasingly complex examples in this chapter. For Example 9-2, we'll move to a solid model; for Example 9-3, we'll create a lighted move; and for Example 9-4, we'll build a texture-mapped model.

Initializing Example 9-1

As with DirectDraw, Direct3D initialization is more than half the work. We have to create an instance of all those Direct3D objects discussed earlier, and we have to build the 3D scene. It's not really that hard; it just takes a long time.

In order to keep all the Direct3D initialization in one spot, let's create a function called **SetupDirect3DRetainedMode**, which takes the handle of the window to render into as its lone parameter. We'll call it from within the main message handler when we receive a **WM_CREATE** message:

```
if(!SetupDirect3DRetainedMode(hWnd))
 PostQuitMessage(0);
```

The function will also return a Boolean value, so we can exit if it should fail.

SetupDirect3DRetainedMode

This is probably the most complex function of the bunch. There's a lot of initialization to be done, plus we have to learn what we're doing along the way. First off, let's look at the code in Listing 9-1:

Listing 9-1 **SetupDirect3DRetainedMode**

```
BOOL SetupDirect3DRetainedMode(HWND hWnd)
{
// Try to create the interface. If failed display an error message and
// return FALSE;
if(Direct3DRMCreate(&pD3DRetainedModeAPI) != D3DRM_OK)
 {
 MessageBox(hWnd,"Could not create Retained Mode Interface!",
  NULL,MB_OK | MB_ICONSTOP);
 return FALSE; // Failed creation
 }

// Create Scene API
if(pD3DRetainedModeAPI->CreateFrame(NULL,&pD3DSceneAPI) != D3DRM_OK)
 {
 MessageBox(hWnd,"Could not create scene!",
  NULL,MB_OK | MB_ICONSTOP);
 return FALSE; // Failed creation
 }

// Create Camera API
if(pD3DRetainedModeAPI->CreateFrame(pD3DSceneAPI, &pD3DCameraAPI)
 != D3DRM_OK)
```

continued on next page

continued from previous page

```
{
MessageBox(hWnd,"Could not create camera frame!",
 NULL,MB_OK | MB_ICONSTOP);
 return FALSE; // Failed creation
 }

// Set the position of the camera
if(pD3DCameraAPI->SetPosition(pD3DSceneAPI, 0.0f, 0.0f, 0.0f)
 != D3DRM_OK)
 {
MessageBox(hWnd,"Could not set camera position!",
 NULL,MB_OK | MB_ICONSTOP);
 return FALSE; // Failed creation
 }

// Create the clipper and associate it with the window
if(DirectDrawCreateClipper(0, &pDDClipperAPI, NULL) != DD_OK)
 {
MessageBox(hWnd,"Could not create clipper!",
 NULL,MB_OK | MB_ICONSTOP);
 return FALSE; // Failed creation
 }

if(pDDClipperAPI->SetHWnd(0, hWnd) != DD_OK)
 {
MessageBox(hWnd,"Could not associate clipper with window!",
 NULL,MB_OK | MB_ICONSTOP);
 return FALSE; // Failed creation
 }

// Create Device and viewport
if(!CreateDeviceAndViewport(hWnd))
 {
MessageBox(hWnd,"Could not create viewport!",
 NULL,MB_OK | MB_ICONSTOP);
 return FALSE; // Failed creation
 }

// Create the scene
if(!BuildScene())
 {
MessageBox(hWnd,"Could not create scene!",
 NULL,MB_OK | MB_ICONSTOP);
 return FALSE; // Failed creation
 }

bD3DReady = TRUE;
return TRUE; // Successful Creation
}
```

The first thing we must create is the Direct3D object, or API. This is a lot like the DirectDraw object as its main job is creating other objects. We'll put it in the variable ***pD3DRetainedModeAPI***, which is a pointer to a Direct3D object (or an **LPDIRECT3DRM**). If **Direct3DRMCreate**, the function creating the Direct3D object, or any of the other functions in the initialization process fails, we just pop up a message box saying so, then bail the program.

After creating the Direct3D object, we'll use it to create the scene. The first step is creating a frame that's the reference for every other frame in the scene (the parent frame of all the others in the scene). We do this by using the `IDirect3DRM` interface (member function) `CreateFrame`.

`CreateFrame` takes two parameters: the new frame's parent frame, and a pointer to a pointer to the new frame. Any frame without a parent is called a *scene* in Direct3D lingo. All you do to create one is pass **NULL** as the first parameter to `CreateFrame`. That's what we did in our example, and we passed a pointer to the frame *pD3DSceneAPI* as the second parameter:

```
if(pD3DRetainedModeAPI->CreateFrame(NULL,&pD3DSceneAPI) != D3DRM_OK)
    ...
```

Now we can position all the other frames we'll create relative to *pD3DSceneAPI*, our scene frame.

Our next order of business is creating the camera. As mentioned earlier, there isn't a special type of object for cameras; you just have to create a frame describing where the camera is. First we create the camera frame, using *pD3DSceneAPI* as its parent since it will be positioned relative to the scene frame:

```
if(pD3DRetainedModeAPI->CreateFrame(pD3DSceneAPI, &pD3DCameraAPI)
    ...
```

Now we need to position the camera in the scene. We'll put it at the center of our little universe at $(0,0,0)$ using the `IDirect3DFrame` interface `SetPosition`:

```
if(pD3DCameraAPI->SetPosition(pD3DSceneAPI, 0.0f, 0.0f, 0.0f)
    ...
```

`SetPosition` is a simple function you'll use a lot in Direct3D to position frames. The frame you're positioning is going to be moved relative to another frame, called the *reference frame*. The first parameter to SetPosition is a pointer to the reference frame you want to use. Position the frame relative to the *center* of the reference frame. The reference frame doesn't *have* to be the parent frame of the frame you're positioning, although it usually is (as in this case). The remaining three parameters are simply the frame's new coordinates (relative to the center of the reference frame in the first parameter).

 Note

You might not have seen numerical values like 0.0f before. The f suffix simply means to pass this number as a floating-point value and is generally just used to avoid compiler warnings and clunky casts.

Positioning the camera like we just did was actually redundant, since it was already at $(0,0,0)$ relative to the scene frame. That's because when you create a child frame it's automatically put at the center of its parent frame, and we created the camera as a child frame of the scene frame. In other words, no need to position it where it already was. The only reason we positioned it at (0,0,0) again was to teach you how to do it.

The next thing we do to initialize our example (in `SetupDirect3DRetainedMode`) is create a regular old DirectDraw clipper, which we'll need later to create the Direct3D device. To create the clipper, we call the DirectDraw API function `DirectDrawCreateClipper`, which takes the same parameters as `IDirectDraw::CreateClipper`. See Chapter 3, "More DirectDraw," if you need to review clippers.

After creating the clipper, all we do is associate it with the program's main window, using `IDirectDrawClipper::SetHWnd`. Again, see Chapter 3 for more on `SetHWnd`.

We'll go over the next two functions, `CreateDeviceAndViewport` and `BuildScene`, in a moment. `CreateDeviceAndViewport` creates the rest of the Direct3D objects we'll need for our program, and `BuildScene` actually puts the visual 3D objects into our scene. Let's take a look at `CreateDeviceAndViewport`.

Initializing the Rest of Direct3D: `CreateDeviceAndViewport`

`CreateDeviceAndViewport` is a pretty simple function if you know what's going on. And after reading this section, you will. Take a look at Listing 9-2, which shows the code.

Listing 9-2 `CreateDeviceAndViewport`

```
BOOL CreateDeviceAndViewport(HWND hWnd)
{
RECT rect;

// Get the curren dimensions of the window,
// and make sure they are valid
GetClientRect(hWnd, &rect);

if(!rect.right  || !rect.bottom)
 return FALSE;

// Create the D3D Retained Mode Device
if(pD3DRetainedModeAPI->CreateDeviceFromClipper(pDDClipperAPI, NULL,
   rect.right, rect.bottom, &pD3DRMDeviceAPI)
   != D3DRM_OK)
 return FALSE;

// Finally, Create the viewport
if(pD3DRetainedModeAPI->CreateViewport(pD3DRMDeviceAPI,pD3DCameraAPI,
 0,0, pD3DRMDeviceAPI->GetWidth(), pD3DRMDeviceAPI->GetHeight(),
 &pD3DViewportAPI) != D3DRM_OK)
 return FALSE;

// Set background depth to an arbitrarily large value
pD3DViewportAPI->SetBack(5000.0f);

return TRUE;
}
```

By now you should recognize what the first few lines are doing: They're putting the screen coordinates of the application window into a rectangle and making sure the window is big enough to draw into. After that, things start looking a little more foreign.

Creating the Device

To create the Direct3D device (which, as you'll recall, is Direct3D's rendering destination) you have your choice of several methods. They all use an already initialized Direct3D object's internal variables to create and set up the device.

Probably the most common way to create a Direct3D device is from a DirectDraw clipper you've already initialized. That way, Direct3D is automatically connected to DirectDraw and the rendering destination, and everything is set up for you. You'll probably use this method about 90 percent of the time. To create a Direct3D device from a DirectDraw clipper, use the `IDirect3DRM` interface `CreateDeviceFromClipper` (we'll discuss this function in a moment).

You can also create a device from a DirectDraw surface, useful if you want to do any DirectDraw stuff onscreen. For this method, use the `IDirect3DRM` interface `CreateDeviceFromSurface`. This method is basically for more advanced programming, because it's more complex than creating the device from a clipper and `CreateDeviceFromClipper` works just fine in most cases. However, we *will* use it in Chapter 15, so you'll get to try this method out too.

There's one more technique you can use to create the device. If you're using Direct3D *Immediate Mode* in your program, you can create a device from your Direct3D (Immediate Mode) object. Since most people use Retained Mode all the time, not many people will want to know about this, so we'll move on.

Anyway, back to the example. We were just about to create the device for our program. We'll do that using `CreateDeviceFromClipper`, passing it the DirectDraw clipper we just built and initialized:

```
if(pD3DRetainedModeAPI->CreateDeviceFromClipper(pDDClipperAPI, NULL,
    rect.right, rect.bottom, &pD3DRMDeviceAPI)
    != D3DRM_OK)
 return FALSE;
```

`CreateDeviceFromClipper` takes five parameters. The following list explains what they are and how we'll use them in the example:

1. *lpDDClipper*—This is the address of the DirectDraw clipper for initializing the new device. In our example, we'll use a pointer to the clipper we just created and initialized.

2. *lpGUID*—The ID of the hardware device to use. Use NULL and Direct3D will always look for the default display hardware.

3. *width*—The width of the device. You can, if you want, have Direct3D draw on just a portion of your window, but usually you'll want it to use the whole thing.

4. *height*—The height of the device.

5. *lplpD3DRMDevice*—A pointer that will be filled with the device if `CreateDeviceFromClipper` succeeds.

Looking at the list above, you should be able to figure out what's going on in the example in the call to `CreateDeviceFromClipper`. Basically, we're creating a device that takes up the entire window and putting it into the pointer variable *pD3DRMDeviceAPI*.

After creating the device, we need to create the viewport, really the last remaining Direct3D object not visible in the scene. To do that, we need to call `CreateViewport`, an interface of `IDirect3DRM`.

 ## IDirect3DRM::CreateViewport

HRESULT CreateViewport(LPDIRECT3DRMDEVICE *lpdev*,
LPDIRECT3DFRAME *lpCamera*, DWORD *dwXPos,* DWORD *dwYPos,* DWORD
dwWidth, DWORD *dwHeight,* LPDIRECT3DRMVIEWPORT*
lplpD3DRMViewport)

`CreateViewport` takes seven parameters:

1. *lpdev*—A pointer to the device onto which this viewport will render. In our example, we'll use the device just created.

2. *lpCamera*—A frame describing the position and direction of the camera. The *real* camera (the one maintained in the viewport) is moved by moving the camera frame. We'll talk more about this when we build the 3D scene.

3. *dwXPos*—The x position of the viewport on the device. As mentioned earlier, you can have multiple viewports on the same device. You might want to put several viewports on the screen in several different places, so they won't always have their upper-left corner at (0,0) and lower-right corner at the bottom right of the device.

4. *dwYPos*—The y position of the upper-left corner of the viewport.

5. *dwWidth*—The width of the viewport.

6. *dwHeight*—The height of the viewport.

7. *lplpD3DRMViewport*—A pointer to the memory to fill with the new `IDirect3DRMViewport`.

As you can see from the example code, we're creating a viewport taking up the entire device (and thus our entire window), using the camera frame created a while back to locate the camera and putting the new viewport in the pointer *pD3DViewportAPI*.

 ## Note

The last item of business in CreateDeviceAndViewport is the call to
IDirect3DRMViewport::SetBack. This function sets the back clipping plane of the viewport: pD3DViewportAPI->SetBack(5000.0f);

The *back clipping plane* of the viewport is the distance away from the camera at which Direct3D stops drawing objects (and by the way, this distance is in arbitrary units you detemine). This means that up to the distance given to `SetBack`, Direct3D will draw everything in sight. After reaching the back clipping plane, however, it won't draw anything. The back clipping plane feature exists so if you have a very large, complex world, Direct3D won't have to draw the whole thing each time it updates the device. For the most part, though, you won't really need it, so set the back clipping plane to some ridiculously large value your objects won't ever reach (like 5,000).

Building the Scene

The function we use to build the scene (imaginatively named `BuildScene`) is located in the file `Scene.cpp`. Since all our Direct3D objects were declared in a different file (`Arch.cpp`), they are all declared again as external variables (externs) in `Scene.cpp` so we can also use them in this file.

Listing 9-3 shows the code for `BuildScene`. Just look it over for now, and we'll dissect it piece by piece in a moment:

Listing 9-3 `BuildScene`

```
BOOL BuildScene(void)
 {
 LPDIRECT3DRMMESHBUILDER pMeshBuilder = NULL; // Mesh builder interface
 LPDIRECT3DRMFRAME pArchFrame = NULL;  // Frame to contain arch

 // Setup rendering options first
 if(!SetRenderingOptions())
  return FALSE;

 // Create the mesh builder
 if(FAILED(pD3DRetainedModeAPI->CreateMeshBuilder(&pMeshBuilder)))
  return FALSE;

 // Load the faces from the vertex array
 pMeshBuilder->AddFaces(23, archVertices, 0, NULL,
  (unsigned long *)faces, NULL);

 // Create a frame
 if(FAILED(pD3DRetainedModeAPI->CreateFrame(pD3DSceneAPI, &pArchFrame)))
  return FALSE;

 // Add the mesh to the frame
 if(FAILED(pArchFrame->AddVisual(pMeshBuilder)))
  return FALSE;

 // Set the position of the frame within the scene
 if(FAILED(pD3DCameraAPI->SetPosition(pD3DSceneAPI, 0.0f, 0.0f, -7.0f)))
  return FALSE;

 // Set orientation
 if(FAILED(pD3DCameraAPI->SetOrientation(pD3DSceneAPI, 0.0f, 0.0f, 1.0f,
```

continued on next page

continued from previous page
```
     0.0f, 1.0f, 0.0f)))
     return FALSE;

  // Release interfaces
  pArchFrame->Release();
  pMeshBuilder->Release();

  return TRUE;
}
```

The scene we're building here is a wireframe arch against a black background. It's not too complex, but it'll get us ready for the next few examples and the 3D game in the last chapter.

The first statement that does something is the call to `SetRenderingOptions`, which we'll discuss after we get done with `BuildScene`. There's nothing in there you need to know about before we can go on, so for now we'll concentrate on building the 3D scene.

 ## Note

You may have noticed the `FAILED` macro in the above code. We'll start using it at times instead of the `!= D3DRM_OK` so it's a little easier to read the code.

Building the Arch Model

First of all, there's a Direct3D object we haven't discussed yet that we need to get out of the way. It's called a *mesh builder* (`IDirect3DRMMeshBuilder`), and it's used to build 3D models.

A *mesh* is a set of polygons that form a model. There are two objects you can use to create and manipulate meshes: mesh builders and plain old meshes (`IDirect3DRMMesh`). A mesh builder is a wrap around a mesh object enabling you to build meshes quicker and more easily. It's a bit slower, but you won't notice the difference as long as you're not doing anything fancy like morphing your meshes.

In our example, we'll use a mesh builder called *pMeshBuilder* to build our arch. After declaring that variable, we also declare a frame called *pArchFrame* to position the arch in our 3D world. To move the mesh, we'll put the arch model into the frame and position the frame (and thus the arch) wherever we want the arch to go.

In the next line of code, we call `IDirect3DRM::CreateMeshBuilder` to create the mesh builder object. Nothing too interesting here, so let's move on.

The next statement calls `IDirect3DRMMeshBuilder::AddFaces`. This is where our model is actually being built, so let's take some time to examine this function call more closely.

Meshes are usually built by supplying the `AddFaces` function with an array of 3D points telling the mesh builder where all the vertices in the object are. You describe the vertices using arbitrary units, but make sure you're consistent throughout your entire program as to their size.

In our program, the array holding the vertices in the arch is at the beginning of `Scene.cpp`, in the array *archVertices*. It's an array of **D3DVECTORS**, a simple type of Direct3D structure holding vertex information. A **D3DVECTOR** is a set of three floating-point numbers, each of which is the x, y, or z coordinate of the vertex (as usual, x is the first coordinate in the structure, y the second, and z the third).

Anyway, in our example, the array definition looks like this (Listing 9-4):

Listing 9-4 The array of vertices

```
D3DVECTOR archVertices[] = { -1.5f, -1.0f, 1.0f, // 0
    -1.5f, 1.0f,  1.0f,  // 1
    -1.5f, 1.0f, -1.0f,  // 2
    -1.5f, -1.0f, -1.0f, // 3
    1.5f, 1.0f, 1.0f,  // 4
    1.5f, 1.0f, -1.0f,  // 5
    1.5f, -1.0f, -1.0f,  // 6
    1.5f, -1.0f, 1.0f,  // 10
    -1.0f, -1.0f, -1.0f, // 11
    -1.0f, -1.0f, 1.0f,  // 12
    1.0f, -1.0f, 1.0f,  // 13
    1.0f, -1.0f, -1.0f,  // 14
    -1.0f, 1.0f, -1.0f,  // 15
    1.0f, 1.0f, -1.0f,  // 16
    -1.0f, 1.0f,  1.0f,  // 17
    1.0f, 1.0f, 1.0f,  // 18
    -1.0f, 0.75f, -1.0f, // 19
    1.0f, 0.75f, -1.0f,  // 20
    1.0f, 0.75f, 1.0f,  // 21
    -1.0f, 0.75f, 1.0f  // 22
    };
```

Since we're creating an array of simple structures with only three floating-point members per structure, it's basically the same thing (in memory, at least) as an array of floats. Thus, we can simply put three floats (one for x, y, and z) in the array for each vertex. (Actually, we could probably make the array one of floating-point numbers, but that might worry the compiler a bit too much.) When the mesh builder reads the array, it will look for the vertices' coordinates in x, y, z order, so make sure you don't get confused about that. It's a good idea to number your vertices with comments (as done above) to make sure you don't mix them up. It's also a good idea because you'll need their array indexes later in the model-building process (that's the array indexes of the **D3DVECTOR**s in the array, though, not the individual floating-point numbers—don't mix them up).

You'll need the vertices' array indexes in the array, since you also have to tell the mesh builder which vertices belong to which polygons (remember, polygons are also called faces), and you need some way to identify each individual vertex from the array.

To tell **AddFaces** which vertices make up each polygon in the mesh, you need to supply **AddFaces** with yet *another* array, this one grouping vertices from the first array into the faces of the polygon.

In our code, the polygon data array (the one grouping vertices into polygons) looks like this (Listing 9-5):

Listing 9-5 The face data for the arch model

```
int faces[] = { 4, 0,  1,  2,  3,  // Far left
  4, 1,  4,  5,  2,  // Top
  4, 6,  5,  4,  7,  // Far right
  4, 3,  8,  9,  0,  // Left bottom
  4, 7,  10, 11, 6,  // right bottom
  4, 3,  2,  12, 8,  // Left front
  4, 13, 5,  6,  11, // Right front
  4, 9,  14, 1,  0,  // Left back
  4, 10, 7,  4,  15, // Right back
  4, 16, 12, 13, 17, // Front top
  4, 14, 19, 18, 15, // Back top
  4, 16, 17, 18, 19, // Top inside
  4, 8,  16, 19, 9,  // Inside left
  4, 10, 18, 17, 11, // Inside right
  0 }; // Terminator
```

As you can see, it's simply an array of integers, since the array is composed solely of indexes into the first array. The face data array goes like this: The first integer in the data for a face tells **AddFaces** how many vertices are in that face. Let's say the first integer is 4, as in our code. The next *four* integers should be indexes into the array of vertices, and those four vertices define the first face of the object. In our example, the next four integers are 0, 1, 2, and 3, telling **AddFace** that the vertices described in the first, second, third, and fourth array entries of the vertex array make up the first face (from that point, **AddFaces** essentially connects the 3D dots). Since we told **AddFaces** the face contained four vertices and we indeed gave it four, it would then know to move on to the next face. In our example, all the faces are rectangular (not by requirement—simply because that's the way our model is shaped), so all our faces have four vertices. After you describe the last face, end the array with a zero to indicate to **AddFaces** there aren't any more faces in the object.

IDirect3DRMMeshBuilder::AddFaces

```
HRESULT AddFaces( DWORD dwVertexCount, D3DVECTOR*
lpD3DVertices, DWORD normalCount, D3DVECTOR* lpNormals,
DWORD* lpFaceData, LPDIRECT3DRMFACEARRAY*
lplpD3DRMFaceArray)
```

Let's take a closer look at **IDirect3DRMMeshBuilder::AddFaces**. It takes six parameters, described below:

1. *dwVertexCount*—The number of vertices in the object (yet another reason to number your vertices).

2. *lpD3DVertices*—The array of D3DVECTORs describing each of the vertices in the object.

3. *normalCount*—The number of normals in the object (don't worry about this or the next one just yet).

4. *lpNormals*—The array of normals in the object.

5. *lpFaceData*—The array of integers telling **AddFaces** which vertices make up which face.

6. *lplpD3DRMFaceArray*—A pointer to a pointer that points to an **IDirect3DRMFaceArray** object. These objects organize faces if you want to manipulate them after the object is built. If you don't pass **NULL** for this parameter, **AddFaces** fills this memory with the face data it got from the arrays.

In our example, we called **AddFaces** with this code:

```
pMeshBuilder->AddFaces(23, archVertices, 0, NULL, (unsigned long *)faces,
NULL);
```

Here's the translation: We tell **AddFaces** that there are 23 vertices in our object and it should find them in the *archVertices* array. We don't have any normals yet (we'll learn what those are in Example 9-3), so we'll pass **NULL** for the normals array. We also don't want to use an **IDirect3DRMFaceArray** object, so we'll pass **AddFaces NULL** for the last parameter.

That's all we do to actually *build* the model. Now we have to position it and set up the rest of our scene.

Positioning the Arch

The next statement in **BuildScene** creates *pArchFrame*, a child frame of the scene frame. This is the frame into which we'll put the arch model. We'll do this using the **IDirect3DRMFrame** interface **AddVisual**, which adds a visual object (a mesh or a texture) to a frame. If the frame is visible, so are any objects inside of it.

All we do to add the arch model to the scene now is call **AddVisual** from our new frame using the arch mesh builder as its parameter and position the camera so the model is in view.

The call to **AddVisual** is really simple, so simple that there's no reason to repeat it. Refer back to Listing 9-3 if you want another look.

Right now, every single frame in our scene (basically just the camera frame and the arch frame) remains at (0,0,0) since we haven't moved them. We can't see the arch with the camera if they're right on top of each other, so we have to move one of them. Since it doesn't matter which, we'll just move the camera farther back on the z axis, to about (0,0,-7). To do this, we call **IDirect3DRMFrame::SetPosition**:

```
if(FAILED(pD3DCameraAPI->SetPosition(pD3DSceneAPI, 0.0f, 0.0f, -7.0f)))
```

This is simple enough, especially considering we discussed **SetPosition** when going over **SetupDirect3DRetainedMode**. Let's move on.

The last *new* function in **BuildScene** is **SetOrientation**. This function (which is an interface of **IDirect3DRMFrame**) rotates the frame from which it's called.

SetOrientation takes (besides a reference frame) two vectors as parameters. These vectors are passed to it as two 3D points.

The second 3D point passed to SetOrientation is the frame's new z axis, or *direction vector*. The direction vector runs through the frame from front to back, so it's possible to turn the frame by rotating the vector. The direction vector's main job is telling the frame which direction it should face, and, along with the up vector (discussed below), making it possible to rotate the frame to any angle. The direction vector for a new frame is initially set to (0,0,1), right in front of the origin on the z axis. To make the frame face the other way, set the direction vector to (0,0,-1)—facing in the negative z direction. It's that simple.

The second point is used as the frame's new y axis, or *up vector*. The up vector skewers the frame through the top and bottom, as in Figure 9-8 (the frame is represented as a box, which it really isn't). The 3D point defining the up vector when a new frame is created is automatically set to (0,1,0), which is straight up since the frame itself is at (0,0,0). If you move the up vector to (0,-1,0), it will be under the frame and the frame will be flipped upside-down. Also, the frame moves with the up vector.

In BuildScene, we're trying to position the camera so it looks directly at the arch model. It's now at (0,0,-7) and we want it to look at the arch, whose frame is still at (0,0,0). Thus, we'll leave its up vector at (0,0,1), and we want it to look straight ahead to (0,1,0). (If you haven't figured it out yet, these are the frame's automatic values it got when created, so this call isn't necessary. But we're doing it anyway just so we can have this fun little conversation.)

FIGURE 9-8

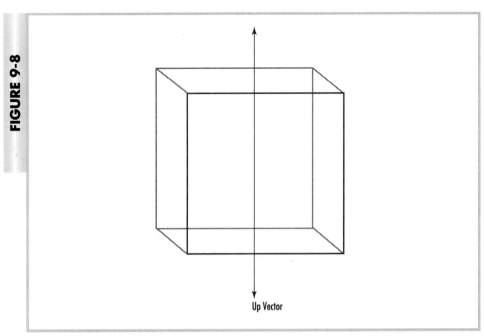

Up Vector

An up vector

Here's the call to `SetOrientation`, which you should be able to decipher by now:

```
if(FAILED(pD3DCameraAPI->SetOrientation(pD3DSceneAPI, 0.0f, 0.0f, 1.0f, 0.0f,
1.0f, 0.0f)))
```

The first set of numbers (0, 0, and 1) is the direction vector, and the second set (0, 1, and 0) is the up vector.

Cleanup

Since the arch is already positioned and we won't move it any more (at least for right now), we can `Release` the arch frame. We also have the mesh completely built, so we can `Release` the mesh builder too.

SetRenderingOptions

The `SetRenderingOptions` function sets up some miscellaneous rendering variables. Listing 9-6 shows the code:

Listing 9-6 `SetRenderingOptions`

```
BOOL SetRenderingOptions(void)
{
// Set Scene background to black
pD3DSceneAPI->SetSceneBackground(D3DRGB(0,0,0));

// Set Drawing mode to wireframe
pD3DRMDeviceAPI->SetQuality(D3DRMRENDER_WIREFRAME);

// Return success
return TRUE;
}
```

The first function, `IDirect3DRMFrame::SetSceneBackground`, simply sets the background color of a scene. It takes a `D3DCOLOR` value, which you can create using the `D3DRGB` macro, similar to the Win32 API macro `RGB`. We want the background to be black, so we'll use `D3DRGB` (0,0,0) as the parameter.

The second call is to `IDirect3DRMDevice::SetQuality`, which sets the level of rendering quality for the device. There are several values you can use for `SetQuality`'s only parameter:

- `D3DRMRENDER_WIREFRAME`—This renders only the lines connecting each object's vertices when the device is rendered. This is the value we'll use for this first example.

- `D3DRMRENDER_UNLITFLAT`—This value renders flat (single-colored) objects without any lighting.

- `D3DRMRENDER_FLAT`—This value renders objects flat, but with lighting.

⚫ `D3DRMRENDER_GOURAUD`—This value renders Gouraud shaded objects. This is currently the highest detail level available

⚫ `D3DRMRENDER_PHONG`—This value renders Phong shaded objects, but isn't supported yet.

There are several rendering options, and the ones listed above are just common combinations of them. You can make up your own combination or use one of the choices above—it's up to you. You'll find a complete list of the flags in your DirectX help file.

Note that each device can have its own rendering quality if you want. This may or may not come in handy, depending on what you're doing. Also, each mesh in a scene can have its own quality. This means you can set the device's rendering quality to Gouraud shading, but still render some objects as wireframe. However, a mesh's rendering quality can only be as high as the device's.

That's all we need to do in this example. Now we'll go back and take a look at the window callback function, because there's a whole bunch of stuff going on there that we haven't seen yet.

WndProc—The Window Callback Function

`WndProc`, contained in `Arch.cpp`, is somewhat complex compared to any callback functions written in previous examples. Let's just take it one message handler at a time, and it won't be too bad.

WM_CREATE

The handler for `WM_CREATE` has just one job—to call `SetupDirect3DRetainedMode` (Listing 9-7):

Listing 9-7 `WM_CREATE` message handler

```
case WM_CREATE:
 // Window creation. If the Direct3D environment cannot be
 // setup, then just stop here and end the program.
 if(!SetupDirect3DRetainedMode(hWnd))
  PostQuitMessage(0);
 break;
```

This is the simplest handler in the function, and you should be able to understand what's going on here by now. Let's move on.

WM_ACTIVATE

`WM_ACTIVATE` is sent when our window gains the input focus after losing it to another window. Since the other window could have messed with the palette while it had focus (Direct3D builds an internal palette that's pretty much invisible to you unless you really want to mess with it), we need to make sure we put back the correct colors.

To do this, we'll create an `IDirect3DRMWinDevice`, which is similar to an `IDirect3DRMDevice` except that it can handle some window messages for a window procedure. It basically handles the `WM_PAINT` and `WM_ACTIVATE` as it does in our example.

Here's the code for our `WM_ACTIVATE` handler (Listing 9-8):

Listing 9-8 The `WM_ACTIVATE` message handler

```
case WM_ACTIVATE:
{
// Handles Activate Message, insures colors are correct.
LPDIRECT3DRMWINDEVICE pWinDev = NULL;

// Stop if the Retained Mode API hasn't been created yet
if(!pD3DRMDeviceAPI)
 break;

// If we get the Windows device, handle the activate message
if(SUCCEEDED(pD3DRMDeviceAPI->QueryInterface(IID_IDirect3DRMWinDevice,
 (void **)&pWinDev)))
 {
 pWinDev->HandleActivate(wParam);
 pWinDev->Release();
 }
}
break;
```

First we make sure the `IDirect3DRMDevice` object created in `SetupDirect3DRetainedMode` is valid, since we'll need it to create the `IDirect3DRMWinDevice` object. If it's not valid, we just bail.

Next, we create a new `IDirect3DRMWinDevice` object. We do this using the COM interface `QueryInterface`, an interface all COM objects must support (it's inherited from `IUnknown`). Its first parameter is the reference identifier of the object you want to create (the prefix `IID_` followed by the object's COM name, `IID_IDirect3DRMWinDevice`), and its second parameter is a pointer to the memory address where `QueryInterface` puts the new object.

In our example, we want to create a new `IDirect3DRMWinDevice` object, so we pass `QueryInterface IID_IDirect3DRMWinDevice` as the first parameter. We're passing *pWinDev* as its second parameter, since that's the pointer to an `IDirect3DRMWinDevice` we declared at the top of the handler. Notice that since you can create any kind of COM object using `QueryInterface`, it takes a *void* pointer as its second parameter, not a specific type of pointer. So when you use `QueryInterface`, you need to cast the second parameter to type (`void**`) no matter what type of object you're creating.

Since we created *pWinDev* by calling `QueryInterface` as an interface of our Direct3D device, it is automatically initialized with our device's properties (basically meaning it's already set up for us to use). So we can just go ahead and use the function we want without worrying about initializing the `IDirect3DRMWinDevice`.

The `IDirect3DRMWinDevice` interface we want to use is called `HandleActivate`, which handles `WM_ACTIVATE` window messages. It takes the `wParam` of the message as its only parameter. When you call it, it fixes the palette so Direct3D can draw with the proper colors again.

Even though we created the IDirect3DRMWinDevice object using QueryInterface, we still need to Release it. Just call Release in the normal fashion and you'll be fine.

WM_PAINT

In WM_PAINT, all we do is paint the window and render the scene. Since you just learned how to use an IDirect3DRMWinDevice to handle WM_ACTIVATE, handling WM_PAINT with one should be a piece of cake.

Listing 9-9 shows the code for our WM_PAINT handler:

Listing 9-9 The WM_PAINT handler

```
case WM_PAINT:
{
LPDIRECT3DRMWINDEVICE pWinDev = NULL;
PAINTSTRUCT ps;

// Do not process if the device doesn't exist, or the window is
// minimized
if(!pD3DRMDeviceAPI || IsIconic(hWnd))
 return DefWindowProc(hWnd, message, wParam, lParam);

// Handle the paint message, should be done before doing any repainting
BeginPaint(hWnd, &ps);
if(SUCCEEDED(pD3DRMDeviceAPI->QueryInterface(IID_IDirect3DRMWinDevice,
 (void **)&pWinDev)))
 {
 pWinDev->HandlePaint(ps.hdc);
 pWinDev->Release();
 }


// Render the scene
pD3DViewportAPI->Clear();   // Clear the viewport
pD3DViewportAPI->Render(pD3DSceneAPI); // Render the scene
pD3DRMDeviceAPI->Update();   // Update the device (window)

EndPaint(hWnd, &ps);
}
break;
```

First, we check that the Direct3D device is still valid and the application isn't minimized. If the application is an icon, we'll just let the default callback function handle the WM_PAINT message (since we don't have anything special we need to paint).

Next, we create a window DC to use for window painting and create an IDirect3DRMWinDevice using QueryInterface as before. Then, we use the IDirect3DRMWinDevice's HandlePaint interface to repaint the window. HandlePaint's job is to repaint anything that needs it. You only have to give it one parameter: a window DC that's valid for the application window. It'll do the rest.

After releasing the `IDirect3DRMWinDevice` object, we call `IDirect3DRMViewport::Clear`. This function clears the viewport (and because of the way we initialized Direct3D, end ups clearing our entire window) and fills it with the current background color.

Next, we want to render the scene. Since the scene was already built in `BuildScene`, we just have to render it to the viewport. To do this, we call `IDirect3DRMDevice::Render`, whose only parameter is a pointer to the scene to render (actually, you pass it a frame, and it renders that frame and all its child frames—in this case we pass it our scene frame). It will then render the scene to the viewport so that as soon as the device is updated, the scene will be visible.

In order to update the device (which is the window in this case), we call `IDirect3DRMDevice::Update`. Update doesn't take any parameters and simply copies the image rendered to it onto the display.

WM_SIZE

When we get a `WM_SIZE` message, we need to re-initialize the device and viewport so they render the right size image for the window. The handler contains a lot of the same code we saw in `CreateDeviceAndViewport` since we're practically doing the same thing.

Listing 9-10 shows the code for the `WM_SIZE` handler:

Listing 9-10 The **WM_SIZE** handler

```
case WM_SIZE:
 {
 // Get current width and height of the window
 int width = LOWORD(lParam);
 int height = HIWORD(lParam);

 // Newly created window may not have any dimensions
 if (!width || !height || IsIconic(hWnd))
  break;

 // Get current width and heigh of device and viewport
        int vWidth = pD3DViewportAPI->GetWidth();
 int vHeight = pD3DViewportAPI->GetHeight();
 int dWidth = pD3DRMDeviceAPI->GetWidth();
 int dHeight = pD3DRMDeviceAPI->GetHeight();

 // If the window hasn't changed size, nothing to do
 // (window and viewport are same size, probably because
 // the window was minimized and has been restored)
 if (vWidth == width && vHeight == height)
  break;

 // If the window is smaller, reuse the same device, but a
 // new viewport
 if (width <= dWidth && height <= dHeight)
  {
```

continued on next page

continued from previous page

```
             // Release the viewport and get a new one
             pD3DViewportAPI->Release();
             pD3DRetainedModeAPI->CreateViewport(pD3DRMDeviceAPI,
               pD3DCameraAPI,
                             0, 0, width, height,
                             &pD3DViewportAPI);

             // Set depth of viewport to arbitrary large value
                       pD3DViewportAPI->SetBack(D3DVAL(5000.0));
           }
         else
           {
           // Window is larger, we need new device and viewport
           pD3DViewportAPI->Release(); // Release the
                 // current viewport
           pD3DRMDeviceAPI->Release(); // and device

           if(!CreateDeviceAndViewport(hWnd)) // Create a new
                     // viewport and
                     // device
             {
             MessageBox(hWnd,
             "Cannot create new viewport and device",
              NULL,MB_OK | MB_ICONSTOP);
              PostQuitMessage(0);
             }
           else
             SetRenderingOptions(); // Setup new device
                       }
         }
         break;
```

After checking that the window is big enough to be drawn into and not minimized, we get the current dimensions of the viewport and store them in some temporary variables.

Next we check that the window's size has indeed changed. If it hasn't, our current device and viewport will work fine as is, and we can exit from the handler.

If the window is now smaller than it was before, we can still use the old device, since it still covers the whole visible area of the window (some of it just won't be visible). All we do is **Release** the viewport and recreate it with the same dimensions as the window (so that part of the image isn't cut off by the smaller window). Since we learned how to create the device in **CreateDeviceAndViewport** (Listing 9-2), we won't go over it again.

If the window is larger now, we need to create a new viewport *and* device. This is because the device will only be as big as the window was before and won't be able to render onto the entire window. All we have to do to initialize everything correctly is **Release** the device and viewport, then recreate them using the new window dimensions. To recreate them, we simply call **CreateDeviceAndViewport** again, which uses the new window dimensions when creating the device and viewport. We also have to reset the rendering options, since they were blown away along with the old device.

WM_KEYDOWN

When the user presses an arrow key, we'll rotate the arch model. This isn't as hard as it sounds and only takes a few lines of code.

Listing 9-11 shows the handler for **WM_KEYDOWN**:

Listing 9-11 The **WM_KEYDOWN** handler code

```
case WM_KEYDOWN:
{
LPDIRECT3DRMFRAMEARRAY pFrameChildren; // Array of frames
LPDIRECT3DRMFRAME      pChildFrame; // The frame we want

// Get array of frames
pD3DSceneAPI->GetChildren(&pFrameChildren);

// Get the particular frame we want (0 - top)
pFrameChildren->GetElement(0, &pChildFrame);

// Rotate based on keystroke
if(wParam == VK_UP)
 pChildFrame->AddRotation(D3DRMCOMBINE_AFTER, 1.0f, 0.0f, 0.0f,
  0.2f);

if(wParam == VK_DOWN)
 pChildFrame->AddRotation(D3DRMCOMBINE_AFTER, 1.0f, 0.0f, 0.0f, -
  0.2f);

if(wParam == VK_LEFT)
 pChildFrame->AddRotation(D3DRMCOMBINE_AFTER, 0.0f, 1.0f, 0.0f,
  0.2f);

if(wParam == VK_RIGHT)
 pChildFrame->AddRotation(D3DRMCOMBINE_AFTER, 0.0f, 1.0f, 0.0f, -
0.2f);

// Release frame array object and invalidate window for repaint
pFrameChildren->Release();
InvalidateRect(hWnd,NULL,FALSE);
}
break;
```

To rotate the arch model, we'll have to rotate the frame the model is in. But before we can do that, we need to get a pointer to the frame the arch is in. The most common way to do this is by working our way down the frame hierarchy from the scene frame, until we reach the arch frame.

To work our way down the frame hierarchy and find the frame holding the arch, we first get all the child frames of the scene frame and put them into a frame array. A frame array is just a convenient way to hold a bunch of frames so we can find a certain one. To fill a frame array with all the child frames of our scene frame, we first have to declare an **IDirect3DRMFrameArray** object at the top of the handler. Then we use the

`IDirect3DRMFrame::GetChildren` interface to fill the frame array with all the scene frame's children:

```
pD3DSceneAPI->GetChildren(&pFrameChildren);
```

The `GetChildren` interface only takes one parameter, a pointer to an `IDirect3DRMFrame` object. It then proceeds to fill the array with all the child frames of the frame from which it's called.

After we have the array filled with all the child frames of the scene frame, we need to find the frame we want—that is, the frame containing the arch mesh. To retrieve the arch frame, we'll use the `IDirect3DRMFrameArray` interface `GetElement`, which gets you a specific frame from the array.

`GetElement` takes two parameters. The first is the index of the frame you want from the array, and the second is a pointer to memory space to put the frame into. The indexes of the array elements (frames) are the same as the order in which the frames were created.

In our example, we want the first frame in the scene (the one holding the arch), so we pass zero as the first parameter to `GetElement`. (The array uses a zero-based index.) We store the frame in the *pChildFrame* pointer:

```
pFrameChildren->GetElement(0, &pChildFrame);
```

Now that we have a pointer to the frame the arch model is in, we can manipulate it however we want. We need to look at the key the user pressed and rotate the frame accordingly.

To determine which key has been pressed, we'll use a few *if* statements that look at the `wParam` of the `WM_KEYDOWN` message for the keycode. All the *if* statements are pretty much the same, so we'll only go over one of them—the one that handles an *Up* arrow key (*wParam* = `VK_UP`):

```
if(wParam == VK_UP)
  pChildFrame->AddRotation(D3DRMCOMBINE_AFTER, 1.0f, 0.0f, 0.0f, 0.2f);
```

When the user presses the *Up* arrow key, we want to rotate the top of the model towards the user and the bottom away from him or her. To rotate the arch frame (pointed to by *pChildFrame*), we'll use the `IDirect3DRMFrame` interface called `AddRotation`. `AddRotation` is a complex function, and we'll need to take a little time to discuss it.

There is something in Direct3D we haven't discussed yet called a *clock tick*. A clock tick is a unit of time—that you specify the length of—after which Direct3D updates the scene and renders to the device. If you want to, you can specify that a frame should do something, such as rotate or translate, every time a clock tick occurs. This makes the frame perform that action continuously, or at least until you stop it.

If you want to tell a frame to rotate every clock tick, use the function `IDirect3DRMFrame::SetRotation`, then call `IDirect3DRM::Tick` whenever you want a clock tick to occur (you'd probably set a timer to call `IDirect3DRM::Tick`). However, we *don't* want the frame to rotate every clock tick (in fact, we aren't even using clock ticks); we want it to rotate when the user presses an arrow key, since we'd otherwise waste a lot of CPU time rendering the same image over and over again. To do this, we have to **use** `IDirect3DRMFrame::AddRotation`, which only rotates the frame *once*.

Frame motion is actually described internally to Direct3D by *matrices*. Matrices are a complex and tricky topic if you haven't recently taken a college algebra course, and needless to say, we don't have time to thoroughly discuss them here. As long as you don't want to do anything too fancy with frame motion, you don't need to bother with them. And if you do, the DirectX help file offers a brief, but helpful, introduction to matrices.

The first parameter to **AddRotation** specifies how to rotate the frame. Actually, it specifies how to combine this new rotation with any action the frame did before (probably from a call to a function setting the frame in motion every clock tick, such as **SetRotation**). And, as just mentioned, this means it tells Direct3D how to combine the matrix describing the frame's previous motion with the matrix describing the motion you want to give it.

Direct3D combines the two matrices by multiplying them together, and matrix multiplication is not commutative (meaning it *does* matter which matrix comes first in the multiplication). That's the reason we have three different values for **AddRotation**'s first parameter instead of just two. Using **D3DRMCOMBINE_REPLACE** replaces the frame's old motion with the new motion you're specifying in the rest of **AddRotation**'s parameters. **D3DRMCOMBINE_BEFORE** combines the two motion matrices with multiplication, but uses the new motion matrix (the one you're describing by this call to **AddRotation**) first in the matrix multiplication. **D3DRMCOMBINE_AFTER** is the same as **D3DRMCOMBINE_BEFORE**, except it uses the new motion matrix as the second matrix in the multiplication.

If you don't have time to thoroughly learn matrices (which many people probably don't) but you still want to combine matrices using **D3DRMCOMBINE_AFTER** or **D3DRMCOMBINE_BEFORE**, it's probably quickest to try both out and see which gets you the results you want.

Okay, **AddRotation**'s first parameter is out of the way. The second, third, and fourth parameters let you specify which axis you want to rotate around (in x, y, z order as usual). Simply use 1 for the axis you want to rotate around and 0 for the other two. For example, if you want to rotate around the y axis, simply use 0 for the second parameter (the x axis), 1 for the third parameter (the y axis), and another 0 for the fourth parameter (the z axis).

The fifth and final parameter for **AddRotation** is the angle at which you want to rotate the frame around the axis, in *radians*. In case you've forgotten—or have never even heard of radians—there are about 6.28 radians in the circumference of a circle (the actual number of radians is 2π). In our example, we'll rotate the arch 0.2 radians, which is about the same as 11 degrees. Generally, you want to keep the angle of rotation pretty small. Otherwise, it'll look choppy when the scene is rendered because it's moved so much since the last frame.

After we move the arch, we need to **Release** the frame array holding the frames in the scene. Otherwise, we will needlessly eat up memory (and this handler will be used every time the user moves the arch, so we'd drain a *lot* of memory over the course of the program).

Finally, we need to make sure the viewport gets updated so the user can see the changes made to the scene. To do this, we simply call the Win32 API function **InvalidateRect**, which sends a **WM_PAINT** message to our window. Since the **WM_PAINT** handler updates the viewport, we'll let it do all the rendering for us.

WM_DESTROY

When our window is closed, we need to clean up all our Direct3D objects and tell our application to close via the standard **PostQuitMessage** function (Listing 9-12):

Listing 9-12 The **WM_DESTROY** handler

```
case WM_DESTROY:
 // The application is terminating. Release the D3DRM interfaces.
 ShutdownDirect3DRetainedMode(hWnd);
 PostQuitMessage(0);
 break;
```

ShutdownDirect3DRetainedMode is a simple little function that **Releases** all our Direct3D objects in the opposite order from which they were created, so there aren't any objects dependent on an object already **Released**. Listing 9-13 shows the code:

Listing 9-13 **ShutdownDirect3DRetainedMode**: The cleanup function

```
void ShutdownDirect3DRetainedMode(HWND hWnd)
{
bD3DReady = FALSE;

// If the interface pointer is not NULL, then release it.
if(!pD3DViewportAPI)
 pD3DViewportAPI->Release();

if(!pD3DRMDeviceAPI)
 pD3DRMDeviceAPI->Release();

if(!pDDClipperAPI)
 pDDClipperAPI->Release();

if(!pD3DCameraAPI)
 pD3DCameraAPI->Release();

if(!pD3DSceneAPI)
 pD3DSceneAPI->Release();

if(!pD3DRetainedModeAPI)
 pD3DRetainedModeAPI->Release();
}
```

There's not much to this function that we haven't gone over in earlier chapters. As mentioned earlier, make sure you don't **Release** an object that another one is using, because that'll definitely cause problems.

Compiling Example 9-1

To compile Example 9-1, be sure that you include **d3drmwin.h**, the Direct3D Retained Mode header file, in your source files and that your compiler knows where it is. You'll also need to include **d3drm.lib**, the library containing Direct3D Retained Mode, in your project.

There's one common problem a lot of Visual C++ users encounter that can be quite confusing at first. If you're using a version of VC++ including an older version of DirectX than the one you're programming with, you'll have two copies of the DirectX headers and libraries on your system—one copy from VC++'s installation and one from your DirectX installation. VC++ will always look at the files from the VC++ installation first, so you need to delete the files from VC++'s **include** and **lib** directories before you can compile anything successfully.

That's it for Example 9-1. Let's move on to Example 9-2, where we'll move to flat polygon rendering.

Example 9-2: Filled Polygons

Example 9-2 is pretty much the same thing as Example 9-1 except that we're rendering the arch as filled polygons instead of as a wireframe mesh. Figure 9-9 shows a screenshot.

You'll notice this model is hard to make out since everything is the same shade of green. This is because we haven't lit the model yet, which we'll do in Example 9-3).

The work we must do to get from a wireframe model to a flat-rendered model is minimal. Basically, all we need to do is assign the model a color and tell Direct3D to render using flat-shaded polygons. Only two functions have really changed: **SetRenderingOptions** and **BuildScene**.

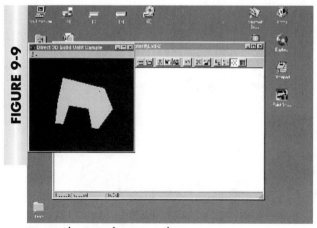

FIGURE 9-9

Example 9-2 doing its thing

SetRenderingOptions

There's only one thing different in `SetRenderingOptions`, but it's the main change in our program. Take a look (Listing 9-13):

Listing 9-13 `SetRenderingOptions`

```
BOOL SetRenderingOptions(void)
{
// Set Scene background to black
pD3DSceneAPI->SetSceneBackground(D3DRGB(0,0,0));

// Set Drawing mode to unlit and flat
pD3DRMDeviceAPI->SetQuality(D3DRMRENDER_UNLITFLAT);

// Return success
return TRUE;
}
```

The only difference is this time, instead of setting the rendering quality to `D3DRMRENDER_WIREFRAME`, which renders everything as an unlit wireframe model, we'll set the rendering quality to `D3DRMRENDER_UNLITFLAT`. Using `D3DRMRENDER_UNLITFLAT` renders everything as an unlit flat-shaded model.

That's all we had to do to change rendering from wireframe to filled polygons. Now we just have to tell Direct3D what color our model will be, which we'll do in `BuildScene`.

BuildScene

`BuildScene` hasn't changed much since the last example. It's only had one function call added. Listing 9-14 shows the code:

Listing 9-14 `BuildScene`

```
BOOL BuildScene(void)
{
LPDIRECT3DRMMESHBUILDER pMeshBuilder = NULL; // Mesh builder interface
LPDIRECT3DRMFRAME pArchFrame = NULL;  // Frame to contain arch

// Setup rendering options first
if(!SetRenderingOptions())
 return FALSE;

// Create the mesh builder
if(FAILED(pD3DRetainedModeAPI->CreateMeshBuilder(&pMeshBuilder)))
 return FALSE;

// Add the faces
pMeshBuilder->AddFaces(23, archVertices, 0, NULL,
 (unsigned long *)faces, NULL);
```

```
// Set all faces to green
pMeshBuilder->SetColor(D3DRGB(0, 1, 0 ));

// Create a frame
if(FAILED(pD3DRetainedModeAPI->CreateFrame(pD3DSceneAPI, &pArchFrame)))
 return FALSE;

// Add the mesh to the frame
if(FAILED(pArchFrame->AddVisual(pMeshBuilder)))
 return FALSE;

// Set the position of the frame within the scene
if(FAILED(pD3DCameraAPI->SetPosition(pD3DSceneAPI, 0.0f, 0.0f, -7.0f)))
 return FALSE;

// Set orientation
if(FAILED(pD3DCameraAPI->SetOrientation(pD3DSceneAPI, 0.0f, 0.0f, 1.0f,
 0.0f, 1.0f, 0.0f)))
 return FALSE;

// Release interfaces
pArchFrame->Release();
pMeshBuilder->Release();

return TRUE;
}
```

The new function call is to `IDirect3DRMMeshBuilder:SetColor`, which sets the color of all the faces of the mesh being built to the specified color. The argument is a `D3DCOLOR` value, which we supply via the `D3DRGB` macro. We'll set the color to solid green.

That's it for Example 9-2. It was a simple step forward from Example 9-1, but Example 9-3 gets a bit more complex (at least in terms of the number of 3D concepts to understand), so make sure you completely understand what's happening in this example before moving to the next.

Example 9-3: Lighting

Example 9-3 contains the biggest changes we'll make to any example in this chapter. We'll add lighting to the scene, enabling us to Gouraud shade the arch model. Adding lighting isn't quite as easy as it might seem, though, so be prepared to learn a lot in this example.

Before looking at any code, there are a few concepts we need to go over.

Normals

In order to light a model, Direct3D needs to calculate the color shade of each vertex in it. This means it goes through the list of vertices and sees how much light shines on each. It then calculates what color each vertex should be, depending on how much light shines on it and the color of the polygon itself (by either setting the model to a solid color or texture mapping).

In order to determine how much light is shining on each vertex, Direct3D needs us to provide it with a list of *vertex normals*. Normals are vectors telling Direct3D which way the object they are normals of is facing. Then Direct3D can just look at the normal to find out which way the vertex faces so it can calculate how much light, if any, is shining on it.

Lights

As you learned earlier, there are two basic lighting modules: RGB and monochromatic (*ramp*). RGB uses color lights and monochromatic uses black and white. We'll use RGB lights since that's the model most supported by 3D hardware (of course, you could always check to see what the user's hardware does and does not support).

There are several types of lights you can use in a scene:

- *Ambient* lights illuminate everything in the scene with the same amount of light.

- *Spotlights,* which we won't use, illuminate a specific circle of light. They point in a certain direction and have a fixed intensity. They look good when pointing at a mesh with a lot of surfaces, but not as good when pointing at a cube or something simple. The reason is that with more vertices, the Gouraud lighting is able to make a rounder spotlight. Otherwise, the results you get with spotlights won't be too different from point or directional lights.

- *Point* lights are just that—points of light. Point lights have a position but no direction, since they are just balls of light. They produce a realistic, though somewhat slow, lighting effect by shading the objects they illuminate.

- *Directional* lights have a direction, but no position. This means they illuminate objects where the light hits the mesh, but they have the same intensity everywhere in the scene. This also means that if the light is underneath a model but pointing down, it will still shine on top of it (since it has no position). Incidentally, directional lights are the fastest lights to render.

- *Parallel point* lights are like directional lights except they also have a position. They achieve just about the same effect as a point light, except they are faster.

In this example we'll use two lights: an ambient light to illuminate the whole scene, and a directional light so we actually see some shading (otherwise, the ambient light would illuminate everything at the same intensity—hence, no shading).

Let's start looking at some actual code from our example.

SetRenderingOptions

In the previous example, `SetRenderingOptions` (the first function call in `BuildScene`) only set the rendering quality and initialized the color of our model. Now, it also has to create the ambient and directional lights and add them to the scene.

Listing 9-15 shows the code for `SetRenderingOptions`:

Listing 9-15 `SetRenderingOptions`

```
BOOL SetRenderingOptions(void)
{
LPDIRECT3DRMLIGHT pAmbient = NULL; // Ambient light
LPDIRECT3DRMLIGHT pDirectional = NULL; // Directional light

// Create a directional light
if(FAILED(pD3DRetainedModeAPI->CreateLightRGB(D3DRMLIGHT_DIRECTIONAL,
  0.4f, 0.4f, 0.4f,
   &pDirectional)))
 return FALSE;

// Add light to main scene
if(FAILED(pD3DSceneAPI->AddLight(pDirectional)))
 return FALSE;

// Create the ambient light source
if(FAILED(pD3DRetainedModeAPI->CreateLightRGB(D3DRMLIGHT_AMBIENT, 0.6f,
  0.6f, 0.6f,
   &pAmbient)))
 return FALSE;

// Add the ambient light to the scene
if(FAILED(pD3DSceneAPI->AddLight(pAmbient)))
 return FALSE;

// Set Scene background to black
pD3DSceneAPI->SetSceneBackground(D3DRGB(0,0,0));

// Set shading mode to gouraud, turn on the lights, solid object
pD3DRMDeviceAPI->SetQuality(D3DRMLIGHT_ON | D3DRMFILL_SOLID
 |D3DRMSHADE_GOURAUD);

// Return success
return TRUE;
}
```

First, we declare two pointers to `IDirect3DRMLight` objects (which obviously represent lights). *pAmbient* is our ambient light source and *pDirectional* is the directional light that provides the shading.

Okay, let's create the directional light. To do this, we'll use the `IDirect3DRM::CreateLightRGB` function. There are two `CreateLight` functions: `CreateLightRGB` and `CreateLight`. `CreateLightRGB` lets you specify the red, green, and blue components of the light color as separate parameters, while `CreateLight` takes a `D3DCOLOR` parameter as the light color. Obviously, there's not a huge difference between the two—they're both there just for the sake of convenience.

`CreateLightRGB`'s first parameter is a constant describing the type of light to create. There are several different values for this parameter:

- D3DRMLIGHT_AMBIENT, which creates an ambient light.

- D3DRMLIGHT_POINT, which creates point light source.

- D3DRMLIGHT_SPOT, which creates a spotlight.

- D3DRMLIGHT_DIRECTIONAL, which creates a directional light.

- D3DRMLIGHT_PARALLELPOINT, which creates a parallel point light source.

Because we're creating a directional light, we need to use D3DRMLIGHT_DIRECTIONAL.

The second, third, and fourth parameters in a call to CreateLightRGB are the red, green, and blue components of the light's color, respectively. We want to create dim white light (the reason will become apparent in a moment), so we'll use 0.4 for all three of these values (feel free to experiment with different values yourself, though).

The last parameter is, as you might suspect, a pointer to the address of an IDirect3DRMLight object for the new light. This will be our new gray directional light.

After the light is created, we need to add it to the scene. We do this by using the IDirect3DRMFrame::AddLight interface. AddLight takes just one parameter, a pointer to the light to add to the frame, and attaches it to the frame. And since we're attaching the directional light to our scene frame, it will go wherever the scene frame goes and point in which ever direction it points. This means that when our program starts up, the directional light will face the model, apparently coming from somewhere behind the camera (or viewport, if you prefer).

Second, now that the directional light source is out of the way, we need to create our ambient light source (to illuminate anything the directional light isn't shining on). We'll give the light's color red, green, and blue values of 0.6, 0.6, 0.6, respectively. That way, the total intensity of light given off in front of the directional light (which has an intensity of 0.4 for each component) will equal 1.0 (0.4 + 0.6)—illuminating everything in front of it at 100 percent intensity.

After creating the ambient light, we add it to the scene in the same way as the directional light. Now both our lights are in the scene and we just have to set the rendering options.

When we called IDirect3DRMDevice::SetQuality in Example 9-2 we used D3DRMRENDER_UNLITFLAT, which, as previously mentioned, is a combination of several different rendering options. Now we'll use a combination of our own so we can achieve just the effect we want.

First of all, we'll use the D3DRMLIGHT_ON flag so Direct3D uses the lights we created. Then we'll use D3DRMFILL_SOLID, which tells Direct3D to render all the models as filled polygons. Finally, we'll use D3DRMSHADE_GOURAUD, which tells Direct3D to utilize the vertex normals we'll supply it to use Gouraud shading. Again, you can look up all the different flags for SetQuality in your DirectX help file if you want.

That takes care of all the changes in SetRenderingOptions. Let's move on to BuildScene, in which we'll add normals to the scene so the Gouraud shading just implemented works.

BuildScene

The only thing that's changed in `BuildScene` is the call to `IDirect3DRMMeshBuilder::AddFaces`. Since that's a relatively small part of the code, we won't list the whole function again, just the call to `AddFaces` (Listing 9-16):

Listing 9-16 The call to `IDirect3DRMMeshBuilder::AddFaces`

```
// Load a mesh from the vertex arrays
pMeshBuilder->AddFaces( 23, archVertices,
    23, archNormals,
    (unsigned long *)faces, NULL);
```

In the last example, the call to `AddFaces` looked like this:

```
pMeshBuilder->AddFaces( 23, archVertices,
    0, NULL,
    (unsigned long *)faces, NULL);
```

As you can see, the second set of parameters have changed form zero and **NULL** to 23 and *archNormals*. This change in parameters was made to accommodate the normals we have to use now for lighting.

We keep the vertex normals in an array, much like our list of vertices. Each normal is a vector, just like a vertex. Listing 9-18 shows our array of vertex normals, *archNormals*:

Listing 9-18 The array of vertex normals

```
D3DVECTOR archNormals [] = { -1.0f, 0.0f,  0.0f, // 0 - Points left
     0.0f, 1.0f,  0.0f, // 1 - Points up
     1.0f, 0.0f,  0.0f, // 2 - Points right
     0.0f, -1.0f, 0.0f, // 3 - Points down
      0.0f, 0.0f,  -1.0f, // 4 - Points toward - z
     0.0f, 0.0f,  1.0f}; // 5- Points toward + z
```

Since we have a square arch, (there aren't any curved surfaces) all our normals point in a single direction (up, down, left, right, +z, or -z). Since all the faces on the arch are straight up and down and none are diagonal (as if we were building a ball, diamond, or the like), each face will use the same vertex normal for all its vertices. For example, take a look at the front, top face of the arch (Figure 9-10).

Assuming we are looking at the model from somewhere on the negative z axis, the front top surface would face us and point in the negative z direction. So for each of the face's four vertices, we would use a normal pointing in the negative z direction (for our example, the fourth normal in the array). Direct3D would then know the vertices (and thus, the surface) face the negative z direction and would shade the face accordingly.

One other note: Vertex normals always rotate with the vertices they're normals of, so you don't have to worry about keeping them pointed the right way. Direct3D takes care of that for you.

FIGURE 9-10

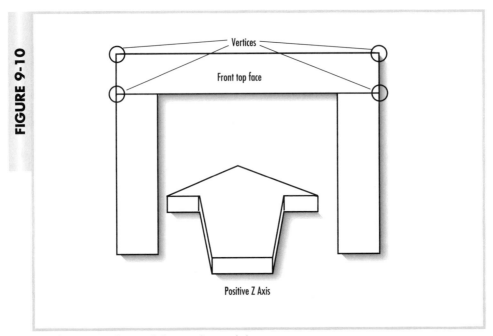

The front, top face of the arch model

Anyway, back to the code. The third parameter to **AddFaces** is the number of normals in the model. Since we have 23 vertices and a normal to go with each, there are 23 normals. The fourth parameter then is the array of normals to be used for the model.

The array of integers describing the faces of the model has changed significantly since last time. Listing 9-19 shows the *faces* array as it stands now:

Listing 9-19 The *faces* array

```
int faces[] = { 4, 0,  0, 1,  0, 2,  0, 3,  0, // Far left
    4, 1,  1, 4,  1, 5,  1, 2,  1,  // Top
    4, 6,  2, 5,  2, 4,  2, 7,  2,  // Far right
    4, 3,  3, 8,  3, 9,  3, 0,  3,  // left bottom
    4, 7,  3, 10, 3, 11, 3, 6,  3,  // right bottom
    4, 3,  4, 2,  4, 12, 4, 8,  4,  // Left front
    4, 13, 4, 5,  4, 6,  4, 11, 4,  // Right front
    4, 9,  5, 14, 5, 1,  5, 0,  5,  // Left back
    4, 10, 5, 7,  5, 4,  5, 15, 5,  // Right back
    4, 16, 4, 12, 4, 13, 4, 17, 4,  // Front top
    4, 14, 5, 19, 5, 18, 5, 15, 5,  // Back top
    4, 16, 3, 17, 3, 18, 3, 19, 3,  // Top inside
    4, 8,  2, 16, 2, 19, 2, 9,  2,  // Inside left
    4, 10, 0, 18, 0, 17, 0, 11, 0,    // Inside right
    0 };      // Terminator
```

Last time for each face, the array contained a number indicating there were *x* number of vertices in the face and *x* number of indexes into the vertex array describing the face itself. Now, however, we have two numbers for each vertex in a face. The first number is, as before, an index into the array of vertices. The second number in the pair, though, is an index into the array of normals. The index corresponds with the normal to be used for that vertex.

For example, consider the first face in the array: 4,0,0,1,0,2,0,3,0. The first number, 4, tells Direct3D there are four vertices in the face. The second and third numbers (0 and 0) describe the first vertex. It's the first vertex in the array of vertices, while its normal is the first normal in the array of normals. The third and fourth numbers (1 and 0, respectively) indicate that the second vertex is the second vertex in the array of vertices and it uses the first normal in the array of normals, and so on.

The call to **AddFaces** is the only thing changed in **BuildScene**. The model's color is still set to solid green, so adding the lights (as we did in **SetRenderingOptions**) results in the arch rendering green with Gouraud shading. The Gouraud shading dictates what shade of green is rendered at each point on the model depending on how much light shines on it.

The Window Procedure

One small thing has changed in the window procedure. When the user presses an arrow key, we have to get a pointer to the frame containing the arch. We did this previously by calling **IDirect3DRMFrameArray::GetElement** like so:

```
// Get array of frames
pD3DSceneAPI->GetChildren(&pFrameChildren);

// Get the particular frame we want (0 - top)
pFrameChildren->GetElement(0, &pChildFrame);
```

But now we have another frame in the **pChildFrame** array: the directional light we created. Since we created the directional light before the arch mesh, and the directional light has a position and is in a frame, the arch frame is now the second frame in the array. Therefore, we have to call **GetElement** using 1 as the first parameter.

Compiling Example 9-3

That's the end of Example 9-3, which is shown in Figure 9-11. It looks a much better than Example 9-2—lighting really does a lot for the realism factor.

Example 9-4 adds texture mapping. This will take a little work too, but not quite as much as the last one.

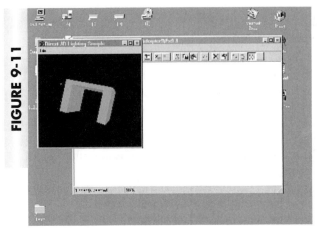

FIGURE 9-11

Example 9-3

Example 9-4: Adding Texture Mapping

For the next example, we'll wrap a texture onto the arch mesh. After this example, we'll be ready (as far as the graphics area is concerned) for Chapter 15 and building a complete game (of course, we still have to work through the sound chapters first).

We'll use the same texture for all the arch's faces. That way we'll conserve disk space, and it'll look as if the arch were made of the same material all the way through. The texture we'll use is in the bitmap **Marble8.bmp**, shown in Figure 9-12.

Before we get into the code, we need to discuss the one confusing aspect of texture mapping: texture coordinates.

FIGURE 9-12

The texture we'll wrap onto the arch

Texture Coordinates

In 3D computer graphics, we use a special coordinate system for textures. It is a 2D coordinate system, but instead of x and y, it uses the letters u and v, respectively. u and v both go from 0.0 in the upper-left corner of the texture to 1.0 in the lower-right corner. For a rectangular texture (all textures must obviously be rectangular, since they're actually image files), the coordinates resemble Figure 9-13.

In order to *wrap* a texture onto a face, you need to specify exactly where each vertex is located on the texture map. If you wanted to wrap a texture onto a square, for example, this would be extremely simple. You'd just use (0,0) as the texture coordinate for the upper-left vertex on the square, (1,0) as the texture coordinates of the upper-right vertex, and so on.

There are actually a bunch of different methods available through Direct3D for wrapping textures onto objects, but the one we'll use is the most basic. The other methods play with the texture coordinate system and get somewhat messy. You'd only use them in more exotic programming situations, so we won't even discuss them.

Now that we've covered the basics, let's go ahead and dig into the code.

SetRenderingOptions

We make one simple change in **SetRenderingOptions**: We increase the intensity of the ambient light from 0.6 per **RGB** component to 0.8. We need to do this since the texture is somewhat hard to see otherwise. The directional light will provide some illumination, but the texture itself is a dark color and needs a little more light to be seen clearly.

FIGURE 9-13

Texture coordinates

BuildScene

BuildScene is where most of our changes have occurred. Take a look at Listing 9-20 for the new code:

Listing 9-20 **BuildScene**

```
BOOL BuildScene(void)
{
LPDIRECT3DRMMESHBUILDER pMeshBuilder = NULL; // Mesh builder interface
LPDIRECT3DRMFRAME pArchFrame = NULL;  // Frame to contain arch
LPDIRECT3DRMTEXTURE pTexture = NULL;  // Texture API

// Setup rendering options first
if(!SetRenderingOptions())
 return FALSE;

// Create the mesh builder
if(FAILED(pD3DRetainedModeAPI->CreateMeshBuilder(&pMeshBuilder)))
 return FALSE;

// Create the texture API
if(FAILED(pD3DRetainedModeAPI->LoadTexture("marble8.bmp",&pTexture)))
 return FALSE;


// Create the mesh from our array
pMeshBuilder->AddFaces( 56, archVertices,
    56, archNormals,
    (unsigned long *)faces, NULL);

// Set color of all faces to white, this is combined with the texture
pMeshBuilder->SetColor(D3DRGB(1, 1, 1));

// Sets the texture
pMeshBuilder->SetTexture(pTexture);

// Set up texture coordinates. Each face is four vertices and is wound
// clockwise. A simple loop sets the texture coordinates to be the same
// for them all.
for(int i = 0; i < 56; i+= 4)
 {
 pMeshBuilder->SetTextureCoordinates(i,0.0f,0.0f);
 pMeshBuilder->SetTextureCoordinates(i+1,1.0f,0.0f);
 pMeshBuilder->SetTextureCoordinates(i+2,1.0f,1.0f);
 pMeshBuilder->SetTextureCoordinates(i+3,0.0f,1.0f);
 }


// Create a frame
if(FAILED(pD3DRetainedModeAPI->CreateFrame(pD3DSceneAPI, &pArchFrame)))
 return FALSE;
```

```
// Add the mesh to the frame
if(FAILED(pArchFrame->AddVisual(pMeshBuilder)))
 return FALSE;

// Set the position of the frame within the scene
if(FAILED(pD3DCameraAPI->SetPosition(pD3DSceneAPI, 0.0f, 0.0f, -7.0f)))
 return FALSE;

// Set orientation
if(FAILED(pD3DCameraAPI->SetOrientation(pD3DSceneAPI, 0.0f, 0.0f, 1.0f,
 0.0f, 1.0f, 0.0f)))
 return FALSE;

// Release interfaces
pArchFrame->Release();
pMeshBuilder->Release();
pTexture->Release();

return TRUE;
}
```

First of all, as you've undoubtedly noticed, we declare a pointer to an `IDirect3DRMTexture` object. `IDirect3DRMTexture` objects are just an interface to an internal `IDirectDrawSurface` object that makes the surface easier to manipulate alongside Direct3D. There are several methods available for creating textures, but we'll do it using the most common method: by loading the texture in from a file.

To load the texture in from a file, we'll use `IDirect3DRM::LoadTexture`. `LoadTexture` accepts two parameters: the name of the file to load (which must be a bitmap or a `.PPM` file) and a pointer to the address to put the new `IDirect3DRMTexture` into. By the way, you don't have to create the `IDirect3DRMTexture` object before calling `LoadTexture`—it's automatically created for you.

After creating the texture, we need to load in the vertices and faces of our arch mesh. Not so fast, though, because we must change the arrays of vertices and faces.

In case you didn't notice, we reused some of the vertices in the vertex array for multiple faces in the first three examples of this chapter. That is, many times (in fact, most of the time) two or more faces shared the same point as a vertex (see Figure 9-14). In previous examples, we just used the same vertex for each face using the point when we built our mesh.

This little trick worked just fine for the last three examples because we weren't doing any texture mapping. Direct3D is kind of finicky about the way texture mapping is done, though. It makes you associate a *single* texture coordinate with each vertex, meaning that even though two faces can share a vertex, they can't use the same one for texture mapping purposes. This complication forces us to expand our vertex array by duplicating all the vertices previously shared, so each face has its own *unique* set of vertices. That way, we can texture map each face without running into problems with shared vertices.

The array of vertices expanded from 23 to 56 to accommodate the new vertices. If you look at the source (which isn't listed here because of space limitations), you'll notice that

FIGURE 9-14

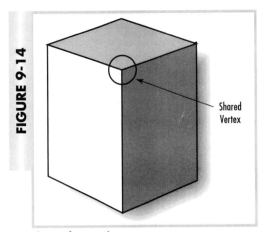

Shared
Vertex

Three faces sharing a vertex

after the original 23 vertices, each of the remaining ones is commented with the number of the vertex it duplicates in order to keep things clear. This is a good idea since it easily lets you change a vertex if needed and find all the duplicate vertices without a problem.

The array of faces has also obviously changed, as it now must use the duplicate vertices. As far as the model goes, that's all that has to be modified to support texture mapping, so now let's look at how we actually wrap the texture onto the arch.

Wrapping the Texture

First of all, we have to call `IDirect3DRMMeshBuilder::SetTexture` to let the mesh builder know which texture to use for the mesh. (This texture will be used for the *entire* mesh; however, you can specify a texture for each individual face if you want.) `SetTexture` simply takes a pointer to an `IDirect3DRMTexture` object as a parameter, then sets up that texture for use in all the texture wrapping operations to follow (on that mesh).

Now we have to associate each vertex in the mesh with a texture coordinate so Direct3D will know how to correctly render the texture. We'll do this via the `IDirect3DRMMeshBuilder::SetTextureCoordinates` interface, which takes three parameters. The first parameter is the index of the vertex to set the texture coordinates for, and the second and third parameters are the u and v coordinates of the vertex on the texture, respectively.

The vertices in the vertex array are listed clockwise (from the upper-left vertex to the lower-left), and for good reason. We don't really want to call `SetTextureCoordinates` 56 times, once for each vertex in the mesh, so we'll use a *for* loop to speed up the process:

```
for(int i = 0; i < 56; i+= 4)
{
pMeshBuilder->SetTextureCoordinates(i,0.0f,0.0f);
pMeshBuilder->SetTextureCoordinates(i+1,1.0f,0.0f);
pMeshBuilder->SetTextureCoordinates(i+2,1.0f,1.0f);
pMeshBuilder->SetTextureCoordinates(i+3,0.0f,1.0f);
}
```

Since all the faces are defined in clockwise order, we can go through the vertices four at a time and set the first (upper-left) vertex in the face's coordinates to (0,0) (in u, v coordinates), the second (upper-right) vertex's coordinates to (1,0), and so on. The *for* loop walks through all the vertices this way, and when it's finished, all the faces will have the texture properly mapped onto their vertices.

Whew! That's it. Since the texture is already on the mesh and we won't need it anymore, we can just `Release` it and be done with it. After that, we're finished with `BuildScene`.

Compiling Example 9-4

This has been a really productive example. Learning how to perform texture mapping is a big step forward in creating realistic 3D scenes (getting texture coordinates out of the way is also a plus).

Summary

Congratulations, you have just graduated from Direct3D preschool! You learned how to initialize Direct3D, build a 3D scene, light the scene, and perform texture mapping. In Chapter 15 (following the sound chapters), you'll learn how to use your newfound knowledge to create the foundation for a real 3D game.

10
A Sound Primer

by Keith Weiner

In this chapter we'll take a look at sound as it relates to computer games in general, and Windows 95 games specifically. Our discussion will cover some sound theory, then get down to sound cards, DOS, Windows, and Windows 95. As you'll see, programming sound with DirectSound in Windows 95 is significantly less work than programming sound under Windows 3.1 or DOS.

Despite the ease of using DirectSound, there is still a body of information you need to know, which we'll introduce later in this chapter.

You could cheat and skip over this chapter. However, I have a hunch you'll appreciate DirectSound all the more after reading about how sound programming used to be done. Plus, programmers should find my survey of digital sound theory useful.

What Is Sound?

To understand how different methods of sound generation work on the PC, it might be helpful to explore exactly what sound is, physically. You may have heard that sound is a *longitudinal pressure wave* created by any object vibrating in a fluid more than 20 and less than 20,000 times per second. What does that mean?

Longitudinal means that the oscillation, or back and forth motion, is in the same line as the direction the wave is traveling. Compare this with the wave that travels down the length of a rope when you tug it. The motion of any individual piece of rope is perpendicular to the path of the wave. This is called a *transverse* wave.

A longitudinal wave will exhibit the Doppler effect, meaning its perceived pitch varies with the emitter's velocity with respect to the listener. Sounds moving away from the listener are perceived as lower than their original pitch, and the opposite is true for sounds approaching you. The greater the velocity, the more severe the effect.

The ultimate in realistic audio production would address this. A discussion of 3D audio positioning and modeling the Doppler effect is beyond the scope of this chapter. Indeed, this stuff is cutting edge as of this writing.

In a pressure wave, the density of the air (or other fluid) varies from the static level. The fact that sound waves are pressure waves means that, unlike light waves, sound needs a medium (such as air) to propagate through. See Figure 10-1.

All physical objects can vibrate to produce sound if scraped, dropped, hit, and so on. What's interesting to us in computer audio, however, is that electronic speakers can reproduce any sound when signals are converted to the correct vibration. Obviously, programming a computer to play sound relies on this.

As you might suspect, waves are *sinusoidal,* that is, composed of the familiar sine wave shape. Furthermore, sine waves can be added together to form complex waves, as shown in Figure 10-2. The converse of this is also true: Any complex wave can be broken down into a finite number of component sine waves. This last point is important in understanding digital sampling, filtering, and *Digital Signal Processing* (DSP)—something else beyond the scope of this chapter.

FIGURE 10-1

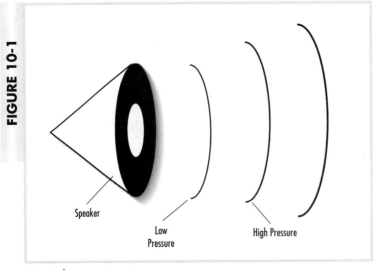

Speaker

Low Pressure

High Pressure

Sound waves in air

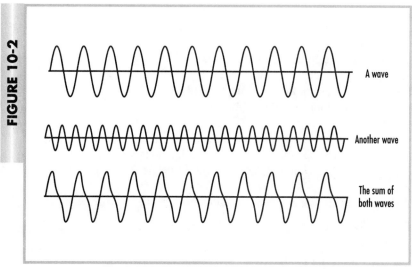

FIGURE 10-2

A wave

Another wave

The sum of
both waves

Two waves and their composite

Digitized Sound

All modern computers are digital. The waves we're tossing around cannot be directly represented in a computer. They must first be *digitized*, or converted to finite numbers.

To digitize a sound, you obtain an electrical signal from a microphone and measure its voltage at precise intervals using an Analog to Digital Converter (ADC). The numbers output by this special circuit can be stored and later sent to a Digital to Analog Converter (DAC). In the DAC, they're converted back into voltages, amplified, and used to drive speakers to produce a reasonable facsimile of the original sound.

Unfortunately, it isn't so simple in practice. The first question is how often do you have to measure your samples? Clearly, one sample per second is totally insufficient for recording anything.

A mathematician named Harry Nyquist determined that to perfectly record a sound, you must sample at twice the highest frequency component it contains. In other words, if your sound contains sine wave components of up to 10kHz, you must sample at 20,000 times a second or higher. If you sample at a lower rate, all frequencies above the *Nyquist frequency* will be *aliased* to a lower frequency, the same way a rapidly spinning propeller aliases to a slower—or even backward—rate of spin. On the other hand, if you sample at a higher rate you're just wasting memory.

To sample audio for use in a computer, there's a two-part strategy for dealing with the Nyquist rate and aliasing. First, choose your sampling rates to match the source material, or vice versa. Do not sample live music at 11kHz! Second, use a *low-pass filter* when recording, to eliminate any frequencies you can't correctly digitize. Any sound board with a microphone input provides filters for this purpose.

Another problem is *quantization noise*. Because you're sampling at a finite rate, the digital data will exhibit a characteristic stair-step shape. The computer can't see any in-between positions. See Figure 10-3.

The vertical lines in Figure 10-3, which are an artifact of the digitizing process, represent an infinite series of frequency components. If you simply convert the data to analog, the extra frequencies sound like noise. You must filter the output to remove quantization noise. Again, sound boards come with filters that do this.

You may have heard of *oversampling* (especially in CD players). This is simply a process of interpolating to create more data points and a smoother curve. The advantage is that this puts the noise at a higher frequency. Since steep cutoff low-pass filters don't sound as clean as the shallow filters used with oversamplers, this is one means of improving sound quality.

The first commandment in producing digital audio for computer playback is thou shalt sample thy sound carefully.

Mixing Sounds

Every innovative game made after 1992 can play multiple sound effects at once. You might wonder how they did this. There is certainly nothing in the average sound board to support this (notable exceptions are the Sound Blaster AWE32 and the Advanced Gravis Ultrasound).

FIGURE 10-3

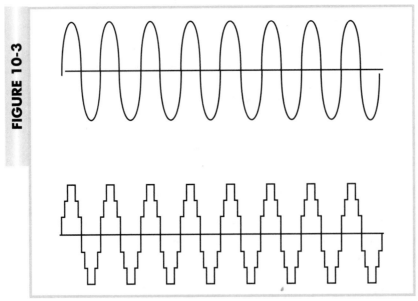

A wave and its digital representation

From a theoretical perspective, mixing sounds is easy. You just add them together. Since each sound is really the sum of a series of sine waves, adding them is quite valid. The following algebra illustrates:

$$X = X_1\sin(\theta) + X_2\sin(2\theta) + \quad + X_n\sin(N\theta)$$
$$Y = Y_1\sin(\theta) + Y_2\sin(2\theta) + \quad + Y_n\sin(N\theta)$$
$$X + Y = (X_1 + Y_1)\sin(\theta) + (X_2 + Y_2)\sin(2\theta) + \quad + (X_n + Y_n)\sin(N\theta)$$

However, there are several problems when doing this on a computer.

Under DOS and Windows 3.1

For better or for worse, most sound boards use Direct Memory Access (DMA) to play sounds. DMA is a feature of the PC's architecture, often used by peripherals to access memory buffers. Normally, DMA is performed as rapidly as the system can go. However, with most sound boards (again the Advanced Gravis Ultrasound is an exception) you program it to send each sample as needed. If you're using 8-bit 22kHz mono sound, then this method will send 22,050 bytes per second.

Playing only one sound, which is less than 64K bytes, causes no problems. Simply copy the sound into a buffer, program up some DMA, and sit back and listen.

But if you want to mix sounds, then you need to be playing *something* at all times—if nothing else, then silence. The trick to doing this is to alternate between playing two buffers, first A, then B, then A again, and so on.

Each time the hardware completes the last byte in a buffer, it generates an *Interrupt ReQuest* (IRQ). At this point, there's so little time to play the next buffer, that even copying the data would be too slow. Obviously, your second buffer had better be ready to go when you receive that interrupt.

I should emphasize that, as hard as this is under DOS, it's even worse under Windows 3.1. Windows is *not* a real-time operating system, so it makes no guarantees as to when your critical code gets its time slices. Without resorting to writing a virtual device driver (VxD), the problems of receiving notification that your current buffer is done and getting the next one playing, are daunting.

After the buffer sequencing problem, your next worry is that IRQs might be *masked* (or disabled) for too long. If you're forced to wait briefly, the outcome will be a click. If longer, you'll hear a distinct gap in the sound. In the bad old days of DOS, programmers (including yours truly) worked many all-nighters on the problem of minimizing the delay between buffers.

The next problem is arithmetic *overflow*. As soon as you add two numbers of unknown range together, you risk an overflow. In sound, it's no different. With 8-bit samples, a value that was supposed to be 0x101 will come out as 0x01. This comes out like a sharp click, and sounds awful.

If you can't have the 0x101, then the next best thing would be to clip at 0xff. It adds some noise, but if it doesn't happen too often and you don't overflow by much, then it sounds okay. Of course, clipping after each addition will slow you down.

In order to minimize how often you get a click or pop (especially under Windows 3.1!) you will want to make your buffers fairly large (enough data to play for a second or more).

However, this exacerbates the problem of *latency*. If each buffer takes one second to play, you might wait up to one second before hearing a sound just mixed in. So you better reduce your buffer size and pour yourself another cup of coffee: It's going to be another late night....

Now that you've worked out how to reliably sequence small buffers, your next problem is that many sounds are longer than your buffer size—especially if you spent your evenings and weekends productively. There is no easy solution to this. Your growing mixer kernel will expand some more in order to handle this problem and all the new border cases it requires.

Of course, we're now talking about taking several sounds—adding them all together, clipping when necessary, and doing it all in real-time, one buffer at a time. This code better be well-optimized, otherwise you'll have no CPU cycles left over for the 3D graphics!

Whew! All this, just to play several sounds at once and have each one heard right after the call to play it.

Under Windows 95

Microsoft was not entirely deaf to the cries of game developers looking for a better way. DirectSound was its answer.

DirectSound does everything just discussed and more, isolating it behind an API so it's accessible to applications programmers. With some caveats, DirectSound makes sound programming much easier. As we'll see in the next chapter, 300 lines of C++ code (plus a header file) are sufficient for creating a bare-bones sound class.

Sound Files

Under Windows 3.1 and 95, the paramount file format for sound is the **WAVE** file. We'll look at the specifics of the file format in the next chapter. But for now, there are some issues to understand about storing sound, and other media, in files.

First, when you read data from a file, you want to know its format. Sound can be stored using either 8 or 16 bits per sample, mono or stereo. As discussed earlier, the sampling rate is critical. If we set the hardware to 44100Hz, but our file was recorded at 11025Hz, its speed and pitch will both be four times too high.

The **WAVE** file is one instance of the *Resource Interchange File Format* (**RIFF**). All **RIFF** files contain one or more *chunks*, or records, within a RIFF file. It was designed this way so that the specification could be amended in the future without breaking legacy software. **RIFF** parsers should be written to ignore any **chunks** they don't understand.

Some chunks (for example, **RIFF** and **LIST**) contain other chunks. The first chunk in a **RIFF** file must be a **RIFF** chunk, containing the rest of the file as one or more subchunks.

A chunk contains a four-character code (**RIFF** for the **RIFF** chunk), a 4-byte length field, and the data. The data field of the **RIFF** chunk begins with a four-character field, which is always **WAVE** for **WAVE** files.

For now, don't worry about the details. The Multimedia Input/Output (MMIO) API is a set of functions handling this work. We'll discuss this API and present code using it in the next chapter.

DirectSound Overview

We'll conclude this chapter with an overview of how DirectSound works and what it offers the programmer. DirectSound can mix several sounds together. As we saw earlier, this is no mean feat. DirectSound can also convert between sampling rates as it mixes, a feature that can be abused into changing the pitch of a sound.

DirectSound is a *Component Object Model* (COM) interface. The two basic ideas behind COM are separating APIs from implementations and providing a binary object standard that works with all programming languages. Since systems programming is often done in C++ these days, it's no coincidence COM fits that language fairly well. It fits C almost as well, with the exception of an extra pointer dereference when you call its methods. COM isn't accessible from Visual Basic.

As you might imagine, this adds some extra complexity for programmers who just want to add sound to their games. In the next chapter, we'll use a C++ class to hide COM's gory details.

DirectSound is a channel-oriented API, meaning it's focused on allocating, playing, and deallocating channels. This isn't really what a game program wants, so our class will also hide most of the details of COM and channel management.

What *does* a game program want? The game we're building in this book (presented in the last chapter) wants a clean API that allows the program to load **WAVE** files by filename, then play, stop, and unload them. In short, it wants a sound-oriented API.

What Does All This Mean?

We've presented some of the theory of digital audio. This will help you understand the production of audio assets for games and multimedia. It's also an essential foundation to understand mixing or any of the more advanced techniques in digital audio. I could have said *you just add up all the samples*, but there are some good mathematics behind *why* that's correct.

We also took a brief tour of how sound programming was once done and why DirectSound was created. Sound programming under Windows 95 is mostly a matter of figuring out how to use an API, rather than solving complex real-time hardware programming problems. Like the blacksmith, the hardware programmer is an endangered species (except for those hired by hardware vendors). It's a shame, but it also makes the field accessible to regular programmers.

The next chapter will delve into the specifics of the **WAVE** file and DirectSound programming. It will also be illustrated with the complete source code to a working sound class.

11

DirectSound

by Keith Weiner

In this chapter, we'll discuss the essentials of writing code to use DirectSound. While the documentation that comes with the DirectX SDK is a satisfactory reference, this chapter serves as a more in-depth guide. It gives you an overview, then takes you through the steps necessary for DirectSound programming.

First, we'll take a brief look under the hood. Understanding the architecture will enable you to use it more effectively. Later, we'll develop a **DIRSOUND** class that encapsulates the details of DirectSound and presents a nice clean API, which is useful in games.

DirectSound Architecture

To your program, DirectSound is a *Dynamic Link Library* (DLL). You link with an *import library* (Microsoft provides one for their Visual C++ compiler). You can then call the functions in the DLL.

In the case of DirectSound, there are only two functions exported from the DLL. All other DirectSound functionality is implemented as part of a *Component Object Model* (COM) interface. Fortunately, you don't need to know much about COM to use DirectSound. One of the two aforementioned functions returns a pointer to an object of type **DIRECTSOUND**. From C++, you can call its methods directly (no pun intended). Figure 11-1 shows how DirectSound fits into your program— very different from a typical DLL!

FIGURE 11-1

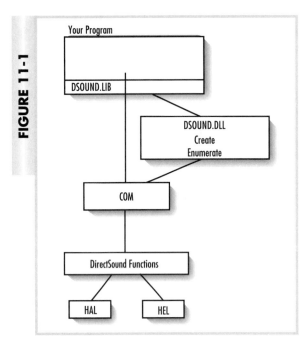

DirectSound in your program

DSOUND.DLL provides the DirectSound API to your program. Internally, it determines what features (if any) the hardware supports. Such functionality is implemented in a *Hardware Abstraction Layer* (HAL) inside the low-level driver. Anything else is performed by the *Hardware Emulation Layer* (HEL) inside the DirectSound DLL, provided by Microsoft. The advantage here is that Microsoft debugs and performance-tunes the tricky stuff in its DLL only once, rather than depending on scores of manufacturers for drivers. The driver simply provides an interface to whatever subset of the DirectSound specification the hardware supports.

The designers of DirectSound are hoping that audio hardware manufacturers will provide hardware mixing of multiple digital audio streams out of on-board RAM. Hardware mixing frees the processor from the burden of doing it in code. However, compared to 3D polygon blitting, hardware audio mixing is a relatively minor speedup.

On *Industry Standard Architecture* (ISA) based sound hardware, hardware mixing must be done from on-board RAM in order to gain any speed improvement. Transferring multiple channels of audio via DMA is slower than mixing it in software on a Pentium. There is also the issue of ISA bus bandwidth. Each CD-quality audio track (16-bit stereo, 44kHz sampling rate) is 176,400 bytes per second. The ISA bus can sustain no more than about six such channels before saturating.

Already, sound boards are being built to plug into the *Peripheral Component Interface* (PCI) bus found in all modern PCs. The PCI bus is easily capable of transferring all sound streams via DMA, where they can be 3D positioned and otherwise processed before being mixed and sent to the DAC. 3D localization, unlike mixing, is a processor-intensive operation greatly benefited by hardware acceleration. Obviously, the hardware must localize each voice in 3-space before the mixing step. Thus, a prerequisite of hardware localization is hardware mixing. We'll return to the topic of 3D audio later in this chapter.

Currently, only a few sound boards support hardware mixing. Most notable are the Sound Blaster AWE32 and the Advanced Gravis Ultrasound. Advanced Micro Devices makes a single-chip audio processor based on the Ultrasound called the InterWave.

For mixing, low latency is even more important than hardware acceleration. *Latency* is the period of time between a sound call and the point at which the user hears the result. Any driver implemented to the DirectSound specification will at least provide a *play cursor* and a *write cursor*. See Figure 11-2 for a diagram of a buffer, with both play and write cursors shown.

The key to any sound mixing scheme (be it under DOS, Windows, or even UNIX) is a looping buffer. As long as you know the offset where the hardware is currently playing, you can safely write sound data ahead of that point. DirectSound provides a way to determine where the system is playing and where it's safe to write. This is impossible for the application to determine by itself, because the sound hardware operates independently of your program. There's simply no way to keep in sync, without a special API call.

Before DirectSound, you could create a circular buffer scheme in Windows, but you could not write to a buffer once it had been played. Since the buffer size was fairly large (to avoid the skipping problem mentioned in the last chapter), you had high latency, and that was that.

DirectSound API

As mentioned earlier, two functions are exported by **DSOUND.DLL**. **DirectSoundCreate** is used to create an instance of the DirectSound object. **DirectSoundEnumerate** queries the available drivers (there may be more than one).

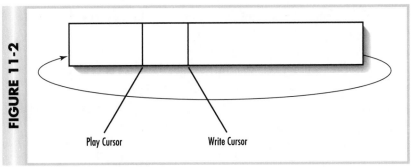

FIGURE 11-2

Play Cursor   Write Cursor

DirectSound buffer scheme

Exported Functions from `DSOUND.DLL`

Most likely you would call `DirectSoundEnumerate` first, so let's take a look at it.

```
BOOL DirectSoundEnumerate(LPDSENUMCALLBACK lpDSEnumCallback, LPVOID lpContext);
```

Your function, which `lpDSEnumCallback` points to, is called once for each DirectSound driver in the system. This mechanism allows you to build a list of choices for the user, though why they didn't do this through one function call is a mystery!

The callback must conform to the following prototype:

```
BOOL DirectSoundEnumCallback(GUID FAR *lpGuid, LPSTR lpstrDescription, LPSTR ⇐
lpstrModule, LPVOID lpContext);
```

The function returns **TRUE** to continue enumerating drivers, **FALSE** to stop. You could present the drivers to the user one at a time and stop if the user finds one he or she likes. But this is a textbook case of poor GUI design. I strongly recommend you build a complete list of drivers, then offer the user a chance to choose one from a listbox.

An improvement to this technique is to pre-screen each driver and highlight the first one you find offering hardware-accelerated mixing and the lowest latency.

The first parameter is a pointer to a *Globally Unique ID* (GUID). This is a very long number that's absolutely, positively guaranteed to be unique among every other GUID, provided they were all generated with the same algorithm. Microsoft provides a utility for this express purpose (**GUIDGEN.EXE**). The GUID pointed to by **lpGUID** identifies the DirectSound driver. When you call `DirectSoundCreate` later you can specify which driver to use, and you can use the GUID you got from this callback (or **NULL** to indicate you want the default).

The second parameter is a string containing a description of the driver suitable for displaying to the user.

The third parameter is a string containing the module name of the DirectSound driver corresponding to this device.

Last is a pointer to application-specific data. This field is unnecessary.

You must be careful to copy the data pointed to by `lpGuid`, `lpstrDescription`, `lpstrModule`, and `lpContext` to your own buffers. The data you get is not guaranteed as valid outside the *extent* (time of execution) of your callback function.

```
HRESULT DirectSoundCreate(GUID FAR *lpGuid, LPDIRECTSOUND *ppDS, IUnknown FAR ⇐
*pUnkOuter);
```

As mentioned previously, you must tell this function which DirectSound driver you want. Each has its own GUID.

The second parameter is the address of a pointer to a **DIRECTSOUND** structure. This function will initialize your pointer with the correct address.

The third parameter must be **NULL**.

Once you call this function, everything you do with DirectSound is through its COM interface, which to a C++ program are methods of the **DIRECTSOUND** object. Before we take a look at these methods, we need to cover one more detail of DirectSound's architecture.

DirectSound Buffers

The *primary buffer* is a looping buffer into which all other buffers are mixed. Its contents are then directly sent to the hardware for playback. A normal application does not need (or want) to worry about messing with this.

A *secondary buffer*, on the other hand, is the fundamental block of DirectSound with which you will work. There is no limit to how many you can create (except for available memory), though finite computing power will effectively limit how many sounds you can mix together. The DirectSound mixer will clip the output if it grows too loud for the hardware to play.

As Figure 11-3 shows, the secondary buffers are mixed into the primary buffer.

Putting each of your sounds into a secondary buffer is definitely the preferred method. However, there is another way, which I'll mention for the sake of being thorough.

You can mix directly into the primary buffer, although this action is subject to some caveats. When you obtain a pointer to the primary buffer's memory (obtaining a pointer to a buffer's memory is an important procedure, which we will discuss momentarily), it effectively prevents your application from sharing DirectSound with other programs on the Windows desktop. Whether or not a game programmer cares about this is another matter.

FIGURE 11-3

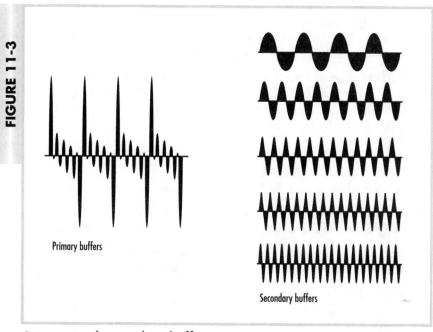

Primary buffers

Secondary buffers

Primary and secondary buffers

There is one major technical problem. The primary buffer is looping at a certain rate. If you fail to keep up with it (because, for instance, Windows schedules another thread for execution), DirectSound will happily repeat the contents of the old buffer. You can bump up your mixer's thread priority to be quite high, but this can cause other problems.

Finally, your custom mixer will not take advantage of any hardware acceleration. For all these reasons, I strongly recommend using secondary buffers.

The `IDirectSound` Interface

As mentioned earlier, DirectSound is a COM object. COM objects provide *interfaces*. One interface provided by DirectSound is the `IDirectSound` interface, which consists of the main methods of DirectSound. DirectSound also provides `IDirectSoundBuffer` and other interfaces, which we'll discuss later.

The first method you might want to call is

- `IDirectSound::GetCaps`, which returns information about the sound hardware's capabilities. The following code instantiates a DirectSound object, then calls `IDirectSound::GetCaps`.

  ```
  DirectSoundCreate(NULL, &lpdirsnd, NULL);
  lpdirsnd->GetCaps(&dscaps);
  ```

- `dscaps` is a structure containing a lot of information. We won't discuss every last piece of it here. For a complete reference, check out the online help file provided with the Direct X SDK. Some of the salient fields are

  - `dwFlags` contains bitfields telling you what kind of hardware mixing is supported, whether DirectSound is emulated in the DLL, what sample sizes and rates are supported by the hardware, whether the driver has been certified by Microsoft, and so on.

  - `dwMaxHwMixingAllBuffers` tells you how many channels the hardware can mix.

  - `dwTotalHwMemBytes` is the size of the hardware's on-board memory.

  - `DwUnlockTransferRateHwBuffers` tells you how fast data is transferred to the sound hardware from system memory, in kilobytes per second.

  - `DwPlayCpuOverheadSwBuffers` tells you the percentage of the CPU installed in the machine that will be used to mix buffers in software.

There's much more stuff in here. The intent of the DirectSound designers was to give you the information for scaling audio support from low-end to high-end systems. See the DirectSound reference section in the DirectX SDK Help file for complete details.

Next, you should call `IDirectSound::SetCooperativeLevel`.

```
Lpdirsnd->SetCooperativeLevel(hwnd, DSSCL_NORMAL);
```

Microsoft recommends the *normal* level, because this is the easiest way to get robust code up and running, plus all applications using this level cooperate. At the normal priority level, DirectSound will not give you write access to the primary buffer. Therefore, you won't need a handle to it, so the rest of this chapter and its accompanying code won't address it.

Next, you will need to create at least one secondary sound buffer.

```
IDirectSound::CreateSoundBuffer(LPDSBUFFERDESC lpdirsndbufdesc, ⇐
LPLPDIRECTSOUNDBUFFER *lplpDirectSoundBuffer, IUnknown *pUnkOuter);
```

The first parameter is a pointer to a DirectSound buffer descriptor structure. Its three interesting fields (read this chapter's example code to see how to make this call) are `dwFlags`, `dwBufferBytes`, and `lpwfxFormat`.

`dwFlags` is how you specify the numerous options. If you just want to make a standard secondary buffer, use a value of **DSBCAPS_CTRLDEFAULT**. The DirectSound reference discusses the other options (such as creating a primary buffer), but you won't need them here.

`dwBufferBytes` specifies the size of the buffer to create.

`lpwfxFormat` is a pointer to a **WAVEFORMATEX** structure. It's normally used to describe a **WAVE** file, but in this function call it was put to good use describing the DirectSound buffer you need. You can specify the audio data format, although DirectSound currently only supports **WAVE_FORMAT_PCM** (in other words, regular audio data). It also lets you specify mono or stereo via the `nChannels` field, the sampling rate via the `nSamplesPerSec` field, and the sample size via the `wBitsPerSample` field. Let's take a look at one of the methods of our **DIRSOUND** class, which will help illustrate:

```
void DIRSOUND::CreateBuffer(WORD channel)
{
  DSBUFFERDESC dsbdesc;
  PCMWAVEFORMAT pcmwf;
  HRESULT hr;

  memset(&pcmwf, 0, sizeof(PCMWAVEFORMAT));
  pcmwf.wf.wFormatTag     = WAVE_FORMAT_PCM;
  pcmwf.wf.nChannels      = ds_CHANSPERSAMPLE;
  pcmwf.wf.nSamplesPerSec = ds_SAMPLERATE;
  pcmwf.wf.nBlockAlign    = ds_CHANSPERSAMPLE * ds_BITSPERSAMPLE / 8;
  pcmwf.wf.nAvgBytesPerSec = pcmwf.wf.nSamplesPerSec * pcmwf.wf.nBlockAlign;
  pcmwf.wBitsPerSample    = ds_BITSPERSAMPLE;

  memset(&dsbdesc, 0, sizeof(DSBUFFERDESC));
  dsbdesc.dwSize        = sizeof(DSBUFFERDESC);
  dsbdesc.dwFlags       = DSBCAPS_CTRLDEFAULT;
  dsbdesc.dwBufferBytes = len[channel];
  dsbdesc.lpwfxFormat   = (LPWAVEFORMATEX)&pcmwf;

  hr = lpdirsnd->CreateSoundBuffer(&dsbdesc, &lpdsb[channel], NULL);
```

continued on next page

continued from previous page

```
if (hr != DS_OK)
{
  exit(-1);
}
}
```

Notice how we initialize the entire structure to zero before using it. This ensures there is no garbage lying around in unused fields.

Make sure you call `IDirectSound::Release()` on every buffer you create, before your program terminates.

The `IDirectSoundBuffer` Interface

`IDirectSoundBuffer` provides an interface, which you will use for all operations using DirectSound buffers. Let's take a look at it.

Before you can do anything with a buffer, you need to fill it with sound. To do this, you must lock a region of the buffer down (in other words, obtain a pointer and notify DirectSound you will be modifying it), write your data, then unlock the region.

```
HRESULT IDirectSoundBuffer:Lock(DWORD dwWriteCursor, DWORD dwWriteBytes, ⇐
LPVOID lplpvAudioPtr1, LPDWORD lpdwAudioBytes1, LPVOID lplpvAudioPtr2, ⇐
LPDWORD lpdwAudioBytes2, DWORD dwFlags);
```

This function obtains a pointer to the buffer that you can use to write data to it. The reason for this extra layer of indirection is that the sound buffer may actually live in the RAM on-board the sound hardware, out of reach by normal C++ pointers. When you unlock the buffer, the driver copies it, usually using DMA, to the sound card.

The first parameter is the offset from the beginning of the buffer to which you wish to start writing—often the write cursor. This is useful if you need to update a buffer once it's begun.

The next parameter is the length of data you want to write to, which should obviously not exceed the size of the buffer itself.

 Note

If you're going to update part of a buffer, try to lock down no more than you will actually write to, because every byte transferred wastes DMA and CPU bandwidth.

For now, we'll skip over the next four parameters because they are return values, and go right to the last parameter. The only flag currently defined,`DSBLOCK_FROMWRITECURSOR`, specifies that you want to start writing at the write cursor position. This will save you the call to `IDirectSoundBuffer::GetCurrentPosition`, if you want to write the next piece in a changing, looping buffer.

The return values need some explanation. Figure 11-4 shows a typical circular buffer. Notice how a single 1K segment can wrap from the end of the buffer to the beginning. That can also happen with `IDirectSoundBuffer::Lock`.

The third and fourth parameters are the address of your buffer pointer and the address of a length variable. These specify the first segment of the write buffer. Depending on the write cursor and the length you specified, DirectSound may need to give you another pointer and size. These are parameters five and six.

Note

It's important to write your code so it can handle a buffer broken into two pieces, because as shown in Figure 11-4, the buffer is broken into two pieces every time the DirectSound buffer wraps.

Once you've locked a buffer for writing, you should write your sound data to it—in the format specified in the `WAVEFORMATEX` structure—and unlock it with `IDirectSoundBuffer::Unlock` as soon as possible.

Now that you have a buffer with sound, it's showtime! To play the sound, call `IDirectSoundBuffer::Play`.

```
HRESULT Play(DWORD dwReserved1, DWORD dwReserved2, DWORD dwFlags);
```

The first two parameters must both be zero, according to the Microsoft documentation. The last parameter may be either `0` or `DSBPLAY_LOOPING`, both of which cause it to loop.

At any time, you can call `IDirectSoundBuffer::Stop`. It saves the play cursor, so that a subsequent call to `IDirectSoundBuffer::Play` resumes playing the sound.

Make sure you call `IDirectSoundBuffer::Release` when you're done with the buffer.

FIGURE 11-4

End   Start

When a circular buffer wraps

The **MMIO** Functions

There's another API we have to go through before developing our **DIRSOUND** class. The **MMIO** functions are not part of DirectSound, but you'll definitely want to use them for playing **WAVE** files since they provide an easy means of finding and reading the PCM (Pulse Code Modulation, or digital sound data) chunks. DirectSound doesn't recognize anything except PCM data; so if you played an entire **WAVE** file, you would get some awful noise along with your sound.

As we discussed in Chapter 8, "Advanced DirectDraw," a **WAVE** file is one type of **RIFF** file. All **RIFF** files consist of chunks. The **MMIO** functions make it easy to find and read the various chunks.

Although the **MMIO** functions are part of the standard Win32 API, they're actually contained in a DLL called **WINMM.DLL** (which was provided with the so-called multimedia extensions to Windows 3.x, and never renamed). Visual C++ provides an import library for this DLL, called **WINMM.LIB**. You'll have to add this file to your project.

As Figure 11-5 shows, the **WAVE** file is just a subchunk of the **RIFF** chunk. It contains two subchunks itself: **fmt** (careful: there's a space after the *t* because all chunks have a four-character code) and **data**. The format chunk is a **WAVEFORMATEX** structure. The data chunk contains the sound samples, suitable for writing into a secondary buffer (if they're uncompressed PCM).

FIGURE 11-5

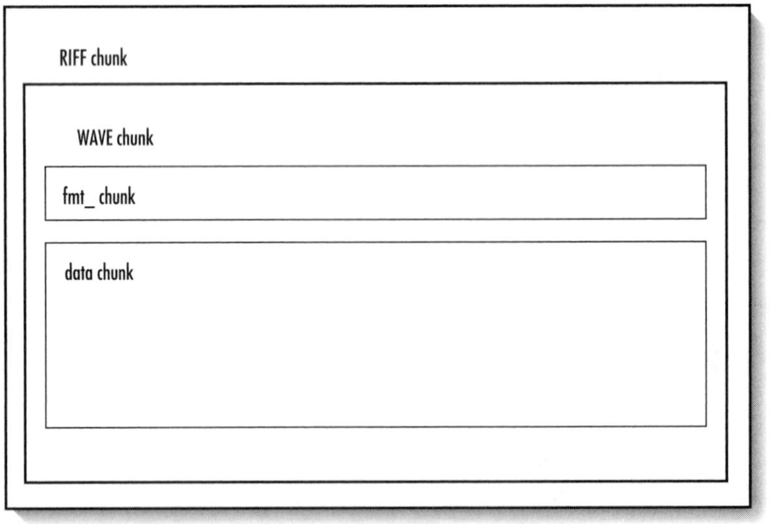

Format of a WAVE-style RIFF file

For our `DIRSOUND` class, we need five `MMIO` functions: `mmioOpen`, `mmioClose`, `mmioDescend`, `MMIOAscend`, and `mmioRead`.

`mmioOpen` turns a filename (or memory handle) into an `MMIO` handle. Its prototype is

```
HMMIO mmioOpen(LPSTR szFilename, LPMMIOINFO lpmmioinfo, DWORD dwOpenFlags);
```

The filename is an ordinary `NULL`-terminated string. `lpmmioinfo` should be `NULL` if you're working with disk files, and `dwOpenFlags` will be `MMIO_READ | MMIO_ALLOCBUF` in our code. This tells it we only plan on reading the file and that it should use the `MMIO`'s internal 8K buffer.

```
MMRESULT mmioClose(HMMIO hmmio, UINT wFlags);
```

When closing a file opened with `mmioOpen`, pass the file handle for the first parameter and zero for the second.

Ascending and *descending* require a brief explanation. The `MMIO` functions recognize and respect the chunk boundaries in the `RIFF` file. When you descend into a chunk, the `MMIO` code positions the file pointer at the beginning of that chunk, and reads the size information. Additionally, the `mmioDescend` function can be used to find the chunk you want, skipping everything in between the current file position and the chunk's start. Ascending out of a chunk reverts the state of the file. You must ascend before moving on to any other chunk.

```
MMRESULT mmioDescend(HMMIO hmmio, LPMMCKINFO lpck, LPMMCKINFO lpckParent, ⇐
UINT wFlags);
```

The first parameter is the handle returned by `mmioOpen`. The second parameter is the address of an `MMCKINFO` structure. Before the call, you must fill the `ckid` (chunk ID) in with the chunk type into which you want to descend, so `mmioDescend` can fill it in. The third parameter is the `MMCKINFO` structure for the parent of the current chunk, or `NULL` if the chunk we seek is at the top level of the file. The last parameter is the specific predefined chunk type desired, or zero. Special types are `MMIO_FINDLIST` and `MMIO_FINDRIFF`.

```
MMRESULT mmioAscend(HMMIO hmmio, LPMMCKINFO lpck, UINT wFlags);
```

To leave the chunk when you're finished, call `mmioAscend`. The first parameter is the handle. The second is the address of the structure filled in when you descended into this chunk. The last parameter must be zero.

The **DIRSOUND** Class

We're now ready to develop the `DIRSOUND` class. We've looked at the DirectSound API in sufficient detail and even understand what it does behind the API and why. We know it does not play directly from `WAVE` files, or even `WAVE` files loaded into buffers, but rather raw PCM data. Finally, we've also looked at the `MMIO` functions that simplify the work of dealing with `WAVE` files.

What Should the **DIRSOUND** Class Do?

Obviously, all well-designed classes attempt to hide the gory details of how they perform their work. Every book on C++ and object-oriented design evangelizes this philosophy. But a good class should also provide an API that's *useful*, something entirely different than serving as a model of exceptional object-oriented design.

Since we're encapsulating the details, users of our class need not be familiar with DirectSound. In fact, they shouldn't have to `#include dsound.h` (though the header file declaring the **DIRSOUND** class might). They also shouldn't have to worry about **WAVE** files or **MMIO**.

What sound class would be useful to a game? What must a game be able to do with sound? Let's take a look at **DS.H**, which declares the class.

```
typedef class DIRSOUND
{
  public:
    DIRSOUND(HWND hwnd);
    ~DIRSOUND();

    WORD LoadWave(char *filename);       //returns channel number
    void UnLoadWave(WORD channel);

    void Start(WORD channel, BOOL looping);
    void Stop(WORD channel);

  private:
    /* ---------- Methods ---------- */
    WORD AllocChannel(void);

    void CreateBuffer(WORD channel);
    void DestroyBuffer(WORD channel);

    void FillBuffer(WORD channel);

    /* ---------- Data ---------- */
    HWND                  hwnd;             //application's window handle
    LPDIRECTSOUND         lpdirsnd;

    /* These fields keep track of each sound */
    BYTE                  *sound[ds_NUMCHANNELS];
    DWORD                 len[ds_NUMCHANNELS];
    LPDIRECTSOUNDBUFFER   lpdsb[ds_NUMCHANNELS];

} DIRSOUND;
```

As this class definition shows, the interface consists entirely of methods; there are no public data fields. This is considered good practice by current software engineering standards. The data members are declared in the private section. If you had ever derived a class from **DIRSOUND**, you would need to revisit this issue.

The **ctor** (abbreviation for constructor) requires a window handle (**HWND**). This is a byproduct of the way DirectSound operates and not something we can easily avoid.

Once the object is instantiated, there are only four methods in the class to worry about. The **LoadWave** method loads a **WAVE** file from disk into an internal buffer, allocates a DirectSound secondary buffer for it, copies the data into it, and returns a handle (actually an index) to the sound. The **UnLoadWave** method frees up the resources used by the **WAVE**, including the DirectSound buffer.

Once a sound is loaded, the **Start** and **Stop** methods can be called to start (with looping optional) and stop the sound.

The class API is clean, simple, and easy to use. There isn't much more to say about it.

The **DIRSOUND** Implementation

But now let's take a look at the implementation. There is *a lot* to say about **DS.CPP**!

```
DIRSOUND::DIRSOUND(HWND hwnd)
{
  DWORD ret;
  WORD x;

  for (x=0;x<ds_NUMCHANNELS;x++)
  {
    lpdsb[x] = NULL;
  }

  ret = DirectSoundCreate(NULL, &lpdirsnd, NULL);

  if (ret != DS_OK)
  {
    exit(-1);
  }

  ret = lpdirsnd->SetCooperativeLevel(hwnd, DSSCL_NORMAL);

  if (ret != DS_OK)
  {
    exit(-1);
  }
}
```

First, the **ctor** initializes all its DirectSound buffer pointers to **NULL**, indicating they're not in use. As you can see from the class definition, there are three private data array members: **sound**, **len**, and **lpdsb**. They hold each **WAVE**'s data, length, and DirectSound secondary buffer.

Note

The **ctor** only initializes the DirectSound buffer array. Since this is sufficient for determining whether or not an index is used, initializing the other two arrays is redundant. Redundancy in code is often the source of defects (bugs), and should usually be avoided.

The **ctor** then creates a DirectSound object (using the default driver for simplicity, though you learned how to give the user a choice of drivers). It finally sets the cooperative level.

 Note

All errors are handled by a simple and expedient method. They cause the program to bomb, using the standard library's ex i t function. This is not robust, consistent with good software engineering practice, or state-of-the-art. But this code was designed to be easy to read, not perfect. Once you understand it, you can add some real error handling.

After the program has created a **DIRSOUND** object, it will then load one or more **WAVE**s. So, here's the code for **DIRSOUND::LoadWave**.

```
WORD DIRSOUND::LoadWave(char *filename)
{
  HMMIO          hmfr;
  MMCKINFO       parent, child;
  WAVEFORMATEX   wfmtx;
  WORD           channel;

  parent.ckid        = (FOURCC)0;
  parent.cksize      = 0;
  parent.fccType     = (FOURCC)0;
  parent.dwDataOffset = 0;
  parent.dwFlags     = 0;

  child = parent;

  hmfr = mmioOpen(filename, NULL, MMIO_READ | MMIO_ALLOCBUF);

  if (hmfr == NULL)
  {
    exit(-1);                  //can't open file
  }
```

So far, we've created two blank **MMCKINFO** structures for use later and opened the **WAVE** file the user specified. At least, we're assuming it's a **WAVE** file.

```
  /* descend into the RIFF */
  parent.fccType = mmioFOURCC('W', 'A', 'V', 'E');

  if (mmioDescend(hmfr, &parent, NULL, MMIO_FINDRIFF))
  {
    mmioClose(hmfr, 0);

    exit(-1);                  //not a WAVE file
  }

  /* descend to the WAVEfmt */
  child.ckid = mmioFOURCC('f', 'm', 't', ' ');
```

```
    if (mmioDescend(hmfr, &child, &parent, 0))
    {
      mmioClose(hmfr, 0);

      exit(-1);                  //WAVE file has no fmt chunk
    }
```

Note how we've descended twice, once into the **WAVE** chunk, then again into the format chunk within the **WAVE**.

```
    /* read the WAVEFMT from the wave file */
    if (mmioRead(hmfr, (char*)&wfmtx, sizeof(wfmtx)) != sizeof(wfmtx))
    {
      mmioClose(hmfr, 0);
      exit(-1);                  //unable to read fmt chunk
}

/* We only handle PCM format WAVEs */
if (wfmtx.wFormatTag != WAVE_FORMAT_PCM)
{
      mmioClose(hmfr, 0);

      exit(-1);                  //WAVE file is not PCM format
    }

    if (mmioAscend(hmfr, &child, 0))
    {
      mmioClose(hmfr, 0);

      exit(-1);                  //unable to ascend
    }
```

We read the format chunk right into the **WAVEFORMATEX** structure and ascend out of the chunk.

```
    /* descend to the data chunk */
    child.ckid = mmioFOURCC('d', 'a', 't', 'a');

    if (mmioDescend(hmfr, &child, &parent, MMIO_FINDCHUNK))
    {
      mmioClose(hmfr, 0);

      exit(-1);                  //WAVE file has no data chunk
    }

    channel = AllocChannel();

    sound[channel] = new BYTE[child.cksize];
    len[channel]   = child.cksize;

    if (sound[channel] == NULL)
    {
      exit(-1);
    }
```

Here, we're finding a free slot for the sound and setting up to store it.

```
/* read the wave data */
if ((DWORD)mmioRead(hmfr, (char *)sound[channel], child.cksize) !=
    child.cksize)

{
  mmioClose(hmfr, 0);
  exit(-1);                      //unable to read data chunk
}

mmioClose(hmfr, 0);

CreateBuffer(channel);
FillBuffer(channel);

return (channel);
}
```

Then, we read the actual sound data into the memory just allocated and close the file. We next make calls to create and fill a DirectSound buffer for the **WAVE**.

 Note

This class, in attempting to hide some of the details from the caller, also makes some assumptions for it. In this case, the caller cannot reuse or overwrite DirectSound buffers. With D IRSOUND, a WAVE is a DirectSound buffer. Look out for this: It is a classic tradeoff in software engineering.

Here's the source code to **DIRSOUND::AllocChannel**.

```
WORD DIRSOUND::AllocChannel(void)
{
  WORD x;

  for (x=0;x<ds_NUMCHANNELS;x++)
  {
    if (lpdsb[x] == NULL)
    {
      break;
    }
  }

  if (x == ds_NUMCHANNELS)
  {
    exit(-1);                    //no channels are available
  }

  return (x);
}
```

It's looking for an unused slot in our private DirectSound buffer array. There are two interesting points about this code.

First, the array is allocated as part of the object. It's always good to avoid lots of memory allocation and deallocation, because they can lead to memory fragmentation. In the case of **DIRSOUND**, it's easy to see that a program using it needs a fixed number of slots. Since a slot takes little memory and slot usage is so predictable within a given program, a fixed scheme like this makes sense.

The second point about this code is that it bails out when it detects there are no slots remaining (an error condition). An alternate scheme (which I do not prefer) would return a -1 or another error condition. The caller then determines whether it received a legitimate slot number or an error and takes appropriate action. For any system with a fixed number of slots, the error condition should be treated as fatal because it indicates you must increase the array size for the program's current configuration. In a dynamic allocation scheme, you should always handle running out of memory gracefully.

DIRSOUND::CreateBuffer allocates a fresh DirectSound buffer, custom-made for the new **WAVE**.

```
void DIRSOUND::CreateBuffer(WORD channel)
{
  DSBUFFERDESC dsbdesc;
  PCMWAVEFORMAT pcmwf;
  HRESULT hr;

  memset(&pcmwf, 0, sizeof(PCMWAVEFORMAT));
  pcmwf.wf.wFormatTag      = WAVE_FORMAT_PCM;
  pcmwf.wf.nChannels       = ds_CHANSPERSAMPLE;
  pcmwf.wf.nSamplesPerSec  = ds_SAMPLERATE;
  pcmwf.wf.nBlockAlign     = ds_CHANSPERSAMPLE * ds_BITSPERSAMPLE / 8;
  pcmwf.wf.nAvgBytesPerSec = pcmwf.wf.nSamplesPerSec * pcmwf.wf.nBlockAlign;
  pcmwf.wBitsPerSample     = ds_BITSPERSAMPLE;

  memset(&dsbdesc, 0, sizeof(DSBUFFERDESC));
  dsbdesc.dwSize        = sizeof(DSBUFFERDESC);
  dsbdesc.dwFlags       = DSBCAPS_CTRLDEFAULT;
  dsbdesc.dwBufferBytes = len[channel];
  dsbdesc.lpwfxFormat   = (LPWAVEFORMATEX)&pcmwf;

  hr = lpdirsnd->CreateSoundBuffer(&dsbdesc, &lpdsb[channel], NULL);

  if (hr != DS_OK)
  {
    exit(-1);
  }
}
```

It initializes a **WAVEFORMATEX** and **DSBUFFERDESC** structure and calls DirectSound for a new secondary buffer. Note how it picks up the size of the **WAVE** from **len[channel]**. An alternate method would be to explicitly pass the size as a parameter to the function. In general, passing parameters to functions beats using global (or even object private) variables. But in the case of **DIRSOUND**, the code is simple enough. Given that we're in danger of coding a bug related to this, it doesn't matter either way.

Finally, the function creates the DirectSound secondary buffer and returns.

After `CreateBuffer`, `DIRSOUND::LoadWave` calls `FillBuffer`; its code appears below:

```
void DIRSOUND::FillBuffer(WORD channel)
{
  LPVOID write1;
  DWORD length1;
  LPVOID write2;
  DWORD length2;
  HRESULT hr;

  hr = lpdsb[channel]->Lock(0, len[channel], &write1, &length1,
                            &write2, &length2, 0);

  if (hr == DSERR_BUFFERLOST)
  {
    lpdsb[channel]->Restore();

    hr = lpdsb[channel]->Lock(0, len[channel], &write1, &length1,
                              &write2, &length2, 0);
  }

  if (hr != DS_OK)
  {
    exit(-1);
  }
```

The interesting thing so far, besides our accepting up to two possible write pointers from `DIRECTSOUND::Lock`, is that we must be prepared for the *buffer lost* error. This error usually occurs if you have allocated memory in the sound board's RAM and another application writes over it. In this case, you must restore it and retry the operation.

Of course, our simple code should never encounter a split buffer (we lock the buffer starting with offset zero) or a lost buffer (we just allocated it). But robust code is designed to handle all cases.

```
  CopyMemory(write1, sound[channel], length1);

  if (write2 != NULL)
  {
    CopyMemory(write2, sound[channel] + length1, length2);
  }

  hr = lpdsb[channel]->Unlock(write1, length1, write2, length2);

  if (hr != DS_OK)
  {
    exit(-1);
  }
}
```

Once the buffer is locked down all we need to do is recopy the sound data, unlock the buffer, and return.

`DIRSOUND::Stop`, `DIRSOUND::UnLoadWave`, `DIRSOUND::DestroyBuffer`, and the `dtor` are trivial functions. Their source code is on the CD in the back of the book.

3D Positioning

Wouldn't accompanying your 3D graphics with 3D sound be exciting?

With a firm grasp of the human hearing mechanism and some good ole' *digital signal processing* (DSP), you can render an audio stream that appears to originate from a specific point. Any number of 3D-localized sounds can be mixed together in a 3D audio soundscape.

The Theory

Let's define some terms. *Azimuth* is the angle in the horizontal plane around the listener's head, as shown in Figure 11-6, looking down at the head.

Elevation is the angle in the vertical plane, as shown in Figure 11-7, looking sideways at the listener's head.

In both figures, we define 0 degrees where convenient, and sweep increasing angles counterclockwise. But, of course, any other consistent scheme would work.

With loudspeakers, placing a sound within an azimuth of +/- 60 degrees is entirely possible. Distance cues are also stable and consistent. But azimuths outside that range, or elevation of any kind, don't function consistently. Some sounds (those containing full spectra) work better than others, and if they're constantly moving around, it helps.

With headphones, the above limitations do not apply. It's possible, in theory, to place a sound anywhere—even behind, above, or below the listener.

It should come as no surprise that the algorithm for 3D audio localization is different for speakers than for headphones.

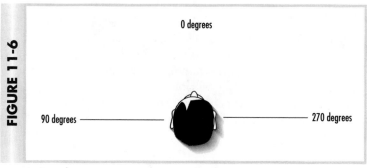

FIGURE 11-6

Azimuth

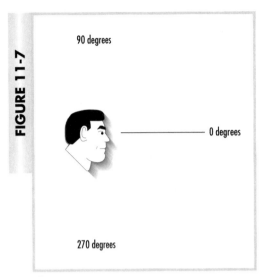

FIGURE 11-7

Elevation

How Do You Localize Audio?

Let's briefly look at how the magic is performed.

You might guess it's easy; the sound is louder in the ear it's closer to. Unfortunately, it's not so simple. There are several *cues* used by the human brain to determine where a sound comes from. Audio positioning is not an exact science.

The ears are only about six inches apart. Most sounds are far enough away that the distance between the ears doesn't account for a significant falloff in sound power.

The next idea is to look at the angle of the sound. The volume at which each ear hears a sound has more to do with the emitter's angle than the distance between the ears.

But even a noise 10 feet left of your left ear sounds almost as loud in your right ear, though there's some *Interaural Intensity Difference* (IID). IID is one cue, but not the most important.

Let's return to that six-inch gap between the ears, which, at the speed of sound in air, is significant compared with the wavelength of a band of frequencies. There is an *Interaural Time Difference* (ITD), which provides the most important azimuth cues.

If you have a subwoofer in your stereo system, try turning off your main speakers and playing some music. If your stereo is really sending the subwoofer just the bass signal, you won't be able to determine where the sound is coming from! The ear does not localize bass information, because the distance between them is too small a fraction of the bass frequencies' wavelength.

You're probably wondering how you can tell whether a sound is behind, or perhaps above, you. After all, any such sound will have identical IID and ITD parameters to a frontal sound.

This is where the odd shape of the outer ear comes into play. Your ear's *pinna* (and to some extent, your head, face, neck, shoulders, and body) acts as a frequency-dependent filter. That is, from any given angle of approach, incoming audio is reduced more at some frequencies than others. Change the angle and all the frequency coefficients change.

Due to the small size of the pinna, the frequency of the audio must be even higher (than for ITD). Also, since this *Head Related Transfer Function* (HRTF) filters each frequency to a different level, it doesn't work with single-frequency audio. For this reason, it's difficult to determine the location of a pure sine wave.

Note

It's comparatively difficult to determine the emitter location without moving your head. That's why you cock your head to one side when listening to faint sounds—the abrupt change in angle helps localize a sound.

So What?

What does all this mean? What do we learn from it?

For starters, we must realize that perfect 3D audio doesn't happen without a head-tracking unit and headphones.

But perfection isn't necessary. Frontal angle and distance cues are quite stable and computationally easy to produce. Beyond that, there are DSP techniques that provide elevation cues or position sounds behind the listener. They're good enough right now to produce an exciting audio experience that will certainly augment any 3D graphics.

And, like everything else in computers, the state of the art advances steadily each day.

The DirectSound3D API

All of this information is useless without a 3D audio API. Microsoft has extended DirectSound for DirectX 3 to include 3D audio capabilities.

Now there's a special type of secondary buffer for 3D audio streams, called **IDirectSound3DBuffer**. You obtain a secondary buffer by first calling **IDirectSound::CreateSoundBuffer**, just as you would for a regular sound buffer. The only difference is you must use the **DSBCAPS_CTRL3D** in the **swFlags** field. Once you have the buffer, you call **QueryInterface** to obtain the **IDirectSound3DBuffer** interface:

```
lpds->CreateSoundBuffer(&dsbufdesc, &lpdsbuf, NULL);
lpdsb->QueryInterface(IID_IDirectSound3DBuffer, &lpds3dbuf);
```

You can use this new interface to control the various 3D parameters, or you can use the **IDirectSoundBuffer** interface to control the non-3D parameters of the sound. Both control different aspects of the same sound.

The primary structure used in controlling a 3D sound buffer is defined as:

```
typedef struct
{
  DWORD       dwSize;     //how many bytes used in this struct
  D3DVECTOR   vPosition;     //coordinates of sound emitter
  D3DVECTOR   vVelocity;     //velocity vector of emitter (for Doppler)
  DWORD       dwInsideConeAngle;
  DWORD       dwOutsideConeAngle;
  D3DVECTOR   vConeOrientation;
  LONG        lConeOutsideVolume;
  D3DVALUE    flMinDistance;  //doesn't get any louder closer than this
  D3DVALUE    flMaxDistance;  //doesn't get any software farther than this
  DWORD       dwMode;

} DS3DBUFFER;
```

The sound cone needs some explanation. An *omnidirectional* sound radiates equally in all directions. However, most sounds are at least somewhat directional. That is, they are louder in the direction they facing.

DirectSound3D supports this phenomenon using a pair of cones. Within the inner cone, the sound is at its stated maximum volume (attenuated for distance). Outside the outer cone, the volume level is specified by the **lConeOutsideVolume** field (zero is maximum, and all values should be less than or equal to zero). Between the two cones, volume is smoothly interpolated between the two levels depending on the angle—quite sophisticated, actually.

The primary API call you use in working with 3D audio is **SetAllParameters**, which takes a pointer to a **DS3DBUFFER** structure, and a **DWORD**, which is either **DS3D_IMMEDIATE** or **DS3D_DEFERRED**, telling DirectSound to immediately apply the new parameters, or wait for a call to **CommitDeferredSettings** (a method of **IDirectSound3DListener** we'll discuss in a moment).

The corresponding call to read all the current 3D parameters for a sound is **GetAllParameters**.

There are individual calls to set and get each parameter, but they are of limited use.

You can create and use as many 3D DirectSound buffers as you wish. However, there is only one listener supported by the system. Let's take a look at the listener.

The **IDirectSound3DListener** object is created from the primary buffer, just as an **IDirectSound3DBuffer** is created from a secondary buffer.

The primary structure used for controlling the listener is

```
typedef struct
{
  DWORD       dwSize;     //how many bytes used in this struct
  D3DVECTOR   vPosition;     //location of listener
  D3DVECTOR   vVelocity;     //for Doppler
  D3DVECTOR   vOrientFront;    //facing of front of listener
  D3DVECTOR   vOrientTop;    //facing of top of listener's head
  D3DVALUE    flDistanceFactor;  //your distance units as fractions of a meter
  D3DVALUE    flRolloffFactor;  //distance rolloff factor compared to real air
  D3DVALUE    flDopplerFactor;  //doppler effect factor compared to real world
} DS3DLISTENER;
```

Both the distance rolloff factor and the Doppler effect factor have ranges of 0 to 10, inclusively.

Just like with 3D buffers, there are **SetAllParameters** and **GetAllParameters** calls, which work in the same way. There are also calls to set and get each parameter individually.

There's one other additional call, **CommitDeferredSettings**. This call will, as the name implies, affect any changes made with the **DS3D_DEFERRED**.

DEV3D

Unfortunately, DirectSound3D will not exploit any 3D DSP functions in the audio hardware. It's a software-only API.

Faced with the perennial tradeoff of quality versus CPU usage, Microsoft made the only choice game developers could accept: sacrifice quality in favor of CPU impact.

There are audio chips whose powerful DSPs can localize several audio streams in 3-space. One of the most notable is from VLSI Technology—it's a PCI-based audio chip that mixes sounds, localizes them, performs wavetable synthesis, and so on.

The DEV3D (named for DiamondWare, Echo Speech, and VLSI) specification was developed by these three companies to address the total lack of hardware support of DirectSound3D.

The specification is vendor-independent and is available in its entirety to the public on the Web at **http://www.dw.com/dev3d**. The DEV3D reference code is also downloadable from this page. The reference code offers an API that looks DirectSound3D and will utilize DEV3D if present, or DirectSound3D if not.

The DEV3D API

Unlike DirectSound3D, DEV3D does not provide function calls. Microsoft's DirectSound API cannot be so extended. DEV3D works by using a block at the end of a DirectSound buffer.

This extra block would play back as awful noise if a DEV3D-compliant driver were not present in the system. Therefore, we need a method to determine whether or not DEV3D is supported. We'll extend this concept and return a structure full of hardware capabilities. Let's look at the query operation first.

```
#define dev3d_QUERY      "DEV3DCompliant?"
#define dev3d_SIGNATURE  "!tnailpmoCD3VED"
#define dev3d_LOCALIZE   "DEV3D Localize!"

typedef struct
{
   char    szMagicString[16];
   DWORD   dwDEV3Dversion;          //hi word is major, lo word is minor
   DWORD   dwMaxHighQuality3D;      //total # of high-quality-localized streams
   DWORD   dwMaxMediumQuality3D;    //total # of med-quality-localized streams
   DWORD   dwMaxLowQuality3D;       //total # of low-quality-localized streams
   DWORD   dwFreeHighQuality3D;     //current remaining capacity
```

continued on next page

continued from previous page

```
DWORD    dwFreeMediumQuality3D;
DWORD    dwFreeLowQuality3D;
DWORD    dwReserved[5];
```

} dev3d_INFO;

At the beginning of the word, you should allocate a DirectSound buffer with a length the size of this structure. Call **Lock** on the buffer, copy the **dev3d_QUERY** string into the **szMagicString** array, then call **UnLock** and then **Lock** again. If **szMagicString** holds the **dev3d_SIGNATURE** string, DEV3D is supported in this system. If so, then the other fields of the **dev3d_Info** structure hold valid values.

You can perform the query operation any time thereafter, whenever you need to determine how many 3D streams are available. All hardware systems can localize only a finite number of sounds at the maximum. After that, localization quality degrades to medium and eventually low. Beyond that, the hardware cannot localize sounds at all.

To localize a given sound, the application allocates its DirectSound buffer with some extra space at the end—enough to hold a **dev3d_LOCALIZE** string, a **DWORD**, a **DirectSound3DBuffer** structure, and a **DirectSound3DListener** structure.

The sound data begins at offset zero, and extends to **buflen − dev3d_EXTRABUF** bytes. The extra space at the end of the buffer is used for communicating the localization information out-of-band.

As mentioned above, the extra bytes at the end of the buffer are used for DEV3D information. The first 16 bytes must be the **dev3d_LOCALIZE** string. This is how the driver knows not to play the data as sound.

The next **DWORD** is a priority value. If the application requests more 3D-localized voices than the DSP hardware can provide, this field helps the driver determine which voices to do at a lesser quality—or not localize at all.

After the priority field comes a **DS3DBUFFER** structure and, finally, a **DS3DLISTENER** structure. You can read or write them any time the DirectSound buffer is locked. To indicate that you don't want to change a field, write a **0xffffffff** to it.

Note

There is only one listener; so each time you write to it, the new values replace the old.

DEV3D is still being finalized as I write this. The finished specification can be found on the Web at **http://www.dw.com/dev3d**.

In Conclusion

So what have we done? We surveyed DirectSound and learned our way around it. By way of a roadmap, Figure 11-8 illustrates the hierarchical nature of the various DirectSound components (mostly COM objects), showing which ones create which.

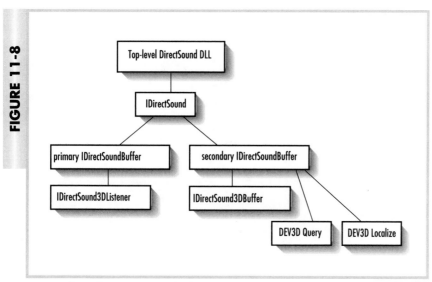

FIGURE 11-8

Hierarchy of DirectSound objects

We've also built a decent class encapsulating DirectSound and **WAVE** file code and learned the important aspects of each along the way.

While a competitive game in today's market is likely to demand more from its sound engine (such as 3D audio), the **DIRSOUND** class will serve well in many applications. Never underestimate the value of having learned how to do it, either.

For a more feature-filled (and easier to use) sound system, you might take a look at the demo of DiamondWare's Sound ToolKit on the CD accompanying this book. It's not only more complete than **DIRSOUND**, but it also supports Windows 3.x and Windows NT, in addition to Windows 95. It's no substitute for learning how to do it yourself, but it's useful if you're more interested in finishing games quickly. In today's highly competitive game market, development time is critical.

By the time you read this, version 2.0 will probably have been released. It includes total DirectSound support, 3D positional audio, plug-in DSP filters, full-duplex record and playback, realtime compression and decompression, and so on.

12

DirectPlay

by Keith Weiner

In this chapter, we'll discuss DirectPlay. But unlike we did for DirectSound, we won't present a reasonably complete class. Why not?

Networking is more complicated than sound. Essentially, a sound API must be able to handle simple commands such as *play this*, *stop playing that*, and so on. On the other hand, a network API must keep two or more state machines in sync.(A state machine transitions between a finite number of states, and its input expectations vary depending on the current state.) It's not that simple to hide the details of this task behind a class wrapper. In any event, networking architecture is beyond the scope of this chapter.

The DirectPlay COM object contains more methods than the DirectSound object, plus there are more issues to handle.

Why DirectPlay?

We thoroughly examined DirectSound in order to understand why it exists and learned that its purpose is to provide low-latency audio mixing. Everything else is already provided by Windows (also known as hardware-independence), can be done by an API vendor (multi-channel mixing), or is less important (hardware-accelerated mixing).

With networking, the TCP/IP, IPX, modem, other hardware drivers, and Winsock provide a formidable and robust platform on which to build your application. So what does DirectPlay do that's so important?

In part, the answer stems from marketing, as with DirectInput. It's certainly a value-added API, but not nearly to the extent that DirectSound is, let alone DirectDraw (probably the component which makes the Games SDK so hot).

On the positive side, DirectPlay offers some functionality beyond connectivity: sessions, groups, player management, and so on. Let's take a closer look at these concepts.

The Basic DirectPlay Model

When your program initializes, it first queries DirectPlay for available drivers. If there's a choice, it lets the user pick whether he or she wants to play over the LAN, Internet, proprietary service, and so on. Finally, it opens the chosen driver.

Next, there may be a choice of *sessions* (or games). Some of them may even be your application. Each might or might not allow new players. Present a list of games to the user. The user may opt to join one of the games or start a new one. All players after this point have the option of joining this new game or one of the others.

Once a player connects to a game, the program queries it to enumerate the players in it. Players can join or leave at any time. You will have to handle this non-trivial issue. In fact, you will also have to handle cases in which the driver loses the connection, especially with modem and Internet drivers.

You must create a player object, which sends all existing players a system message so they know to add you to their internal data structures. Sending a network message is easy. All you need is a buffer with data and the ID of the recipient (or zero for all players). A single function call can guarantee it's been received. Note that some data will be irrelevant if not received immediately. However, you will achieve optimum performance if you send these messages *unreliably*, saving the time and network bandwidth that gets wasted if the message is resent.

Receiving, on the other hand, is more complicated (though easier than it could be). You never know when you will receive a network message, so you can't just poll in a hot-loop waiting for one to come in. However, you can fire off a background thread that blocks until a message is received. We'll also look at a way to periodically poll (such as from a WM_TIMER message handler). Chances are your program will have a list of what it needs to accomplish each time through the main loop. Receiving network messages will definitely be on the list. In many applications, batch processing the messages received since the last poll is a reasonable method. Our code expects a heartbeat call (like during WM_TIMER) and will call your function through a pointer once for each player message (it handles system messages).

This is the bare minimum. What doesn't it address?

Almost everything. Starting with sessions. DirectPlay supports saving a session to the registry, but this was originally intended for things like phone numbers in modem games. Saving the state of a game is itself a deep topic. Things quickly grow more complex when there are several players. Ask yourself whether it's reasonable to allow 11 out of 12 players to resume a saved game.

The player list is the next exciting issue. You start out knowing the players in the game before you. It's all well and good that some code in your program detects when new players join. But how do you handle this at the higher levels? It's much easier to allow new players to join for a period of time, until the player who created the session hits the *go* button. At this point, new players cannot join anymore (there's a DirectPlay method to call for this), and the game action commences. Of course, you can opt to allow players to join at any time. This chapter will not address the implications of such a decision.

Players can drop out, too. Although the code in this chapter only exits in this case, a commercial game program needs to do something more robust. For example, when new players join in the middle of the game, there are data structure issues at the higher level.

Although the code in this chapter doesn't exploit it, DirectPlay lets you put players into groups. Team A and Team B might be one scheme, or perhaps all players in a given room in the dungeon form one group. Maintaining groups is work, but sending to a group can sometimes save much more network bandwidth than sending to several players individually (and sometimes results in DirectPlay just sending the individual messages).

Of course, sending and receiving are the biggest problems. What messages do you send? How do you handle receiving any of them? This is where you will spend the bulk of your efforts—designing the protocol and architecture. Should each machine send all the world data during each frame? Or just what's changed? Which machine should control which objects and enemies? How do you stay synchronized? How do you handle when network latency is slower than any acceptable frame rate?

The list goes on and on. A comprehensive treatment of this topic could fill a book.

Instead, we'll cover the specifics of the DirectPlay API and write the lowest level of code on top of it. It will add some value, but it will make few architectural decisions.

DirectPlay API Overview

As in DirectSound, the DirectPlay DLL exports two functions: enumerate and create. They serve the same purpose, too.

Exported Functions

```
HRESULT DirectPlayEnumerate(LPDPENUMDPCALLBACK enumdrivers, LPVOID context);
```

This function takes a pointer to a function that is called once per installed DirectPlay driver. The second parameter is a user-supplied data structure, or **NULL**.

Your enumeration functions look like:

```
BOOL PASCAL EnumDrivers(LPGUID lpguid, LPSTR name, DWORD majver, DWORD minver,
LPVOID context);
```

For each DirectPlay driver, there is a GUID, a human-readable name, and a version number. Your function should return **TRUE** to continue enumerating, **FALSE** to stop.

```
HRESULT DirectPlayCreate(LPGUID lpguid, LPDIRECTPLAY *lplpdp, IUnknown
*outer);
```

You specify which driver to open by its GUID. The **create** function returns a pointer to a DirectPlay object, which is how you'll perform the other operations. The last parameter is there for future compatibility with COM aggregation features. For the current version of DirectPlay, it must be **NULL**.

Salient Methods

As I hinted earlier, I won't cover all of DirectPlay's methods—only the ones we need to get up and running. As with all other non-trivial APIs, you start with the basics and learn the rest as needed (no programmer knows what every last Windows API call does, but everyone has called **SendMessage** or written a **WM_PAINT** handler).

```
HRESULT IDirectPlay::Release(void);
```

If you called **DirectPlayCreate**, you must call this function when you're done.

```
HRESULT IDirectPlay::EnumSessions(LPDPSESSIONDESC lpdpsession, DWORD dwtimeout,
LPDPENUMSESSIONSCALLBACK enumsessions, LPVOID context, DWORD flags);
```

The first parameter is a pointer to a structure describing the type of sessions you're looking for. You certainly don't want to find sessions of people playing someone else's game! The structure contains:

```
DWORD      dwSize;
GUID       guidSession;
DWORD      dwSession;
DWORD      dwMaxPlayers;
DWORD      dwCurrentPlayers;
DWORD      dwFlags;
char       szSessionName[DPSESSIONNAMELEN];
```

Given that the structure may change size in future versions, the **dwSize** member is a good way to ensure DirectPlay does not cause an access violation trying to reach members that aren't there. This implies that future fields will be backward-compatible.

Each session has a GUID, which is how you will later specify the one you want to join. **dwSession** will be returned by DirectPlay later when you create or join a session.

dwMaxPlayers and **dwCurrentPlayers** tell you something about the state of the game you're entering. Later, if you create a new session, you must fill in **dwMaxPlayers**.

For this call, **dwFlags** must be set to **DPENUMSESSIONS_ALL**. Later, when you want to create or join a session, you will use **DPOPEN_CREATESESSION** or **DPOPEN_OPENSESSION**.

szSessionName is either input or output, depending on whether you are creating the game or entering it after someone else created it. For this call, it's output.

There are other fields, but they are not normally used.

The next parameter to **IDirectPlay::EnumSessions** is **dwtimeout**, which gives the timeout value in milliseconds. Internally, DirectPlay broadcasts its query for sessions. It waits a finite period of time before concluding it knows what's out there. Different connection mechanisms, of course, have radically varying latencies. All machines on a single-segment Local Area Network (LAN) should respond in no more than a few milliseconds. On the other hand, in a game in which the players are connected to the Internet by modem, enumerating all available sessions on a given server might take many seconds.

The third parameter is a pointer to a user-provided enumeration function.

Pass **NULL** for the **context** parameter. For **flags**, use **DPENUMSESSIONS_AVAILABLE** (for games in progress) or **DPENUMSESSIONS_PREVIOUS** (for games previously saved in the registry). Saving games in the registry is not fully supported yet by DirectPlay.

Your enumeration function looks like:

```
BOOL EnumSessions (LPDPSESSIONDESC lpdpsession, LPVOID context, LPDWORD
lpdwtimeout, DWORD flags);
```

You'll get a session descriptor structure, with the GUID, maximum players, current number of players, and session names filled in. These will help you determine whether or not to join.

Ignore the **context** parameter.

The **timeout** parameter here is given through a pointer. You can change the value if you want, though I'm still not clear on when you should do so. Microsoft is silent on this topic.

The flags **field** is supposed to be a mechanism in which DirectPlay tells you the enumeration has timed out. Plus, it allows you to reset the timeout period. But you have no more information at the timeout than when you began the enumeration, and thus no reason to wait for more stragglers to enumerate. You can safely ignore it.

Once you've enumerated the available sessions (and somehow presented them to the player), he or she has enough information to decide which one to join, or whether to start his or her own. The following DirectPlay method is the next call you must make:

```
HRESULT IDirectPlay::Open(LPDPSESSIONDESC dpsessiondesc);
```

This call is used for creating a new session, as well as joining an existing one. **dpsessiondesc** is a pointer to a session descriptor structure, as we saw earlier. In this case, you need to supply the session GUID to get back the session number.

If you call **IDirectPlay::Open**, eventually you must call **IDirectPlay::Close** (which takes no parameters).

Once you're connected to a session, the next step is to create a player object.

```
HRESULT CreatePlayer(LPDPPID lpdpid, LPSTR friendlyname, LPSTR formalname,
LPHANDLE lpevent);
```

The first parameter is the address of the variable holding the player's newly created ID.

The two names are used only for display to the user, and they need not be unique. It's up to you to decide when it's appropriate to display one or the other. *Jonathan Smith (Jonny) has entered the game* and *Jonny shot you for 10 points of damage* might be appropriate usage of the formal and friendly names.

The **lpevent** parameter was not used in this chapter's code, mostly to avoid extra complexity. It's a handle to a single-event object (created and maintained by the application), which you can supply. When the player object receives network messages, DirectPlay can signal it. This is useful if you have a background thread for networking; it calls **WaitForSingleObject**. And it is much more efficient than hot-looping on a call to **DirectPlay::Receive**.

If you call **IDirectPlay::CreatePlayer**, then you must later call **IDirectPlay::DestroyPlayer**. It takes one parameter, the **DPID** returned when you created the player. If you're joining an existing game, you will also need to determine the players already in the session.

```
HRESULT IDirectPlay::EnumPlayers(DWORD sessionid, LPDPENUMPLAYERSCALLBACK
enumplayers, LPVOID context, DWORD flags);
```

The first parameter is the session ID, returned by `IDirectPlay::OpenSession`.

Next is the pointer to your enumerate function.

Ignore the context parameter. `flags` can be one of `DPENUMPLAYERS_GROUP`, `DPENUMPLAYERS_PREVIOUS`, or `DPENUMPLAYERS_SESSION`, specifying that you want the groups as well as the players and you want the players stored in the registry (although Microsoft says this is not yet supported). Otherwise, the list for the specified session should be pulled from the nameserver. Use a zero to simply enumerate the players in the game.

The user-supplied enumeration functions look like:

```
BOOL EnumPlayers(DPID dpid, LPSTR friendly, LPSTR formal, DWORD flags, LPVOID
context);
```

In the first parameter, DirectPlay passes the player's ID.

The next two parameters are the short and long versions of the player's name (in ASCII text).

The `flags` field can be one of `DPENUMPLAYERS_GROUP`, `DPENUMPLAYERS_LOCAL`, or `DPENUMPLAYERS_REMOTE`, specifying that group and player names should be enumerated, only local players should be enumerated, or only remote players should be enumerated. Since these are parameters to a callback function called by DirectPlay, Microsoft's documentation is unclear on what the flags mean. I can only conclude that DirectPlay is telling your callback what it was instructed to do when you called `IDirectPlay::EnumPlayers`. At the time of this writing, DirectX was still evolving, to say nothing of the state of its documentation!

Now, we're finally onto the meat and potatoes: sending and receiving messages. We'll look at the immediate problem of sending and receiving data buffers using DirectPlay. Designing a set of messages, creating an architecture to manage them, and keeping synchronized are all non-trivial issues.

```
HRESULT IDirectPlay::Send(DPID idfrom, DPID idto, DWORD flags, LPVOID data, DWORD
len);
```

The first two parameters are your player ID and the recipient's ID. Use zero to send to everyone in the session.

The `flags` field can be one of `DPSEND_GUARANTEE`, `DPSEND_HIGHPRIORITY`, or `DPSEND_TRYONCE`. Respectively, this field specifies that: you want a reliable send; the send must get there as soon as possible (even if it wastes some network bandwidth to go right away); or the message should be sent once, in which case we don't care if it's received.

A good example of when to use reliable and unreliable sends can be found in the backgammon application I developed (it was written for OS/2, but the principles are the same). When one player drags a piece around, the other sees it move on his or her screen. I used an unreliable message for this, because the position is updated again as soon as the player moves his mouse one more pixel. However, when a piece is dropped, I use a reliable message since it's critical that both computers have the same board positions in their memory.

Since Microsoft does not say how large messages can be, some caution is appropriate. Most underlying network architectures have limits to the packet sizes they can send (thus, there is an efficiency issue for Winsock and DirectPlay). Modems are not, in general, reliable. Since error checking—and resend requests—are done only for an entire packet, sizes are limited (modem file transfer protocols usually do not exceed 1K, unless they successfully send several smaller packets first). The code for this chapter uses 1K as its maximum buffer size.

The **data** and **len** fields specify the message to be sent.

```
HRESULT IDirectPlay::Receive(LPDPID lpidfrom, LPDPID lpidto, DWORD flags, LPVOID data, LPDWORD len);
```

You call this method to receive a message. The first two parameters tell the function which messages you want to see (or use zero for all messages), as well as your own ID. Remember, DirectPlay does not know your player ID unless you pass it as a parameter. Future versions will undoubtedly support multiple players on a single machine, playing against others on their own machines (especially as we see Windows 95 and NT merge into one operating system).

The **flags** field may be one of **DPRECEIVE_ALL**, **DPRECEIVE_FROMPLAYER**, **DPRECEIVE_PEEK**, or **DPRECEIVE_TOPLAYER**, indicating that: You're interested in all messages, you're only interested in those from a certain player, you want a preview without removing the message from DirectPlay's queue, or you want only messages sent to a certain player ID (system messages are sent to ID zero).

data is a pointer to a message to hold the buffer. **len** is the address of the variable holding the length of your buffer. The function returns the actual length of the message received.

The Goal

We'll do this a little bit differently than we did for DirectSound, when we developed a reasonable class you could actually use in a real game. Given everything we've seen about DirectPlay (and everything we haven't), there's no way we could develop anything nearly as comprehensive—or as likely to be useful.

Instead, what we'll do is develop a *value-added* wrapper for DirectPlay, which isolates the application program from many of the details of network programming using DirectPlay, provides a few work-saving mechanisms, but does not encapsulate a network object. In other words, we'll develop some C++ functions, but not a C++ class (assume what you will about my position in the C++ *everything should be an object* debate).

We still haven't touched upon the following issues: lost connections, players joining or dropping out in the middle of a game, a messaging protocol, a mechanism for enqueing then later dispatching a number of messages at once (in real-world networks, one 1K message is much faster than 100 10-byte messages), a background thread for receiving messages, synchronization, a *mailbox* mechanism so individual objects in the game can receive messages, ways to deal with the uncertainty caused when an opponent's message wasn't received before the next frame, the DirectPlay lobby (we'll discuss the lobby in more detail later), and so on. In short, we won't address the problems caused by supporting network play, only the raw mechanism for exchanging messages on a network.

The Code

Let's look at the code for **DP.CPP**. We'll take it somewhat out of order because I think the best order to present the code isn't the best for code style.

Like most function libraries, this one needs to be initialized before being used.

```
void dp_Init(dp_MESSAGECALLBACK *mcb)
{
  DWORD ret;

  messagecallback = mcb;

  numdrivers  = 0;
  numsessions = 0;
  numplayers  = 0;

  lpdirplay = NULL;

  ret = DirectPlayEnumerate(EnumDrivers, NULL);

  if (ret != DP_OK)
  {
    exit(-1);
  }
}
```

As you can see from the parameter list, we ask the user of the module to supply a pointer to a function. We'll call that function whenever the player has received a message not handled internally at this library. The capability to call a function by a pointer is one of the wonderful features separating C from, say, Pascal or BASIC, though this mechanism isn't used as often in C++ code. Here we'll use it to avoid making assumptions about what the application might want to do when it receives a network message. We initialize some variables and document their uses below.

Finally, we enumerate the DirectPlay drivers available on the machine. Notice how we bail out if we receive a DirectPlay error. This code is hardly commercial quality, but it's easier to read and explain. It's amazing how code grows in sheer size and complexity when all the little touches are added for robustness and reliability. This call will result in one or more calls to our enumeration function, so let's look at it next.

```
static BOOL PASCAL EnumDrivers(LPGUID lpguid, LPSTR name, DWORD majver,
                               DWORD minver, LPVOID context)
{
  memcpy(&dpdriver[numdrivers].guid, lpguid, sizeof(dpdriver[0].guid));

  dpdriver[numdrivers].name = new char[strlen(name) + 1];
  strcpy(dpdriver[numdrivers].name, name);

  if (++numdrivers == NUMDRIVERS)
  {
    return (FALSE);
```

```
    }
    else
    {
      return (TRUE);
    }
}
```

Note how the function is declared **static**. This eliminates the risk that its name will clash with a function in another source file. I always prepend the module name onto publicly visible names (like **dp_Init**) and declare all internal-use functions with the **static** storage class.

First, the function copies the GUID and driver name. DirectPlay does not guarantee the validity of these pointers outside this enumeration call.

Each driver is stored in a separate structure member in an array. We need to ensure that we don't write past the end of it, though it's extremely unlikely there will be more than 16 DirectPlay drivers on a user's machine.

When the application is done with the library, it should deinitialize it.

```
void dp_Kill(void)
{
  DWORD x;

  for (x=0;x<numplayers;x++)
  {
    delete [] player[x].friendly;
    delete [] player[x].formal;
  }

  for (x=0;x<numdrivers;x++)
  {
    delete [] dpdriver[x].name;
  }

  DestroyPlayer();
  CloseSession();
  CloseDriver();
}
```

It needs to deallocate the memory used by the driver names and player names. Then, it needs to close down DirectPlay, which has probably allocated a player, session, and driver (each of those functions checks to make sure).

After initializing the library, the application will probably want to give the user his or her choice of drivers.

```
char *dp_GetDriverName(DWORD drivernum)
{
  return (dpdriver[drivernum].name);
}


DWORD dp_GetNumDrivers(void)
{
  return (numdrivers);
}
```

There's a function call to determine how many drivers exist and a call to get the name of each. This is surely easier to use than the enumeration scheme DirectPlay provides.

Once you've presented the available drivers to the user and determined his or her choice, the library lets you open it by the ordinal number you used to get its name.

```
void dp_OpenDriver(DWORD drivernum)
{
  HRESULT ret;

  ret = DirectPlayCreate(&dpdriver[drivernum].guid, &lpdirplay, NULL);

  if (ret != DP_OK)
  {
    exit(-1);
  }

  sdesc.dwSize  = sizeof(sdesc);
  sdesc.dwFlags = DPENUMSESSIONS_ALL;

  ret = lpdirplay->EnumSessions(&sdesc, TIMEOUT,
                                EnumSessions, NULL,
                                DPENUMSESSIONS_AVAILABLE);

  if ((ret != DP_OK) && (ret != DPERR_NOSESSIONS))
  {
    exit(-1);
  }
}
```

After the call to **DirectPlayCreate**, we have a pointer to a DirectPlay object. All calls after this point will be to methods of that object.

This function also enumerates the available sessions. This is a good example of value-added wrapper. **dp_EnumerateSessions** could have been a separate function. But why should it be? There is no conceivable reason user why a would want to open a driver but not want to follow up with a query of available sessions for it.

The enumeration function is similar to the one for drivers.

```
static BOOL PASCAL EnumSessions(LPDPSESSIONDESC lpdpsgamedesc,
                                LPVOID lpcontext, LPDWORD lpdwtimeout,
                                DWORD flags)
{
  if (lpdpsgamedesc == NULL)
  {
    return (FALSE);            //timeout is the end of the road
  }

  memcpy(&dpsdesc[numsessions], lpdpsgamedesc, sizeof(dpsdesc[0]));

  if (++numsessions == NUMSESSIONS)
  {
    return (FALSE);
  }
```

```
  else
  {
    return (TRUE);
  }
}
```

The function, like the other enumerators, is declared with the Pascal calling convention. C and C++ use, by default, a convention allowing for a variable number of passed parameters.
`printf` is a good example of this. In order to pull this magic off, the compiler has to generate code pushing them onto the stack in the opposite order occurring in the source code.
Thus, the first parameter popped off the stack by the called function is the first parameter to the function. That's how the called function knows to interpret its arguments (for
example, `printf` gets the format string with the `%d` and `%s` fields in it).

Regardless of which convention is better (the C convention allows for a feature not possible with the Pascal method), caller and callee must agree on one to use.

The function first checks if the session descriptor pointer is **NULL**, indicating that
DirectPlay's enumeration has timed out. If not, it copies the descriptor into its own private
array.

```
char *dp_GetSessionName(DWORD sessionnum)
{
  return (dpsdesc[sessionnum].szSessionName);
}


DWORD dp_GetNumSessions(void)
{
  return (numsessions);
}
```

We do the same thing for sessions as for drivers. After the user has decided on the session, you should call:

```
void dp_OpenSession(DWORD sessionnum)
{
  HRESULT ret;

  dpsdesc[sessionnum].dwFlags = DPOPEN_OPENSESSION;

  ret = lpdirplay->Open(&dpsdesc[sessionnum]);

  if (ret != DP_OK)
  {
    exit(-1);
  }

  ret = lpdirplay->EnumPlayers(sdesc.dwSession, EnumPlayers, NULL, 0);

  if (ret != DP_OK)
  {
    exit(-1);
  }
}
```

Again, you declare which session to open using its ordinal from the enumeration. After the call to open the session we start the player enumeration, just as we do with the sessions after the call to open the driver. The code for the player enumeration is

```
static BOOL PASCAL EnumPlayers(DPID dpid, LPSTR friendly, LPSTR formal,
                                DWORD flags, LPVOID context)
{
  player[numplayers].dpid = dpid;

  player[numplayers].friendly = new char[strlen(friendly) + 1];
  player[numplayers].formal   = new char[strlen(formal) + 1];

  strcpy(player[numplayers].friendly, friendly);
  strcpy(player[numplayers].formal, formal);

  numplayers++;

  if (++numplayers == NUMPLAYERS)
  {
    return (FALSE);
  }
  else
  {
    return (TRUE);
  }
}
```

We have to allocate space to store the short and long name for each player (which will be deallocated later).

If the player instead wants to create a new game (or if there isn't an existing one, there isn't any choice), call this instead:

```
void dp_CreateSession(void)
{
  HRESULT ret;

  sdesc.dwSize  = sizeof(sdesc);
  sdesc.dwFlags = DPOPEN_CREATESESSION;

  ret = lpdirplay->Open(&sdesc);

  if (ret != DP_OK)
  {
    exit(-1);
  }
}
```

Notice how the code does not bother enumerating the players—there aren't any players in a new session—but is otherwise very similar to dp_OpenSession.

Assuming that the player has joined an existing game, expect the following two functions. One theme repeated often in software engineering literature is *creativity causes bugs!* If you can design an API so it does the expected, do so. And so, there are **dp_GetNumPlayers** and **dp_GetPlayerName**, which follow the precedent set for drivers and sessions.

```
void dp_GetPlayerName(DWORD playnum, char **friendlyname, char **formalname)
{
  *friendlyname = player[playnum].friendly;
  *formalname   = player[playnum].formal;
}


DWORD dp_GetNumPlayers(void)
{
  return (numplayers);
}
```

The only trick is supplying two name values, which can't easily be done via the function's return value. So we modify the caller's two **char **** parameters.

Sending a message, as alluded to earlier, is easy:

```
void dp_Send(DWORD playnum, void *data, DWORD len)
{
  HRESULT ret;

  if (len > MAXBUFFERLEN)
  {
    len = MAXBUFFERLEN;
  }

  ret = lpdirplay->Send(dpid, player[playnum].dpid,
                        DPSEND_GUARANTEE, data, len);

  if (ret != DP_OK)
  {
    exit(-1);
  }
}
```

Notice how we're clipping all messages to the maximum length as necessary. This isn't really robust, but it will prevent problems. It might be better to break messages that are too long into *n* pieces and send each one separately. The receiver could put them back into one piece. But this quickly gets complicated. First, you'll need a header indicating that a message is part of a bigger piece. You'll need to order the messages and put them into the bigger piece on the other end. You'll need two message numbering schemes: one for the actual packets sent, and one for the larger messages the pieces comprise. And, as we'll see, the receiving end would get even more complicated—it's quite difficult to determine when to call the user with *here's your message*.

Such additional functionality is a good candidate for its own module. In an expanded networking hierarchy, the lowest level (**DP.CPP**) would probably just publish the maximum allowed buffer size through a function call made after the **dp_OpenDriver**. This would allow it to query the system and perhaps even try some performance benchmarks, in order to calculate the maximum buffer size. The next module up (say **NETMSG.CPP**) would be responsible for breaking down and assembling large messages, checksumming, requesting resends, handling timeouts, and so on. That's probably enough for one module to do.

For receiving messages, there is no **dp_Receive**. Why?

Because the **DirectPlay** system sometimes sends a message that is not meant for the application (such as **DPSYS_ADDPLAYER**, telling you that a new player just joined the game), we need to receive these messages with some predictability. Waiting until the user calls **dp_Receive** might not be sufficient. Instead, the library provides **dp_Update** (I use the convention of calling a function **Update** if it should be called regularly, like from a **WM_TIMER** handler). In the case of this DirectPlay library, the function will call the application back when it has a message for it. This is a nice way of making network messages event-driven, like the rest of any Windows program. This mechanism could easily have been implemented as a window message, but it would need to have the user's window handle and a message number.

Anyway, to the code:

```
void dp_Update(void)
{
  static data[MAXBUFFERLEN];
  DPMSG_ADDPLAYER *add;
  DPMSG_GENERIC *msg;
  DPID dpidfrom;
  DPID dpidto;
  HRESULT ret;
  DWORD len;
  DWORD x;
```

data was declared with **static** storage class. It's always a good idea to take large arrays and structures off your stack frame—where local variables normally live—and put them in their own storage. It helps avoid stack overflows, too.

```
  len = MAXBUFFERLEN;

  ret = lpdirplay->Receive(&dpidfrom, &dpidto, DPRECEIVE_ALL, data, &len);

  if (ret == DPERR_NOMESSAGES)
  {
    return;
  }
```

We don't know if there are, in fact, any messages for us. Most of the time, this function will simply return.

As hinted at earlier, a more sophisticated architecture is to have a background thread block until DirectPlay signals there is a message. The background thread would dump it into a buffer of some sort and return to wait mode. The update function would then call the user back next time it's called. The reason the background thread wouldn't call the user's function itself is to avoid all the re-entrancy (additional calls on executing code during an interrupt) issues. A good API and the code behind it should always strive to minimize potential problems.

```
  if (ret != DP_OK)
  {
    exit(-1);
  }

  if (dpidfrom == 0)
  {
```

```
    /* System message */
    msg = (DPMSG_GENERIC *)data;

    switch (msg->dwType)
    {
      case DPSYS_SESSIONLOST:
      {
        exit(-1);        //not the best way to handle it...

        break;
      }
      case DPSYS_ADDPLAYER:
      {
        EnumPlayers(add->dpId, add->szLongName, add->szShortName, 0, NULL);

        break;
      }
      case DPSYS_DELETEPLAYER:
      {
        exit(-1);          //not even close to the best way to handle this!!!

        break;
      }
    }
}
```

This code bails when it gets a message it doesn't like. Game players won't tolerate such behavior. The tricky thing happening here is that, when the code gets the message that a new player has joined, it just calls the `EnumPlayers` function (the same one called back by DirectPlay). If confined to a single source file, this sort of thing won't necessarily cause problems.

The more significant problem is that the application doesn't know there is a new player in the game, and therefore does not know to call `dp_GetPlayerName` or update its own data structures.

Probably the best way to handle this situation, if you decide to let players join in the middle of a game, is to call back a special user-supplied function that's only used for player adds and drops. You'll have to support this in any Multi-User Dungeon (MUD) game.

```
    else
    {
      for (x=0;x<numplayers;x++)
      {
        if (player[x].dpid == dpidfrom)
        {
          (*messagecallback)(x, data, len);

          return;
        }
      }
    }

    //if we get here, the message was not from any player we know...
}
```

This last bit of code determines which player number (as the application understands it) the message came from and calls the user-supplied function.

Without any further knowledge of how this system behaves, it looks like if we reach the comment at the end, we'll have an error condition. A reasonable way to handle this error would probably be to throw it into a log file while debugging, but ignore it otherwise.

Finally, notice how the function does not check whether there's more than one message. In a real-time game, it's critical to get all the messages as soon as they arrive. Otherwise, 15 messages could take a $1/4$ second to trickle in (assuming that **dp_Update** is called about 60 times per second).

The Lobby

The *lobby* is the single most important addition to DirectPlay 3. It allows a separate program to handle all areas of determining who to play a game with, what game to play, how to handle network addresses, and so on. This separate lobby program can then spawn the game program, sparing it some GUI work reinventing the wheel.

The **IDirectPlayLobby** interface (and the **DirectXRegisterApplication** function call), new for DirectPlay 3, provides the functionality that makes this possible.

The Game Program

The lobby needs to know which DirectPlay games are installed. The setup program for each game must therefore call **DirectXRegisterApplication**. This function puts the application name, **GUID**, and other information needed to run into the system registry.

Now let's look at the game program itself.

First the game calls **DirectPlayLobbyCreate**. Next it calls the **IDirectPlayLobby::GetConnectionSettings** method. If it returns the error **DPERR_NOT-LOBBIED**, the application was not launched by a lobby. Release the **IDirectPlayLobby** interface, then proceed from here as discussed earlier in the chapter.

Otherwise, you can optionally change the number of players allowed, whether or not players may even join after this point, and so on with the **IDirect PlayLobby::SetConnectionSettings** call. Finally, you must call **IDirectPlayLobby::Connect**, which will return a pointer to an **IDirectPlay2** interface.

At this point, create a player. You already know what to do from there.

The Lobby Program

I have this vision (yes, I still have my sanity): Someone puts in the time and effort to develop a lobby program and server the *right* way, no holds barred. Imagine being able to download a universal lobby client program from the Web—a classy GUI-based effort with all the bells and whistles, including multichannel chat, different rooms, maybe even BBS-style message areas, advertising banners, and so on.

It can handle every DirectPlay application that will ever be written. It knows what games are installed on your machine and easily lets you list all the other players. In no time you've put together teams for the game you want to play, all players click the Launch button, and the games begin.

Using the TCP/IP protocol, the lobby program logs into the lobby server with an IP address configured at setup time (and probably stored in the registry). This lobby client/server system is meant for the Internet, but can also work on any TCP/IP LAN. Since most game players don't have multi-kilobuck corporate (let alone home!) LANs to play on, and long-distance telephone service is expensive, the Internet is the most important multiplayer game delivery mechanism. (Ever wonder why it's so much cheaper to exchange data all over the world for 200 *hours* a month than to call long distance for 200 *minutes*? The answer is taxes, but I digress.)

The lobby client first creates an `IDirectPlayLobby` interface just like the application, although it will use different calls. To build a list of games compliant with the `IDirectPlayLobby` launch method (lobbyable games), it will use a call to `IDirectPlayLobby::EnumLocalApplications`.

The lobby client should then call `DirectPlayEnumerate`, to build a list of the available service providers. `IDirectPlayLobby::EnumAddressTypes` will build a list of the address types required for each service provider. Our hypothetical lobby client is probably looking for the service provider(s) that work through the Internet (though this could be configurable at runtime—the important point is it wants to know that all players can physically address each other). The `DPAID_Inet` address type means the given service provider uses Internet addressing.

The client will then tell the server the player's name (probably stored in the registry), IP address, list of games available, and so on. The user will spend some time reading messages, chatting with potential players, and so on. Eventually, the server will give all the client programs the addresses of the other players, which is where DirectPlay programming comes in.

`IDirectPlayLobby::CreateAddress` will convert the IP address (in string format) to something usable by DirectPlay. Finally, the `IDirectPlayLobby::RunApplication` will actually load and execute the game program.

I haven't written code to do all this stuff. It's complex, and far beyond the scope of a simple chapter on DirectPlay. Interested readers will want to peruse the `DPLAUNCH` sample, included with DirectX 3. Although it's nothing near what I described here, it shows all the functions being called in context.

Conclusion

We've surveyed DirectPlay and determined how to use it to connect to multiple players on any supported network. Unlike with DirectSound, we have not examined how things would otherwise have worked. Interested readers should pick up one of the books on Winsock or network programming architectures.

Given the team nature of today's game development environment, one programmer will have to become an expert in network programming. His or her input would impact the overall program design. The network programming itself would likely consume a few months in a state-of-the-art program.

We've developed some code that calls into the DirectPlay component, and determined along the way that this is really just the beginning. There is a lot more code to write in order to actually complete a network game.

We've raised many—but undoubtedly not all—of the issues involved in networking a game with DirectPlay. But running into major unforeseen engineering problems at the last minute is one of the joys known to software developers.

13
Artificial Intelligence

It's fun to play games with other people over a network, modem, or the Internet, but sometimes you can't find anyone to play with. What then? Well, most games have a single player mode for such a situation, in which you compete against the computer instead. Of course, if you're used to playing against people and the computer is as dumb as your toaster, you won't stay entertained long. That's where artificial intelligence (AI) comes in.

Although AI is used for all kinds of things in the computer world, it's most commonly used for games. AI ranges in complexity from a tic-tac-toe engine to one that talks and carries on a meaningful conversation with you. If you're only writing an action game, then you won't need to write a very advanced AI engine. But if you're writing a chess game or a strategy war game, you might want to make your engine a bit more intelligent. The type of AI used varies with each game; it's up to you to decide which techniques you want to use.

In all honesty, the artificial intelligence in most games isn't really *intelligent* per se. Real artificial intelligence, the kind developed in labs and universities, would be much too processor-intensive for games. Instead, game programmers try to simulate artificial intelligence by giving the game a kind of intelligent behavior. We hope the techniques in this chapter will show you how to implement the level of intelligence you want in your game. Just be aware, however, that AI isn't *real* artificial intelligence, just a sort of intelligent behavior.

Throughout the chapter, we'll look at a few of the most common types of artificial intelligence, including:

- Chasing the player
- Avoiding (eluding) the player
- Adding chance to the algorithm
- Convergence

- Divergence
- Patterns
- States
- Using probability to select states
- Vision

We'll look mainly at using AI in 2D games, because a third dimension adds a lot of complex topics beyond the scope of this book. However, this chapter will include several hints on how to implement the 2D techniques we're discussing in 3D games. Also, some of the basic algorithms for techniques such as chasing and avoiding can be converted to 3D simply by adding the third dimension (Z) into the mix.

One other thing you should keep in mind throughout this chapter: The more complex the AI engine, the more processing time it needs. If you're writing a fast-moving action game, you don't want such an advanced AI that it significantly drops the frame rate. If you're writing a game that doesn't rely on fast screen updates, such as a board or strategy game, then it won't matter as much. Besides, you'll probably *need* a more advanced AI. Again, it's up to you to weigh these factors and decide.

Tracking the Player

The simplest way to implement AI is to *track* the player—in other words, make the computer enemies chase or avoid the player.

Chasing the Player

To chase the player, you just need to know his or her location and the location of the computer enemy. Let's say the situation looks something like Figure 13-1, with the player at (*player_x, player_y*) and the enemy a little down and to the right at (*enemy_x, enemy_y*). Assume we're using the traditional 2D coordinate system with (0,0) at the upper-left corner.

As you can see from the picture, the enemy has to move in both directions (*x* and *y*) to reach the player. To find where the enemy should move to so it can get closer to the player, we must calculate its movement in each direction separately.

First, we check to see whether the enemy is above or below, and to the left or the right, of the player. We then move the enemy accordingly. The bare-bones code segment in Listing 13-1 shows how to do this—it's pretty self-explanatory.

Listing 13-1 Chasing the player

```
if( enemy_x < player_x )      // If the enemy is to the left of player
    enemy_x++;                //  move it to the right
else if( enemy_x > player_x ) // If the enemy is to the right of player
    enemy_x--;                //  move it to the left
```

FIGURE 13-1

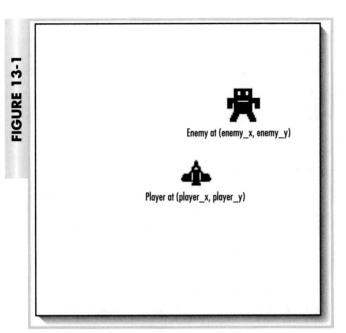

Enemy at (enemy_x, enemy_y)

Player at (player_x, player_y)

Player and enemy locations

```
if( enemy_y < player_y )      // If the enemy is above the player
    enemy_y++;                // move it down
else if( enemy_y > player_y ) // If the enemy is below the player
    enemy_y--;                // move it up
```

If this were part of a real game, you'd probably see if the enemy were right on top of the player and then kill the player or at least penalize him or her somehow. In our code, though, the enemy just sits on top of the player until he or she moves again.

Another thing you'll notice is that it makes a big difference how fast you move the enemies. In Listing 13-1, we only moved the enemy one coordinate unit in each direction, each time the code ran. In a real game, however, you'll probably move enemies at many different speeds, depending on several factors. For example, in the classic arcade game *Space Invaders,* the aliens got faster and faster as the player progressed through the levels, until they moved at such a dizzying pace the player could hardly keep track of them. You could do something similar in your game, for instance, have different speeds for walking and running. There are numerous ways to use the enemies' speed in your game.

A more advanced chasing technique involves anticipating where the player will go based on the direction in which he or she is currently moving, instead of simply heading toward his or her current position. You'll also need to devise this kind of algorithm if you want your enemies to *aim* at the player, since the missiles will almost never hit the player if they're just aimed at where he or she *was*, instead of where he or she *will be*.

You should keep in mind that the player should be able to move faster than enemies, or the enemies will eventually catch up to the player no matter what (unless you create some kind of time limit level). Remember, it's no fun if you can't win!

Avoiding the Player

Avoiding the player, the exact opposite of chasing the player, is simple as well. All you really need to do is reverse the code in Listing 13-1 as follows (Listing 13-2):

Listing 13-2 Avoiding the player

```
if( enemy_x < player_x )      // If the enemy is to the left of the player
    enemy_x--;                //  move it farther to the left
else if( enemy_x > player_x ) // If the enemy is to the right of the player
    enemy_x++;                //  move farther to the right

if( enemy_y < player_y )      // If the enemy is above the player
    enemy_y--;                //  move it farther up
else if( enemy_y > player_y ) // If the enemy is below the player
    enemy_y++;                //  move it farther down
```

If you want to use this code in your game, you should add some lines that make sure the enemy doesn't move off the edge of the screen. Otherwise, the enemy will continue to run away from the player forever, right off into infinity.

Adding a Little Chaos

Life is seldom predictable, so your AI shouldn't be either. It makes for more interesting interaction with the computer if you don't know what's coming next. For this reason, you'll probably want to add a bit of chance to your AI engine.

To do this, you need a random number generator. You can either write your own routine—there are several that people have already written in circulation on the Net—or use the standard C library function **rand**. **rand** gives you a seemingly random number, derived from a number called the *seed*. You can either give **rand** a seed each time you call it (using the **srand** function), or you can let **rand** get its own seed from the system clock. The system clock should work just fine for any game, but you can go ahead and give **rand** a seed by some other method if you wish.

One handy little algorithm to keep in mind: If you use **rand** in a statement such as

```
num = rand % MAX_NUM
```

num will be a number between zero and **MAX_NUM**. This is an extremely useful line of code you'll use often to find a random number between two other numbers.

There aren't any hard and fast rules about where to add calls to **rand** in your program. You can add or subtract a random number to or from an object's speed, or determine an enemy's direction with a random number. Don't use chance *exclusively* when determining these factors, however, because your AI will seem totally random and purposeless, and therefore unintelligent (also known as AS, or Artificial Stupidity), which is not what we're shooting for. To create a truly lifelike engine, you need to use other AI techniques along with chance.

To give a brief example of how you could use **rand** to spice up your AI routines, let's modify the earlier snippet of code that had the enemy chase the player (see Listing 13-1).

One possible way to inject chance into this routine is by adding a small random number to each direction in which the enemy moves. The enemy will still eventually reach the player, but it'll take a roundabout route that won't seem quite so artificial. This will also make it harder for the player to target the enemy, since the enemy won't appear to be taking any direct path. Listing 13-3 shows the modified code:

Listing 13-3 Adding chance to a chasing routine

```
if( enemy_x < player_x )      // If the enemy is to the left of player
   enemy_x += (rand % 2) + 1; //  move it to the right
else if( enemy_x > player_x ) // If the enemy is to the right of player
   enemy_x -= (rand % 2) + 1; //  move it to the left

if( enemy_y < player_y )      // If the enemy is above the player
   enemy_y += (rand % 2) + 1; //  move it down
else if( enemy_y > player_y ) // If the enemy is below the player
   enemy_y -= (rand % 2) + 1; //  move it up
```

As you can see, instead of just adding or subtracting 1 or 2 from the enemy's position, we add or subtract **(rand % 2) + 1**. **rand % 2** gives us a random number between 0 and 2. Adding 1 ensures that the enemy will move at least 1 coordinate unit (in case **rand** comes up with 0). This means the enemy can move 3 coordinate units at most, 1 at the least.

Just remember this is only *one* way to add chance to your AI routine. The possibilities are endless, so don't let yourself be restricted by something you read in a book.

Teamwork

Making your computer enemies work together makes a huge difference in how intelligent they seem. Most humans, when they're on a team, try to work together to prevent the other team from winning. The same should hold true with your AI entities. Although it's a little tougher to implement than just one enemy working solo, the results are well worth the trouble.

You can get as tricky as you want with your teamwork implementation. You can have enemies pair up to attack the player, or swarm the player all at once. You can even have one enemy distract the player while the others sneak up from behind. It's all up to you, but again, bear in mind that you need to strike a balance between intelligence and processing power.

There are two basic types of AI teamwork. There's *convergence*, in which the enemies all head toward one common point (often used when the enemies are supposed to attack the player). And then there's *divergence*, in which all the enemies scatter away from a common point (often used in retreat situations).

Convergence

Basically, all you do to implement convergence and divergence code is make the enemies chase or avoid a common point. There are some more complex ways to achieve the same results, but they're really not worth the trouble. They involve a lot of intricate math, and the speed gains yielded really aren't that impressive. Let's take a quick look at how to make a swarm of enemies converge on the player (see Listing 13-4):

Listing 13-4 Converging on the player

```
for( int j = 0; j < NUM_ENEMIES; j++ )
{
    if( enemy[j].x < player_x )
        enemy[j].x++;
    else if( enemy[j].x > player_x )
        enemy[j].x--;

    if( enemy[j].y < player_y )
        enemy[j].y++;
    else if( enemy[j].y > player_y )
        enemy[j].y--;
}
```

As you can see, the only change is that the enemies are stored in an array (presumably holding **NUM_ENEMIES** enemy structures). Somewhere earlier in the code you'd need to put them all somewhere, either randomly or with hard-coded positions.

Of course, there are many possible variations to this code. You could store a lot of information specific to each enemy in its structure, such as its speed, the chance factor (which we didn't even use in this code), or just about anything else. There's a lot of room for innovation in this code. It would be vastly improved just by writing a C++ class for enemies, so they could move themselves just by calling some member function.

Divergence

Divergence is just the opposite of convergence, so all you would do to implement it is use the avoidance routine instead of the chasing routine, as in Listing 13-5:

Listing 13-5 Diverging from the player

```
for( int j = 0; j < NUM_ENEMIES; j++ )
{
    if( enemy[j].x < player_x )
        enemy[j].x--;
    else if( enemy[j].x > player_x )
```

```
        enemy[j].x++;

    if( enemy[j].y < player_y )
        enemy[j].y--;
    else if( enemy[j].y > player_y )
        enemy[j].y++;
}
```

Again, you'll have to add some code to make sure the enemies don't run clear off the edge of the screen if you plan to use this. It might also be beneficial to make them diverge toward some other spot to regroup after they've scattered, depending on the situation.

Patterns

One technique used a lot in action games to create realistic movement on the part of computer enemies is hard-coded patterns. These patterns are simply pre-recorded movements—dodging, pivoting, swooping, punching, and so on—that look very lifelike. Computer enemies programmed with hard-coded patterns are spared the trouble of calculating movements on the fly. Even though this is sort of cheating, it's *very* effective. Hard-coded patterns are used all the time in games, especially fighting and sports games in which the computer enemies are constantly performing complex actions.

 Note

Direct3D gives you an easy way to use patterns by using animations loaded from a file. See the earlier Direct3D chapters for more information.

Although you *could* code an AI engine that produces the same results as using patterns, it would probably be so slow it would detract significantly from the frame rate. This especially applies to sophisticated 3D games since there are so many different variables that you'd need to consider.

Patterns are usually stored in some sort of data structures loaded in from a file. You choose a pattern depending on what the player does. You can still use other AI techniques, such as avoidance and convergence, but using patterns once in a while (or even more often) will really give your enemies life. There are also certain situations in which you'll always use patterns, like when an enemy dies (for example, a plane just about always goes into a tailspin).

The format you use to load and store patterns in your game is entirely up to you (except if you decide to use an API route—see the Note above). It will change from game to game, especially between 2D and 3D games. 3D game patterns tend to be much more complex since they end up storing information for all (or almost all) the vertices of an object. Patterns also tend to get quite large for complex objects such as humans, because they require incredibly involved actions and literally thousands of vertices (for a detailed model). As you can see, it's beyond the scope of this book to show you how to implement a pattern system.

States

One of the most advanced AI techniques this chapter discusses is the use of *states*. States hold information about what an enemy is, or should be, doing. An enemy is always in some kind of state, and you use its present state to determine what action (or pattern) it will perform next.

For example, let's consider a scenario in which an enemy tank is chasing the player, also in a tank (see Figure 13-2).

Right now the enemy is chasing the player (thus the state named *Chasing*). There are a number of things that could happen here. If the enemy gets within firing range, it would probably be a good idea to change its state to *Attacking*. Or, if the *player* starts firing, you might want to change the enemy's state to *Retreating*, and possibly have it go into some sort of evasive pattern.

That's where the whole trick of using states comes in: It's difficult to decide which state the enemies should enter next. Generally, each state has a set of conditions that must be met in order for the enemies to enter into it. Sometimes you'll have rules saying if the creature is in one state, it must next move into a subsequent state (for example, if an enemy has been hit and is in the *Dying* state, it'll move to the *Dead* state next). Other times you might want to select a state randomly, just to keep things interesting (you might choose between *Hunting* and *Resting*, for example). As you've probably noticed by now, AI is very case-specific, and there aren't any hard and fast rules about using it.

FIGURE 13-2

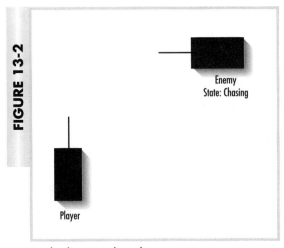

Enemy
State: Chasing

Player

Tank chasing the player

Choosing States Using Probability

You probably don't want your enemies to be predictable, so you'll have to choose the next state they enter somewhat randomly (save for special situations like death). Of course, you don't want them to be *completely* random, otherwise they won't appear intelligent at all. What to do?

A special method of state selection used a lot in games, *probabilistic state selection,* simply chooses from a number of different states based on each one's probability of occurring (we'll call it the state's *probability factor*). You do this by assigning each state a number—usually a decimal number in tenths—designating its chances of occurring. The probability factors of all the states should add up to 1. Probabilistic state selection is also useful for deciding on an enemy's plan of attack, or any number of other things that must be chosen with some degree of intelligence.

For example, consider Table 13-1, which shows four different states and their probability of occurring (notice all the probability factors add up to 1):

Table 13-1 States and their probabilities of occurring

State	Probability
Chasing	0.4
Avoiding	0.1
Attacking	0.3
Random	0.2

When you select a state, you choose one based on its probability factor. As you can see, *Chasing* has the greatest chance of occurring—in fact, it occurs about 40 percent of the time since its probability factor is 0.4. Individually, none of the other states are as likely to occur but if you look at them together, one of them *will* occur 60 percent of the time. Everything tends to even out in the end.

To implement probabilistic state selection in code, you'd make a table containing the states from which you want to select. Actually, it will probably contain #defines corresponding to states because putting the actual state structures in the table would get pretty hairy.

Listing 13-6 is a brief example showing how to use probabilistic state selection (using the states from Table 13-1 and their probability factors). It creates a table (using an array) and fills it with the five states, putting in each the specific number of times corresponding to its probability factor. Then it randomly selects one of the states using rand. Take a look:

Listing 13-6 Using probabilistic state selection

```
int state_table[10] = {CHASING, CHASING, CHASING, CHASING, AVOIDING,
                       ATTACKING, ATTACKING, ATTACKING, RANDOM, RANDOM};

int state = state_table[ rand() % 10 ];
```

The probability factor requires 10 elements in the array since the probability factors of all the states add up to 1. For each tenth in each state's probability factor, we stick it into the array once. This way, we can select one of the states by randomly pulling it from the array.

If you want your enemies to adapt to their environment or the current state of the game, one possible way is to change the states' probability factors. If the enemies are more likely to retreat in a certain situation, such as when the player gets a power-up, you might want to turn up the *Retreating* state's probability factor a couple of notches and turn down another state's probability factor the same amount (just so the total of all the factors remains 1). All you'd do to change the code in Listing 13-6 is give the array **state_table** a new set of values corresponding to the modified probability factors.

Vision

The enemies have no sense of vision with the way the AI routines have been programmed so far. If the player is behind a wall, as in Figure 13-3, or behind the enemy, the enemy can still *see* the player, even though the player isn't in its field of vision. Not very fair to the player if enemies have this kind of radar, is it?

You might want to use the sight factor by making the enemy's field of vision vary, depending on several conditions. For example, you might want the enemy to see farther if in a plane, rather than a truck or boat. You might also want enemies with x-ray vision that can see through walls, and so on. There's a lot you can do with it, so go ahead and be creative.

There are a number of ways to give enemies vision. Doing it in 2D is a whole lot simpler than 3D since the extra dimension isn't involved. For the sake of discussion, we'll just consider a 2D game for now. It's up to you to move these techniques into the third dimension.

Perhaps the most common way to give enemies vision in 2D games is to divide the entire game world into square cells, as in Figure 13-4. Using this scheme, every object in the game is contained in a cell (there might be more than one object in a cell, and objects can take up more than one cell). This makes it easy to find out what the enemy sees, because all you have to do is calculate which cells are in its field of vision. You usually do this by including cells in a pyramid shape fanning out from the enemy in the direction it's facing (see Figure 13-5).

FIGURE 13-3

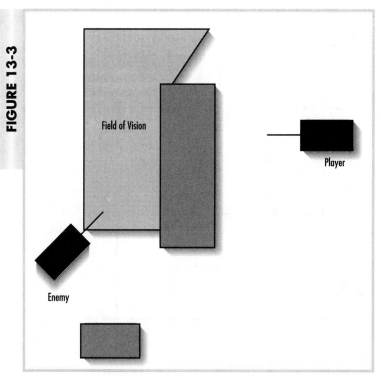

Field of Vision

Player

Enemy

The enemy's field of vision

The only complicated step here is calculating the pyramidal field of vision. That's because you want to be sure that if there's an obstacle in the field of vision, the enemy can't see around it, which sometimes gets sticky.

Once you've nailed down 2D vision, extending this cell technique into the third dimension really isn't too hard. All you have to do is use some 3D objects—such as cubes—instead of 2D cells to find out what your enemies can see.

FIGURE 13-4

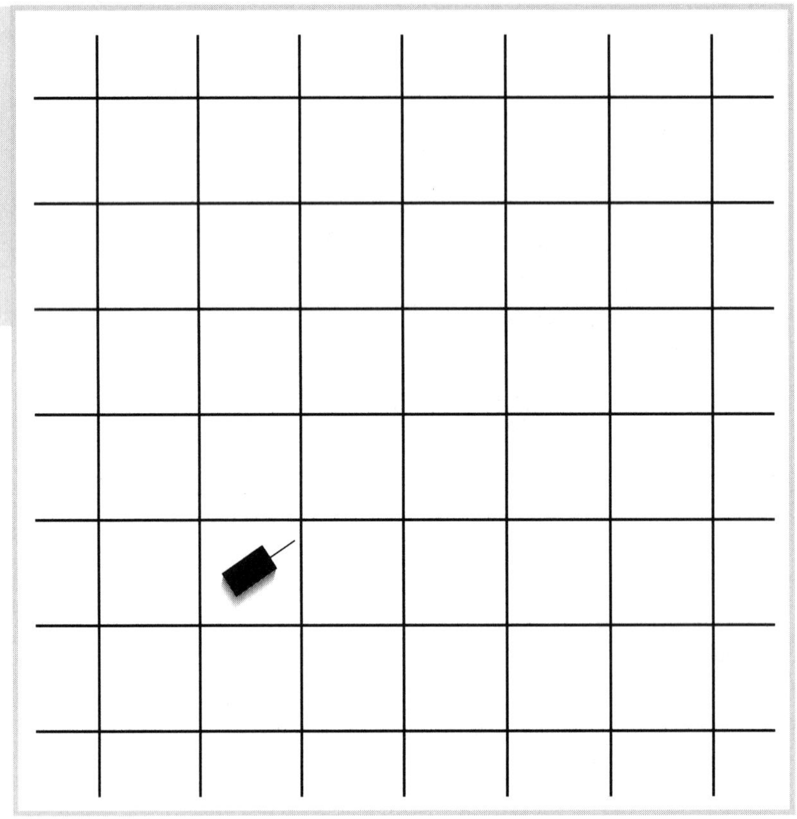

A cellular game world

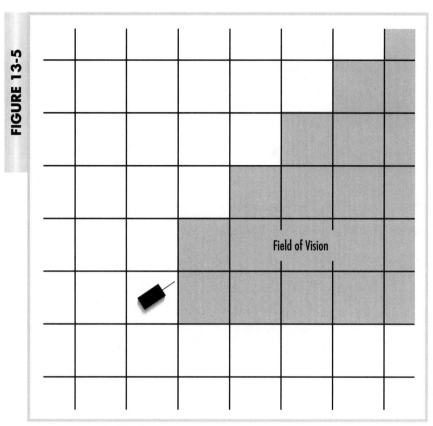

FIGURE 13-5

Field of Vision

The enemy's field of vision

Summary

We covered a lot of ground in this chapter. We talked about most of the common AI techniques including chasing and avoiding the player, using states, and adding vision.

As you've probably seen, a lot of AI is case-specific. It's hard to say what techniques are best for you without looking at your game individually. Hopefully, though, this chapter has given you a solid foundation you'll use to devise your own AI techniques.

14

Distributing Your Game

So you have a game. Now what? Now you need to get it ready for distribution and decide whether to release it yourself or have someone else do it for you. That's what this chapter is all about. We'll cover some of the aspects of game programming that are often overlooked, including:

- Creating an installation program
- Using `DirectSetup`
- Using `AutoPlay`
- Choosing a channel of distribution

You'll be able to present a more polished and refined game after reading this chapter, and be more knowledgeable about how to sell your game.

First, let's take a look at what's involved in writing an installation program for your game.

Installation Programs

Installation programs, or setup programs, are often overlooked by game programmers. Often the installation program is a cheesy little text-based application, the result of the minimum amount of work the programmer could get away with. This really isn't wise. The setup program is the first part of the game a user sees, somewhat of a reflection on the entire game. Besides that, a poorly written installation program can be *extremely* frustrating for the user—

maybe even frustrating enough to make him or her stop right there if the game is share-ware or something similar in nature. And if your game is being sold commercially, you'll either get tons of returns or be flooded by e-mail from hundreds of irate customers.

Writing an actual installation program can get extremely complex and is far beyond the scope of this book. There are plenty of wonderful libraries and tools out there that can alle-viate some of the tedium frequently associated with writing installation programs. Instead of writing user-interface code and file copy code yourself, you can simply tell the tool or library what to do and have it generate a complete installation program for you. One such program, InstallShield, is an excellent tool that comes free with the Win32 SDK and is high-ly recommended as a cheap alternative to writing an installation program yourself. See your Win32 SDK for more information.

Whether you decide to write your installation program from scratch or use some kind of tool, there are a few things you'll need to be sure it does. Let's take a look at them now.

DirectX Installation

The DirectX runtime libraries are the files allowing a user to work with DirectX on his or her system. These are usually DLLs, unlike the programming libraries, which are **LIB** files used to build your application. In order to run any program using DirectX, you must have the runtime libraries installed on the user's system.

Since DirectX is a relatively new technology, it's possible users don't have it installed on their systems yet. Thus, before they can run your game, they'll have to install the DirectX DLLs. That's where **DirectSetup** comes in.

DirectSetup

Luckily, Microsoft provides us with a convenient API (**DirectSetup**) that automatical-ly installs the runtime libraries into their proper locations on the user's hard drive. We still have to write the user interface code for the installation program, but **DirectSetup** auto-matically copies all the DirectX files and sets up the environment (registry settings, and so on).

DirectSetup basically consists of one function, **DirectXSetup**. There's also one other function, **DirectXDeviceSetup**, that you would only use if you were installing DirectX device drivers for a piece of hardware you or your company manufactured. Most game programmers, however, will only have use for **DirectXSetup**, so it's the only one we'll cover in this book.

One short note before we go on to discuss **DirectXSetup**: When you use **DirectXSetup**, you need to #include the header file **DSETUP.H**, which contains all the definitions for **DirectSetup**. You also need to link the library file, **DSETUP.LIB**, to your project when you compile.

DirectXSetup

DirectXSetup is declared as follows:

 ## DirectXSetup

```
int WINAPI DirectXSetup( HWND hWnd, LPSTR root_path,
DWORD dwFlags )
```

DirectXSetup takes three parameters:

- *hWnd*—handle of parent window for setup dialogs.

- *root_path*—string containing the root path to install DirectX components from. This is the directory in which the Direct3D, DirectDraw, DirectSound, and DirectPlay DLLs are located.

- *dwFlags*—indicates which DirectX components will be installed. Legal values are DSETUP_DDRAW (DirectDraw), DSETUP_DSOUND (DirectSound), DSETUP_DPLAY (DirectPlay), DSETUP_DIRECTX (all components), and DSETUP_REINSTALL (install even if any existing components are the same version).

DirectXSetup's return value is important because it tells us whether or not the DirectX components were successfully installed. If DirectXSetup wasn't successful, the return value will give us a pretty good idea of what went wrong. Here's a list of possible error return values:

- 0—successful and no reboot is required.

- 1—successful and reboot *is* required.

- DSETUPERR_BADWINDOWSVERSION—the user is using a version of Windows that isn't supported by DirectX.

- DSETUPERR_SOURCEFILENOTFOUND—one of the source files (from the installation root directory) couldn't be found.

- DSETUPERR_BADSOURCESIZE—a source file's size was incorrect or couldn't be found.

- DSETUPERR_BADSOURCETIME—a source file's data and time couldn't be read or was incorrect.

- DSETUPERR_NOCOPY—a file's version couldn't be read, or the file being copied over had a newer version.

- DSETUPERR_CANTFINDINF—an .INF (setup information) file couldn't be found in the correct location off the root directory (DirectXSetup expects to find several .INF files it uses in subdirectories of the root directory).

- DSETUPERR_OUTOFDISKSPACE—DirectXSetup ran out of disk space during installation.

- DSETUPERR_CANTFINDDIR—DirectXSetup couldn't find the root directory.

- DSETUPERR_INTERNAL—some unspecified internal error occurred.

It's a good idea to put your call to DirectXSetup in a switch statement and give the user a dialog with information about the installation result. That way the user can either try fixing the problem or use the program as is, depending on whether or not the installation was successful.

Before we look at an example, we need to take a look at **DirectXSetup**'s second parameter, **root_path**, and some related files. **DirectSetup** expects to find a number of files and subdirectories in the directory you give it for this parameter, and it just won't work if they aren't there. Thankfully, Microsoft has grouped all these files and directories into one directory on the DirectX SDK CD, named **REDIST**, which is right off of the root directory. This makes life much simpler. All you have to do is copy **REDIST** into a directory on the CD on which your game is being shipped (or into your archive, if you choose that distribution method), and pass **DirectXSetup** the location of *that* directory.

DirectXSetup also expects to find a number of DLLs in the same directory your installation program is in. These DLLs all have the prefix **DSETUP** and are the only files in the **REDIST** directory itself (all the driver and runtime DLLs are in subdirectories of **REDIST**). You must copy these files to the same location as your installation program executable in order for **DirectSetup** to function properly.

When your installation program calls **DirectXSetup**, **DirectSetup** will show several progress dialog boxes as it installs the DirectX components (Figure 14-1). These progress dialogs also have Cancel buttons that cancel the rest of the DirectX installation if the user wants. You don't have to write any code for these dialog boxes; **DirectSetup** does it all.

Okay, let's look at a brief snippet of code that calls **DirectXSetup**. Let's suppose we're installing off a CD, and we've copied the **REDIST** directory from the DirectX SDK CD to a directory by the same name on the game CD. Assuming your installation program's window handle is named *hwnd* and the user chooses to install all of the DirectX components, the code will look something like Listing 14-1:

Listing 14-1 Calling **DirectXSetup**

```
DirectXSetup( hwnd, "\REDIST", DSETUP_DIRECTX );
```

Of course, you certainly want to check for errors. That way, if one occurs, the user will probably know how to remedy the situation so he or she can successfully install the DirectX components.

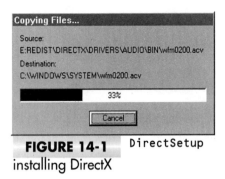

FIGURE 14-1 DirectSetup installing DirectX

AutoPlay

AutoPlay is a feature similar to **DirectInput** in that it's actually part of Windows 95, not the DirectX SDK. It allows CDs to automatically run an executable program when inserted into the CD-ROM drive. You'll probably only use **AutoPlay** if you're distributing your game on CD-ROM (see the section, *Distributing Your Game,* later in this chapter).

 Note

AutoPlay is required if you want to put the Windows 95 logo on your game. (The Windows Logo requirements are summarized in the Appendix.)

AutoPlay works by looking at the user's CD-ROM drive every five seconds to see whether a new CD has been inserted. If it has, **AutoPlay** looks for the file **AUTOPLAY.INF** on the root directory of the CD and runs whatever executable the file tells it to. Incidentally, it *does* take a small amount of time for Windows 95 to check the drive (which, as just noted, it does every five seconds). Theoretically, this could affect the performance of your game, so you may want to tell your user to turn it off.

There's a way to turn off **AutoPlay** using the registry, but that's a whole different topic. If you want to learn how to turn off **AutoPlay**, consult the DirectX help file or the MSDN CD, both of which tell you how.

AUTOPLAY.INF

As mentioned earlier, **AUTOPLAY.INF** is the file **AutoPlay** looks at if it finds a new CD in the drive and must be located in the CD's root directory. **AUTOPLAY.INF** contains a few simple commands telling Windows 95 which executable to run on the CD. Usually the program being executed will either install your game (probably using **DirectSetup** and your custom installation program) or start your game's executable, depending on whether or not your game has already been installed. There are several ways to find out if your game has been installed. In fact, most installation tools provide easy ways to do this.

AUTORUN.INF looks like a standard Windows **.INI** (initialization) file. That is, it has headers in brackets setting off a bunch of values, or commands as **DirectSetup** calls them. Each value has a name and an equal sign (=) denoting it. You'll understand immediately once we look at an **AUTORUN.INF** file.

A typical **AUTORUN.INF** file looks something like this:

```
[autorun]
open=install.exe
icon=install.ico
```

First comes the header, **[autorun]**. This tells **AutoPlay** the commands are about to start. After the header, of course, come the **AutoPlay** commands themselves.

There are only four **AutoPlay** commands. The first and most important is **open**, which tells **AutoPlay** what executable to start when the CD is inserted. As mentioned earlier you'll probably want to write a program that determines if your game is installed and then, depending on what it discovers, either runs or installs the game.

The next command is called **icon**. As you've probably noticed, the icon representing a CD-ROM drive in Windows 95 changes when you insert a new CD. The **icon** command selects the icon Windows should use when identifying your game's CD. The icon can be the name of an icon file, a bitmap file, an executable, or a DLL. If you specify an executable or a DLL, you need to put the (zero-based) index of the icon you want to use after the file name. Here's a sample **icon** command that loads the second icon in the file **BOVINE.EXE**:

```
icon=bovine.exe 1
```

The commands we still haven't covered all have to do with adding a custom menu option to your CD's *context menu*. Your CD's context menu is the menu users see when they right-click on your CD's icon. By default, this only has a few standard options (**Open**, **AutoPlay**, and so on); however, you can use these special commands to add options that do whatever you want.

The first custom context menu command we'll look at is **shell\verb**, which specifies what the text appearing on the menu should say. Like other menus, you can use the ampersand (&) to denote which key will select the menu option (the shortcut key). This line makes the menu option say **Read me** and uses **R** as the shortcut key:

```
shell\verb=&Read me
```

The other command, which works closely with **shell\verb**, is called **shell\verb\command**. This command specifies the executable that will run when the menu option is selected. All you do is give this command the path to the executable you wish to run when your custom menu option is selected. This line would open the file **README.TXT** using Notepad:

```
shell\verb\command=notepad readme.txt
```

The last of these custom menu option commands is **shell**, which sets the default menu option. This command exists just in case you want to override the default menu option, which is **AutoPlay**. You need to give it the same text you gave **shell\verb** for the custom option you want as the default. In keeping with the **Read me** example, the **shell** command looks like this:

```
shell=&Read me
```

Let's quickly look at a short example **AUTORUN.INF** file that demonstrates everything we just learned.

Say we want to run **INSTALL.EXE** when the CD is inserted, and we want the first icon in the same file to represent the CD. We also want to add a new default menu option, which opens the file **README.TXT**. The following **AUTORUN.INF** file is what we'd use:

```
[autorun]
open=install.exe
icon=install.exe
```

```
shell\verb\command=notepad readme.txt
shell\verb=&Read me
shell=&Read me
```

That's about all there is to implementing **AutoPlay**. It's definitely not one of the most complex components of DirectX, but it's necessary if you want to meet the Windows 95 logo requirements (see Appendix).

Online Help

In Windows programs, it's always a good idea to include some form of online context-sensitive help. Users have come to rely on it—and besides, it could help relieve some of the product support costs for your game (more on this later).

There are various ways to write online help, none of which are that simple, unfortunately. It's similar to writing HTML (Hypertext Markup Language) code, which, as you know if you've worked on the Web at all, has a slew of different commands and features.

 Note

Speaking of HTML, Microsoft has plans to move its entire operating system (including online help) over to the HTML format in the next release of Windows. So it might not actually be a bad idea to look into writing your online help as HTML instead of the traditional online help format, especially if you plan on releasing your program on more than one platform.

There are several tools you can use to help ease the burden of writing online help, available in shareware, freeware, or commercial versions. It would be wise to search the Net for one that suits your needs since writing online help by hand is an *extremely* tedious process. But, if you want to write it by hand, go ahead and consult your Win32 SDK documents for more information.

Distributing Your Game

Probably the important decision you'll make during the course of developing your game is how to distribute it. There are two main types of distribution: shareware and commercial. We'll discuss the pros and cons of each, as well as how to go about tackling them.

 Note

If you're a corporate game developer, this section won't be of much use to you because your company will have a marketing department handling all these matters.

Shareware

Shareware is probably the most widely used method of distribution. It lets users test drive your game for a specified time before requiring them to register (send you money).

There is some shareware that depends solely on the honor system for registrations. Going this route is a little risky, though. In fact, there are some alternative ways of getting users to register. Most of these involve distributing a limited or crippled (or, in more politically correct terms, functionally challenged) game, thereby forcing the user to register in order to get the fully operational version.

Games are usually limited by only including a few levels in the shareware version. Hopefully, once the user completes all the levels in the shareware version, he or she will be hooked and will register in order to get the rest of the game.

Another technique that's used quite a bit is holding back some of the best features of the game in the shareware version. id's DOOM (a shareware legend) did this by having two guns that were only available in the registered version. The features you hold back don't have to be weapons, however—they can be anything. You could restrict the characters the user can be in the shareware version and reserve the others for the registration version (this method, in fact, is employed in a lot of fighting-style games).

Some games don't include the full documentation with the shareware version. This probably isn't quite as effective, though, and will most likely frustrate people more than entice them to buy your program. Besides, most games don't need a whole lot of documentation, so it's not a very practical idea.

Another method of getting players to register is to use nag screens. However, this method is mostly used in utility-type programs and might not work too well for games. Every time the user runs the program, a nagging dialog box pops up urging him or her to register. Usually the user can't get the nag screen to disappear until after a certain number of seconds has passed. Some programs also have an OK button on the nag dialog, which the user must press to dismiss it (some programs even move the button around each time they run, so the user has to study the nag screen for a moment or two). Hopefully, the user will get so sick of looking at the nag screen he or she will register the program. But, as I mentioned, this method doesn't work so well for games, because people spend a lot more time playing the game than staring at the nag screen.

The last technique we'll examine, which is becoming increasingly popular, is time-limiting the program. You distribute a fully functional version of your game, but it stops working after a given number of days or uses. The drawback is that it's difficult to implement this approach successfully. Most of the time users find ways to hack or get around the time-limiting scheme so they can continue to use your program. Their methods can be as simple as setting back the computer's clock, and as complex as digging into the game with a hex editor. Either way, you must be sure you can successfully hide the time-limiting scheme from experienced users before you decide to try this technique.

Distribution

Once you've decided to distribute your game as shareware, you need a way to get it into people's hands. The most common (and probably most effective) way to distribute shareware is across online services or the Internet. Millions of people use online services such as CompuServe and America Online, offering a sizable group of potential customers. If you can get your game widely distributed on the Internet, you'll be exposed to an even bigger group of people. If you can spare the expense, you may want to set up a Web and FTP site once your game's ready for distribution, so people who want it can easily access it. If you set up a Web site, you also get a lot of free advertising space you can use to your advantage.

There are also a few mail order companies that sell shareware on disks. You might be interested in calling some and possibly using them to distribute your game. That way you can get your game into the hands of computer users who don't have (or use) modems.

If you developed a good game, it will probably spread by itself once it hits the Net and online services. When people find a game they like, they usually pass it along and discuss it with others. Word-of-mouth is probably the biggest source of advertising you'll find, plus it's totally free.

Product Support

You'll probably have to set up some type of product support if you don't release your game commercially. For shareware authors, this usually just means releasing your e-mail address to purchasers, although you might want to get another phone line if you expect a lot of problems (I hope you won't).

You can also set up a Web site, which, as mentioned earlier, is also a great way to generate a lot of publicity for your game, plus it's a place from which people can download it. A Web site is expensive, though, so unless you expect a lot of revenue from the game, you might just want to use your e-mail address.

Commercial

If your game gets released commercially (in shrinkwrap on store shelves), you'll make a lot more money than if you release it as shareware. A lot of potential buyers might not have modems (or at least high-speed modems necessary for downloading large games), so distributing a game as shareware pretty much rules them out. Also, if your game takes up several hundred megabytes of space on a CD (perhaps because of rendered movie sequences or some kind of multimedia), it's much less likely to be pirated and distributed illegally across the Net or bulletin board systems because it takes so long for data to be sent over modems—hundreds of megabytes of data could take days to send across a modem.

Getting your game distributed commercially isn't the easiest thing to do. Hundreds, even thousands, of people send games to game publishers hoping to make big bucks. A lot of these games are garbage, though, and never get published. If the publisher can wade through the garbage to find your little gem underneath, you have a good chance of getting your game published.

When you shop around for a publisher, you may want to try more than one. Chances are, you won't get a response from several of them due to the volume of submissions they receive. There are plenty of small publishing companies out there who are more than willing to distribute anything, but you probably won't get the same kind of exposure or return you'll get from a big-name publisher.

Submitting a Proposal

When you decide to try to get a certain publisher (or publishers) to distribute your game, you need to submit a proposal to them. A proposal is just a letter outlining your game and giving some details about it. Every company has a different set of items it looks for in a proposal—you should call any prospective publishers and ask them about this.

Usually, though, a proposal includes at least the storyline, the premise of the game, how it's played, some art from the game, and possibly a demonstration. After you've sent in a proposal, you'll just have to wait and see what happens. If you don't hear anything for over a month, it's a good idea to call the publisher and find out what's going on. Many publishers also require you to sign a release form so that if they reject your game and something similar comes out later, you can't accuse them of stealing your idea.

If a publisher accepts your proposal, you'll sign a contract that specifies advance amounts and royalty percentages. Make sure you understand everything (or better yet, hire a lawyer), because it's much too easy for a publisher to back you into a legal corner if you just sign the contract without even looking at it.

Only when your game is on store shelves will you start making money. The standard way to get paid in a game publishing deal is by royalty. That means for every copy of the game sold, you get a small percentage of the proceeds. The rest goes to the publisher to cover their profit, production, salaries, and any number of other things. Even though you aren't getting the total cost of the game, you'll probably make more money than you would distributing it through shareware because so many more copies will be sold.

Note

As mentioned earlier, there are small, independent publishers who are always willing to publish your game. If you *do* decide to go with one of them, you'll probably get a larger royalty, though you probably won't sell as many copies.

If you can't get your game published by a publisher, you should either revamp it and try again or release it as shareware and start another project.

Summary

Well, now you have all the knowledge needed for writing a polished, releasable game. You know how to use **AutoPlay** and **DirectSetup**, and have enough information to make an informed decision about how to distribute your game and get the most money out of the whole deal.

In the next (and last) chapter you'll learn how to put Direct3D, DirectDraw, and DirectSound together to write a complete 3D game. You should then have enough information to write your own game and put to use the ideas we discussed in this chapter.

15
Putting It All Together

Ready to get going with Direct3D? I hope so, because we'll take on a really big project in this chapter. The example in this chapter is bigger than anything we've done—or will do—in the entire book.

In this chapter we'll write a game—simple although it may be—encompassing DirectDraw, Direct3D, and DirectSound. The game part of the program is pretty simple: The user has two minutes to collect as many gold coins from a dungeon as he or she can (there are ten in all). After two minutes, the game ends and a message pops up telling the player how many of the coins were collected.

That may sound too simple, but rest assured this game covers many of the different topics you'll come across when programming a *real* game. The dungeon is a Doom-like environment the user can freely explore with the arrow keys. There are even doors for the user to walk through and collision detection so that the user grunts when he or she runs into a wall. Figure 15-1 shows a screenshot.

To keep things short and simple, there isn't any code in this example to check for the best display mode—it's a program "by programmers, for programmers" as they say. You'll need to run it in a 256-color mode, and the example will take it from there (it sets the resolution in the initialization routines). Hopefully, it'll work correctly for you. The only thing that could mess up the program is your video driver since, as mentioned in the introduction, DirectX is fairly new and hardware manufacturers haven't quite mastered the art of writing video drivers for it yet.

Well, there's more code than we have room to thoroughly cover, so let's get down to business.

FIGURE 15-1

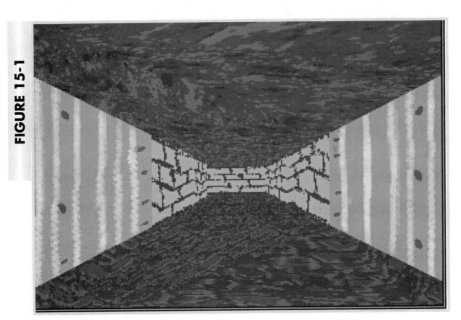

The virtual environment

Getting Started

The program starts in `WinMain`, so that's a good a place as any for us to begin. We'll trace the function calls from there until we're through the entire program.

You should be able to easily recognize what's happening in `WinMain` by now (and if you don't, go back to Chapter 2 where we talked about it). Take a look at Listing 15-1 and see if you can figure it out:

Listing 15-1 `WinMain`

```
int APIENTRY WinMain(    HINSTANCE        hInstance,
    HINSTANCE        hPrevInstance,
    LPSTR            lpCmdLine,
    int              nCmdShow)
{
MSG             msg;            // Message Structure
WNDCLASS        wc;             // Window Class structure


// Register Window style
wc.style            = CS_HREDRAW | CS_VREDRAW;
wc.lpfnWndProc      = (WNDPROC) WndProc;
wc.cbClsExtra       = 0;
wc.cbWndExtra       = 0;
wc.hInstance        = hInstance;
```

```
wc.hIcon               = NULL;
wc.hCursor             = LoadCursor(NULL, NULL);
wc.hbrBackground       = NULL;
wc.lpszMenuName        = NULL;
wc.lpszClassName       = lpszAppName;


// Register the window class
if(RegisterClass(&wc) == 0)
 return FALSE;

// Create the Window
g_hWnd = CreateWindow(lpszAppName, lpszAppName,
 WS_VISIBLE,
 0, 0, dwScreenWidth, dwScreenHeight,
 NULL, NULL, hInstance,NULL);


// If window was not created, quit now
if(g_hWnd == NULL)
 {
 MessageBox(NULL,"Could not create window!",NULL,MB_OK
  | MB_ICONSTOP);
 return FALSE;
 }


// Process application messages until the application closes
while(GetMessage(&msg, NULL, 0, 0))
 {
 TranslateMessage(&msg);
 DispatchMessage(&msg);
 }

return msg.wParam;
}
```

The only real difference from previous **WinMain**s is this one does all the window creation right in **WinMain** itself. The previous versions doled that task out to separate functions, but there are already so many other functions in this program that it's better if we can keep as much stuff as possible in one single function. That way we won't get lost in all the function calls.

The message pump sends all the window's messages to the **WndProc** callback function, so let's take it from there.

The Window Callback

The window callback function, **WndProc**, is the central hub of our program. Everything that happens is related to it in some way, so let's trace the different messages and come back to **WndProc** when we've finished. That way we can keep everything in perspective and not lose our place in this enormous program.

Here's the complete listing for `WndProc`, taken from the `Ddmain.cpp` file on the CD. Just skim over it once for now, and we'll cover it piece by piece throughout the chapter (Listing 15-2):

Listing 15-2 The window callback function **WndProc**

```
LRESULT CALLBACK WndProc(        HWND     hWnd,
    UINT    message,
    WPARAM  wParam,
    LPARAM  lParam)
{
static HDC hDC = NULL;              // Device context

switch (message)
 {
 case WM_CREATE:
  // Initialize Direct Sound
  if(!bInitializeDirectSound(hWnd))
   MessageBox(hWnd,"Could not initialize Direct Sound",
    NULL,MB_OK | MB_ICONEXCLAMATION);

  // Window creation.If Direct3D environment can't be setup,
  // then just stop here and end the program.
  if(!SetupDirect3DRetainedMode(hWnd))
   PostQuitMessage(0);

  // Initialize navigation module
  SetupNavigator();

  // Hide the cursor
  ShowCursor(FALSE);

  // Set timer to fire after 120 seconds (two minutes)
  SetTimer(hWnd,101,nTime,NULL);

  // Game is now in play
  bInPlay = TRUE;

  break;

 case WM_ACTIVATE:
  {
  if(!bD3DReady)
   return (DefWindowProc(hWnd, message, wParam,
    lParam));

  // Handles Activate Message, insures colors are correct.
  LPDIRECT3DRMWINDEVICE pWinDev = NULL;

  // If we get the Windows device, handle activate message
  if(SUCCEEDED(pD3DRMDeviceAPI->QueryInterface(
   IID_IDirect3DRMWinDevice, (void **)&pWinDev)))
```

```
  {
  pWinDev->HandleActivate(wParam);
  pWinDev->Release();
  }                        }
 break;

// Game Over
case WM_TIMER:
 {
 RECT wndRect    // Get screen size
 char caOutput[128];       // Buffer for output string
 HDC hDC;                  // Handle to GDI Device Context

 // Get the device context and the window dimensions
 hDC = GetDC(hWnd);
 GetWindowRect(hWnd, &wndRect);


 // Redraw current scene on the back buffer. This is in
 // case the current surface is not the GDI surface. If it
 // isn't, then redrawing the scene prevents the scene from
 // jumping back one frame before displaying the score
 pD3DViewportAPI->Render(pD3DSceneAPI);  // Render scene
 pD3DRMDeviceAPI->Upda        // Update the device (window)

 // Make sure GDI capable surface is in the front
 pDD->FlipToGDISurface();

 // Display ending text. Background is transparent, color
 // is white, and message is centered. This is just good
 // old fashioned Windows GDI.
 SetBkMode(hDC,TRANSPARENT);
 SetTextColor(hDC,RGB(255,255,255));
 sprintf(caOutput,"Game Over!\n\nYour Score was %d out of
    %d!\n(Press ESC to return to Windows)",
  nScore,nPossible);
 DrawText(hDC,caOutput,-1,&wndRect,DT_CENTER);
 ReleaseDC(hWnd, hDC);

 // Game is over... Stop the timer, stop the background
 // music, and set the bInPlay flag to false.
 KillTimer(hWnd,101);
 StopBackgroundMusic();

 bInPlay = FALSE;
 }
 break;

case WM_PAINT:
 {
 if(!bD3DReady)
  return (DefWindowProc(hWnd, message, wParam,
   lParam));
```

continued on next page

continued from previous page

```
          LPDIRECT3DRMWINDEVICE pWinDev = NULL;
          PAINTSTRUCT ps;

          // Do not process if the device doesn't exist, or the
          // window is minimized
          if(!pD3DRMDeviceAPI || IsIconic(hWnd))
           return DefWindowProc(hWnd, message, wParam, lParam);

          BeginPaint(hWnd, &ps);

          // Handle the paint message
          if(SUCCEEDED(pD3DRMDeviceAPI->QueryInterface(
           IID_IDirect3DRMWinDevice, (void **)&pWinDev)))
           {
           pWinDev->HandlePaint(ps.hdc);
           pWinDev->Release();
           }

          EndPaint(hWnd, &ps);

          // Render the scene (probably just the first time)
          pD3DViewportAPI->Clear();            // Clear viewport
          pD3DViewportAPI->Render(pD3DSceneAPI);  // Render scene
          pD3DRMDeviceAPI->Update    // Update device (window)

          // Move back buffer (where drawing is occuring to front)
          pSurf->Flip(NULL,DDFLIP_WAIT);

          // Start music after scene is painted the first time
          if(!bMusicStarted)
           {
           bMusicStarted = TRUE;
           StartBackgroundMusic(hWnd);
           }

          }
          break;

      // When arrow keys are pressed, rotate the object around
      case WM_KEYDOWN:
       {
       if(!bD3DReady)
        return (DefWindowProc(hWnd, message, wParam,
          lParam));

       // If game over, allow no movement, only ESC key valid
       if(!bInPlay)
        {
        // Escape key, exit the program
        if(wParam == VK_ESCAPE)
         {
         PostQuitMessage(0);
```

```
    break;
    }

 break;
 }

// Move Forward and backwards
if(wParam == VK_UP)
 if(GetKeyState(VK_SHIFT) & 0x8000 // Shift runs
  RunForward();   // forward
 else
  StepForward();


if(wParam == VK_DOWN)
 if(GetKeyState(VK_SHIFT) & 0x8000)   // Shift runs
  RunBackward();   // backward
 else
  StepBackward();

// Turn left or right
if(wParam == VK_LEFT)
 if(GetKeyState(VK_SHIFT) & 0x8000)  // Shift
  SwingLeft();       // swings faster
 else
  TurnLeft();

if(wParam == VK_RIGHT)
 if(GetKeyState(VK_SHIFT) & 0x8000)  // Shift swings
  SwingRight();            // faster
 else
  TurnRight();

// Escape key, exit the program
if(wParam == VK_ESCAPE)
 {
 PostQuitMessage(0);
 break;
 }

// Update the players position
pD3DCameraAPI->AddRotation(D3DRMCOMBINE_REPLACE, 0.0f,
 1.0f, 0.0f,fGetAngle());
pD3DCameraAPI->SetPosition(pD3DSceneAPI, fGetXPos(), 1.5f,
 fGetZPos());


// Render the scene
pD3DViewportAPI->Clear  // Clear the viewport
pD3DViewportAPI->Render(pD3DSceneAPI);  // Render scene
pD3DRMDeviceAPI->Update  // Update the device (window)
```

continued on next page

continued from previous page

```
            // Move back buffer (where drawing is occuring to front)
            pSurf->Flip(NULL,DDFLIP_WAIT);
            }
            break;

        case WM_DESTROY:
            // Application terminating. Release D3DRM interaces.
            ShutdownDirect3DRetainedMode(hWnd);
            ShutdownDirectSound();
            StopBackgroundMusic();
            ReleaseDC(hWnd,hDC);
            PostQuitMessage(0);
            break;

        // Posted when the music stop playing. Reissue "play" command.
        case MM_MCINOTIFY:
            if(wParam == MCI_NOTIFY_SUCCESSFUL)
             ReplayBackgroundMusic(hWnd);

            break;

    default:            // Passes message on if unproccessed
        return (DefWindowProc(hWnd, message, wParam, lParam));
    }

    return (0L);
}
```

Since the first message that ever gets received by the callback function is **WM_CREATE**, let's take care of it now.

WM_CREATE

When our window is first created, we need to set up all our DirectX objects and our navigation system. To set up DirectSound, we first call **bInitializeDirectSound**. (For further explanation of DirectSound refer to Chapter 11.) Then, we set up DirectDraw and Direct3D by calling **SetupDirect3DRetainedMode**, a leftover from the last example.

After setting up DirectX, we call **SetupNavigator**, which initializes the system we'll use to interact with the user. We then hide the cursor so when we switch to fullscreen mode the player's view is unobstructed by the pointer.

Last, we get the game ready to play by setting up a timer for two minutes (the length of the game) and setting the *bInPlay* Boolean to **TRUE**. When all the time has elapsed (setting off the timer and sending a **WM_TIMER** message), we'll set *bInPlay* to **FALSE** so we know the game is over and then display the score.

Now let's move on to the initialization code. Probably the most interesting of the initialization functions is **SetupDirect3DRetainedMode**, which, as you know, is called from the **WM_CREATE** message handler.

SetupDirect3DRetainedMode

SetupDirect3DRetainedMode, which you probably remember from Example 9-4, takes care of setting up the Direct3D environment. This time, though, it also has to set up all the DirectDraw stuff, so it's a heck of a lot longer. We'll just take it chunk by chunk, and hopefully you'll understand everything that's going on.

Listing 15-3 shows the first bit of code in SetupDirect3DRetainedMode:

Listing 15-3 The first chunk of **SetupDirect3DRetainedMode** code

```
BOOL SetupDirect3DRetainedMode(HWND hWnd)
{
// Get interface to Direct Draw
if(DirectDrawCreate(NULL, &pDD, NULL) != DD_OK)
 {
 MessageBox(hWnd,"Could not create Direct Draw Interface!",
  NULL,MB_OK | MB_ICONSTOP);
 return FALSE;
 }

// Get interface to Direct Draw 2
pDD->QueryInterface(IID_IDirectDraw2, (void **)&pDD2);
if(pDD2 == NULL)
 {
 MessageBox(hWnd,"Could not create Direct Draw 2 Interface!",
  NULL,MB_OK | MB_ICONSTOP);
 return FALSE;
 }

// Set to full screen and exclusive cooperative level
if(pDD2->SetCooperativeLevel(hWnd, DDSCL_EXCLUSIVE | DDSCL_FULLSCREEN)
 != DD_OK)
 {
 MessageBox(hWnd,"Could not set exclusive mode!",
  NULL,MB_OK | MB_ICONSTOP);
 return FALSE;
 }

if(pDD2->SetDisplayMode(dwScreenWidth, dwScreenHeight, 8, 0, NULL)
 != DD_OK)
 {
 MessageBox(hWnd,"Could not set display mode!",
  NULL,MB_OK | MB_ICONSTOP);
 return FALSE;
 }
```

First of all, Direct3DRetainedMode creates the global IDirectDraw object using DirectDrawCreate (the *pDD* pointer is declared at the top of Ddmain.cpp, as are all the other DirectDraw and Direct3D objects used throughout the program). If it can't create the object, SetupDirect3DRetainedMode puts up a message box saying so and bails.

Next, we create an `IDirectDraw2` object. We haven't discussed these so far in the book since there wasn't a need.

Besides the normal `IDirectDraw` and `IDirectDrawSurface` objects, introduced in the first release of DirectX (DirectX 2), there are also `IDirectDraw2` and `IDirectDrawSurface2` objects. These objects are simply extensions of their predecessors that add a little bit of functionality. We'll need one of the functions only provided by the `IDirectDraw2` interface, which is really the only reason we'll use it.

Anyway, to create an `IDirectDraw2` object, we create the regular old `IDirectDraw` object, then use the `IDirectDraw` object's `QueryInterface` method to create a new `IDirectDraw2` object.

Once we have the `IDirectDraw2` object ready, we go ahead and use it to call `SetCooperativeLevel`. As you can see, we're making our application exclusive and initializing it to fullscreen mode. That way, we have full control over the palette and everything else and are running in fullscreen mode so our game has the user's undivided attention.

After calling `SetCooperativeLevel`, we need to set the display mode. *dwScreenWidth* and *dwScreenHeight*, which we'll use in our call to `SetDisplayMode` to indicate the screen's width and height, are declared at the top of **Ddmain.cpp** and defined as 320 and 240, respectively. We'll also use a 256-color display mode, as indicated by the third parameter. The fourth parameter is new with `IDirectDraw2` and indicates what the monitor's refresh rate should be. If you use zero for this parameter, as we are, it tells DirectDraw to use the version of `SetDisplayMode` from `IDirectDraw`, and not `IDirectDraw2` (in other words, zero makes DirectDraw ignore this parameter). The last parameter, which is also new, is always zero in this version of DirectX.

Now that we have the basic DirectDraw elements of the program up and running, let's set up our surfaces. Listing 15-4 shows the next chunk of `SetupDirect3DRetainedMode` code:

Listing 15-4 The second chunk of `SetupDirect3DRetainedMode`

```
// Surface descriptor. Setup for complex double buffer, and D3D
// abilities.
DDSURFACEDESC ddsd;

memset(&ddsd,0,sizeof(ddsd));
ddsd.dwSize = sizeof(ddsd);
ddsd.dwFlags = DDSD_CAPS | DDSD_BACKBUFFERCOUNT;
ddsd.ddsCaps.dwCaps = DDSCAPS_COMPLEX | DDSCAPS_FLIP |
    DDSCAPS_PRIMARYSURFACE | DDSCAPS_3DDEVICE;
ddsd.dwBackBufferCount  = 1;
pDD2->CreateSurface(&ddsd, &pSurf, NULL);

if(pSurf == NULL)
  {
  MessageBox(hWnd,"Could not create Direct Draw 2 Interface!",
   NULL,MB_OK | MB_ICONSTOP);
  return FALSE;
  }
```

```
// Get pointer to back buffer too
DDSCAPS ddscaps;
ddscaps.dwCaps = DDSCAPS_BACKBUFFER;
pSurf->GetAttachedSurface(&ddscaps, &pBackBuffer);
```

First of all, we zero out the **DDSURFACEDESC** structure so we have a clean chunk of memory with which to work. After that, we initialize its members so that **CreateSurface** will create a complex, flippable surface that's the primary surface. You've probably noticed the new *ddsCaps.dwCaps* flag, DDSCAPS_3DDEVICE. This flag means the surface can be rendered onto by Direct3D. (You guessed it—this time we'll render the scene onto a surface instead of directly onto the window.)

After calling **CreateSurface** to create the surface, we need to grab a pointer to the back buffer for future use. That done, we move on to the last chunk of code (shown in Listing 15-5), which looks exactly like the **SetupDirect3DRetainedMode** function from the last example in Chapter 9 (which was Example 9-4):

Listing 15-5 The last section of **SetupDirect3DRetainedMode**

```
// Create the retained mode API
if(Direct3DRMCreate(&pD3DRetainedModeAPI) != D3DRM_OK)
 {
 MessageBox(hWnd,"Could not create Retained Mode API!",
  NULL,MB_OK | MB_ICONSTOP);
 return FALSE;
 }

// Create Scene API
if(pD3DRetainedModeAPI->CreateFrame(NULL,&pD3DSceneAPI) != D3DRM_OK)
 {
 MessageBox(hWnd,"Could not create Frame!",
  NULL,MB_OK | MB_ICONSTOP);
 return FALSE;
 }

// Create Camera API
if(pD3DRetainedModeAPI->CreateFrame(pD3DSceneAPI, &pD3DCameraAPI)
 != D3DRM_OK)
 {
 MessageBox(hWnd,"Could not create Camera API!",
  NULL,MB_OK | MB_ICONSTOP);
 return FALSE;
 }

// Set the position of the camera
if(pD3DCameraAPI->SetPosition(pD3DSceneAPI, 0.0f, 0.0f, 0.0f)
 != D3DRM_OK)
 {
 MessageBox(hWnd,"Could not position camera!",
  NULL,MB_OK | MB_ICONSTOP);
```

continued on next page

continued from previous page

```
   return FALSE;
   }

// Create the clipper and associate it with the window
if(pDD2->CreateClipper(0, &pDDClipperAPI, NULL) != DD_OK)
   {
   MessageBox(hWnd,"Could not create Retained Mode Interface!",
    NULL,MB_OK | MB_ICONSTOP);
   return FALSE;
   }

// Create clipper API
if(pDDClipperAPI->SetHWnd(0, hWnd) != DD_OK)
   {
   MessageBox(hWnd,"Could not create Retained Mode Interface!",
    NULL,MB_OK | MB_ICONSTOP);
   return FALSE;
   }

// Create Device and viewport
if(!CreateDeviceAndViewport(hWnd))
   {
   MessageBox(hWnd,"Could not create Retained Mode Interface!",
    NULL,MB_OK | MB_ICONSTOP);
   return FALSE;
   }

// Get Direct Draw interface and set the video mode
bD3DReady = TRUE;

// Create the scene
if(!BuildScene())
   {
   MessageBox(hWnd,"Could not create Retained Mode Scene!",
    NULL,MB_OK | MB_ICONSTOP);
   return FALSE;
   }

return TRUE; // Successful Creation
}
```

First off, this code creates the **IDirect3DRM** object we'll need before we can create anything else. Then, it creates the scene frame in the ***pD3DSceneAPI*** pointer (again, all these variables are declared at the top of **Ddmain.cpp**).

After creating the scene frame, we create the camera frame, which goes inside of the scene frame. We're positioning it at (0,0,0) for now, smack-dab in the middle of our 3D world.

Next, we create our clipper. We do this the same way as we did last time, only this time we call **CreateClipper** as a member of our **IDirectDraw2** object, instead of the old **IDirectDraw** object.

After we create the clipper, we need to get it set up for our application window. We do this by calling `IDirectDrawClipper::SetHWnd` as before, using zero and our window handle as the parameters.

Now that the clipper is ready to go, we call `CreateDeviceAndViewport`, the function that, obviously, creates the device and viewport. We'll take a look at that function in just a moment.

As long as `CreateDeviceAndViewport` succeeds, all the Direct3D objects are completely set up and initalized. Thus we'll set the Boolean variable *bD3DReady*, which we'll use throughout the program to determine if Direct3D is set up, to `TRUE`.

Last, we call `BuildScene` to initialize our 3D world, then return `TRUE`. We'll go over `BuildScene` a little later.

CreateDeviceAndViewport

You should be able to recognize what's happening in `CreateDeviceAndViewport`. Listing 15-6 shows the code:

Listing 15-6 `CreateDeviceAndViewport`

```
BOOL CreateDeviceAndViewport(HWND hWnd)
 {
RECT rect;

// Get the curren dimensions of the window, and make sure
// they are valid
GetClientRect(hWnd, &rect);

if(!rect.right  || !rect.bottom)
 return FALSE;

// Load the palette from a single texture that contains all the colors
// used by the app.
LPDIRECTDRAWPALETTE pDDPalette;
pDDPalette = LoadPaletteFromBMP(pDD, "Textures.bmp");

// Set the palette for front and back surfaces
pSurf->SetPalette(pDDPalette);
pBackBuffer->SetPalette(pDDPalette);

// Create the device from the back buffer. This will cause D3DRM to
// render into the back buffer
if(pD3DRetainedModeAPI->CreateDeviceFromSurface(NULL,(IDirectDraw
 *)pDD2,pBackBuffer, &pD3DRMDeviceAPI) != D3DRM_OK)
 return FALSE;

// Make sure device is double buffered
pD3DRMDeviceAPI->SetBufferCount(1);

// Finally, Create the viewport
```

continued on next page

continued from previous page

```
if(pD3DRetainedModeAPI->CreateViewport(pD3DRMDeviceAPI,pD3DCameraAPI,
 0,0, pD3DRMDeviceAPI->GetWidth(), pD3DRMDeviceAPI->GetHeight(),
 &pD3DViewportAPI) != D3DRM_OK)
 return FALSE;

// Set background depth to the maximum distance the player will ever be
// able to see within the dungeon. This establishes the far clipping
// plan as near as possible, without interferring with seeing the
// entire dungeon.
pD3DViewportAPI->SetBack(70.0f);

// Set fron clipping plane very close.
pD3DViewportAPI->SetFront(0.5f);

// Release out palette interface
pDDPalette->Release();

return TRUE;
}
```

The first thing **CreateDeviceAndViewport** does is get the dimensions of our window, since, as you know, we'll need them quite a bit throughout **CreateDeviceAndViewport**.

Next we want to create a palette for our application. With that in mind, there's a file called **Textures.bmp** containing all the textures in the game. Since all the textures, and therefore all the colors, in the game are in this file, we can extract the palette from this file and use it as our main palette. As long as the image-editing software built a decent palette for the image, the palette we get from the file should work just fine.

To extract the palette from the file, there's a new function called **LoadPaletteFromBMP** (in **Ddmain.cpp**). It's a pretty simple function to figure out once you know how to load bitmaps (which you should, by this point in the book). You should have no trouble figuring it out with Chapters 4 and 5 as a reference, so it's up to you to dissect it if you feel the urge. For this example, all you need to know about **LoadPaletteFromBMP** is it takes an **IDirectDraw** object and the name of the bitmap file from which to extract the palette as parameters, and returns a newly created **IDirectDrawPalette** object.

Now that we have the palette we'll use, we need to associate it with the front and back buffers so they'll use it. That way they'll look right when we render our 3D world filled with the textures in **Textures.bmp** onto them.

Now we'll create the Direct3D device. In the Direct3D chapter (Chapter 9) we always used **CreateDeviceFromClipper** to create the device. Now, however, since we want to render the 3D scene onto a surface, we'll use the **IDirect3DRM** interface **CreateDeviceFromSurface**. **CreateDeviceFromSurface** creates the device and initializes it so it renders onto a back buffer passed as one of its parameters.

CreateDeviceFromSurface accepts four parameters: the **GUID** of the device driver (**NULL** for the default driver), a pointer to the **IDirectDraw** object that created the back buffer (we're casting our **IDirectDraw2** object to an **IDirectDraw** object), a pointer to the back buffer being rendered to, and a pointer to the memory being filled with the new device.

Since we'll be rendering to a complex **IDirectDrawSurface**, it's a good idea to call **IDirect3DRMDevice::SetBufferCount** to let the device know how many back buffers we're using. We'll use one for `SetBufferCount`'s only parameter to let the device know there's only one back buffer. However, remember that we didn't *have* to call `SetBufferCount`—one back buffer is the default, so you only have to call `SetBufferCount` if you use more than one back buffer in the complex surface. It never hurts to be safe, though.

After taking care of the device, we create the viewport. The call to `IDirect3DRM::CreateViewport` is almost identical to the call from Example 9-4, so we won't even discuss because space is limited.

In Chapter 9, we set the back clipping plane of the viewport to a ridiculously large number since it didn't even matter what it was. Now, though, we'll set it to 70 units away so Direct3D doesn't have to render everything in the entire scene. The user can only see 70 units away at 320x240 resolution (you'll have to experiment to find the right value for other resolutions), so it doesn't make sense to set the clipping plane any farther away (it just takes more time to render each frame for the same results).

The front clipping plane is set to 0.5. The only way the user can get that close to anything is if he or she stands right on top of it; however, we don't want to render an object if the user is right in the middle of it. Thus, we use a small value for the front clipping plane.

Since we already associated the palette with both buffers in our complex surface, we can get rid of it. We then return `TRUE`, as we were obviously successful if the code ran through to this point.

BuildScene

Now we need to go back and look at `BuildScene`, called from inside of `SetupDirect3DRetainedMode`. You can find it in `Scene.cpp` on the CD.

This monstrosity of a function will take a little while to get through. Probably the most difficult part of writing a 3D game is building the actual 3D world. As you'll see, it's *very* complex, and it's easy to get confused if you don't pay close attention.

Every part of our 3D world is a mesh, which, as you'll recall from Chapter 9, is a 3D model. We'll use several meshes repeatedly in our world (for example, a wall or the corner of two walls), which is much more economical in terms of space than building an entire 3D world with a modeling program (although that's a common way of doing things).

The 3D dungeon itself is in a two-dimensional array declared in the file `Nav.cpp` on the CD. The array is a grid of integers that act as a sort of code telling us what mesh appears where in our dungeon.

Each mesh has its own integer appearing in the array wherever the mesh appears in the scene. For example, 8 signifies a north-facing wall, 14 signifies a north-facing door, 7 signifies just the floor and ceiling with no walls, and so on. There is a slew of possible values we'll have to look for in the array, each with its own distinct meaning.

Listing 15-7 shows the array defining our 3D dungeon:

Listing 15-7 The 3D scene as represented in the array

```
int iDungeon[MAX_ROW][MAX_COL] = {
{ 3, 10, 5, 0, 0, 3, 10, 5, 0, 0, 0, 0, 0, 0, 3, 10, 5, 0, 0, 0, 0, 0 },
{ 8, 7, 9, 0, 0, 8, 7, 9, 0, 0, 3, 2, 2, 16, 23, 7, 9, 0, 0, 0, 0, 0 },
{ 4, 21, 6, 0, 0, 4, 21, 6, 0, 0, 1, 0, 0, 0, 4, 11, 6, 0, 0, 0, 0, 0 },
{ 0, 14, 0, 0, 3, 2, 17, 0, 0, 0, 1, 0, 0, 0, 0, 0, 0, 0, 0, 0, 0, 0 },
{ 0, 1, 0, 0, 1, 0, 0, 0, 0, 0, 1, 0, 0, 0, 0, 0, 0, 0, 0, 0, 0, 0 },
{ 0, 1, 0, 0, 1, 0, 0, 0, 0, 0, 1, 0, 0, 0, 0, 3, 10, 5, 0, 0, 0, 0 },
{ 0, 4, 2, 2, 7, 2, 2, 10, 2, 2, 6, 0, 0, 0, 0, 8, 7, 9, 0, 0, 0, 0 },
{ 0, 0, 0, 0, 1, 0, 0, 1, 0, 0, 0, 0, 0, 0, 0, 4, 21, 6, 0, 0, 0, 0 },
{ 0, 0, 0, 0, 15, 0, 0, 1, 0, 0, 3, 2, 2, 2, 2, 18, 2, 5, 0, 0, 0 },
{ 0, 0, 0, 3, 22, 5, 0, 1, 0, 0, 1, 0, 0, 0, 0, 0, 0, 1, 0, 0, 0 },
{ 0, 0, 0, 8, 7, 9, 0, 1, 0, 0, 1, 0, 0, 0, 3, 10, 5, 0, 1, 3, 10, 5 },
{ 0, 0, 0, 4, 11, 6, 0, 1, 0, 0, 1, 0, 0, 0, 8, 7, 9, 0, 20, 23, 7, 9 },
{ 0, 0, 0, 0, 0, 0, 0, 1, 0, 0, 1, 0, 0, 0, 4, 21, 6, 0, 1, 4, 11, 6 },
{ 0, 0, 0, 0, 0, 0, 0, 4, 2, 2, 7, 2, 2, 2, 2, 24, 2, 2, 6, 0, 0, 0 },
{ 0, 0, 0, 0, 0, 0, 0, 0, 0, 0, 1, 0, 0, 0, 3, 22, 5, 0, 0, 0, 0, 0 },
{ 0, 0, 0, 0, 0, 0, 0, 0, 0, 0, 1, 0, 0, 0, 8, 7, 9, 0, 0, 0, 0, 0 },
{ 0, 0, 0, 0, 0, 0, 0, 0, 0, 0, 1, 0, 0, 0, 4, 11, 6, 0, 0, 0, 0, 0 },
{ 0, 0, 0, 0, 0, 0, 0, 0, 0, 0, 25, 0, 0, 0, 0, 0, 0, 0, 0, 0, 0, 0 }};
```

Don't worry too much about decoding it just yet. You may, however, find it interesting to come back to this listing and see if you can figure out what the dungeon will look like after we get done with the rest of **BuildScene**.

As mentioned earlier, it is possible to create a mesh in a 3D modeling program and load it in from a file. However, at the moment there aren't too many modeling programs that can save meshes in Direct3D's file format, so we must build them inside the program as lists of vertices and faces. When modeling programs capable of producing the right type of file are more common, however, you can model 3D objects and worlds without worrying about this type of array translation.

For right now, though, we'll have to deal with this complex situation. **BuildScene** is basically one big switch statement that loops through the array holding the integer codes for our 3D world and *decodes* the various mesh codes. It then calls the appropriate functions to build the correct mesh and place it in our dungeon.

Let's take **BuildScene** step by step as we did with **SetupDirect3DRetainedMode**, and hopefully it'll be easier to handle. Listing 15-8 shows the first bit:

Listing 15-8 The first bit of **BuildScene**

```
BOOL BuildScene(void)
{
LPDIRECT3DRMMESHBUILDER pMeshBuilder = NULL; // Mesh builder interface

// Setup rendering options first
if(!SetRenderingOptions())
 return FALSE;

// Create a frame
```

```
if(FAILED(pD3DRetainedModeAPI->CreateFrame(pD3DSceneAPI,
 &pDungeonFrame)))
 return FALSE;

// Setup the textures
if(FAILED(pD3DRetainedModeAPI->LoadTexture("Floor.bmp",&pTxtFloor)))
 return FALSE;

if(FAILED(pD3DRetainedModeAPI->LoadTexture("Ceiling.bmp",
 &pTxtCeiling)))
 return FALSE;

if(FAILED(pD3DRetainedModeAPI->LoadTexture("Wood.bmp",&pTxtWood)))
 return FALSE;

if(FAILED(pD3DRetainedModeAPI->LoadTexture("Walls.bmp",&pTxtWall)))
 return FALSE;

if(FAILED(pD3DRetainedModeAPI->LoadTexture("gold.bmp",&pTxtGold)))
 return FALSE;
```

At the outset, we first declare a mesh builder. We'll use the mesh builder to build the entire dungeon. We'll use the frame *pDungeonFrame*, declared at the top of `scene.cpp`, to hold the dungeon after building it.

Next, we call `SetRenderingOptions`, which should look very familiar to you by now. Take a quick glance at it in Listing 15-9:

Listing 15-9 `SetRenderingOptions`

```
BOOL SetRenderingOptions(void)
{
// Set Scene background to black
pD3DSceneAPI->SetSceneBackground(D3DRGB(0,0,0));

// Set shading mode to flat with no lights (faster than shading
// textures for very little additional visual effect)
pD3DRMDeviceAPI->SetQuality(D3DRMRENDER_UNLITFLAT);

// Return success
return TRUE;
}
```

`SetRenderingOptions` sets the scene background to black (although it makes no difference since the player is completely surrounded by walls). It also sets the rendering quality to flat rendering with no lighting. That's partly for the speed gains achieved when you don't use lights, but mostly for the sake of brevity. If you use lights your world will definitely look more realistic, but it also takes a lot more vertices and code (as you saw in Chapter 9). Consider adding lights to the game a challenge.

Anyway, after calling `SetRenderingOptions`, `BuildScene` creates the frame that will hold the dungeon mesh once it's built. We'll create the dungeon piece by piece using the mesh builder and stick it into this frame.

The last bit of code before we dive into the gigantic switch statement loads all five textures for the game from their bitmap files into four **IDirect3DRMTexture** pointers. The pointers are all declared at the top of **Scene.cpp**. We'll only need them while building the mesh, so we'll release them at the end of **BuildScene**.

Let's move on to the next chunk of code. This section contains two *for* statements that loop through the two-dimensional dungeon array and call the big switch statement (Listing 15-10):

Listing 15-10 Starting to build the world

```
for(int r = 0; r < 18; r++)
 for(int c = 0; c < 22; c++)
  {
  switch(iDungeon[r][c])
   {
   case 0:
    break; // Do nothing, most common. No drawing,
     // player will not even be allowed to
     // move into these squares

   case 1: // North-South facing Corridor
    if(!bGetNSCooridorMesh(pMeshBuilder))
     return FALSE;
    break;

   case 2: // East-West facing Corridor
    if(!bGetEWCooridorMesh(pMeshBuilder))
     return FALSE;
    break;

   case 3: // North-West Corner
    if(!bGetNWCornerMesh(pMeshBuilder))
     return FALSE;
    break;

   case 4: // South-West Corner
    if(!bGetSWCornerMesh(pMeshBuilder))
     return FALSE;
    break;

   case 5: // North-East Corner
    if(!bGetNECornerMesh(pMeshBuilder))
     return FALSE;
    break;

   case 6: // South-East Corner
    if(!bGetSECornerMesh(pMeshBuilder))
     return FALSE;
    break;
```

As you can see, the dungeon array is called *iDungeon* and is 18x22 elements in size. The two *for* loops simply loop through each element in the array, and the *switch* statement sees what's in the array at element (r, c).

If the current array element contains the integer 0, there's absolutely nothing in the world at that spot. That point in the world is completely outside the dungeon, so we don't have to build any meshes for it. So we simply *break* and move onto the next element.

Since there's so many possible meshes to build, we'll just take a look at one of them. Let's trace through the code that will be executed if the current array element is 1.

If the current array element is 1, we are told to put a north-south facing corridor (Figure 15-2) in the 3D world at this position. A north-south corridor has two walls on the east and west sides (facing north-south) and is open at the north and south ends.

Instead of building every possible mesh in the *switch* statement itself, we've delegated that task to several functions—one function per mesh. As for the north-south corridors, they're built by the function **bGetNSCorridorMesh**.

bGetNSCorridorMesh is shown in Listing 15-11.

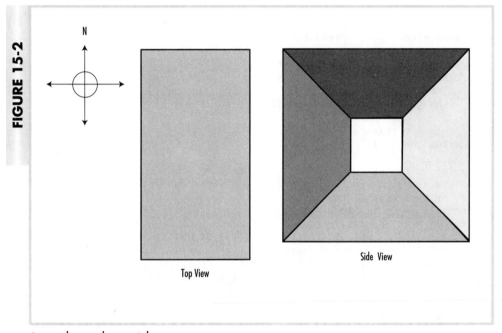

N

Top View

Side View

A north-south corridor

Listing 15-11 bGetNSCorridorMesh

```
BOOL bGetNSCorridorMesh(LPDIRECT3DRMMESHBUILDER& pMeshBuilder)
 {
 D3DVECTOR Vertices[] =
    {-3.0f, 0.0f, -3.0f, -3.0f, 3.0f, -3.0f,//Left wall
    -3.0f, 3.0f, 3.0f, -3.0f, 0.0f,  3.0f,

    3.0f, 0.0f,  3.0f, 3.0f, 3.0f,  3.0f, // Right wall
    3.0f, 3.0f, -3.0f, 3.0f, 0.0f, -3.0f,
    };

 intFaces[] = {4, 0, 1, 2, 3, // Inside left
    4, 4, 5, 6, 7, // Inside right
   0};   // Terminator


 // Create the mesh builder
 if(FAILED(pD3DRetainedModeAPI->CreateMeshBuilder(&pMeshBuilder)))
  return FALSE;

 // Set color of all faces to white, this is combined with the texture
 pMeshBuilder->SetColor(D3DRGB(1, 1, 1));

 // Create the mesh from our array
 pMeshBuilder->AddFaces( 8, Vertices,
    0, NULL,
    (unsigned long *)Faces, NULL);

 // Sets the texture
 pMeshBuilder->SetTexture(pTxtWall);

 // Set up texture coordinates. Each face is four vertices and is wound
 // clockwise. A simple loop sets the texture coordinates to be the same
 // for them all. Coordinates are for wall panel
 for(int i = 0; i < 8; i+= 4)
  {
  pMeshBuilder->SetTextureCoordinates(i,0.0f,0.0f);
  pMeshBuilder->SetTextureCoordinates(i+1,1.0f,0.0f);
  pMeshBuilder->SetTextureCoordinates(i+2,1.0f,1.0f);
  pMeshBuilder->SetTextureCoordinates(i+3,0.0f,1.0f);
  }

 return TRUE;
 }
```

The arrays at the beginning set up the vertices and faces of the mesh. As you can see from the comments, there are only two walls: the wall on the west side of the mesh, and the wall on the east side. We'll call a separate function in just a moment to add the floor and ceiling.

After getting the vertex and face arrays set up, **bGetNSCorridorMesh** creates the mesh builder. Obviously, every single mesh-building function, including **bGetNSCorridorMesh**, will need a mesh builder. So we'll just use one universal mesh builder variable, *pMeshBuilder*, which we'll `Release` at the end of the main *switch* statement so another mesh-building function can reuse it next time.

After creating the mesh builder, we set the basic color of the mesh to white, which is added to the textures to make them appear a light color.

After getting the mesh builder set up, we add all the vertices and faces to the mesh. Since our mesh is then built, all we have left to do is wrap the wall texture onto it (since this particular mesh is made up of walls only). To map the texture onto the mesh, we first map texture coordinates to each vertex. This is practically the same code used in the last example of Chapter 9, so you should understand what's happening.

Finally, `bGetNSCorridorMesh` returns `TRUE` to let `BuildScene` know everything went fine and it's all right to continue the world-building process.

That's all there is to adding a north-south facing corridor to our dungeon. Every other mesh is built basically the same way. For example, if the index element we're on is a 2, then we're told to build a corridor facing east-west. To do that, we call the function `bGetEWCorridorMesh`, which is the same as `bGetNSCorridorMesh` except the vertices in the mesh are arranged so the walls are on the north and south sides.

All the rest of the *case* statements through case 11 cover another kind of mesh representing part of our 3D world. Because of space constraints, we won't go over all of them (except for 7, which you'll be able to figure out after we discuss the rest of the meshes). Feel free to take a peek at `scene.cpp` on the CD, if you want to see them all.

There's one thing you need to note before we go on. At the end of the *switch* statement (after a mesh has been built), we always translate (move) the mesh just built to its proper place in the 3D world. If we don't do this, the mesh builder will create each mesh on top of all the others, right in the center of the world, which would obviously look quite wrong. So we move the mesh to where it should be, based on its position in the array of meshes. We'll examine this in more detail a little later.

Anyway, back to the *switch* statement. There are no elements numbered 12 or 13 in the world. Elements 14 through 24 all involve doors, which are more complex and require a few extra steps to build. Let's look at how to build one, and hopefully you'll pick up on the others easily.

Let's take a look at element number 14, a north-south corridor with a door on the north side—where the north wall should be. The code used to build the mesh is shown is Listing 15-12:

Listing 15-12 Building a corridor with a door on the north side

```
case 14: // North Door
 if(!bGetNDoorMesh(pMeshBuilder))
  return FALSE;

 // Translate vertices into position
 TRANSLATE();

 // Add the mesh to the frame
 if(FAILED(pDungeonFrame->AddVisual(pMeshBuilder)))
  return FALSE;
```

continued on next page

continued from previous page

```
// Release this mesh builder and get a new one        pMeshBuilder->Release();
if(!bGetNSCorridorMesh(pMeshBuilder))
 return FALSE;
break;
```

In order to decrease the amount of code to write, we don't have a separate function for every possible mesh with a door in it. Instead, there are four functions that build a door into an existing mesh on its north, south, east, or west side. Since we're creating a corridor with a door on the north and a wall on the south, we'll need to call two functions, one to create the corridor and one to create the door.

First off, we call the function **bGetNDoorMesh**, which creates a door facing north. A door is basically the same as a wall except it has a different texture mapped onto it (*pTxtWood*). The meshes themselves don't make any difference—we'll distinguish between walls and doors in the navigation portion of our program. Since we already learned how the basic mesh-building functions work, we won't bother looking at the door functions.

After building the door mesh, we need to translate it to its proper place in our dungeon (like we do at the end of the *switch* statement). We do this now instead of waiting for the end of the *switch* statement to do it because we still must create another mesh (the corridor mesh), and the end of the *switch* only takes care of one. To translate the mesh, we call the macro **TRANSLATE**, defined at the top of **Scene.cpp** (Listing 15-13):

Listing 15-13 The **TRANSLATE** macro

```
#define TRANSLATE() { if(FAILED(pMeshBuilder->Translate((((float)c*6.0f)
 +3.0f,0.0f,(((17.0f- (float)r)*6.0f)+ 3.0f)))) return FALSE; }
```

As you can see, **TRANSLATE** calls the **IDirect3DRMMeshBuilder::Translate** interface to move the mesh to its proper location. It uses the *for* loop variables to accomplish this by multiplying them by the width and height of the cells we've created (a *cell* is one mesh). This will place the mesh in the world according to its place in the array of meshes. By the way, this is the same macro we'll use at the end of the *switch* statement to translate the mesh.

Now that the door mesh is ready in its proper place, we need to add it to the scene. Usually this, like translation, is handled at the end of the *switch* statement. However, since we still must build another mesh, we have to do it here. We simply add it as a child of the dungeon frame using **IDirect3DRMFrame::AddVisual**.

After putting the door mesh into the scene, we have to **Release** the mesh builder so we can use it to build the wall on the south side of the mesh. Then, all we have to do to complete the mesh we're building is call **bGetNSCorridorMesh**, which will create the north-south corridor. (It doesn't matter that this function creates a north wall too, it won't be visible behind the door.)

That's all the meshes we need to learn how to build—you should be able to figure the rest out for yourself. The *default* switch case sets *pMeshBuilder* to NULL, so we know not to translate the mesh and add it to the scene after the *switch* statement (which would probably cause a GPF or two).

After the *switch* statement, we still must translate the mesh into its proper position and add it to the dungeon. Also, you might have noticed we didn't create a floor or ceiling for any of the meshes built. Ceilings and floors are common to every single mesh in the world, so we add them here instead of cluttering up the *switch* statement with them.

Listing 15-14 shows the code after the *switch* statement:

Listing 15-14 The code at the end of the *switch* statement

```
if(pMeshBuilder != NULL)
{
// Translate vertices into position
TRANSLATE();

// Add the mesh to the frame
if(FAILED(pDungeonFrame->AddVisual(pMeshBuilder)))
return FALSE;

pMeshBuilder->Release();

if(!bGetFloorMesh(pMeshBuilder))
return FALSE;

// Translate vertices into position
TRANSLATE();

// Add the mesh to the frame
if(FAILED(pDungeonFrame->AddVisual(pMeshBuilder)))
return FALSE;

pMeshBuilder->Release();

if(!bGetCeilingMesh(pMeshBuilder))
return FALSE;

// Translate vertices into position
TRANSLATE();

// Add the mesh to the frame
if(FAILED(pDungeonFrame->AddVisual(pMeshBuilder)))
return FALSE;

pMeshBuilder->Release();
}
```

First of all, this code translates the mesh in the mesh builder into position (the entire *switch* statement is still in the *for* loops, don't forget, so the loop indices are still valid). Then it adds the mesh to the dungeon frame. Finally, it releases the mesh builder so we can use it to build our floor and ceiling meshes.

We build the floor and ceiling by calling the functions **bGetFloorMesh** and **bGetCeilingMesh**, respectively (translating the meshes, adding them to the dungeon frame, and **Releasing** the mesh builder in between, of course). After adding the ceiling to the scene, we **Release** the mesh builder so we can use it next time.

Once we've run through all the elements of the world array and emerge from the *for* loops, the scene will be completely built. However, we still have two more things to do: We need to put the gold coins in the dungeon and set up the camera.

To add the gold coins we call the function `AddGoldFrames`, which we'll review in a moment. For now, let's look at the camera part of the code. We already created the camera in `SetupDirect3DRetainedMode`, so all we have to do now is position it in our dungeon (Listing 15-15):

Listing 15-15 Creating gold coins and positioning the camera

```
// Add the frames with gold coins to the dungeon
AddGoldFrames(pDungeonFrame);

// Set the position of the frame within the scene
if(FAILED(pD3DCameraAPI->SetPosition(pD3DSceneAPI, fGetXPos(), 1.5f,
 fGetZPos())))
 return FALSE;

// Set orientation
if(FAILED(pD3DCameraAPI->SetOrientation(pD3DSceneAPI, 0.0f, 0.0f, 1.0f, 0.0f,
 1.0f, 0.0f)))
 return FALSE;
```

The `fGetXPos` and `fGetYPos` functions used here return the user's current position. His or her position (on both axes) is given as a floating-point number. These functions are part of the navigation system in `Nav.cpp`, which we'll look at in a little while. There are some initial position values in `Nav.cpp` that `fGetXPos` and `fGetZPos` use that initially set the player in a corridor.

The call to `SetOrientation` sets the camera's up vector to point straight up and points it along the z axis.

After `Releasing` the objects we no longer need, we return `TRUE`. Now our scene is completely set up, and all we have left to initialize is the navigation system. But before we look at that, let's go over the function that sets up our gold coins, `AddGoldFrames`.

AddGoldFrames

There will be ten gold coins scattered throughout the dungeon. Instead of specifying their positions in the mesh array, however, we'll place them in the dungeon in random positions each time the game runs. That keeps things more interesting than if the coins stayed the same place each time.

To keep track of the coins (we need to remove them once the player picks them up and stuff like that), there's a new structure in `Nav.h` called `GoldLocations`. This structure contains a frame for the coin itself, as well as the location of the coin in the dungeon and a Boolean variable indicating whether the coin has been found yet (`TRUE` if the coin is found). Listing 15-16 shows the structure:

Listing 15-16 The `GoldLocations` structure

```
struct GoldLocations
{
LPDIRECT3DRMFRAME pGoldFrame;
int nRow;
int nCol;
BOOL bFound;
};
```

To hold the ten coins in the dungeon, there's an array of ten `GoldLocations` structures, called *GoldFrames*, declared at the top of `scene.cpp`. The code in `AddGoldFrames` basically fills each of these ten structures and sticks the meshes into the dungeon. Then, we can use the `GoldLocations` structures to find out information about the coins scattered throughout the dungeon. Listing 15-17 lists the code for `AddGoldFrames`:

Listing 15-17 `AddGoldFrames`

```
void AddGoldFrames(LPDIRECT3DRMFRAME& pDungeonFrame)
{
LPDIRECT3DRMMESHBUILDER pMeshBuilder = NULL; // Mesh builder interface
int r,c;

// Seed the random number generator
srand( (unsigned)time( NULL ) );

// Create the frames
for(int i = 0; i < 10; i++)
 {
 // Create Individual frame
 if(FAILED(pD3DRetainedModeAPI->CreateFrame(pD3DSceneAPI,
  &(GoldFrames[i].pGoldFrame))))
  return;

 // Get a mesh with gold coin on floor
 bGetGoldFloorMesh(pMeshBuilder);

 // Find a random position with a gold coin
 do {
  r = int(  ((float)rand() / (float)RAND_MAX)
   *(float)MAX_ROW);
  c = int(  ((float)rand() / (float)RAND_MAX)
   *(float)MAX_COL);
  }
 while (iDungeon[r][c] == 0);

 // Translate to correct position in dungeon
 pMeshBuilder->Translate(((float)c*6.0f)+3.0f,0.0f,
  (((17.0f- (float)r)*6.0f)+ 3.0f));

 // Store coordinates, frame pointer, and mark as not found.
 GoldFrames[i].nRow = r;
```

continued on next page

continued from previous page

```
        GoldFrames[i].nCol = c;
        GoldFrames[i].pGoldFrame->AddVisual(pMeshBuilder);
        GoldFrames[i].bFound = FALSE;

        // Add frame to dungeon
        pDungeonFrame->AddChild(GoldFrames[i].pGoldFrame);


        // Get next mesh and frame
        pMeshBuilder->Release();
    }
}
```

The code really isn't that different from anything you've seen before. First it seeds the random number generator so we can obtain random locations for the coins, then it moves into a loop to initialize all ten coins.

The loop creates a frame for the coin, then creates a mesh using **bGetGoldFloorMesh**. **BGetGoldFloorMesh** simply creates a standard floor with a different texture mapped onto it (a bitmap of the floor texture with a gold coin on top).

After creating the mesh, the code then finds a random location for the coin in one of the cells from the element array we used to build the original dungeon. While doing so, it also makes sure the mesh at the random location isn't 0 (which would indicate that specific location is outside the dungeon) and tries again if it is. It keeps going until it finds a suitable location for the coin.

After finding a place for the coin, we translate it into its proper position within the world. We then fill the **GoldLocations** structure with information about the new coin so it's there when we need it.

Last, we add the new coin frame to the dungeon as a child of the dungeon frame and release the mesh builder since we no longer need it.

SetupNavigator

You might recall the line of code from the **WM_CREATE** handler calling the function **SetupNavigator**. **SetupNavigator** is a function initializing some variables we'll need in order to interact with the user.

Listing 15-18 shows the code for **SetupNavigator**:

Listing 15-18 **SetupNavigator**

```
void SetupNavigator(void)
{
//    2 * PI
float fStep =
6.28318530718f / 36.0f; // 1/36thnd of a rotation. The reason
    // we chose 36 is because it is relatively
    // small, and evenly divisable by 4. If we
    // choose a value that is not evenly
```

```
        // divisable by 4, then east/west movement
        // could not be straight, but at a slight
        // angle from north/south

   for(int i = 0; i < 36; i++)
    {
    fAngleLookUp[i] = fStep*(float)i;
    fSineLookUp[i] = sin(fAngleLookUp[i]);
    fCosineLookUp[i] = cos(fAngleLookUp[i]);
    }

   g_iRotIndex = 0;
   }
```

When the user turns, we'll have to use a bit of trigonometry to find out which way he or she is facing. Trigonometry functions (especially sine and cosine) are notoriously slow, which is bad for games—especially 3D games. What we basically want to do is pre-calculate all the trigonometry variables we'd otherwise get by calling the trigonometry functions. That way, we can just look up the pre-calculated variables, bypassing all the function overhead.

We'll limit the player to facing in 36 different directions. (36 directions isn't bad at all—the player won't even notice it, and you *could* make that number higher if you really wanted to.) We'll use three different arrays to hold angle information: one for the value of the angles themselves, one for the sine of the angles, and one for the cosine of the angles (each is 36 elements long to hold the 36 angles).

The *fStep* variable is the distance between each of the 36 angles. This value is in radians, since Direct3D doesn't understand degrees. One complete revolution (a circle) is 2π radians, so *fStep* is equal to $1/36$ of 2π.

The *for* loop's job is filling up each of the three *lookup tables*. It fills the *fAngleLookUp* array with the value of the current angle (calculated by multiplying *fStep* by the *for* loop index). The *fSineLookUp* array holds the sine of each of the angles from the *fAngleLookUp* table, while the *fCosineLookUp* array holds the cosine of each of the angles. We'll use the values from both these arrays when we move the user.

The *g_iRotIndex* variable is what we'll use to indicate which direction the user is currently facing. It's just an index into the lookup tables—*not* the value of the angle itself. We'll simply update it when the user turns so we have the angle he or she is facing handy, plus its sine and cosine.

The WM_PAINT Message

We're done with all the initialization, so let's move on to the WM_PAINT message handler. When we get a WM_PAINT message, all we need to do is let Direct3D handle the message for us and render the scene. Of course, we're rendering the scene into a complex surface now, so it's a little more complex than in Example 9-4.

Listing 15-19 shows the code making up the WM_PAINT handler:

Listing 15-19 The **WM_PAINT** handler

```
case WM_PAINT:
 {
 if(!bD3DReady)
  return (DefWindowProc(hWnd, message, wParam, lParam));


 LPDIRECT3DRMWINDEVICE pWinDev = NULL;
 PAINTSTRUCT ps;

 // Do not process if the device doesn't exist, or window is minimized
 if(!pD3DRMDeviceAPI || IsIconic(hWnd))
  return DefWindowProc(hWnd, message, wParam, lParam);

 BeginPaint(hWnd, &ps);

 // Handle the paint message
 if(SUCCEEDED(pD3DRMDeviceAPI->QueryInterface(IID_IDirect3DRMWinDevice,
  (void **)&pWinDev)))
  {
  pWinDev->HandlePaint(ps.hdc);
  pWinDev->Release();
  }

 EndPaint(hWnd, &ps);

 // Render the scene (probably just the first time)
 pD3DViewportAPI->Clear();   // Clear the viewport
 pD3DViewportAPI->Render(pD3DSceneAPI); // Render the scene
 pD3DRMDeviceAPI->Update();   // Update the device (window)

 // Move back buffer (where drawing is occuring) to front
 pSurf->Flip(NULL,DDFLIP_WAIT);


 // Start music after scene is painted the first time
 if(!bMusicStarted)
  {
  bMusicStarted = TRUE;
  StartBackgroundMusic(hWnd);
  }
 }
 break;
```

The first thing we do is make sure Direct3D is all ready to go (by looking at the **bD3DReady** Boolean we set to either **TRUE** or **FALSE** in **SetupDirect3DRetainedMode**). If it isn't, we can't do anything with Direct3D anyway so we let the default window procedure handle the message. And as always, we won't do anything if our window is minimized or we don't have a device with which to work.

Next, we get a **PAINTSTRUCT** structure to work with from **BeginPaint**. Then, we create an **IDirect3DRMWinDevice** and use it to handle the **WM_PAINT** message (**Releasing** it afterwards).

Now it's time to actually render the scene. After we clear the viewport, we render the scene onto it via **IDirect3DRMViewport::Render**. Then we update the device so the user can to see the changes.

Remember when we created the complex surface and used **CreateDeviceFromSurface** to create the device? Well, we also told **CreateDeviceFromSurface** to render into the back buffer of our complex surface. So right now, the rendered image is just sitting in our back buffer, invisible to the user. In order to make it visible, we merely have to call **IDirectDrawSurface::Flip**.

Last, we'll start the music. You didn't know we had music? Well, we do, and if this is the first time we received a **WM_PAINT** message, then we'll call the **StartBackgroundMusic** to turn it on. **StartBackgroundMusic** uses the Windows multimedia functions to play a **MIDI** file in the background, but since the main focus of this chapter is the graphics end of the program, we won't here. If you want to, however, you can easily consult your Windows API reference and learn more about this kind of thing.

Handling the **WM_ACTIVATE** Message

The **WM_ACTIVATE** message, as you'll recall, is sent when our application gains the input focus. Listing 15-20 shows the code, essentially the same as it was in the last example from Chapter 9, Example 9-4:

Listing 15-20 The **WM_ACTIVATE** handler

```
case WM_ACTIVATE:
 {
 if(!bD3DReady)
  return (DefWindowProc(hWnd, message, wParam, lParam));

 // Handles Activate Message, insures colors are correct.
 LPDIRECT3DRMWINDEVICE pWinDev = NULL;

 // If we get the Windows device, handle the activate message
 if(SUCCEEDED(pD3DRMDeviceAPI->QueryInterface(IID_IDirect3DRMWinDevice,
  (void **)&pWinDev)))
  {
  pWinDev->HandleActivate(wParam);
  pWinDev->Release();
  }
 }
 break;
```

As you can see, all this code does is send the message to an **IDirect3DRMWinDevice** for processing as before. We already went over this code in Chapter 9, so let's move on to the last segment of our program: handling user input.

Interacting with the User

If you've every played Doom, then you already know how to use this program. It uses the standard Doom-style game controls wherein the left and right arrow keys turn, the up and down arrow keys move forward and backward, pressing (SHIFT) speeds up your movement, and the (ESC) key exits the program.

There are several functions in **Nav.cpp** we'll call to move the user—we won't actually do anything to move the player in the handler itself. We'll take a look at each of these functions from **Nav.cpp** in turn.

Move

Move is a function that won't be called by the **WM_KEYDOWN** handler directly, but rather from within the functions the handler calls. **Move** is in charge of actually *moving* the player, so it's only called when the player moves forward or backward (he or she won't actually move if turning, but will just rotate in one place).

Let's take a look at **Move** in Listing 15-21:

Listing 15-21 **Move**

```
void Move(float fCellColDelta, float fCellRowDelta)
{
// Some workspace for figuring new position. These may be rejected if
// player is trying to walk through walls.
float ftmpNewCellCol, ftmpNewCellRow;
int ntmpNewMapCol, ntmpNewMapRow;

// Add to current cell position
ftmpNewCellCol = g_fCellCol + fCellColDelta;
ftmpNewCellRow = g_fCellRow + fCellRowDelta;

// Get old map positions
ntmpNewMapCol = g_iMapCol;
ntmpNewMapRow = g_iMapRow;


// Check for roll over or under on cell positions
// Column roll overs
if(ftmpNewCellCol > 5.0)
  {
  ftmpNewCellCol = 1.0f;
  ntmpNewMapCol++;
  }
```

```
// Column roll under
if(ftmpNewCellCol < 1.0)
 {
 ftmpNewCellCol = 5.0f;
 ntmpNewMapCol--;
 }

// Row roll overs
if(ftmpNewCellRow > 5.0f)
 {
 ftmpNewCellRow = 1.0f;
 ntmpNewMapRow--;
 }

// Row roll under
if(ftmpNewCellRow < 1.0f)
 {
 ftmpNewCellRow = 5.0f;
 ntmpNewMapRow++;
 }


///////////////////////////////////////////////////////////
// New position has been calculated. Check for valid move.
// If the move is invalid, sound a grunt and return without
// changing the real position.

// Check for map boundary, row
if(ntmpNewMapRow > MAX_ROW || ntmpNewMapRow < 0)
 {
 sndGrunt();
 return;
 }

// Check for map boundary, column
if(ntmpNewMapCol > MAX_COL || ntmpNewMapCol < 0)
 {
 sndGrunt();
 return;
 }

// Check for walking through a wall into a non-map space
if(iDungeon[ntmpNewMapRow][ntmpNewMapCol] == 0)
 {
 sndGrunt();
 return;
 }


///////////////////////////////////////////////////////////
// All is well, update the position
g_fCellCol = ftmpNewCellCol;
g_fCellRow = ftmpNewCellRow;
```

continued on next page

continued from previous page

```
g_iMapCol = ntmpNewMapCol;
g_iMapRow = ntmpNewMapRow;

// Since this is where movement from one cell to another is
// coordinated, it's the best place to check for scoring.
if(bCheckForScore(g_iMapRow, g_iMapCol))
 {
 sndScore();
 nScore++;
 }

// End of function
} }
```

Move takes two parameters: the distance the player has moved in the *x* (column) direction, and the distance the player has moved in the *z* (row) direction. As always, positive values indicate up and right, negative values indicate down and left.

First of all, you have to get acquainted with the variables we're using to designate the player's position in the dungeon. As you know, there are several cells in our world, each containing a specific mesh (a door, a coin, a corner, and so on). Each of the cells is 6 units wide in both the *x* and *z* dimensions.

Before we can move the player, we need a system to tell where he or she is at any given moment. To do this, we'll indicate his or her location on each axis as a decimal number, with the part before the decimal point identifying the cell he or she is currently in, and the part after the decimal point identifying where he or she is in the cell (how far into the cell he or she is).

You have to keep in mind that these numbers are relative to the size of each cell (which, as you'll recall, is six units wide in each direction). For example, the location (3.2, 8.6) indicates the user is in the first cell on the x axis, two-tenths of the way into the cell. It also indicates the player is in the second cell on the z axis, six-tenths of the way through the cell.

As you'll see in a little while, we'll need these two separate parts of the player's location (the part before the decimal point and the part after) in two different variables. So we'll store the *x* and *z* location of a cell where the player is in the *g_iMapCol* and *g_iMapRow* variables, respectively (these are the parts of the location *before* the decimal point). We'll store the part of the player's location *after* the decimal point (the player's location *within* the cell) in *g_fCellCol* and *g_fCellRow*, for the x and z axes, respectively.

The two variables passed into **Move** are floating-point numbers arranged the same way as the locations just discussed. The only difference is the cell and intra-cell locations are given in one number, not split into two separate variables. The two floating-point numbers passed via parameters specify how far the player should move on the x and z axes, and in what direction (depending on whether the numbers are positive or negative).

To move the player, we first add the changes in position passed into his or her old position and store the new position in the *ntmpNewMapRow* and *ftmpNewCellRow* variables. After adding up the new position and saving the old one, we need to see whether or not the player changed cells as a result of the movement (he or she could have just moved a little within the cell). If he or she did change cells, we need to update both sets of position variables (for the cell position and the position within the cell) to mirror the his or her new location. For example, if the user moves one cell over to the right, we set *ftmpNewCellCol* (the temporary variable holding the player's position within the cell) to 1 to indicate the player is to the left of the new cell. We also increment the *ntmpNewMapCol* variable (the temporary variable indicating which cell the user is currently in) by 1 so we know which cell he or she is in. You should be able to figure the rest out for yourself.

Next we need to make sure the user didn't run into a wall. If he or she did, we want to play the grunt sound and restore the position variables to what they were at the start of **Move**. Otherwise, we just let the user move right through the wall, which isn't what we want.

There are a few things we check to make sure the user is still in valid playing space. First of all, the player's current cell must be located at a position greater than zero and less than the maximum number of cells—in both directions. There are two #defines that define the maximum number of cells on each axis. They're called **MAX_ROW** (for the x axis) and **MAX_COL** (for the y axis) and are basically the dimensions of the array used to put together the mesh for our dungeon. If *ntmpNewMapRow* is less than zero or greater than **MAX_ROW**, or if *ntmpNewMapCol* is less than zero or greater than **MAX_COL**, the user has gone out of bounds. Therefore we need to grunt and return from the function (preventing any actual movement, which occurs at the end of the function, from taking place).

Also, we need to make sure the user hasn't moved into a cell with the value zero in the array of meshes, since a zero indicates non-valid space (actually, it indicates area outside of the dungeon). If we let the user move there he or she would be moving outside of the dungeon mesh, and we won't allow that. Therefore, we grunt and return from **Move**.

Now that we put the user's new position into temporary variables and made sure he or she is still in bounds, we need to update the *real* position variables. Right now the player's new position is only stored in the temporary variables used to make sure everything worked out all right, but nothing's will actually change unless we update the *real* position variables. You should be able to look at the code yourself and figure out which temporary variables match which permanent ones.

Last, we check if the user moved into a cell containing one of the ten gold coins. To do this, we call the function **bCheckForScore**, which returns **TRUE** if the location passed to it contains a gold coin. If the player did indeed pick up a coin, we play the coin sound using the **sndScore** function (see the sound chapters) and increment the player's score (kept in the variable *nScore* and initialized to zero at the top of **ddmain.cpp**).

Well, that's the end of **Move**, the guts of our program when it comes to moving the player. Let's take a quick look at the **bCheckForScore** function just so you know what's happening there (Listing 15-22):

Listing 15-22 **bCheckForScore**

```
BOOL bCheckForScore(int row, int column)
{
// Loop through all 10 locations and check each one
for(int i = 0; i < 10; i++)
  {
  if(GoldFrames[i].nRow == row && GoldFrames[i].nCol == column
  && GoldFrames[i].bFound == FALSE)
    {
    GoldFrames[i].bFound = TRUE;

    // Remove coin from scene graph
    pDungeonFrame->DeleteChild(GoldFrames[i].pGoldFrame);
    GoldFrames[i].pGoldFrame->Release();

    return TRUE;
    }
  }
return FALSE;
}
```

As you can see, all the code does to find out if the user stumbled upon a coin is loop through all ten coins to see if their column and row variables match the player's current position. If they match, the player got a coin.

If the player did get a coin, we set the coin's *bFound* member to **TRUE** so we know it was found. We also delete the coin's frame from the scene so it disappears, and **Release** it so we don't have to do that later. Then, we return **TRUE** since the player did indeed find a coin.

Now let's move on to the functions that actually call **Move**, such as **StepForward** and **StepBackward** (called from the **WM_KEYDOWN** handler).

StepForward

StepForward does what the name implies: makes the player take one step forward. We'll call it from the **WM_KEYDOWN** message handler when the player presses the up arrow key. It's a pretty simple function, with only one line of code. It's shown in Listing 15-23:

Listing 15-23 **StepForward**

```
void StepForward(void)
{
Move(2.0f*fSineLookUp[g_iRotIndex], 2.0f*fCosineLookUp[g_iRotIndex]);
}
```

This function uses the direction the user is facing to come up with two values: one value for the change in *x* position, and one value for the change in *z* position.

The first value, **2.0f*fSineLookUp[g_iRotIndex]**, takes the sine of the direction the user is facing (**fSineLookUp[g_iRotIndex]** is a value from the sine table we built) and multiplies it by 2 to come up with a reasonable distance for the user to move in the *x* direction. If you're up on your trigonometry, you know using the sine of the angle the user is facing will move him the correct distance in the *x* direction. Otherwise, you'll have to accept the fact that this works (or go dig out your old trigonometry book).

The second value is exactly the same as the first except we look up the *cosine* of the angle the user is facing, instead of getting the sine of our angle. Doing this will move us the correct distance in the *z* direction.

RunForward

There is one other function that also moves the player forward, called `RunForward`. This is the function we'll call when the user holds down the SHIFT key as he or she presses the up arrow key. It's shown in Listing 15-24:

Listing 15-24 RunForward

```
void RunForward(void)
{
StepForward();
StepForward();
}
```

As you know, we want the player to move forward faster when he or she holds the SHIFT key while moving. `RunForward` is using `StepForward` to do all the work by simply calling it twice, one call right after the other. This will have the effect of moving the player forward twice as fast as plain old `StepForward` would.

StepBackward

`StepBackward` is the function we use when the user presses the down arrow key. It simply makes the player move backward the same distance `StepForward` would make him or her move forward.

Listing 15-25 lists the code for `StepBackward`:

Listing 15-25 StepBackward

```
void StepBackward(void)
{
Move(-(2.0f*fSineLookUp[g_iRotIndex]),
 -(2.0f * fCosineLookUp[g_iRotIndex]));
}
```

As you can see, this is exactly the same code used in `StepForward` except it moves the player in the exact *opposite* direction.

RunBackward

When the user holds down the SHIFT key while moving backward, we want to move backward twice as fast. There's a function for this purpose called `RunBackward`, which works in exactly the same way as `RunForward`—it just calls `StepBackward` twice to make the player move faster.

The Rotation Functions

There are two rotation functions we'll use to rotate the player when he or she presses the left or right keys. They're pretty simple since all they do is update the *g_iRotIndex* variable, our index into the lookup tables.

TurnLeft

TurnLeft, as you can probably guess, turns the player to his or her left. All we have to do is decrease *g_iRotIndex* by 1, which has the effect of turning him or her 10 degrees to the left (since we only used 36 values in our lookup tables).

Listing 15-26 lists the code for TurnLeft:

Listing 15-26 TurnLeft

```
float TurnLeft(void)
{
g_iRotIndex--;

if(g_iRotIndex < 0)
 g_iRotIndex = 35;

return fAngleLookUp[g_iRotIndex];
}
```

After decreasing *g_iRotIndex*, we check to see if it's less than zero. If it is, then we need to wrap it around to the last element of the lookup tables (35), since the player has turned in a complete circle. We also return the new angle the user is facing from TurnLeft, in case that might be useful in the calling function.

SwingLeft

Just like the functions to move forward and backward, the rotation functions also have a matching pair of functions we'll use when the player presses SHIFT as he or she turns. When the player holds SHIFT while turning left, we'll call the SwingLeft function, which turns left at twice the speed of TurnLeft. And as you may have guessed, all SwingLeft does is call TurnLeft twice.

TurnRight

TurnRight is pretty much the same function as TurnLeft. Instead of subtracting 1 from the angle variable (*g_iRotIndex*), we increment it by 1. This will turn the player to the right, which is exactly what we want to do.

Listing 15-27 shows the code for TurnRight:

Listing 15-27 `TurnRight`

```
float TurnRight(void)
{
g_iRotIndex++;

if(g_iRotIndex > 35)
 g_iRotIndex = 0;

return fAngleLookUp[g_iRotIndex];
}
```

You should be able to figure out what's going on here by yourself. If you can't, go take a look at `TurnLeft` again.

SwingRight

Don't forget, there's a matching function for `TurnRight` called `SwingRight`. It calls `TurnRight` twice to make the player turn twice as fast.

We're done with the navigation functions now, so let's look at the code from the window callback procedure calling it.

Handling the `WM_KEYDOWN` Message

When we get the `WM_KEYDOWN` message, the player probably wants to either move or quit. Therefore, most of the handler code will call the navigation functions just discussed.

Listing 15-28 shows the first part of the `WM_KEYDOWN` handler, the part handling the actual keystrokes (the second part updates the player's position):

Listing 15-28 The `WM_KEYDOWN` handler

```
case WM_KEYDOWN:
 {
 if(!bD3DReady)
  return (DefWindowProc(hWnd, message, wParam, lParam));

 // If game is over, allow no more movement, only ESC key is valid
 if(!bInPlay)
  {
  // Escape key, exit the program
  if(wParam == VK_ESCAPE)
   {
   PostQuitMessage(0);
   break;
   }
  break;
```

continued on next page

continued from previous page

```
    }

    // Move Forward and backwards
    if(wParam == VK_UP)
     if(GetKeyState(VK_SHIFT) & 0x8000)  // Shift runs forward
      RunForward();
     else
      StepForward();

    if(wParam == VK_DOWN)
     if(GetKeyState(VK_SHIFT) & 0x8000)  // Shift runs backward
      RunBackward();
     else
      StepBackward();

    // Turn left or right
    if(wParam == VK_LEFT)
     if(GetKeyState(VK_SHIFT) & 0x8000)  // Shift swings faster
      SwingLeft();
     else
      TurnLeft();

    if(wParam == VK_RIGHT)
     if(GetKeyState(VK_SHIFT) & 0x8000)  // Shift swings faster
      SwingRight();
     else
      TurnRight();

    // Escape key, exit the program
    if(wParam == VK_ESCAPE)
    {
    PostQuitMessage(0);
    break;
    }
```

The first statement (besides the one making sure Direct3D is ready) sees if the game is being played. If not, the game is over and the score is being displayed. If the game is over, we don't want to let the player move, we only want to let him or her press [ESC], which exits the program.

As you can see, most of the other *if* statements decide which function to call depending on the state of the [SHIFT] key. That part is pretty straightforward. And if the player presses [ESC], we send a message telling Windows to shut us down.

Now that the easy stuff's out of the way, let's move on to the meat of our handler, the section of code that actually moves the player and re-renders the scene. It's shown in Listing 15-29:

Listing 15-29 The second half of the **WM_KEYDOWN** handler

```
    // Update the players position
    pD3DCameraAPI->AddRotation(D3DRMCOMBINE_REPLACE, 0.0f, 1.0f,
     0.0f,fGetAngle());
```

```
pD3DCameraAPI->SetPosition(pD3DSceneAPI, fGetXPos(), 1.5f, fGetZPos());

// Render the scene
pD3DViewportAPI->Clear();    // Clear the viewport
pD3DViewportAPI->Render(pD3DSceneAPI); // Render the scene
pD3DRMDeviceAPI->Update();    // Update the device (window)

// Move back buffer (where drawing is occuring to front)
pSurf->Flip(NULL,DDFLIP_WAIT);
}
break;
```

The call to **AddRotation** is the line of code that actually rotates the player, if he or she is turning. We're simply setting the player's rotation to the angle held in the angle lookup table we built (the **fGetAngle** function just returns *fAngleLookUp[g_iRotIndex]*). This rotates the player to the angle given in the angle lookup table. Since we updated *g_iRotIndex* in one of the movement functions, it already points to the correct angle.

The call to **SetPosition** repositions the player in case he or she moved forward or backward. It sets the player's *x* position to the value returned by **fGetXPos**, the *y* position to 1.5 (the player's height throughout the entire game), and the *z* position to the value returned by **fGetZPos**.

The previous two functions took care of moving the player. Now all we have to do is reflect the player's new position by rendering the scene. You should know how to do this by now: We simply clear the viewport, render the scene to it, then update the device. And, don't forget, we now have to flip the complex surface so the back buffer (which we rendered into) is visible.

Let's move on to the **WM_TIMER** message, which handles the game element of our program.

The **WM_TIMER** Handler

When two minutes have elapsed since the beginning of the game, the timer sends a **WM_TIMER** message to our callback procedure. When we receive that message, we want to freeze the game and tell the player his score: *Your score is x out of 10! (Press <ESC> to return to Windows)*. After that, all the player can do is exit.

Listing 15-30 shows the code for the **WM_TIMER** handler:

Listing 15-30 The **WM_TIMER** handler code

```
case WM_TIMER:
{
RECT wndRect;                    // Get screen size
char caOutput[128               // Buffer to construct output string
HDC hDC;                         // Handle to GDI Device Context

// Get the device context and the window dimensions
hDC = GetDC(hWnd);
```

continued on next page

continued from previous page

```
        GetWindowRect(hWnd, &wndRect);


        // Redraw the current scene on the back buffer. This is in case
        // the current surface is not the GDI surface. If it isn't, then
        // redrawing the scene prevents the scene from jumping back one frame
        // before displaying the score
        pD3DViewportAPI->Render(pD3DSceneAPI); // Render the scene
        pD3DRMDeviceAPI->Update    // Update the device (window)

        // Make sure GDI capable surface is in the front
        pDD->FlipToGDISurface();

        // Display ending text. Background is transparent, color is white,
        // and message is centered. This is just good old fashioned Windows
        // GDI.
        SetBkMode(hDC,TRANSPARENT);
        SetTextColor(hDC,RGB(255,255,255));
        sprintf(caOutput,"Game Over!\n\nYour Score was %d out of %d!\n
        (Press ESC to return to Windows)",nScore,nPossible);
        DrawText(hDC,caOutput,-1,&wndRect,DT_CENTER);
        ReleaseDC(hWnd, hDC);

        // Game is over... Stop the timer, stop the background music,
        // and set the bInPlay flag to false.
        KillTimer(hWnd,101);
        StopBackgroundMusic();

        bInPlay = FALSE;
        }
        break;
```

First of all, we grab a DC to draw on the window and find out how big it is. Then, we render the scene onto the back buffer. We have to do this in case the GDI surface is flipped out at the moment, since the scene wouldn't have been rendered onto it yet and would still contain the *previous* rendering. Since the GDI always renders onto the GDI surface (the back buffer) we'd write the score message onto the previous frame, which would look somewhat odd when flipped (the end result would be the player seeing the frame he or she saw two frames ago, with text written on it).

After rendering the scene onto the back buffer, we flip the complex surface to the GDI surface. We do this to ensure the text we're about to write is visible to the player and not just sitting in the back buffer.

After flipping to the GDI surface, we draw the score onto it. All the GDI code does is draw the player's score in a white font in the center of the screen, along with a message to press the ESC key to exit. You've seen a lot of this stuff before in the DirectDraw chapters, and you can refer back to them if you don't quite understand it.

After releasing the DC, we kill the timer so we aren't eating up system resources. Then, we kill the background music (refer back to the **DirectSound** chapters for a discussion of StopBackgroundMusic) and set *bInPlay* to FALSE so the player can't move any more.

That's pretty much it for the meat of our program. All we have to do now is go over a couple more handlers and we're done!

The `MM_MCINOTIFY` Handler

When we started the background music in `StartBackgroundMusic`, we told Windows to notify us when it stopped so we could start it up again. That's all the `MM_MCINOTIFY` message does. So all we do in this handler is call `ReplayBackgroundMusic` (essentially the same code as `StartBackgroundMusic`) to replay the background `MIDI`.

The `WM_DESTROY` Handler

The `WM_DESTROY` handler has a few things it takes care of: It stops the music, cleans up all the DirectX objects we created, and calls `PostQuitMessage`. After that, we're outta here.

Listing 15-31 shows the code:

Listing 15-31 The `WM_DESTROY` handler

```
case WM_DESTROY:
// The application is terminating. Release the D3DRM interaces.
ShutdownDirect3DRetainedMode(hWnd);
ShutdownDirectSound();
StopBackgroundMusic();
ReleaseDC(hWnd,hDC);
PostQuitMessage(0);
break;
```

First, the `WM_DESTROY` handler calls the `ShutdownDirect3DRetainedMode` function to `Release` all the `Direct3DRM` objects we created in `SetupDirect3DRetainedMode`. After that, it calls the `ShutdownDirectSound` function to `Release` all the DirectSound objects used to play the sounds. `StopBackgroundMusic` then stops the background `MIDI` we kept going throughout the game.

Summary

That's it! Make sure you've included all the necessary libraries in your project file (including `Ddraw.lib` this time) and compile it. Now that you have this basic game foundation to work with, it won't be much harder for you to expand and build on it. Tweak it, play around with it, and have fun! You can learn a lot just by messing around.

Windows 95 Logo Requirements

You'll probably want to be able to say your game is Windows 95-compatible so you can get that nifty little label on the box, especially if you release your game commercially. In order to do this, you need to meet a few requirements Microsoft has set to make sure applications behave properly. This appendix will bring you up to speed with those requirements and give you an idea as to what you need to do to meet them.

First of all, there are two distinct levels of compatibility: *Windows 95 Compatible* and *Designed for Windows 95*.

Under the Windows 95 Compatible level, your program does not meet the Windows 95 logo requirements. It might be a DOS or Windows 3.1 program, or it might just not meet all the requirements for a Windows 95 logo (see Figure A-1). As long as your program actually runs under Windows 95 without crashing every two minutes, you're probably at this level of compatibility.

FIGURE A-1

The Windows 95 logo

The second, and preferable, level of compatibility is the one meeting the logo requirements, Designed for Windows 95. If your program is at this level, you can stick the hallowed Windows 95 logo on your program's box.

Logo Requirements

In a nutshell, your game needs to meet these requirements in order to get the logo:

- Be a true Win32 32-bit Windows application
- Correctly use the Windows 95 user interface
- Be compatible with Windows NT
- Support long file names
- Have an install and uninstall program

First of all, your game has to be a true 32-bit Windows application. This means it must be compiled in PE (Portable Executable) format. You'll need to check your compiler to make sure it supports PE format, but most Windows 95 and Windows NT compilers do.

Your game has to support several user interface features introduced with Windows 95. It has to have two separate icons: one small icon for the start and system menus and one large icon for normal use. You also have to use the colors and metrics the user sets with the Display Properties dialog. You have to use the common dialogs wherever possible, and Microsoft would really like you to use the right mouse button to bring up a context menu (that one's strongly suggested). There are several more guidelines Microsoft would appreciate you following; however, they really aren't necessary for the logo—see your Windows SDK documents for more information.

Your application needs to be compatible with both Windows 95 *and* Windows NT. Since NT will support DirectX in version 4.0 (which is probably outdated by the time you read this), you need to make sure your game runs on Windows NT. If for some reason you have to use a new API or something specific to either OS, you just need to make sure your game doesn't crash and burn when it runs on the other.

You have to support long file names. You really don't need to do much to meet this requirement; just don't limit your file name buffer memory to only 11 or 12 characters. If you use the Windows 95 common dialogs (another requirement) and the standard Windows 95 API, you're pretty well set since they automatically use long file names.

You should include Plug and Play support. This is really a recommendation, not a requirement, but it's a good idea just the same. Using Plug and Play, Windows will send you messages notifying you of several important events, such as the user's changing display resolution, or adding or removing some hardware from the system. Your program should be able to respond appropriately.

There are several other requirements for the logo, such as OLE 2.0 support and Universal Naming Convention support, but they are required only if your program's primary purpose is creating and editing documents. Games usually don't meet this criteria, however, so you don't have to worry about them. If you meet the requirements listed in this chapter, you should do just fine.

It's really not all that hard to meet all these requirements. Since you're writing a game, you have lucked out because you don't have to meet as many requirements as, say, someone who is developing a word processor. As always, for more information about these or any of the other requirements, see your Windows 95 SDK documentation.

Using the Logo

Before you actually go ahead and *use* the logo, you'll have to get a license from Microsoft. If you're really interested, write to Microsoft's logo department at:

Systems Marketing
Windows Logo Department
Microsoft Corporation
One Microsoft Way
Redmond, WA 98052-6399

You can also fax your inquiry to (206) 936-7329.

You'll have to contact Microsoft and assure them that your program meets all the logo requirements.

Index

X-Z

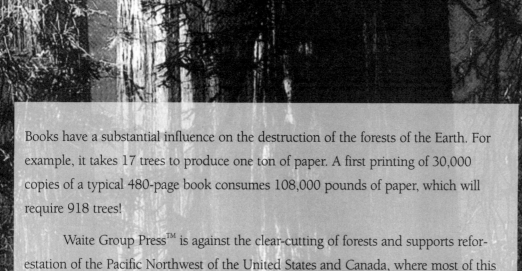

Books have a substantial influence on the destruction of the forests of the Earth. For example, it takes 17 trees to produce one ton of paper. A first printing of 30,000 copies of a typical 480-page book consumes 108,000 pounds of paper, which will require 918 trees!

Waite Group Press™ is against the clear-cutting of forests and supports reforestation of the Pacific Northwest of the United States and Canada, where most of this paper comes from. As a publisher with several hundred thousand books sold each year, we feel an obligation to give back to the planet. We will therefore support organizations that seek to preserve the forests of planet Earth.

Message from the
Publisher

WELCOME TO OUR NERVOUS SYSTEM

Some people say that the World Wide Web is a graphical extension of the information superhighway, just a network of humans and machines sending each other long lists of the equivalent of digital junk mail.

I think it is much more than that. To me, the Web is nothing less than the nervous system of the entire planet—not just a collection of computer brains connected together, but more like a billion silicon neurons entangled and recirculating electro-chemical signals of information and data, each contributing to the birth of another CPU and another Web site.

Think of each person's hard disk connected at once to every other hard disk on earth, driven by human navigators searching like Columbus for the New World. Seen this way the Web is more of a super entity, a growing, living thing, controlled by the universal human will to expand, to be more. Yet, unlike a purposeful business plan with rigid rules, the Web expands in a nonlinear, unpredictable, creative way that echoes natural evolution.

We created our Web site not just to extend the reach of our computer book products but to be part of this synaptic neural network, to experience, like a nerve in the body, the flow of ideas and then to pass those ideas up the food chain of the mind. Your mind. Even more, we wanted to pump some of our own creative juices into this rich wine of technology.

TASTE OUR DIGITAL WINE

And so we ask you to taste our wine by visiting the body of our business. Begin by understanding the metaphor we have created for our Web site—a universal learning center, situated in outer space in the form of a space station. A place where you can journey to study any topic from the convenience of your own screen. Right now we are focusing on computer topics, but the stars are the limit on the Web.

If you are interested in discussing this Web site or finding out more about the Waite Group, please send me e-mail with your comments, and I will be happy to respond. Being a programmer myself, I love to talk about technology and find out what our readers are looking for.

Sincerely,

Mitchell Waite

Mitchell Waite, C.E.O. and Publisher

200 Tamal Plaza
Corte Madera, CA 94925
415-924-2575
415-924-2576 fax

Website:
http://www.waite.com/waite

CREATING THE HIGHEST QUALITY COMPUTER BOOKS IN THE INDUSTRY

Waite Group Press

Come Visit
WAITE.COM
Waite Group Press
World Wide Web Site

Now find all the latest information on Waite Group books at our new Web site, **http://www.waite.com/waite.** You'll find an online catalog where you can examine and order any title, review upcoming books, and send e-mail to our authors and editors. Our FTP site has all you need to update your book: the latest program listings, errata sheets, most recent versions of Fractint, POV Ray, Polyray, DMorph, and all the programs featured in our books. So download, talk to us, ask questions, at **http://www.waite.com/waite.**

The New Arrivals Room has all our new books listed by month. Just click for a description, Index, Table of Contents, and links to authors.

The Backlist Room has all our books listed alphabetically.

The People Room is where you'll interact with Waite Group employees.

Links to Cyberspace get you in touch with other computer book publishers and other interesting Web sites.

About WGP

New Arrivals

Backlist Room

People Room

FTP

Order

Subject Room

Links to Cyberspace

The FTP site contains all program listings, errata sheets, etc.

The Order Room is where you can order any of our books online.

The Subject Room contains typical book pages that show description, Index, Table of Contents, and links to authors.

This is a legal agreement between you, the end user and purchaser, and The Waite Group®, Inc., and the authors of the programs contained in the disk. By opening the sealed disk package, you are agreeing to be bound by the terms of this Agreement. If you do not agree with the terms of this Agreement, promptly return the unopened disk package and the accompanying items (including the related book and other written material) to the place you obtained them for a refund.

SOFTWARE LICENSE

1. The Waite Group, Inc. grants you the right to use one copy of the enclosed software programs (the programs) on a single computer system (whether a single CPU, part of a licensed network, or a terminal connected to a single CPU). Each concurrent user of the program must have exclusive use of the related Waite Group, Inc. written materials.

2. The program, including the copyrights in each program, is owned by the respective author and the copyright in the entire work is owned by The Waite Group, Inc. and they are therefore protected under the copyright laws of the United States and other nations, under international treaties. You may make only one copy of the disk containing the programs exclusively for backup or archival purposes, or you may transfer the programs to one hard disk drive, using the original for backup or archival purposes. You may make no other copies of the programs, and you may make no copies of all or any part of the related Waite Group, Inc. written materials.

3. You may not rent or lease the programs, but you may transfer ownership of the programs and related written materials (including any and all updates and earlier versions) if you keep no copies of either, and if you make sure the transferee agrees to the terms of this license.

4. You may not decompile, reverse engineer, disassemble, copy, create a derivative work, or otherwise use the programs except as stated in this Agreement.

GOVERNING LAW

This Agreement is governed by the laws of the State of California.

LIMITED WARRANTY

The following warranties shall be effective for 90 days from the date of purchase: (i) The Waite Group, Inc. warrants the enclosed disk to be free of defects in materials and workmanship under normal use; and (ii) The Waite Group, Inc. warrants that the programs, unless modified by the purchaser, will substantially perform the functions described in the documentation provided by The Waite Group, Inc. when operated on the designated hardware and operating system. The Waite Group, Inc. does not warrant that the programs will meet purchaser's requirements or that operation of a program will be uninterrupted or error-free. The program warranty does not cover any program that has been altered or changed in any way by anyone other than The Waite Group, Inc. The Waite Group, Inc. is not responsible for problems caused by changes in the operating characteristics of computer hardware or computer operating systems that are made after the release of the programs, nor for problems in the interaction of the programs with each other or other software.

THESE WARRANTIES ARE EXCLUSIVE AND IN LIEU OF ALL OTHER WARRANTIES OF MERCHANTABILITY OR FITNESS FOR A PARTICULAR PURPOSE OR OF ANY OTHER WARRANTY, WHETHER EXPRESSED OR IMPLIED.

EXCLUSIVE REMEDY

The Waite Group, Inc. will replace any defective disk without charge if the defective disk is returned to The Waite Group, Inc. within 90 days from date of purchase.

This is Purchaser's sole and exclusive remedy for any breach of warranty or claim for contract, tort, or damages.

LIMITATION OF LIABILITY

THE WAITE GROUP, INC. AND THE AUTHORS OF THE PROGRAMS SHALL NOT IN ANY CASE BE LIABLE FOR SPECIAL, INCIDENTAL, CONSEQUENTIAL, INDIRECT, OR OTHER SIMILAR DAMAGES ARISING FROM ANY BREACH OF THESE WARRANTIES EVEN IF THE WAITE GROUP, INC. OR ITS AGENT HAS BEEN ADVISED OF THE POSSIBILITY OF SUCH DAMAGES.

THE LIABILITY FOR DAMAGES OF THE WAITE GROUP, INC. AND THE AUTHORS OF THE PROGRAMS UNDER THIS AGREEMENT SHALL IN NO EVENT EXCEED THE PURCHASE PRICE PAID.

COMPLETE AGREEMENT

This Agreement constitutes the complete agreement between The Waite Group, Inc. and the authors of the programs, and you, the purchaser.

Some states do not allow the exclusion or limitation of implied warranties or liability for incidental or consequential damages, so the above exclusions or limitations may not apply to you. This limited warranty gives you specific legal rights; you may have others, which vary from state to state.

MACMILLAN COMPUTER PUBLISHING USA

A VIACOM COMPANY

Technical ---- Support:

If you cannot get the CD/Disk to install properly, or you need assistance with a particular situation in the book, please feel free to check out the Knowledge Base on our Web site at **http://www.superlibrary.com/general/support**. We have answers to our most Frequently Asked Questions listed there. If you do not find your specific question answered, please contact Macmillan Technical Support at **(317) 581-3833**. We can also be reached by email at **support@mcp.com**.

SATISFACTION REPORT CARD

Please fill out this card if you wish to know of future updates to
Win32 Game Developer's Guide with DirectX 3, or to receive our catalog.

First Name: _____ Last Name: _____

Street Address: _____

City: _____ State: _____ Zip: _____

E-Mail Address _____

Daytime Telephone: (   ) _____

Date product was acquired: Month _____ Day _____ Year _____ Your Occupation: _____

Overall, how would you rate Win32 Game Developer's Guide with DirectX 3?

☐ Excellent   ☐ Very Good   ☐ Good
☐ Fair   ☐ Below Average ☐ Poor

What did you like MOST about this book? _____
_____
_____

What did you like LEAST about this book? _____
_____
_____

Please describe any problems you may have encountered with installing or using the disk: _____
_____

How did you use this book (problem-solver, tutorial, reference...)?
_____

What is your level of computer expertise?
☐ New   ☐ Dabbler   ☐ Hacker
☐ Power User   ☐ Programmer   ☐ Experienced Professional

What computer languages are you familiar with? _____
_____

Please describe your computer hardware:

Computer _____ Hard disk _____
5.25" disk drives _____ 3.5" disk drives_____
Video card _____ Monitor _____
Printer _____ Peripherals _____
Sound Board _____ CD ROM_____

Where did you buy this book?
☐ Bookstore (name): _____
☐ Discount store (name): _____
☐ Computer store (name): _____
☐ Catalog (name): _____
☐ Direct from WGP   ☐ Other _____

What price did you pay for this book? _____

What influenced your purchase of this book?
☐ Recommendation   ☐ Advertisement
☐ Magazine review   ☐ Store display
☐ Mailing   ☐ Book's format
☐ Reputation of Waite Group Press   ☐ Other

How many computer books do you buy each year? _____

How many other Waite Group books do you own? _____

What is your favorite Waite Group book? _____

Is there any program or subject you would like to see Waite Group Press cover in a similar approach? _____
_____
_____

Additional comments? _____
_____
_____

Please send to: Waite Group Press
200 Tamal Plaza
Corte Madera, CA 94925

☐ **Check here for a free Waite Group catalog**

BEFORE YOU OPEN THE DISK OR CD-ROM PACKAGE ON THE FACING PAGE, CAREFULLY READ THE LICENSE AGREEMENT.

Opening this package indicates that you agree to abide by the license agreement found in the back of this book. If you do not agree with it, promptly return the unopened disk package (including the related book) to the place you obtained them for a refund.

Notice: Use of Microsoft's Licensed Materials is subject to the terms of the end user license agreement contained in the DirectX 3 SETUP utility on the accompanying CD-ROM.